Mallarmé

Mallarmé

The Poet and His Circle

Rosemary Lloyd

Cornell University Press
Ithaca and London

First published 1999 by Cornell University Press

Printed in the United States of America

Library of Congress Cataloging-in-Publication Data
Lloyd, Rosemary.
    Mallarmé : the poet and his circle / Rosemary Lloyd.
       p.   cm.
    Includes index.
    ISBN 0-8014-3662-1 (cloth)
    1. Mallarmé, Stéphane, 1842–1898.   2. Poets, French—
19th century—Biography.   I. Title.
PQ2344.Z5L56   1999
841'.8—dc21
    [B]   99-35644

Cornell University Press strives to use environmentally responsible suppliers and materials to the fullest extent possible in the publishing of its books. Such materials include vegetable-based, low-VOC inks and acid-free papers that are recycled, totally chlorine-free, or partly composed of nonwood fibers. Books that bear the logo of the FSC (Forest Stewardship Council) use paper taken from forests that have been inspected and certified as meeting the highest standards for environmental and social responsibility. For further information, visit our website at www.cornellpress.cornell.edu.

Cloth printing   10   9   8   7   6   5   4   3   2   1

Facing Page: Dedication of La Musique et les lettres *by Stéphane Mallarmé.* The Academy, *to which the volume is inscribed, was an English periodical founded in 1869. Edmund Gosse published an article on Mallarmé in it on January 7, 1893. Courtesy the Lilly Library, Indiana University, Bloomington.*

for Claude and Vincenette Pichois

To the Academy)
from their friend

With these keys we may partially unlock the mystery.
—Edgar Allan Poe, *Eureka*

If a man does not make new acquaintances as he advances through life, he will soon find himself alone. A man, Sir, should keep his friendship in constant repair.
—Samuel Johnson, quoted in James Boswell,
Life of Samuel Johnson

Facts have their importance. —But that is where the biography comes to grief. [. . .] Therefore, as things are, the best method would be to separate the two kinds of truth. Let the biographer print fully completely, accurately, the known facts without comment: Then let him write the life as fiction.
—Virginia Woolf, *Notebooks*

Contents

Illustrations   ix

Acknowledgments   xi

Abbreviations   xiii

INTRODUCTION: Corresponding   1

INTERLUDE ONE • Reading in Mallarmé's Letters   19

CHAPTER ONE • Writing in Exile   27

INTERLUDE TWO • Depression   66

CHAPTER TWO • Finding a Voice   77

INTERLUDE THREE • Father and Daughter   109

CHAPTER THREE • Forging an Aesthetic   121

INTERLUDE FOUR • Love and Friendship   156

CHAPTER FOUR • Becoming a Symbol   166

INTERLUDE FIVE • "A Passerby Seeking Refuge": Poetry, Politics, and Bombs   202

CONCLUSION: Remembering the Dead   217

Appendix: "Crise de vers"   227

Notes   235

Selected Bibliography   245

Index   255

Illustrations

Following Page 108

1. *Portrait of Mallarmé by Edouard Manet*
2. *Portrait of Paul Verlaine by Louis Anquetin*
3. *Drawing of Villiers de l'Isle-Adam by Paterne Berrichon*
4. *Caricature of François Coppée*
5. *Illustration from* Le Corbeau *(1875)*
6. *Cover of* La Plume *(1893)*
7. *Drawing of Stuart Merrill*
8. *Caricature of the publisher Léon Vanier*
9. *Drawing of Georges Rodenbach*
10. *Paul Nadar photograph of Mallarmé toward the end of his life*
11. *Drawing of Henri Cazalis*
12. *Drawing of Henri de Régnier*
13. *Painting of Méry Laurent by Edouard Manet*
14. *Photograph of Geneviève Mallarmé*
15. *Fan signed by Mallarmé and others*
16. *Saxony clock*

Acknowledgments

This book could not have been written without the immaculate scholarship of Lloyd Austin, whose edition of the correspondence is such a fascinating source of information for anyone interested in fin-de-siècle thought and art. To him, and to the numerous scholars, librarians, and friends who have shared their knowledge and insights with me, I owe a great debt of gratitude. Earlier versions of certain chapters in this book were read to audiences in Toronto (Canada), Edinburgh (Scotland), Stockholm (Sweden), and Iowa City (United States), and I am grateful for the comments I received. I would also like to express my thanks to Nancy Boerner of Indiana University's main library; Lisa Brower, Julia Simic, Saundra Taylor, and all the wonderful staff of the Lilly Library; Geneviève Moly-Averso and Marie-Anne Sarda of the Musée Mallarmé; Marie-Thérèse Stanislas, whose interest in Geneviève Mallarmé was of special help to me; Bernhard Kendler of Cornell University Press; and my colleagues and friends Jill Anderson, Mylène Catel, Mary Ann Caws, Ross Chambers, Jane Fulcher, Michael Graf, Michèle Hannoosh, Bertrand Marchal, Gordon Millan, Larry Porter, and Jean-Luc Steinmetz. It's a special pleasure to record my thanks to Jan Mitchell, who gave me invaluable help as my research assistant, and to Bill Cagle, who over many years as Lilly Librarian built up the wonderful collection of nineteenth-century French books and manuscripts housed in Bloomington's Lilly Library.

Some of the letters from which I quote excerpts appeared in an earlier form in my *Selected Letters of Stéphane Mallarmé* (Chicago: University of Chicago Press, 1988). © 1988 by the University of Chicago. All rights reserved. I am grateful to the Press for permission to use these excerpts here. The National Endowment for the Humanities awarded me a fellowship that enabled me to devote myself full time to this project, and to them, as well as to Indiana University, which granted me a sabbatical, I am deeply grateful.

As always, my husband, Paul, deserves more thanks than I can express. Claude and Vincenette Pichois have long provided leadership and unstinting friendship to *dix-neuvièmistes* throughout the world, and this book is a small token of appreciation for all they have given.

Abbreviations

Mallarmé's punctuation, capitalization, and syntax are idiosyncratic, but part of his meaning. I have preserved them in my translations wherever possible. All translations are my own except where indicated otherwise. A translation of Mallarmé's "Crise de vers" (Crisis of verse) is included at the end of the volume.

Annales   Henri de Régnier, *Annales psychiques et occulaires* (Unpublished diaries) (Paris: Bibliothèque nationale, MSS nouvelles acquisitions françaises, 14974–80).

Corr.   Stéphane Mallarmé, *Correspondance,* ed. L. J. Austin, H. Mondor, and J. P. Richard, 11 vols. (Paris: Gallimard, 1959–85).

CC   Stéphane Mallarmé, *Correspondance complète (1862–1871): Suivie de Lettres sur la poésie (1872–1898),* ed. Bertrand Marchal, pref. Yves Bonnefoy (Paris: Gallimard, 1995).

DSM   *Documents Stéphane Mallarmé,* ed. Carl Paul Barbier et al., 7 vols. (Paris: Nizet, 1968–80).

EL   Henri Mondor, *Eugène Lefébure: Sa vie, ses lettres à Mallarmé* (Paris: Gallimard, 1951).

HC   Lawrence Joseph, *Henri Cazalis: Sa vie, son œuvre, son amitié avec Mallarmé* (Paris: Nizet, 1972).

LML   Stéphane Mallarmé, *Lettres à Méry Laurent,* ed. Bertrand Marchal (Paris: Gallimard, 1996).

OC   Stéphane Mallarmé, *Œuvres complètes,* ed. Henri Mondor and Jean-Aubry (Paris: Gallimard, 1945).

VM   Henri Mondor, *La Vie de Mallarmé* (Paris: Gallimard, 1942).

Mallarmé

Corresponding

What can we know of a human being?
—*Jean-Paul Sartre,* L' Idiot de la famille

Do we then know nobody?—only our own versions of them,
which, as likely as not, are emanations from ourselves?
—*Virginia Woolf,* Notebooks

Late in 1888 the young Belgian poet and critic Albert Mockel wrote to Stéphane Mallarmé, the leading Symbolist poet of the day, asking if he could publish a brief portrait of him, and if so, whether he could be sent some notes to guide his study.[1] Mallarmé replied, "Since you're kind enough to take on the task of writing my portrait, you shouldn't seek out information or write yet another of those biographies we see all too often here. Draw me as I appear to you from a distance and from the point of view of literature, that's where the interest lies" (*Corr.,* III: 277). While this response is in part an expression of the modesty and courtesy typical of Mallarmé, it is also indicative of the degree to which he sought to control the public image of his own life and of the relationship between poetry and experience. His letters, especially those he wrote after returning from the provinces to Paris in 1871, bear eloquent if sotto voce witness to the degree of self-fashioning that went into his presentation of his past, his personality, and his poetry. Clearly, too, he had no desire to find himself thrust into the banality of what had become the standard form of biographical criticism. After all, he was writing at a time when literary criticism had by and large become dominated by the thinking of Charles-Augustin Sainte-Beuve, who sought to gain an understanding of the writer's work through his or her life, and whose disciples had gone yet further, focusing on the life almost to the exclusion and certainly to the detriment of the work. While he conceded that the work needed to be set in its intellectual context,[2] Mallarmé contended that "the poet draws sustenance from his or her Individuality, which is both secret and anterior, more than from external or simply long-standing circumstances, even when they elevate that Individuality, even when they are admirable" (*Corr.,* IX: 74). Yet he accepted that there were times when biographical information was useful or necessary. Writing about the enigmatic final years of the poet Arthur Rimbaud, he confronted the eternal question of biography with his customary modesty and gentle smile: "I know at the very least how gratuitous it is to substitute oneself, comfortably, for someone else's conscience. [. . .] To organize someone else's life into intelligible and convincing fragments, in order to translate it, is nothing less than impertinence: all that remains for me to do is push this kind of misdemeanor as far as it can go. Only, I do seek out the facts" (*OC,* 517).

The facts about his own life can be succinctly stated: Stéphane Mallarmé was born in 1842, in Paris. His mother died when he was five, and he was raised partly in boarding schools, partly by his father and stepmother, and partly by his maternal grandparents. His only sister, Maria, died when she was thirteen and he fifteen. In 1862, the year in which his first poems were published, he went to London to prepare his career as a teacher of English, and the following year he married Maria Gerhard, a German woman seven years his senior. From November of that year until 1871 he taught at various schools in provincial France, devoting much of his spare time to writing poetry and above all to developing a personal aesthetics. The couple's daughter, Geneviève, was born in November 1864 and their son, Anatole, in July 1871. After the fall of the Commune, Mallarmé and his family returned to Paris, where he was to spend the rest of his life, dividing his time between the city and the village of Valvins, overlooking the Forest of Fontainebleau. In 1879 Anatole Mallarmé died, a death that plunged both parents but especially Marie into deep and prolonged depression.

An unenthusiastic teacher, Mallarmé taught English at various Paris schools until he succeeded in being allowed to take early retirement in 1893. From the late 1870s he began gathering writers, artists, and musicians around him at weekly evening gatherings, which became famous as the "Mardis" (Tuesdays). When he died in 1898 he left behind a body of published work, which was small in quantity but was to have a seminal influence on subseqent poetry, and an unshaken reputation for the friendship and encouragement he so generously gave those who came to him.

When it came to talking about his own life, Mallarmé exercised the same control that marks his poetry. The autobiography he provided for Paul Verlaine is, as Austin Gill has shown in *The Early Mallarmé,* a meticulously crafted piece, with an air of spontaneity and directness that to some extent masks how carefully it was constructed. Its value lies not so much in what it tells us about Mallarmé's life as in what it reveals about the poet's desire to control, manipulate, and make meaning of the world's apparent incoherence and inconsistencies. He begins, after affirming his own date and place of birth (March 18, 1842, in Paris), with the classic evocation of the family tree, presented as an uninterrupted line of functionaries working in government administration and in public records. That one of his ancestors signed the death warrant of Louis XVIII may possibly not have been known to him, although that particular regicide does feature in the nineteenth-century Larousse Encyclopedia. In any case, Mallarmé does not mention it, seeking out instead those who used their pens for neither administrating, recording, nor condemning to death but for allowing the publication of books under the reign of Louis XVI or for writing the kind of lighthearted verse found in almanacs and gift albums. One is described as an extravagantly Romantic author of a volume entitled *Angel or Demon.* Clearly Mallarmé is singling himself out both from the pen-pushers who worked as minor functionaries and from any other creative writers the extended family may have contained. His true family, so his autobiography implies, is that of the poets and writers of the previous generation, the Romantics, and, because of a chance meeting, the popular songwriter Pierre-Jean de Béranger.

In conversation, Mallarmé seems to have repeated two anecdotes from his childhood, both of which he undoubtedly selected and vetted quite carefully. They concern dissimulation, imagination, and the reconstruction of unwelcome fact. We are told that when his mother died, five-year-old Stéphane was so embarrassed at the lack of emotion he felt that he threw himself on the floor and tore his hair to convince his audience that he was grief-stricken. The anecdote is interesting in what it conveys about the adult mind, if not the child's. Mallarmé explains the lack of emotion by saying that he had been sent "elsewhere" and had had little time to get to know his mother. Being sent "elsewhere" meant being sent to a wet-nurse, still a widespread custom at that time despite Rousseau's promotion of breast-feeding over half a century before. Indeed, the adult Mallarmé and his wife sent their own children to a wet nurse. We should not therefore read this allusion as an attack on his parents or as a depiction of himself as outcast. But because many infants spent several years with their wet nurses and were returned abruptly and without explanation to their parents, there are records of children suffering considerable distress at being separated from what they had come to regard as their own families. Judith Gautier, Mallarmé's contemporary, makes the point with particular force in her romanticized autobiography, depicting the return to the family bosom as a fall from grace and describing the wet nurse as the "sole beloved."[3] In Mallarmé's account of the loss of his mother, there is therefore a phantom image of the separation from the wet nurse. The child who threw himself on the floor and wept may having been pretending as far as his birth mother was concerned, but he may also, even though unaware of it, have been weeping for a loss that was indeed deeply felt, that of his wet nurse. In any case, this story emphasizes the child's and certainly the adult's desire to convince others, and to behave in a way he thought expected of him.

The second anecdote is similar in purpose. Sent to a modish private school, the boy Stéphane—no doubt under the influence of bullying—described himself as the "comte de Boulainvilliers." The name was taken from a hamlet near Passy, the village on the outskirts of Paris where Mallarmé's family was currently living. The aristocratic handles are entirely invention, but again they show a boy in search of acceptance by his peers and of control over his circumstances.

Charles Baudelaire, in meditating on the role of biography for his adaptation of Thomas de Quincey's *Confessions of an English Opium Eater,* suggests that "biography will serve to explain and, so to speak, to verify, the mysterious adventures of the brain. It's in the notes concerning childhood that we'll find the seeds of the adult's strange reveries, and, to put it better, the seeds of his genius."[4] The mysterious adventures of the brain, the strange reveries of artistic genius, draw attention to the Symbolist portrait painter, for whom, as Mallarmé cogently puts it, the invasion of personal privacy committed by some biographers appeared as simply impertinent. Indeed, Mallarmé's autobiographical notes seek to show a childhood that was essentially an apprenticeship to poetry, a childhood spent filling little notebooks with verses, only to have them confiscated by teachers whose failure to comprehend foreshadows that of the adult Mallarmé's reading public. The continuous lineage of his ancestry, in other words, finds a parallel in the poet's continuous, alchemical search for what he calls, with the unbounded ambition of simplicity, the Book: "a book which would truly be a book, architectural and premeditated, and not an anthology of chance inspirations, however marvelous those inspirations might be" (*OC,* 663). What this book would offer its readers, he insists, is "the Orphic explanation of the earth, which is the poet's sole duty and the literary game *par excellence*" (*OC,* 663). Whatever else the piece he wrote for Verlaine may offer in terms of indicating Mallarmé's interest in ballet and music, the joy he finds in boating at Valvins, and the importance of certain friendships and more generally of the Tuesday evening gatherings, it is clearly this nugget that he wants his reader to remember—this cryptic formula that invites and justifies contemplation of the poet's existence.

At the end of his memorial lecture for his friend, the novelist and playwright Villiers de l'Isle-Adam, Mallarmé acknowledges that his audience has been deprived of what he knew to be the attraction of public talks, the anecdotes about the individual under discussion. My goal in writing this book has not been to retell the anecdotes of Mallarmé's biography, a task already ably undertaken by several commentators, including Henri Mondor in 1941, by Kurt Wais a decade later, and more recently by Austin Gill, Gordon Millan, and Jean-Luc Steinmetz.[5] Gill's two-volume study, *The Early Mallarmé,* explores the poet's childhood and adolescent writings, thus providing the foundation for an exploration of the mature work. Mondor's classic biography of the poet, for all its richness and intrinsic value, is rooted in the social and gender prejudices of the time it was written. Wais's elegant study, written in German, expands on Mondor's but remains primarily descriptive rather than analytical. Millan's much more recent bibliography is primarily aimed at a general readership and is concerned above all with setting Mallarmé in his social and historical context. The poet and critic Jean-Luc Steinmetz has published a beautifully produced and very detailed biography that expands on Mondor's but, like Mondor's, attempts to show the poet's development through his daily experiences and contacts. Unfortunately, this work appeared too late for me to incorporate its findings here.

My objective is to explore the image of the poet conveyed by the letters he sent and received and, to a lesser extent, by the diaries and recollections of those who knew him, so as to retrace the intellectual life of one of the most influential and endearing of poets. Views expressed in Mallarmé's letters have too often been quoted in isolation as definitive convictions, whereas they are more accurately seen as ideas-in-progress, responses and reactions to a correspondent's work or conversation. Recreating and focusing on that context reveals a rather different Mallarmé and liberates him from the moral, political, and aesthetic seclusion too frequently imposed on him. Much of what his contemporaries have said about Mallarmé I have left aside, as my central concern is with the poet himself and with the ways in which his letters may be read as explorations and extensions of the prose and poetry he wrote for publication.

Mallarmé's letters and many of his poems are also very much extensions of his friendships, and to understand them fully we need to consider his concept of friendship, traces of which can found on many objects associated with him. Thus on an elegantly decorated fan we find Mallarmé's unmistakable signature surrounded by those of writers, artists, musicians, actors, and journalists, transforming an everyday object into a symbol of the nourishing and sustaining friendships that were such a central part of the cultural movements in late-nineteenth-century France (Figure 15).[6] More than any other poet I know, Mallarmé relished, cherished, and commemorated friendship, leaving words of affection on a wide variety of objects and using the expression and the relationships of friendship to explore, sharpen, and test his rhetorical and aesthetic convictions. At the beach at Honfleur he found pebbles on which he would write brief rhymes for friends left behind: "Je préfère au parc Monceau / Votre pré, Madame Ponsot" (Dearer to me than the Park Monceau / Is your meadow, Madame Ponsot) (*OC*, 173). Invitations to visit would be couched in the form of lighthearted rhymes: "Que ce cher Monsieur Marcel Schwob / Eperonne vers nous son cob" (Let that dear Mister Marcel Schwob / Spur on toward us his fine cob) (*OC*, 164). Jugs of calvados, Easter eggs (each featuring one line of verse, and carefully numbered so that the poem could be reconstituted), teapots, the golden forms of crystallized fruit—"Sur un rameau vers vous incliné par Marie / Pas plus que l'amitié ce fruit d'or ne varie" (On a branch bent down to you by Mary / This golden fruit, like friendship, will not vary) (*OC*, 130)—as well as the more traditional books and photographs all inspired his warm wit and delight in playful rhyme. He loved making quatrains of his friends' postal addresses, even when their names, or those of their streets, posed formidable problems for rhythm or rhyme: Mme Wrotnowski, Hector Giacamelli, and Princess Poniatowska all found themselves happily paired with a rhyme that somehow manages quite joyously to suggest a spontaneous gift that caused the poet nothing but pure delight. It was doubtless that gift of making other people feel charming that enabled this quiet, unassuming man to gather around him on Tuesday evenings in his house on the rue de Rome a wide cross section of the writers, artists, and musicians of fin-de-siècle France, Belgium, and England.

While love letters, real and fictional, have long attracted close critical attention for both their rhetorical gestures and structures and their social and psychological insights, letters of friendship, particularly friendship among poets and artists working in isolation but with common aims, have been more frequently the focus of popular and biographical than of critical interest. Yet the question of how aesthetic ideas are debated and developed is of central importance to our understanding not only of a particular period but also of the nature of those ideas themselves. When the ideas in question are those of Symbolism, the literary and artistic movement that united so many diverse talents in fin-de-siècle France and Belgium before spreading through the whole of Western culture, the letters take on a particular value, thanks in large measure to the epistolary gifts of that movement's major figures, especially those of Mallarmé. And not just epistolary gifts either: what many of these writers possessed and cultivated in wonderful measure was the ability to convey friendship even in the briefest of formulas.

Mallarmé, whose work and friendship so powerfully influenced aesthetic theory and practice in the last decades of the nineteenth century, was the focus not only of the Tuesday gatherings but also of a voluminous correspondence. Many of his contemporaries, both close friends and total strangers, sent him copies of their books or invited him to exhibitions of their works of art or performances of their music. His responses to these works were frequently regarded as statements of great aesthetic importance, handed around from friend to friend and religiously kept or copied. Furthermore, several of those who attended Mallarmé's Tuesday gatherings also exchanged valuable letters with one another, kept diaries, or published memoirs about the age and its artistic movements. What, then, was the role of the many hundreds of letters they exchanged and in which they debated, often with passion and sometimes in anger, the aesthetic, ethical, and political questions they considered central? What relationship, if any, exists between, on the one hand, not merely the subject matter of these exchanges but also their rhetoric and, on the other hand, the creative writing their authors also produced? How much, in other words, can they be seen as a testing ground for the great experiments of Symbolism? To what extent do the letters reveal affinities and influences or, on the contrary, the anxious desire to break free of influence and the conscious or unconscious use of a correspondent's themes and rhetoric to reach a state of artistic independence?

In a characteristically suggestive and beautifully expressed article celebrating the completion of Lloyd Austin's edition of Mallarmé's eleven-volume correspondence,

Alison Fairlie proposes a close reading of these letters from the poet to friends and followers:

> IT WILL BE WORTH TRACING, through the final volumes of the *Correspondance,* particular sequences of letters, from those to early correspondents (Verlaine, Coppée . . .) through sustained discussion in middle life with those poets he selects for their suggestive qualities, potential or realized (Henri de Régnier receives an outstandingly rich series of reflections; Kahn, Verhaeren, Rodenbach, Vielé-Griffin, Guérin—and many others—are given recurrent appreciations), to the last years with the especial emergence of Valéry. [. . .] Such sequences of letters to individuals may particularly illuminate Mallarmé's own poetic practices.

"Most valuable of new possibilities," she adds, "would be an analysis of how, in letters of thanks, Mallarmé's indications of the art of suggestion in themselves exemplify that art."[7]

The poet and critic Yves Bonnefoy, in his preface to Bertrand Marchal's edition of selected letters, confirms that "Mallarmé's letters are often of extraordinary interest. In some of those written during his years in Tournon and Besançon, in particular, he has given us with regard to his exploration of the confines of mind and matter, and on poetry as he conceives of it, and on the poems he was trying to write at the time, information that nothing of his work, strictly speaking, can replace or even allow us to glimpse" (*CC,* 7).

Taking its initial inspiration from these remarks, my book is concerned above all with exploring the interrelationships of letters and literature, with the transformation of epistolary rhetoric into poetic creativity, and with reaching a closer understanding of the nature of both Symbolism and friendship. For Mallarmé in particular, and for many of these writers more generally, the letters trace a vital form of biography, revealing that life of the mind that was for most of the Symbolists the very essence of existence.

One of Mallarmé's early friendships, and one that lasted until the other poet's death, was with Paul Verlaine (Figure 2).[8] To the outsider, much would seem to separate these poets: Mallarmé was dapper, decorous, intellectual, and intensely private and self-effacing, while Verlaine was exuberant, passionate, untidy, frequently drunk, and the subject of so much public scandal. Yet this was one of Mallarmé's most important friendships, and he, perhaps more than any of their contemporaries, saw what Verlaine was attempting in his poetry and valued that far too much to be disconcerted by the frequently publicized details of his friend's private life. A look at his first letter to Verlaine, especially in the context of the poets' contrasting personalities and their future friendship, reveals several of the possibilities and problems of exploring the correspondence.

This letter to Verlaine dates from the closing years of France's Second Empire, December 1866, when Mallarmé was twenty-four. Victor Hugo, still in exile, had just published his novel *Les Travailleurs de la mer.* Baudelaire, deeply incapacitated by the stroke he had suffered while in Belgium, had only a few more months to live. The previous year had seen the publication of Leo Tolstoy's *War and Peace,* the presentation of Edouard Manet's provocative painting *Olympia,* the end of the American Civil War, and the assassination of Abraham Lincoln. François Coppée (Figure 4), another of Mallarmé's correspondents and his exact contemporary, had already published his first volume of verse, *Le Réliquaire,* modeled on the style and themes of the Parnassian poet Charles Marie Leconte de Lisle. Two other publications, however, pointed forward more clearly to the turbulent days of the Commune: the intransigent Jules Vallès had produced his series of evocations of Parisian outcasts and eccentrics, *Les Réfractaires,* and Suzanne Voilquin had completed her autobiographical feminist response to Saint-Simonianism, *Souvenirs d'une fille du peuple.* Earlier in 1866 the first volume of *Le Parnasse contemporain,* an anthology of contemporary poetry, had appeared under the exuberant editorship of Mallarmé's friend Catulle Mendès and had included poems by both Verlaine and Mallarmé. Under pressure from the United States, Napoleon III had withdrawn his support for Maximilien, the self-styled emperor of Mexico. Blacks had been granted voting rights in the United States, and the first transatlantic cable had been laid. Manet's *Le Fifre* had been rejected by the annual Salon, prompting Emile Zola to publish his articles in support of the artist in the daily newspaper *L'Evénement.* Jacques Offenbach's lively operetta *La Vie parisienne* had been performed for the first time. Pyotr Ilich Tchaikovsky and Anton Bruckner had both completed their first symphonies, and Fyodor Dostoyevsky had published *Crime and Punishment.*

Not surprisingly, Verlaine's first volume of verse reflects the dominant influence of Hugo and Leconte de Lisle, showing the current fascination with the myths of India as well as those of Greece, and restoring the Romantic image of the poet— "L'amour du Beau, voilà sa foi, / L'Azur son étendard, et l'Idéal, sa loi!" (The love of Beauty is his faith, / his standard is the Azure, and the Ideal, his law!)[9]—regardless of Baudelaire's recent transformation of the artist into ragpicker or Théodore de Banville's image of the poet as street performer.

While it begins as a thank you letter for the copy of *Poèmes saturniens* that Verlaine had sent him, Mallarmé's letter rapidly assumes the tone and gestures of friendship:

December 20, 1866
Dear sir and poet,
Allow me to see in the exquisite kindness you showed in sending a copy of your book to me, although we are strangers, as much a literary sympathy, as the wonderful presentiment of an unknown friendship. You forestalled me in my desire to shake your hand, a desire I'd formed after reading your poems in

Le Parnasse. Let me thank you twice over—and more than that!—because these *Saturnine* poems saved me for several days from the ineptitude to which I'm condemned by the worries of setting up home, and healed me of the shame inflicted by reality. (*CC,* 331)

This is where the shift comes, almost imperceptibly, when the standard words of thanks are transformed by the entry into Mallarmé's private life. The reference to the "wonderful presentiment of an unknown friendship" transforms the salutation, creating in its own way that radical shift from the familiar and banal to the unexpected but magically appropriate that stamps Mallarmé's poetry. Cliché, as Baudelaire knew, is "an anthill dug out by generations of ants,"[10] to be both valued and sidestepped for precisely those reasons, and here in his *captatio benevolentiae* Mallarmé masterfully draws on the familiarity of the anthill so as to switch his language from the ant runs of routine to the very different familiarity of true friendship. Here Mallarmé suggests, as he will do later with Valéry and with his Belgian friends, that a friendship newly formed often seems to have existed forever. Even so, this suggestion could in itself be a mere formula, an affectation of universal fraternity of the sort so famously proclaimed by Hugo and so furiously detested by Baudelaire. Mallarmé's letter to Verlaine, however, continues in ways that provide, as Hugo's letters so undeniably do not, that glimpse into the other's personality that betokens real friendship.

Just as Verlaine's volume rescued the poet in provincial exile from the upheaval caused by everyday existence and allowed him to return to the realms he wanted uniquely to inhabit—those of the mind and of art—so, conversely, does it guarantee Verlaine an intimate view into that other world, the world of shameful reality:

So IT WASN'T AT TOURNON that your book found me but at Besançon, surrounded by the backs of picture frames, broken pieces of furniture— visits—which I can't avoid if I'm to obtain any tranquillity from those who hold my fate and my work in their hands. I feel so tired, not yet having a room furnished with my thoughts, but living in a corridor, that I would prefer the greatest of struggles to that of writing a letter. When I do, I feel as if I'm crossing blades with an enemy, so painful is it for me to appear in my present state. Let me, therefore, leave my wit in its scabbard, covered with spider webs and dust, and don't hold against me the torpor of my expression. (*CC* 331–32)

Torpor is hardly the word that comes to mind in reading this remarkable evocation of Mallarmé's public and private life. This is the life of teaching he had chosen because it would leave him more time for writing, a decision that must fill those involved in the profession with a sense of sardonic foreboding. Transferred through the provinces at the will and whim of a ministry more concerned (and who can blame them?) with their employees' gifts as teachers than with their power as poets, distanced from the intellectual stimulus and support of Paris, and forced by his wife and child's dependence on him to pay at least lip service to the conventions of small-town society, Mallarmé tumbled into that deep depression which for him eventually resulted in the formulation of new beliefs, a new religion, and a new language.

Here, in his letter to Verlaine, the upheaval of moving to Besançon is at once a physical reality and an impetus to transform a state of mind into a series of symbols. This is one of the reasons why Mallarmé's letters shed so much light on his mind. It's not necessarily what they say or how they evoke the physical reality in which he worked but that they show how symbols that were to become familiar in his later poetry are deeply rooted in his everyday experience. Of course this familiarity is to some extent already obvious to anyone reading the poems outside their contemporary context. Most of Mallarmé's symbols, after all, stem from commonplace reality: sunsets, mirrors, lace curtains, flower vases. But in a letter such as this to Verlaine, these elements of daily life are not impersonal but closely tied to the poet's personal and private life. The window and the lace curtain that appear in "Une dentelle s'abolit" (Lace abolishes itself), in other words, could be seen as mere abstractions, elements of a standard bedroom:

Une dentelle s'abolit
Dans le doute du Jeu suprême
A n'entr'ouvrir comme un blasphème
Qu'absence éternelle de lit.

Cet unanime blanc conflit
D'une guirlande avec la même,
Enfui contre la vitre blême
Flotte plus qu'il n'ensevelit.

(Lace abolishes itself
In the doubt of the Supreme Game
Merely half-opening, like an act of blasphemy
On the eternal absence of a bed.

This unanimous white conflict
Of one garland with the same,
Fled against the pale window
Floats more than it buries itself away.) (*OC*, 74)

The letter indicates that these elements are not just standard equipment but begin as the fabric of Mallarmé's personal world before undergoing the subtle transformations that make them, if not impersonal, at least certainly universal.

The pictures piled higgledy-piggledy around him, together with the broken furniture, come sharply into focus in this brief reference before undergoing that transformation of the real into the ideal that marks the best of Symbolist poetry, a metamorphosis that happens with the expression "une chambre meublée de ma pensée" (a room furnished with my thoughts). The phrase itself starts as, if not a cliché, at least a *lieu commun* of nineteenth-century imagery. The idea of the mind as a room, a chamber, an architectural space, would certainly be familiar to Mallarmé's correspondent, but what seizes the attention is the shift the poet has made. Here the image concerns less the room that represents the mind than a living space furnished with the poet's thoughts. The allusion seems to be to those ancient tracts on memory, where the student creates the image of a vast library in which everything he or she needs to recall is placed on specific shelves.[11] This is the image that is to be so brilliantly and idiosyncratically transformed in the later sonnets, particularly "Ses purs ongles" (Her pure nails) and "Mes bouquins refermés" (My books closed again), an image Mallarmé is already working out through the medium of this surprisingly intimate first letter to Verlaine.

"Living in a corridor," the expression Mallarmé uses to portray his situation at the moment of writing the letter, is also fraught with echo and suggestion, with a comfortable intimacy that has little to do with the superficial and quotidian and everything to do with the intimacy of the intellect, the acknowledgment of a common quest, and the acceptance that individuals, even close friends, take different approaches to this quest. The corridor is at once firmly connected to everyday reality and an image of that sense of passage: from province to province, from this world to the next, from one concept of poetry to another. Mallarmé uses here the French word *corridor,* as he will later for his poem in memory of Théophile Gautier, where the "magic hope of the corridor" is the belief in the passage from this world to another (*OC,* 54). In the letter, as a result of one of those typical Mallarméan slippages through the word's layers of alternate meanings, the poet sees himself as living in a fortified space ready for imminent conflict, running the gauntlet, participating in a *corrida.* He could have chosen the term *couloir* and played with the idea, suggested by the cognate verb *couler,* of slipping and flowing into the liquid morass of his social existence, but this apparently least militaristic of writers selects instead the term that will lead on to the extended metaphor of armed fight. His fight is that inflicted on him by the need to write a letter (a common complaint in this voluminous correspondence) instead of devoting his writing time to creative work. Yet, of course, creative work demands another kind of battle, transforms the writer into a different kind of warrior, as Mallarmé goes on to affirm, when he turns the letter almost imperceptibly and with characteristic elegance back to Verlaine.

To continue with my swashbuckling comparisons—sorry! (but it's over a month now since I made a comparison!) let me tell you how happy I was to see that with all the old forms, those well worn favorites, that poets inherit from each other, you felt you had to forge a new and virgin metal, fine blades unique to yourself, rather than go on digging into those well worn grooves, leaving an old and ill-defined aspect to things. (*CC* 332)

Here, too, Mallarmé is clearly meditating on the relationship between the formulaic and the freshly forged, between cliché and creativity. Verlaine's *Poèmes saturniens* play with several standard forms, brought back into the repertory by poets who dominate the mid-nineteenth century, Hugo and Banville, Gautier and Baudelaire: the five-line stanza with the fifth line repeating the first, the villanelle, in which three-line stanzas are followed by a concluding quatrain, and the sonnet (but the *sonnet libertin* rather than the standard form that Banville was to describe in his *Petit Traité de versification française,* or the sonnet that opens with its tercets instead of its quatrains, the goldfish standing on its head so admired by Joris Karl Huysmans's eccentric protagonist Des Esseintes in his novel *A Rebours* [*Against the Grain*]). For Mallarmé, who will later watch as younger poets explore *vers libéré* and *vers libre,*[12] and who, in 1894, will report to audiences in Oxford and Cambridge the amazing news that "on a touché au vers" (they're experimenting with the line of poetry) (*OC,* 643), the alexandrine remains the special sword the poet draws from its case only when circumstances demand perfection. The "old forms"—sonnets, rondeaux, rondels, and so forth—are those Mallarmé most often turns to, despite Un *coup de dés,* which Mallarmé himself describes as his contribution to the prosodic experiments of his age. Even such innovative structures as those used in "L'Après-midi d'un faune" and "Hérodiade" are innovative within the familiar framework of the alexandrine. Like clichés, the standard poetic forms, according to Mallarmé, offer the value of an inheritance, a treasure chest handed down from generation to generation, but equally like clichés, their faded engravings cannot merely be followed but must be used to re-create, to reforge in Mallarmé's language something at once familiar and unique. As will so often be the case, Mallarmé uses his evocation of Verlaine's verse to sharpen his own thinking, making of it not so much a sounding board that echoes his own voice as a testing ground that either reinforces his own convictions or compels a reformulation of them.

Equally typical of the letters written to Verlaine after his return to Paris in 1871 is the imperceptible movement from praise to a suggestion of concern: the "it doesn't matter at this stage, but if you continue along this road you may hit a quagmire further on" that occurs under such a variety of different formulas:

Y OU'VE MASTERED YOUR WEAPONS NOW, and are free to deepen them (sometimes they have that air of boldness that sits so well only in a first volume). But your book is, in all its beauty and in the romantic meaning of the term, a first volume, and one which on many evenings has made me regret the vanity that has determined me to hand over my work only when it is complete and perfect, and when it can only decline. (*CC* 332–33)

The apparent mixed metaphor of deepening weapons is justified here through the earlier reference to the grooves (*ciselures*), but what seizes the attention is the unpretentious but unmistakable differentiation between writer and recipient. Friendship, as this affirmation and acceptance of difference insists, is also what makes not just possible but unproblematic the calm acceptance of variance. There is, of course, a degree of posturing in the choice of word *vanity,* for this decision not to publish anything until the whole is complete and perfect is indeed vain, in all senses of the word. Yet it is also part of Mallarmé's modesty, the modesty that pushes him to describe his poems as "studies aiming at something better, as one tries out one's pen nibs" (*OC,* 77).

The letter's closure is typical of its writer's mentality and his preferences. Throughout his long correspondence there is as a constant refrain the desire to meet and talk, the insistence that what is central to life (poetry, literature, art) demands the informal forum of fireside and conversation rather than the enforced formality of paper and pen. And, too, there is that closing *captatio benevolentiae,* that offer of the "balm of time" (*OC,* 75) that consists in suggesting an intimate knowledge of the recipient's work. Mallarmé will repeatedly show by quotation, suggest by allusion, or, as here, simply affirm that he has entered into the volume he has been sent and learned it by heart (and who, more than Mallarmé, can rescue that tired formula from its hackneyed surface and restore it to its original force and beauty?):

A ND MOREOVER, I WOULD SO LOVE to send you in exchange for your gift something other than this miserable and banal letter to which I dare append my signature only in order to find once more a pretext for shaking your hand from the very depths of my heart, and in *friendship,* do you accept it? while awaiting that good conversation at some better time—and it will be better, even if I were to be condemned forever to my present stupidity, for the sole reason that I'll see you! At the moment I'd have the courage only to recite to you all the lines I know by heart from *Poèmes saturniens,* preferring, so greatly am I still at odds with myself, to cling to the intense pleasure they give me, rather than to explain that pleasure.

You will receive, once I've finished this winter's work, a true reading, and until then you will live around me like my absent friends. (*CC* 332–33)

"Vous vivrez autour de moi comme mes amis absents" (You will live around me like my absent friends): This, too, is a sentiment familiar to all readers of Mallarmé's correspondence, as over the years he repeats to many friends and acquaintances that the work they've sent him builds around him a room, a tower, a garden of their thought.

Verlaine, or at least his volumes of verse and prose, was indeed to spend much of the ensuing decades *"autour de"* Mallarmé. Aspects of the rest of their correspondence I consider in Chapter 1, but for the moment I want to concentrate on this letter as typical of Mallarmé's early correspondence to fellow poets. While the letters to such close friends as Henri Cazalis reveal more of Mallarmé's personal life and chart in detail the evolution of his aesthetic thinking away from Parnassian and Baudelairean models and toward a poetry of suggestion and implication, this letter is far more indicative of his later exchanges. From the salutation acknowledging Verlaine as a fellow poet, through the brief but illuminating glimpse into the intellectual reality of Mallarmé's existence, mediated by a physical reality that serves only to provide the metaphors, not to set limitations or parameters, and into the pithy expression of admiration for the poems Verlaine has sent him, the letter sets out a series of rhetorical gestures that will serve to delineate his epistolary model.

As he became better known, as volumes of poetry and packets of novels poured in, as letters piled up on his desk, Mallarmé, that apparently prolific writer of letters, was to lament more and more frequently the duty of replying to all his correspondents and to resort more and more to formulas. Yet even in the most structurally formulaic of his letters there is always a personal touch, a play on words, a quotation, an allusion that indicates that the letter received has been read, the pages of the volume at least cut and leafed through, the poems dipped into and savored. The burden of courtesy may have weighed heavily on the shoulders of the somewhat finicky figure we see wrapped in a shawl in Paul Nadar's 1895 photograph of him (Figure 10), but what Mallarmé so clearly relished was the alchemical transformation of such burdens into precious stones, like the transformation of mere arbitrary sounds into the single, entirely appropriate line of verse. In Mallarmé's age, after all, the letter was, after conversation, the supreme form of communication, and with the aid of a mail service whose efficiency modern paper methods cannot hope to emulate, letters offered a form of exchange that was rapid, subtle, complex, and lasting. While he may not have imagined that even the most superficially banal of his letters—a request for tickets, the acknowledgment of a basket of fruit—would be meticulously preserved and subsequently annotated with all the knowledge and authority of a Lloyd Austin or a Bertrand Marchal, there is little doubt that he perceived most of his later letters as potentially public, vehicles to test ideas and possibilities for an audience that might be critical but that would be both far more demanding and forgiving than the broader public of the literary review and the published volume. It is this awareness, together with the shared sense of an adventure in writing and interpreting, that gives his letters a particular energy and that invites us to explore them more deeply in the context of his prose and verse writing as well as in that of their literary and artistic context. One could argue—critics have, indeed, argued—that Mallarmé's letters (apart from those sent from the provinces to close friends) lack the sense of the daily struggle to create that so wonderfully marks Gustave Flaubert's correspondence, or the grinding poverty and bitterness pervading Baudelaire's letters, and that somehow miraculously crystallized out as *Les Fleurs du mal*. But whereas Flaubert and Baudelaire are what they are because of the powerful egocentricity of their natures, Mallarmé defines his own egocentricity in terms of those to whom he writes, and in so doing he sheds a particular light on his age and its literature, art, and critical writing. As Armand Renaud puts it when still a young poet, Mallarmé's letters frequently offer a "delicious mixture of poetry and friendship" (*DSM*, 7: 216) that makes them quite different in nature from those of either Baudelaire or Flaubert.

Most of his letters date from the period of France's Third Republic, the republic of Protestants and teachers, an age scarred by the defeat not just of the army in the Franco-Prussian War but of the values of expansionism and capitalism that had dominated the empire of Napoleon III. With a shift in power away (in part) from the upper bourgeoisie toward a more liberal intellectual elite, away from the exploitation of the many for the benefit of the few and toward a greater demand for mass education and reformed factory laws, France was at last putting into effect, often for reasons far removed from their initial impetus, ideas that had been formulated in the years leading up to the Revolution of 1789. These decades saw a rapid expansion in literacy, for it was during these heady years that the education minister, Jules Ferry, proclaimed in a speech made to parliament on December 20, 1880, "For us the book, do you hear me, the book, whatever its nature, is the fundamental and irresistible means of freeing the intelligence." With far less censorship than under Napoleon III, many so-called little reviews flourished, and if the Impressionists were still putting their works on show in venues other than the official salons, those venues at least existed and were often at least as exclusive as the official ones. It was a time of great experimentation in the arts, an age of literary cabarets and clubs, but it was also, particularly toward the end of the century, a political moment when the sense of liberation turned to anarchy, terrorism, and bigotry. It saw the return of the question of what role violence should play in effecting political change, a question debated across Europe, from Karl Marx and Friedrich Nietzsche to Leo Tolstoy, and agonizingly pondered by George Sand forty years before in novels such as *Les Maîtres-Sonneurs* (*The Master Pipers*), and while Mallarmé has often been seen as shutting himself off from anything as vulgar as politics, it is undeniable that his letters and his prose writing reflect a continuing sharp awareness of the power of the assassin's bomb and an ongoing inner debate about the effectiveness of literature in comparison with so powerful a weapon. Central also to Mallarmé's thinking is the debate concerning the relative roles of music and literature, particularly poetry. Given the immense popularity of Wagner and his overweening ambitions, Mallarmé, whose love of music seems to have been deep and spontaneous, found himself frequently meditating on ways to reach a contemporary and a future public. The poet's innate courtesy, coupled with his subtle but insistent irony, makes many of his published statements in this regard slippery reading. His letters, while equally subject to the distortions of courtesy and irony, add further glimpses into his thinking.

Whether he is commenting on art or literature, music or politics, bicycles or top hats, Mallarmé's language is complex, multilayered, at once deeply felt and self-effacing. Reading it in such a way as to navigate the pitfalls and shoals of his wit and irony demands a constant close attention, a sensitivity to the slightest of signals, and a knowledge of the contemporary baggage and varnish attached to certain terms and phrases. While sentences from his letters, particularly the early ones to friends of his own age, are frequently taken as limpid and unchanging statements of aesthetic or epistemological conviction and practice, I argue that the letters are, in their own way, as complex, demanding, and subject to multiple interpretations as many of his poems and articles. Moreover, a letter is always written with a particular reader in mind; its tone, its function, its very formula and structure are in some measure determined by the current relationship between writer and intended recipient. In reading over poets' shoulders (as the poet Paul Valéry argued we must even when reading creative writing), we may be blinded by their physical presence, but less so than if we refuse to see them, and their intended reader, at all.

If we want to reach a deeper understanding of Mallarmé's letter writing (and to some extent, because of his influence on his friends and followers, of the letters of other Symbolists), it is worth considering the ways in which he refers to the act of letter writing and the place his correspondence occupies in his life. Unsurprisingly, what is most striking is the switch in nature between his letters before and after his return to Paris. The isolation he felt in the provinces, the driving need to overcome that isolation as far as possible through a communication of minds with chosen correspondents, and the evident desire to build long-lasting friendships all shape the nature and importance of those early letters, even though we already find in them the refrain of laments at the number of letters needing to be written. Later, when increasing fame brought a vast increase in the letters he received and extended his range of correspondents well beyond those he chose himself, we find a growing refrain of regret for the time and energy that letter writing exacted. But even within those complaints we might note the range of imagery used to depict the act of writing and receiving letters. The magic power of the name so frequently and so unforgettably evoked in Mallarmé's critical writing and in *Poésies* in such expressions as "awaken for the Rose and the Lily the mystery of a name" (*OC*, 55), also plays a role in letter writing: "I've long had ready an envelope on which your name strutted in a tempting fashion" (*CC*, 139). Letters often open with a deprecating statement insisting that they are not real letters but mere scribbles (*gribouillages*) to fill a need, even if they can't attain the perfect form their writer would ideally give them. There are endless variations on "This isn't a letter" (*CC*, 355, 371). But letters also mark a sense of ceremony, the celebration of important dates that Mallarmé was to value so highly in his depictions of festivities and crowds: "Let me take advantage of the new year to shake your hand, from far away—from the depths of Boredom" (*CC*, 217); "I'm tearing off a white leaf from the frightening volume of my new year's day correspondence, just to write you a mere two words. I've met charming creatures, creatures who have loved me, how can I not remember myself to them once a year?" (*CC*, 271);

"Although I took your hand a few days ago, as if in a Dream, I don't want this new year's day to pass without your receiving a line from me" (*CC*, 273).

However brief, however conventional the reason for writing, letters to close friends are for Mallarmé notes in a continuing song. To Villiers, whom he was later to depict as a man accustomed to dream, he states, "A letter between the two of us is a banal melody that we allow to wander as it will, while our two souls, which understand themselves so wonderfully, create a natural and divine bass beneath its vulgarity" (*CC*, 278). For greater intimacy, he suggests jokingly to the provençal poet Théodore Aubanel, "I'm scribbling a little message for you in pencil, so as to avoid seeming to place a letter between us, and so we can chat more intimately" (*CC*, 311; compare 414).

In his twenties, the arrival of letters and the invitation to reply to them are often a source of joy, a means of escape from the narrowness and boredom of the provinces:

> MORE THAN EVER, A FEW MINUTES AGO, I was crushed by the provinces. My head in my hands, I was sunk in a brown study, when trumpets, bursting out at my windows, ran through me and shook from my eyes an old tear, gathered by many an ordinary hour and by worries remote from Anguish, by stupidity. Your volume appeared on the table and I'm taking advantage of its charming invitation to leave my torpor through a conversation with its poet, and to abandon myself as well, if I'm not mistaken, to my emotions in the company of the friend I feel I have in you. (*CC*, 328)

The absence of letters is lamented as a threat to friendship, but one that can easily be overcome by a meeting of minds: "Don't let's put centuries between us! Of course there is a land where we must often meet, but since it seems that our two reveries may cross each other without their diaphanous selves feeling so much as a slight shiver, let's have recourse to the writing desk" (*CC*, 440). And, as in the first letter to Verlaine, the letter that offers, renews, or reaffirms friendship often brings with it a sudden, intense glimpse into Mallarmé's existence, not so much the physical and humdrum existence as that of the mind's personal landscape: "Because you did not come, filling the dark stairway with your well-known footstep, to tell us as you opened the door: 'It's me,' because I'm all alone as I close my book on my Sunday, I'll light the lamp before dinner, I won't listen to Marie or Vève telling me about their walk when they get home, and I'll put this sheet of paper between us" (*CC*, 451). As a bridge between friends, as a corridor from one mind to another, these early letters may be playful and sportive, self-mocking and unbuttoned, but they are above all youthful. With the defeat of France in the Franco-Prussian War; with the death of his friend, the precociously talented young artist Henri Regnault, and with the return to Paris, Mallarmé's letters change. It is not that they are less revealing or less warm, but there is in them something undeniably different in quality. They become, perhaps, more gemlike, more self-contained, shifting from the self-obsession of the Faune toward the self-possession of the Master of *Un coup de dés*. Above all, I would argue, they reflect that determination we notice in Mallarmé on his return to Paris from the provinces to take control of his life, his image, and his destiny. These letters are not so readily mined for pithy aesthetic formulas and as a result are less well known. But I intend here to read them within the broader context of Mallarmé's earlier letters, the prose and poetry he published, and the letters and works he received.

Reading in Mallarmé's Letters

Lire—
cette pratique—
—Œuvres complètes, *386*

Understanding Mallarmé's letters, so many of which are responses to works of literature, demands some understanding of how he read, what he looked for, what attracted his attention, and what he tended to skate over. Yet exploring the nature of
someone else's reading habits demands a leap of imagination and an attention to detail that is not often discussed in either literature or criticism.[1] The delights of the
mind and of the flesh are staple fare for much of literature. The joys of the table and
the bed, the pleasure of painting or swimming, the sense of achievement at climbing
a mountain or mastering a boat are captured in countless tales and evoked in countless lyrics. Yet reading them we might meditate on the relative paucity of descriptions of another pleasure: that of reading itself. Artists give us glimpses of readers lost
in a book (what better way of getting your model to sit still?)—Pierre-Auguste
Renoir's painting *The Children's Afternoon at Wagemont,* for instance, or Gustave
Courbet's famous image of Baudelaire deep in a massive tome on the edge of his canvas *The Artist's Studio.* Films sometimes use it as a device to move into the plot, as
happens in *The Never Ending Story* (1984), or to suggest cultural differences: Here
one might think of the pages flicking across the scene in Nicolas Roeg's *Walkabout*
(1971), as the white boy tells the Aboriginal a fairy tale he has read. But where is
it that art reveals *how* other people read and in particular how poets and writers
themselves read? Montaigne may have been right when he asserted in his essay "De
l'expérience" that there are more books on books than on any other subject, but as
A. S. Byatt maintains in *Possession,*

N OVELS HAVE THEIR OBLIGATORY TOUR-DE-FORCE, the green-flecked gold
omelette *aux fines herbes,* melting into buttery formlessness and tasting of
summer, or the creamy human haunch, firm and warm, curved back to reveal
a hot hollow, a crisping hair or two, the glimpsed sex. They do not habitually

elaborate on the equally intense pleasure of reading. There are obvious reasons for this, the most obvious being the regressive nature of the pleasure, a *mise-en-abyme* even, where words draw attention to the power and delight of words, and so *ad infinitum,* thus making the imagination experience something papery and dry, narcissistic and yet disagreeably distanced, without the immediacy of sexual moisture or the scented garnet glow of good burgundy. And yet, natures such as Roland's are at their most alert and heady when reading is violently yet steadily alive.[2]

In this and in many other areas Marcel Proust breaks free from what novelists, in Byatt's term, "habitually" do. His first-person narrator is also one of those who is "at their most alert" or at least most intense when alive to reading and its effects: "in sleeping I hadn't stopped meditating on what I had just been reading, but those meditations had taken a particular form; it seemed to me that I myself was whatever the book had been talking about: a church, a quartet, the rivalry between François Ier and Charles-Quint."[3] Wallace Stevens's beautiful poem "The House was quiet" explores a similar imbrication of reader and book, but in a different register:

The house was quiet and the world was calm.
The reader became the book; and summer night

Was like the conscious being of the book.
The house was quiet and the world was calm.[4]

His poem "The Reader," less analytical and less exegetical, distills even more forcefully the experience of reading: "All night I sat reading a book, / Sat reading as if in a book / Of somber pages."[5] Like Proust's Marcel as a child, Stevens's reader moves through the interstices of reading, "as if in a book," daydreaming through the cracks of reading, through the gaps that are misunderstood or in Marcel's case omitted as his mother censors George Sand's novel *François le champi* as she reads, prudishly leaving out links and explanations that would make sense of the story but that would also close it, transforming somber pages into mere white light.

Writers do, of course, and particularly in autobiography, give us glimpses into how they read, allow us, to use the title of Robert Graves's essay collection, to "read over their shoulder." Thumbnail sketches of the reader leap out from a range of texts: Simone de Beauvoir as a child, lost in the world of *Little Women,* Jules Vallès's unforgettable vignette of Jacques Vingtras punished for an offense at school by being locked in a room where he finds *Robinson Crusoe* and loses all sense of time and place, Arthur Rimbaud's robust if fleeting vision of the seven-year-old poet dreaming of sea voyages in the enclosed space of the attic, or Baudelaire's even briefer allusion to the child in love with maps and engravings.[6] But what I have in mind here is the desire to know not just the sense of joy and discovery and heady excitement, but how, to quote Baudelaire, writers transform the "*volupté*" of reading into "*connaissance*," intense pleasure into understanding. With Baudelaire we have, if not a clear sense of how this works, at least something stronger than an inkling, a series of suggestions and hints that he himself analyzes in his art and literary criticism with his characteristically lucid desire to comprehend. Why is it, he asks, thinking of the poetry of Marceline Desbordes-Valmore, that our reading sometimes awakens responses that seem to run counter to our deeply held convictions and loudly proclaimed opinions? Or, and here it is Hugo's poetry that has goaded him into going deeper into his initial response, why is it that what others uphold as great poetry and that we ourselves intermittently glimpse as such still does not satisfy us? Baudelaire's reading habits, disorganized and fragmented by the exigencies of his chaotic lifestyle, find a fragmented reflection not only in his literary criticism but also in his translations of Edgar Allan Poe and Thomas de Quincey, where the slips and errors that separate their idiosyncratic English from Baudelaire's far more classic French not only remold them as writers into palpably different figures but also indicate that in gazing into the language of the other Baudelaire was also gazing into his own language. In this case, it is not so much that the translator is a traitor, as the Italian proverb puts it; it is more that other writers are always magic mirrors that let him present himself more tellingly.

Perhaps even more than Baudelaire, the image we have of Mallarmé is of a reader. If there is, to my knowledge, no portrait, painted or photographed, that shows him in the act of reading, there is Paul Gauguin's haunting image of him with Poe's raven close behind him, as if reading over his shoulder, as if suggesting that what he has read, like the raven, will leave him nevermore. We know a great deal about what books he had in his library. Many of them are still there in Valvins, in what has now become the Musée Mallarmé. We can deduce from the more than eleven volumes of correspondence and from the numerous accounts of his Tuesday evening gatherings much of how he talked about reading. We can grasp from the care he paid in his own publications to such physical matters as typeface, spacing, paper quality, binding, and ornamentation that for him reading was not just a question of focusing on the words: Gérard Genette's notion of the paratext was already fully familiar to him. And the way in which his poetry takes up familiar themes, responds to challenges set down by other poets, and plays with the poetic language and structures of his day allows us to perceive aspects of his reading as if it were a watermark glimpsed through the paper. The challenge, I think, lies in using these indications to reach a deeper awareness of how he read and how he experienced those moments when, like Wallace Stevens's reader, he "became the book."

A very early critical piece, an appreciation of his friend Emmanuel Des Essarts's *Les Poésies parisiennes,* shows him drawing on a series of indications and suggestions before even beginning to read the text. Although he would later argue that a book needs no introduction by another voice, he asserts here—and there's no reason to think he changed his mind later on—that a preface by the author plays an essential role in helping the reader to find out what the writer "set out to do" (*OC,* 249). There's no timidity on his part about intentional fallacies: "I've always had a deep love for prefaces. When there is no preface and you have the good fortune to find a book as sincere as this one, you seek out the idea in the title, which encapsulates it, and in the epigraphs, which reveal it" (*OC,* 249). It is of course noticeable that Mallarmé himself rarely offered his reader such clues, naming his collection of poems simply *Poésies,* frequently supplying no titles for his sonnets, and delighting in bestowing on his volumes of criticism such bland, modest names as *Pages, Crayonné au théâtre,* and *Variations sur un sujet.* Part of the value for Mallarmé of focusing on the title is that it allows him to meditate, at least for a while, on what the poetry might do, rather than facing the rather more embarrassing task of responding to what Des Essarts actually had done: "clearly delineated contours, a sure sense of rhythm, and a certain breadth unfolding as do great monuments: that," he suggests, "is the sum of what one might expect" (*OC,* 250). Meditation based on a title, an epigraph, or a hint in the text or paratext becomes a constant theme in his criticism and especially in his correspondence; it finds what is perhaps its best-known formulation in the closing poem of *Poésies,* initially entitled "Autre sonnet" (Another sonnet) and now known only by its opening line: "Mes bouquins refermés sur le nom de Paphos" (My books closed once more on the name of Paphos):

Mes bouquins refermés sur le nom de Paphos,
Il m'amuse d'élire avec le seul génie,
Une ruine, par mille écumes bénie
Sous l'hyacinthe, au loin, de ses jours triomphaux.

Coure le froid avec ses silences de faulx,
Je n'y hululerai pas de vide nénie
Si ce très blanc ébat au ras du sol dénie
A tout site l'honneur du paysage faux.

Ma faim qui d'aucuns fruits ici ne se régale
Trouve en leur docte manque une saveur égale:
Qu'un éclate de chair humain et parfumant!

Le pied sur quelque guivre où notre amour tisonne,
Je pense plus longtemps peut-être éperdument
A l'autre, au sein brûlé d'une antique amazone.

(My books closed once more on the name of Paphos,
I delight in summoning up, with nothing but my genius,

A ruin, blessed by a thousand foams
Under the far-off hyacinth of its days of triumph.

Let the wind speed by with its silence of sickles,
I will not howl in empty denial
If this very white ecstasy level with the soil maintains
That no site has had the honor of my false landscape.

My hunger which cannot be sated with the fruit found here
Finds in their erudite absence an equal savor:
Let one of them burst forth with perfumed human flesh!

My foot on some fire-dog where our love burns quietly,
I ponder even longer perhaps and lost in thought
On the other, on the burnt breast of an Amazon of antiquity.) (*OC*, 76)

"Summoning up, with nothing but [his] genius" an imaginary landscape, or dreaming, with his foot on the fire dogs, of "the burnt breast of an Amazon of antiquity": This is Mallarmé's archetypal image of the reader moving beyond the text and into the theater of his or her own imagination.

It is not that Mallarmé merely uses hints in the text he is reading as a springboard into daydreaming: as his early prose piece, *Symphonie littéraire,* demonstrates, these reveries generally stem from a more standard exploration of the text, offering in other words a response based on, but going beyond, analysis. The section of the *Symphonie littéraire* that deals with *Les Fleurs du mal* is both an admiring pastiche of one of Baudelaire's own critical techniques and a creative meditation on the text. Baudelaire's reading of Marceline Desbordes-Valmore's poetry, a reading that represents her imaginary world as a landscape and especially as a garden, seems to be the starting point for Mallarmé's own representation of *Les Fleurs du mal* as "a surprising landscape that comes to life under the gaze with the intensity of those created by that deep drug, opium" (*OC*, 263). His exploration of Baudelaire's landscape leaves him with a more general question—"What, therefore, is the fatherland?"—one that precipitates the study's final paragraph, a meditation with both book and eyes closed. Reading becomes, in the admirable formulation of Mallarmé's January 1888 letter to the Belgian poet Emile Verhaeren, "after a great delight, a prolonged study amidst the lamplight" (*Corr.*, III: 162). As that curious but typically Mallarméan use of "amidst" (*parmi*) suggests with its hints of reading through and by means of, but also surrounded by, the lamp is at once the physical object lighting the book, the context in which it is read, and the imaginative reader's active response to what is read, a symbol for the light of intelligence.

"After a great delight (*jouissance*)": Like Baudelaire's term *volupté, jouissance* is strongly physical, and it is not a random choice either. The *Symphonie littéraire* had already used it, more than twenty years earlier, to convey the poet's sense of impotence when reading "the inaccessible masters whose beauty fills me with despair" (*OC,* 261). Addressing the modern Muse of impotence who is about to read his response to these great masters, the narrative voice here announces, "You will find in it the delights of a purely passive soul which is as yet merely a woman and which tomorrow may be a beast" (*OC,* 261). The feminization of the reader, thus gendered because of the passivity generally associated with reading, is a frequent image in nineteenth-century writing, from Honoré de Balzac's addresses to his *lectrices,* through Baudelaire's more complex image of the astrologers whose reading of a woman's eyes leads to their fall and who seek escape from potential Circes in order, precisely, not to be changed into beasts, to Huysmans's Des Esseintes, whose feverish and extensive reading is revealed as yet another aspect of his impotence. In the misogynistic terms that run through so much late-nineteenth-century writing, passive reading is construed as feminine, an essential first step, but one that must be followed up by active analysis, a process gendered as virile. It would seem, therefore, that reading fully demands for Mallarmé a doubly gendered response.

It has been argued that much of what Mallarmé wrote to other poets when thanking them for the countless stream of books that were sent to him consists of nothing more than reflections about himself. This may be true enough in the case of some of the minor poets, or others whose themes and style were far removed from Mallarmé's, so that the only way to respond without being downright rude was to transform them into a mirror. But writers like Emile Verhaeren, Georges Rodenbach, and Henri de Régnier inspired letters that demand images based on quite different optical devices—if not microscopes revealing previously unknown truths then at least telescopes opening onto new horizons. Certainly Mallarmé's reading of Régnier's poetry, with its slowly evolving form of *vers libre,* led to a long series of letters exploring the nature of poetry and the value of the alexandrine, and this at a time when Mallarmé was working on the much revised study "Crise de vers," an essay that attempts to account for the development of free verse and at the same time to show its potential, its limitations, and its weaknesses.

Mallarmé's reading, it would seem from these letters and from the critical articles I've quoted thus far, is active and analytical, a playing out in the theater of his mind, to use his own expression (*OC,* 300), of what he feels a writer is attempting to achieve. It is also, perhaps inevitably, focused on techniques and artistry. We rarely get the sense of him being lost in the book's narrative or themes, except perhaps in his references to his adolescent reading of Charles Baudelaire or Théodore de Banville, Victor Hugo or Théophile Gautier. The correspondence, together with such contemporary accounts as those of Henri de Régnier, Edmond Bonniot (who was to marry Mallarmé's daughter), and Edouard Dujardin (best known for his development of interior monologue, in a novel that inspired James Joyce's use of the technique), lead us to think that for him the real delight lay not so much in the reading as in discussing what was read, through letters if necessary but even more pleasurably in the presence of the writer him or (rarely) herself. Although Mallarmé wrote his journalistic articles to earn money, I do not think anyone can be in much doubt that sharing his ideas with others in this way also caused him a real sense of joy, however much he might have complained about any task that reduced the time he could devote to poetry. Moreover, those articles allowed him to explore the concept of reading in a broader sense, turning the analytical skills to work on theater, mime, and dance.

He is in a sense also developing here the technique of the poets he admired as an adolescent: Banville, in his remarkable short story exploring the art of tightrope walker Hébé Caristi, and Gautier, in his theater criticism and the ballet *Giselle,* had both suggested ways of looking at the body as a signifier, even if they didn't explicitly analyze or theorize their thinking in this regard. And while Baudelaire's criticism focuses on the reading of texts, paintings, and in one case music, he does provide a starting point for reading a performer's body not just as displaying emotion but as symbolizing political or metaphysical revolt in his prose poem "Une mort héroïque" (A heroic death). But Mallarmé—more inward-looking, more determined not just to extract the connaissance from the volupté but to link that knowledge to a profound truth about human destiny, symbolized through an external sign—takes the metaphor of reading further than any of them. His remarkable piece Hamlet begins by playing on the concept of his own return to Paris in time for the theater season, a return forced on him by the coming of autumn, the season when his daughter, Geneviève, would rather pointedly indicate to him that it was time to leave Valvins by failing to replace the flower displays as they died. His conceit of reading autumn as a symbol of the brevity of human life is saved from cliché and banality by the intensity of the expression and by its function within the article itself, serving as an invitation to read symbolically in ways that are familiar to all of us from such banal examples as the fall of the leaves, but that, Mallarmé implies, we fail to extend into the life of the mind: "Far from everything, Nature, in autumn, prepares her Theater, sublime and pure, waiting to illuminate, in solitude, moments of meaning and prestige, so that a lucid eye may penetrate their sense (and it's a notable one, the destiny of man), so that a Poet may be recalled to mediocre pleasures and cares" (*OC,* 299). Within this context of interpretation, *Hamlet,* the play par excellence for Mallarmé, can be seen to embody the theater's sole subject: "the antagonism of dream in man, with the fatalities of his existence handed out by misfortune" (*OC,* 300).

Mallarmé's lucid eye also presents the ballet as a spectacle to be read. In his study "Ballets" he (famously) argues that

> the ballerina is *not a woman who dances,* for these juxtaposed reasons that she
> *is not a woman,* but a metaphor resuming one of the elementary aspects of our
> form, a blade, cup, flower, etc., and because *she does not dance,* suggesting, by

the miracle of shortcuts or leaps, with a corporeal writing what it would take paragraphs in dialogued or descriptive prose: she's a poem set free from all the apparel of a scribe (*OC,* 304).

"Blade, cup, flower": Quintessential motifs in Mallarmé's poetry, they are revealed in this suggestive evocation as metaphors we are invited to read, not just in the poems but in nature, where they, like the stars that constantly draw the gaze of the Mallarméan hero, demand interpretation as crucial elements of human existence.

When the curtain falls on play or ballet, when the books are closed or the letters set aside, when the fire of love burns quietly, the reader who is Mallarmé, or at least the image he provides of himself within the poems, chooses to retreat into the theater of the mind, to summon up with nothing but his imagination a triumphant summer landscape or merely a symbol of lost beauty. We may never find Mallarmé lost in a book, but we do find him, once the book has been closed, lost in thought, as he puts it in "Mes bouquins refermés," "plus longtemps peut-être éperdument" (perhaps for even longer, passionately).

CHAPTER ONE

Writing in Exile

> No one will ever achieve greatness who does not
> at least checker his life with solitude.
> —*Thomas De Quincey,* Confessions
> of an English Opium Eater

> The only inspiration and safeguard is solitude.
> One learns nothing from others.
> Mallarmé has often told me that.
> —*Henri de Régnier,*
> Annales psychiques et occulaires

Between 1861 and 1871, the years that saw the protracted arguments with his family over his career, his marriage to Maria Gerhard, and the bouts of deep depression and self-doubt that blighted his time in the provinces, Mallarmé enjoyed the companionship of a fairly tight-knit group of young friends: the artist Henri Regnault, the charming future Egyptologist Eugène Lefébure, and the now-forgotten poet Henri Cazalis, who published under the pseudonym of Jean Lahor (Figure 11). Less close at this stage, but certainly part of his group of friends, were Emmanuel Des Essarts, a prolific and genial *homme de lettres* who had first met Mallarmé when the latter was a schoolboy in Sens and Des Essarts was a young teacher there, and Catulle Mendès, whose energy and insight were largely responsible, together with those of Louis-Xavier Ricard, for launching the anthology of contemporary poetry, the *Parnasse contemporain,* and who subsequently played such an important role in championing the operas of Richard Wagner. (Much later, in his autobiographical letter to Paul Verlaine, Mallarmé listed as his "great friendships" [*OC,* 664] those with Mendès, Villiers de l'Isle-Adam, and Edouard Manet.) While living in the south of France, moreover, Mallarmé made the acquaintance of the group of poets known as the Félibrige, who were working to reintroduce as a literary language the dialect spoken south of the river Gironde during the middle ages, now known as Occitan or

Provençal. And he began writing to François Coppée and Verlaine, two poets with whom he was to remain in contact for more than twenty years.

Anyone reading Mallarmé's letters from this period will be struck by the importance these various correspondences held for the young poet, and by the strength of the central image he creates in them of an ongoing and vitally necessary conversation. With the move back to Paris, Mallarmé continued that conversation with different people and in ways that are more difficult to trace. Nevertheless, creating a network of minds that cared about art and literature seems to have been essential to him throughout most of his adult life. While he was later to describe this period in the provinces as a "life of complete monotony" (*Annales,* Notebook 9), both the enforced solitude and the letters he wrote established an indispensable basis for the development of his poetry.

The letters Mallarmé sent and received in the 1860s reflect a closeness of interest, a desire to share experiences, and a robust sympathy that recall the close, analytical, and formative friendships of late adolescence worldwide. Frequently explored for their insights into Mallarmé's developing aesthetic convictions, and into the intellectual and spiritual crisis he experienced during those years in the provinces, these letters have less often been the focus of the kind of attention I wish to pay to them—an attention that centers on their nature as exchanges, on their rhetorical gestures, and on the creation of a shared territory of language and imagery. In this chapter, I begin by concentrating above all on the correspondence with Lefébure and Cazalis, the two friends in whom Mallarmé most often confided at this period. Lefébure's letters were published by Henri Mondor in his biography of this engaging figure, and when read in conjunction with those Mallarmé wrote to him, they offer a sharply etched image of a friendship based on a meeting of minds and tastes, rather than on that sense of similar lived experience which is more important in the letters between Mallarmé and Cazalis. Those of Cazalis appear in Lawrence A. Joseph's edition, supplementing his biography of this interesting if minor poet. After focusing on the exchanges of these three letter writers I examine the correspondence with some of Mallarmé's other early friends, and with the two poets, Coppée and Verlaine, whose epistolary friendship with Mallarmé also dates from these early years and helps form his letter-writing style. His later letters to these poets, moreover, suggest a certain continuity of rhetoric.

Stéphane Mallarmé and Eugène Lefébure both attended the lycée in the city of Sens, and, although they were not in the same class at school (Lefébure was some four years older than Mallarmé), they appear to have established an increasingly close friendship in the mid-1860s. From 1866 to 1871 they wrote regularly to each other, and at least immediately after the death of Lefébure's young wife, the correspondence seems to have been conducted for a time on a fortnightly basis. Close enough to address each other by their given names, they nevertheless preferred the "cher ami" and never adopted the intimate form of the second-person pronoun, what the eminent Baudelaire scholar Claude Pichois has termed the "*tu horrible*." Lamentably, very few of Mallarmé's letters to his friend have been found, although almost none of Lefébure's seem to be missing. Why Lefébure, who became aware very early of his friend's great poetic gifts (*EL,* 171), should have destroyed or mislaid these letters is a mystery. In his biography, Mondor cites Lefébure's son as claiming that his father's memory was so good that he had no need of the letters themselves to remember exactly what Mallarmé had written to him, but that seems an unlikely reason for destroying the letters given Lefébure's awareness of the destiny awaiting his correspondent. Lawrence Joseph, in his biography of Cazalis, suggests more plausibly that when Lefébure was arrested by the Germans in early 1871 and his papers seized, the letters from Mallarmé may also have been taken (*HC,* 147n).

Their friendship stopped abruptly at the end of 1871, apparently because Lefébure, who, in the years between his first wife's death and his second marriage, had several long-term affairs, attempted to introduce one of his young women to the Mallarmé household. Mallarmé appears to have informed Lefébure—subtly, no doubt —that such a gesture was inappropriate. Forced to choose between his friend and his mistress, Lefébure, not without considerable pain, chose the latter, because, as he puts it with admirable dignity, "I have obligations to her, whereas where you're concerned, my poor friend, I would have had only requests, that's to say, services to ask of you" (*EL,* 333). This action brought to a sudden end not only the close epistolary contact between the two men but also the warm and mutually loving relationship between Mallarmé's young daughter, Geneviève, and the man she had always called "Bour." Mondor, while giving no reason for his interpretation or any documentation of other sources he may be using, implies that the disapproval came from Marie Mallarmé (*EL,* 81). But Mondor's misogyny is palpable in all his comments about Méry Laurent and about women poets such as Marceline Desbordes-Valmore, and the three letters in which Lefébure refers to the situation give no hint that anyone other than Mallarmé himself was behind this decision. Whatever the truth of this episode, it is impossible to read Mondor's dry, understated, and euphemistic account without a sense of enormous waste. Twenty years later, when Lefébure lost one of his sons, Mallarmé, who by then knew whereof he spoke, wrote to him with complete sympathy and with that sense of deep friendship that might come only from such long-term relationships. But it was too late at that stage for this particular friendship to be revived. What a mistake it is to believe in permanence— "Quelle erreur que de croire à la fixité!" (*EL,* 259)—as Lefébure exclaims in a remarkable letter written from Cannes in 1867.

Whatever brought the friendship to an end, those letters that have been found from among the many the two exchanged establish a context of images and memories that color much of Mallarmé's later letters to friends, confirmed or potential. Lefébure's character, passionate and introspective, extremely sensitive to the beauty of woman and of nature, self-deprecating and somewhat impractical, comes across clearly in his letters. Cazalis jokingly describes him as "the good, the excellent, the most pious and Hegelian, the most placid and gentle, the stoutest and fattest, the very simple and very erudite, the highly philosophical and Egyptologist Lefébure" (*EL*, 221). From the first of Lefébure's letters that Mondor publishes, one dating from 1862 and written in Auxerre, there is a sense of not only deeply shared interests but also a youthful, totally unexamined conviction that older poets will be as open and welcoming to their juniors as Lefébure and Mallarmé were to each other. If Mallarmé needs the complete works of Poe, Lefébure suggests, he has only to ask Baudelaire for a copy, and while doing so he should seize the opportunity to discover if the author of *Les Fleurs du mal* believes in the devil. For a modern reader, only too aware of Baudelaire's sardonic view of the younger generation of poets, this is both touching and funny. After all, the Baudelaire of the prose poem "Perte d'auréole" (Loss of a halo) depicts his narrator losing his halo and thus finding it possible to enter dens of iniquity, while musing on the ludicrous possibility of someone else finding and wearing that mark of holiness. This has long been interpreted to refer to poets like Mallarmé and Emmanuel Des Essarts taking over Baudelaire's unenviable role as what Verlaine would later term a *poète maudit*. Given Baudelaire's somewhat rebarbative sense of humor, it is in any case unlikely that he would have taken kindly to such a question, even from the gentle soul who later answered, with such tongue-in-cheek seriousness, a journalist's question about the role played in modern society by the top hat (*OC*, 881). According to Henri de Régnier, Mallarmé told him that it was during his time in the provinces that he first came across Baudelaire's volume of poetry, although a letter written in London shows that he already had a copy then (*CC*, 151), and he was certainly familiar with individual poems long before that.[1] Régnier's account is worth quoting here, if only because of what it reveals about Mallarmé's own fashioning of the memories of his time in the provinces: "Mallarmé talks to me of Baudelaire and the strange fascination he felt on discovering his book, which was unknown to him, tucked away in a provincial bookshop. It was like a possession, something that could drive you insane" (*Annales*, October 1887). Consciously or not, the older Mallarmé seems to have evolved a vision of this period in the provinces that was significantly different from that revealed in his letters of the time. Attributing to it the "possession" that Baudelaire's volume of poetry exerted over him is central to that transformation.

What matters here is less Lefébure's naïveté than his sense, which Mallarmé clearly shared throughout his life, that between poets, established or tyro, there ought to be a sense of community, a setting aside of the usual barriers between generations and social classes, a collaboration that had about it nothing of the hostile or the demeaning. Later, in his support for an international society of writers[2] and his letters to the young poets who wrote to him, Mallarmé clearly champions—better still, embodies—such a conviction. And there seems to be strong grounds for arguing that without these early, nurturing epistolary exchanges such a view might not have gained the strength that it did.

The love and admiration these young poets felt for Baudelaire, less than a decade after *Les Fleurs du mal* was first published in volume form, and well before he had achieved anything like the place he holds today, is nowhere more evident than in the letters that refer to the cerebral hemorrhage he suffered in the church of Saint Loup in Belgium. Lefébure, writing from Cannes on March 17, 1866, sums up with beautiful and moving simplicity the existential absurdity of Baudelaire's stroke and the loss it represents to him personally as well as to literature in general:

I FEEL SIMULTANEOUSLY THUNDERSTRUCK and exasperated, like you, by that brutal blood clot that needed only to burst from its vein to extinguish the Prince of Dreams, proving with hateful obviousness once again, that genius is a magnificent illness and that it is fatal.

At the sudden solitude that formed around me, I realized that I was losing a father and the blow is such that I don't have the heart to write anything else to you, for I know you too are distraught. (*EL,* 210)

Mallarmé's letter to Lefébure telling him that Baudelaire had died has not yet been found, but the tone and substance are clear enough from Lefébure's reply. What strikes a modern reader in this context is the frequency and seeming ease with which Lefébure quotes not only from *Les Fleurs du mal* but also from the prose poems, which were published in volume form only in 1869, although they had appeared in periodicals through the late 1850s and early 1860s. In 1870, for instance, Lefébure alludes elegantly and apparently effortlessly to the prose poem "Bénédicta." Referring to himself, he notes that he has "discovered elements of [his] personality that were so revolting that [he] had to step back, despite all [his] good will, and cry out, like the poet on Benedicta's grave: 'No, no, no!'"(*EL,* 317; see also 299). This shared source of quotations, vocabulary, and imagery plays an important role in the creation of that sense of companionship that leads Mallarmé to remark at one point that Lefébure is his true brother.

The letters between the two friends are rich in comments on recent publications both by their contemporaries and by such established poets as Victor Hugo. These comments shed much light on their growing and changing beliefs about the function and nature of poetry. Nevertheless, for all their intrinsic interest, it isn't merely these discussions that lift the correspondence as such out of the ordinary, but also the intensity and originality of their image of the nature and function of friendship.

Reading the letters we have in the order in which they were written, we can watch unfolding an image of the nature of friendship and its place in the intellect that slots in perfectly to Mallarmé's more general image of the mind as room, lined with books, mirrors, and pictures. What is more, it is a conceit that is also closely tied to the personal imagery of his friend. Thus, for instance, in the letter in which Lefébure half playfully greets his friend in the name of the twenty-fifth Egyptian Dynasty, a joke indicative of a fascination that was soon to become a vocation, he draws for Mallarmé a series of hieroglyphs, including one based on his own name. This hieroglyph contains a depiction of a stork, an image Mallarmé takes up some eighteen months later and blends with his own fascination with Edgar Allan Poe's "The Raven":

> MELANCHOLY STORK OF THE IMMOBILE LAKES, doesn't your soul perceive itself in their mirror, with too much boredom—a boredom whose vague twilight disturbs the magical and pure charm and thus reminds you that it's your body that stands there, abandoned, on one foot, while the other is folded, ill, under your feathers? Come back to the sense of reality and listen to the guttural and friendly voice of another old bird, at once heron and raven, as it lands beside you. Let's hope the entire picture doesn't fade from your sight in the eddies and furrows of suffering! Before abandoning ourselves to our murmurings, the true conversations of birds that resemble reeds and are mingled with their vague stupor when we return to life from our fixed position on the pond of dream—on the pond of dream where all we catch is our own image, not even so much as the silver scales of fish!—let's at least ask ourselves, nevertheless, how we are, in this life! (*CC,* 346–47)

Melancholy birds murmuring in the reeds, gazing at their reflections in the motionless lakes of dream, the two friends, according to Mallarmé, speak to each other in "half-words exchanged amidst silences" (*CC,* 465), but they are more likely to picture themselves exchanging these suggestions behind closed doors. As in Mallarmé's verse poetry, the letters to Lefébure suggest that the ideal space for reverie and for deep communication is the study, not the great outdoors or even the controlled outdoor space of the garden. Writing to his friend in October 1865, Mallarmé offers a particularly seductive invitation that is clearly at once physical and imaginary:

> DELICATE ONE, ARE YOU WAITING for fires and winter before indulging in those good conversations around the chimney place? But you'll already have autumn, not the yellow and red autumn of the trees, but the foggy autumn of the waters. From my window, instead of greenery, which is unknown in this region, we have, like a vast pond, the river Rhône. This window is destined for you. [. . .] My room is so big and so high that I'm still a stranger in it, and have not yet populated it with my thought and my words. Come and make it mine, for you are almost me, just so that I can work. (*CC,* 255)

While there can be no doubting the sincerity of Mallarmé's wish to see his friend, there is also in this image a suggestion that the window out onto the world, together with the room populated with thoughts are less those of any external reality than those provided by the exchange of letters. It's a suggestion taken up by Lefébure himself. In May 1866, for instance, Lefébure writes from Cannes, where as he claims his body resides while his mind wanders freely in Cairo:

D ON'T BE SURPRISED TO FIND ME writing to you, it's simply a visit I'm paying you. So open the door for me, let me into your charming living room, darkened by its Chinese blinds that make it cool, let me curl up like a cat in one of your Louis XV arm chairs, and let my vague conversation float towards you to the rhythm of your adorable clock in Saxon porcelain, which seems molded with a paste of flowers. (*EL*, 214)[3]

After complaining about the weather and his own lack of aesthetic progress, he continues: "You can see quite clearly that I need to send what little remains of myself to stroll outdoors, and where will I find a more agreeable welcome and a dearer friend than in the calm old castle whose windows open onto the Rhône?" (*EL*, 215).

Later that year, in response to news about Mallarmé's appointment to Besançon, he brushes aside his friend's crotchety complaints about the need to undergo the disorder of moving: "So what if your room is turned topsy turvy, so what about the architecture of the dreams you'd constructed about you [. . .]; your position, as the bourgeois would say, is strengthened and assured, and you should take pleasure in that" (*EL*, 230–31). But he also sympathizes with a vision in which thoughts cling to the walls, and lines of poetry hang from spider webs, and he offers to give his friend, in place of the sunsets that he will no longer be there to see, sunrises over the sea with their "wonderful views of freshness and of boats swimming in light" (*EL*, 232). Mallarmé's later suggestion in the sonnet "Remémoration d'amis belges" (Remembering Belgian friends) of the multiple parallels between his friendship with Belgian poets and the architectural space of the city of Bruges seems very close to this mode of thinking, this concept of friendship as space, just as his prose poem "Frisson d'hiver" (Winter shiver), which he seems to have written by 1864, evokes both the Saxony clock and the trembling spider webs.

Yet while the outside world is frequently perceived from the inside, through windows, one aspect of it was greatly loved by both poets, and not only dominates many of Mallarmé's finest sonnets but also enabled his recovery from the debilitating depression he suffered through much of the latter 1860s.[4] Sun and sky, sunrises and sunsets, especially those seen over the Rhône or, even more powerfully, over the sea at Nice or Cannes, frequently illuminate the letters between Lefébure and Mallarmé, and nowhere so beautifully as in the letter Lefébure wrote from Cannes on January 24, 1866. While it is unlikely that a Romantic poet would refer to this as "décor," with all that word's suggestion of stage scenery, Mallarmé's reference to it as such is important, underlining his long-held conviction that the poet's task consists in transforming the real into the ideal, making of the pasteboard scenery supplied by nature the glories of the ideal, imagined woods. Lefébure is, in a sense, already doing this, and certainly preparing the way for Mallarmé. His description, while in no way pretentious, is quintessentially literary, showing the countryside as an objective correlative of his mood, moving easily into the metaphoric and setting his description in the context of Théodore de Banville's scintillating descriptions of France's Mediterranean coastline, published in *Le Monitor universel* in 1860:

S HALL I TELL YOU ABOUT what you call my décor, and that Banville has already painted with a style that's too eager to sparkle? I'll slide over it, for you know the South: you know that its charm lies in its magnificent azure, spread over round rumps covered with pines and olive trees, between which, at this early hour when I'm writing to you, a misty light thrusts its way with the radiance of a victory song: on the far horizon there sleeps the long blue mountain of the Mediterranean. [. . .] I don't know whether, like me, you've had the chance to admire those circles of stars that the noonday sun scatters in a leaping shower on the crests of the waves and that distance transforms into far-off golden islands until they disappear at the horizon. At the very least, you've seen and felt better than I have those lovely sunsets that transform the blood-stained gold of their clouds into complex Edens, and you know how the Dream flies towards them as if to an extraterrestrial land inhabited by angels, who are our souls. (*EL*, 204–205)

Extraterrestrial land or not, natural beauty is clearly for Lefébure, as it was for the poet of the "Faune," a source of erotic pleasure, as the round rumps and the thrusting misty light suggest.

Two years later, referring to the time he had spent at Cannes with Lefébure, Mallarmé quotes a line by their mutual friend Cazalis that sums up his new aesthetics and that reveals how accurately Lefébure had read Mallarmé's potential awareness of such beauty: "They travel through the Infinite to create new Heavens" (*CC*, 385). That creation of new heavens, new ideals, new Edens, has clearly been assisted not just by the opportunity that Lefébure's presence in Cannes offered Mallarmé but also by this exploration through their letters of a landscape that is at once that of a physical reality and still more importantly part of the construction of friendship itself.

I suspect, however, that had their letters always been so elevated, the friendship would have been less close. They read each other's poems with sympathy, but also with a desire to improve and if necessary chastise the other as poet, and despite a fair degree of shared melancholy, each is, fortunately, also capable of boyish humor and a robust refusal to let the other wallow in the pleasures of misery. Lefébure, writing to Mallarmé during his friend's long period of deep depression, gives him a gentle and salutary shake: "Anyone who makes of poetry his life's noble career, must, on pain of immediate suicide, call a halt from time to time to the destination that wears him away, and say to himself, like a Balzac character whose name I've forgotten: 'Lift up your head, friend!'" (*EL*, 258). Elsewhere, in a quite unexpectedly funny paragraph, he compares Mallarmé's portrait to that of Tennyson, whose poem "Marianna" Mallarmé was to translate in 1874 and whose eulogy he wrote on the poet's death in 1892: "I noted a curious similarity between your portrait and that of the gentle

Tennyson, whose poetry, I believe, is somewhat the opposite of yours. Only his hair is much curlier than yours" (*EL,* 172).

Intentional or unintentional comedy aside, Lefébure frequently sought to place his friend in the context of contemporary art, and he did so in ways that make clear that from an early stage he was well aware that Mallarmé was seeking above all a poetry of condensation, one that transmuted the real into the ideal. In May 1864 he responds with warm and intelligent enthusiasm to Mallarmé's piece of creative criticism, *Symphonie littéraire,* but adds an illuminating criticism: "You talk of sounds of a rare *justice.* You know that the word is 'justness' (*justesse*) but you *wanted* to say 'justice,' but it could be taken for a grammatical error. What a devilish condenser you are, housing three or four folds of an idea in a single word!" (*EL,* 178–79). Mallarmé's indirect response can be found in a reply to Lefébure's reading of the contemporary philosopher and historian Hippolyte Taine. Whereas the future Egyptologist had accused Taine of stressing the work of art as intellectual reflection, and not allowing enough importance to the spontaneous *impression* that inspires art (*EL,* 187), Mallarmé insists that

> TAINE SEES THE IMPRESSION as the only source of works of art, and that he doesn't pay enough attention to reflection. It's in front of the sheet of paper that the artist creates him or herself. Taine for instance doesn't believe that a writer can change his manner completely, and that's false, as I've observed in watching myself. As a child at school, I wrote stories 20 pages long, and was famous for never knowing when to stop. Well, since then haven't I on the contrary gone too far in the direction of my love of condensation? (*CC,* 227)

This kind of response to a correspondent's comments is frequent in Mallarmé's letters, and while the response is often quoted in studies devoted to the poet's aesthetic thinking, it usually appears in isolation, with the result that there is rarely sufficient acknowledgment of the central role played by such comments from other people. Mallarmé's aesthetics, however, as a reading of these letters reveals, are frequently the outcome not just of the master thinking alone in a closed room but of a continuing debate that is in part a debate among friends discussing central questions in private letters or small groups, and in part that of a much broader intellectual and social context. Within that context Lefébure's role was especially important.

Lefébure's perceptive and stimulating comments on Mallarmé run all through the correspondence, often taking the form of a series of comparisons:

> YOU NEED THE POWERFUL PLENITUDE OF DELACROIX, whereas in general each poet is content to take one face of beauty and go deeply into it. Leconte de Lisle delineates with a firm and achromatic line the musculature of his subjects, transforming them into Michelangelo-like anatomical figures. Banville takes pleasure in apotheoses and splendors. Gautier, that happy sage, wants to

see only the lines that enclose and the colors that adorn creatures. Mme Valmore, forgetful of forms, feels only the soul. Mendès seeks the beautiful in the perfection of rhythm and rhyme. You, on the contrary, enfold everything in your embrace, composition, line, color, soul, form, and you join to it that intense coloration that your distilled spirit casts on everything. It's hard to be more of a poet, my friend. (*EL,* 213–14)

There is, I think, a similar conviction in a letter he wrote later that year, 1866, in which he suggests what lies at the heart of Mallarmé's highly original treatment of metaphor: "You've cut off the earth-laden roots of your flowers, whereas Mme Valmore, for example, Hugo, etc. . . show us their feelings in their entirety, and tie all their loose ends" (*EL,* 252). Lefébure's insights into his friend's nature and his sharp awareness of the originality of his poetry clearly created an atmosphere in which Mallarmé felt comfortable exploring his ideas about both poetry and letters. The few letters he wrote to Lefébure that remain, seen in conjunction with Lefébure's letters, build an image of the kind of space such an exchange can create.

Between Mallarmé and Henri Cazalis, the poet to whom Lefébure once jokingly referred as "that fine ithyphallic monkey [. . .] constantly swinging upside-down from all the lianas of poetry, and climbing up every idea" (*EL,* 215) and of whom Mallarmé himself said, "his soul is made of adorably limpid moonlight" (*CC,* 166), the exchange is different in nature—more concerned, perhaps, with the personal and somewhat less with the aesthetic. It, too, however, points forward to the later correspondence. While Cazalis was more active as a poet than either Lefébure or the young Mallarmé, publishing several volumes of his verse and prose poetry as well as imaginative translations of Persian and Italian poetry, there can be little doubt that, despite his admiration for his friend's gifts, he was less able than Lefébure to comprehend what Mallarmé envisioned. It's clear, too, that the friendship between the two men, a friendship that seems to have faded quietly away once they were close enough to visit each other rather than write, was based primarily on memories of shared emotional experiences.

When Mallarmé was living through the somewhat stormy beginning of his relationship with Maria Gerhard, Cazalis was deeply but ambivalently in love with a young Englishwoman called Ettie Yapp. Although both young men were clearly scarred by the misogyny of their age, a misogyny exemplified by Jules Michelet, for instance, in his studies *L'Amour* and *La Femme,* with their presentation of woman as weak, by nature ill, and in need of constant masculine aid and control, it is arguable that Mallarmé to some extent moved beyond such misogyny during the early years of his marriage, whereas Cazalis seems to have remained to a considerable degree its victim. The exploration of marriage, of the woman's function in a relationship, and of eroticism more generally plays an important role in Cazalis's letters. It must be said, moreover, that modern readers looking at the letters the two men exchanged cannot help finding it hard to gauge the degree of emotional attachment expressed.

Whereas Lefébure chose the simple address "cher ami" (dear friend), Cazalis's letters and those of Mallarmé to him are sprinkled with terms such as "chéri" (darling) and "mon bien aimé" (my beloved). The endearments, the references to hugs and kisses, and the intensity of the expressions of friendship remind us that in looking at the past we are always looking through the wrong end of the telescope.[5] It's hard not to suspect that Cazalis at least was sexually attracted to Mallarmé, and that his ambivalent reaction to Ettie, his inability to accept either her intelligence or her emotional intensity, and his assertion that he has loved her as a virgin too long to feel he would continue to love her as a sexual partner all stem from suppressed or acknowledged homosexual drives. I would guess that once Mallarmé returned to Paris the high emotionalism that could be maintained in the letters became inappropriate, at least to Mallarmé, and that whether or not he was aware of Cazalis's feelings the friendship could not survive personal rather than paper meetings. However that might be, it is at least worth noting in passing that Lawrence Joseph claims that Proust based his character Legrandin in part on Cazalis,[6] making of him not merely the example of a man torn in two directions (in Legrandin's case between poetry and engineering)[7] but also yet another of his homosexual characters.[8] Proust's depiction of the Legrandin the narrator knew in his childhood is pertinent here, too:

> TALL, WITH A FINE STATURE, a thoughtful, narrow face with long white moustaches, his eyes blue and with an air of disenchantment, exquisitely polite, a conversationalist such as we had never heard before, he was in the eyes of my family, who always quoted him as an example, the archetypal gentleman, regarding life in the most noble and delicate way. My grandmother merely criticised him for speaking a little too well.[9]

When Mallarmé first met him in 1862, Cazalis, who first came to the poet's attention through their mutual friend Emmanuel Des Essarts, had already published (anonymously) a brief tract entitled *Lettres aux Français sur l'histoire romaine, les idées impériales*.[10] This tract, according to Mallarmé, increased his desire to meet a friend of whom Des Essarts had already spoken so highly. In a letter to Cazalis written in May 1862, he asserted, "I know in advance that my surprise, long ago aroused by the portrait Emmanuel drew of you, and transformed into fraternal admiration when I read a certain *Lettre* printed by the publisher of *Les Misérables,* will grow daily once I see with my own eyes everything that's exquisite and generous in you" (*CC*, 48). How carefully had Mallarmé read this *Lettre aux Français*? How aware was he of the racism it contains?[11] It may be, as in other instances to come, that the reference to the publication is no more than an act of politeness.[12] What seems more likely to have attracted the attention of the young Mallarmé is first the belief in a meritocracy composed of intellectuals and artists and second Cazalis's scorn for the philistinism and materialism of the Second Empire. Mallarmé himself, after all, was to publish in 1862, the same year in which his friendship with Cazalis began, his brief article

Hérésies artistiques: L'Art pour tous, with its resounding conclusion: "Let the masses read moral tracts, but for goodness sake don't give them our poetry to spoil" (*OC,* 260).[13]

Their letters reveal a shared love of poetry and art, the search for emotional stability, and the pleasure drawn from various mutual friendships, especially with the highly gifted artist Henri Regnault, who died at the battle of Buzenval right at the end of the Franco-Prussian War in 1871. Rhetorically, they are characterized by an informality, a plethora of endearments and marks of affection, and a series of expressions and images that are as much concerned with creating as with depicting friendship. "I beg you, let's not remain so far from each other, so long without each other," writes Cazalis in December 1863 (*HC,* 168), adding three months later: "Our friendship is becoming very platonic, and in truth we're behaving like two lovers who would like to leave each other. Three letters in three months! A month between each letter! With the result that when we do write to each other, our letters, in any case very polite, are chilly enough to turn you to ice" (*HC,* 186). Letters are at once, in Cazalis's view and one suspects also in that of the young Mallarmé, not just a proof of friendship but a means of forming—one might even say fabricating—friendship. The sentiment is certainly echoed by Mallarmé in a May 1865 letter to Cazalis:

A LONG TIME HAS PASSED WITHOUT LETTERS. I beat my breast. It's true that during Geneviève's baptism Emmanuel spoke so much to me about you, and you were so much present at our little celebration, that I felt our far-off laziness less sharply. I'm awaiting lifelessly the hour of your arrival. When I think that you will be speaking in this very room, now so empty, in which I write to you, I'm filled with pride,—but I'm sad, too, for it will only be a dream and then you'll leave! And I'll pick up my life again, wasted through boredom! (*CC,* 239–40)

The desire not merely to emulate but also to evoke the nature of conversation in their letters is clear once more in a letter from Mallarmé dated May 14, 1867:

JUST AS, IF WE WERE NEAR EACH OTHER, we'd abandon ourselves, hand in hand, to endless conversations, in a long avenue ending in a fountain, just so does the terror of a sheet of white paper, which seems to demand lines of poetry so long dreamed of, and which will contain merely a few lines of a friendship that has ended by becoming so much a part of yourself that you forget it, as you forget the rest of yourself, just so does that terror keep you away from a sacrilege! (*CC,* 341)

The image of the long avenue ending in a fountain is striking; it suggests Mallarmé's determination to find symbols for states of mind, a determination evidenced also in his *Symphonie littéraire,* with its desire to describe a landscape corresponding to the experience of reading, say, *Les Fleurs du mal.* Of course that image may also be erotic, suggesting homoerotic ties between the two young men, and offering an explanation for the ending of the friendship after Mallarmé's return to Paris.

If the letter as fireside chat is a frequent image in the correspondence between the two men, that does not preclude disagreements and criticisms. Cazalis, while describing himself to Mallarmé as an "enthusiastic admirer of [his] poetry" (*HC,* 188), nevertheless allows himself to offer some severe criticism of his friend's poem "Las de l'amer repose" (Weary of the bitter rest). The difference between Cazalis's taste and that of his friend is immediately clear to any reader of Cazalis's poetry, for although he describes as "faultless" (*HC,* 188) Mallarmé's "Vers à une putaine," subsequently entitled "Angoisse" (lines that most of Mallarmé's readers would probably prefer him not to have written and certainly not to have published), he warns his friend of tendencies he considers obvious in the poem "Las de l'amer repos," even reinforcing his arguments by calling on the authority of Hugo's sycophant, the minor and now forgotten poet Auguste Vacquerie:

Y OU NEED TO REWRITE THE BEGINNING: I would defy you to talk as you've written those lines: put the whole of the beginning into prose and you'll see what you get. Take care: you've got into the habit of sentences that are too long at first, and then far too abrupt: too many incidental clauses all hanging on each other, and creating a thick dark undergrowth that's so intertwined your reader can hardly advance through it and soon begs for mercy. Vacquerie, I think, has already pointed that out to you, and Renaud who admires you as much as I myself do, told me he'd talk to you about it, too. (*HC,* 188)

Mallarmé's response to this criticism is indirect but unmistakable. In a letter written to Cazalis on April 25, 1864, he refers to "Armonia" which Cazalis had sent him in mid-April. In this prose poem Cazalis struggles to create a complex but ultimately meaningless series of internal repetitions, as the following extract illustrates:

L 'INFINI RÉSONNE COMME UN OCÉAN, un océan le soir, quand le vent fraîchit: l'infini résonne comme une forêt; une forêt le soir, quand remuent ses feuilles;—l'infini résonne, et qui l'a écouté, qui l'a écouté peut chanter lors,— l'âme inondée par le rythme divin. (The infinite echoes like an ocean, an ocean in the evening, when the wind grows cool: the infinite echoes like a forest; a forest in the evening, when its leaves stir;—the infinite echoes, and whoever has listened to it, whoever has listened to it can then sing,—with a soul inundated with the divine rhythm.) (*HC,* 200)

Mallarmé's comment on these somewhat flaccid lines is diplomatic and charitable, but it also clearly delineates differences between his own concepts and those of

Cazalis. It's a letter, moreover, that shows him pondering precisely those links between justice and justness on which Lefébure focuses a mere month later:

I FIND YOUR SENTENCES TOO SHORT, and their harmony is at times a little breathless. What I'm telling you there applies to the artist and not to the dreamer in you who is completely superior. *The sentence,*—which imbeciles take to be plastic—*of Th. Gautier,* but which for me is miraculously balanced, has a justness of touch which contains an element of justice, and offers the perfect model of a soul that lives in Beauty. *The sentence that Balzac uses in Séraphita*—less serene but digging into the deepest abysses and reaching the seventh heaven of mysticism—that's what would make your dream, in the eyes of the few who are artists, even less material.

The height of art here consists in allowing the reader to see, by means of an impeccable possession of all the faculties, that you are in ecstasy, without having shown how you've reached those summits. Well, often your short sentences raise their arms towards the Ideal, take a deep breath, and seem from time to time to take flight. Make them soar. (*CC,* 179)

He makes the same criticism, but less bluntly, a few months later, when Cazalis has again sent him some prose poems. The gentler tone comes, I think one can say with some certainty as it becomes standard in his later letters, less from friendship than from a feeling that the criticism will do no good, that Cazalis will not be able to show the final state without having shown the process, the achievement of which is and will remain for Mallarmé the essence of art:

I CONFLATE YOUR PROSE AND VERSE POEMS, because your verse is, when all's said and done, merely your wingèd prose, more rhythmical and caressed with assonances. It's rather haphazardly dreamed, and doesn't suggest those deep studies of the modern poets.—There's not the shadow of a criticism in that statement.

If you were to publish a volume of poetry, I'd be worried; but in your work in prose, these unfinished lines, harmonious and adorned with rhyme as they are, will only be so many wing beats of the mind as it seeks to rise higher still.

But what lovely things! (*CC,* 231)

We all recognize that rhetorical device that consists in adding a word or two of praise after a series of criticisms, by way of a pat on the head after a rebuke.

While most of these criticisms are barely visible to the naked eye, there are clear warnings here to a poet ready to listen, and clear indications, too, of Mallarmé's own aesthetic program, in the rejection of chance reverie and the suggestion of the need for deep study. The correspondence reveals how important his letters to Cazalis, like those to Lefébure, were in helping Mallarmé define his poetic vision more sharply. It is not just that he needed another mind against which to defend his ideas. His correspondents' letters also stimulate, provoke, and encourage responses to direct comments. The rhetoric of letter writing is closely intermingled here, therefore, with the rhetoric of criticism and thus with the elaboration of poetic principles and convictions for which Mallarmé at that stage in his life had no other forum.

We can see this aspect of their correspondence in a letter written by Mallarmé in January 1864, accompanying his poem "L'Azur":

De l'éternel Azur la sereine ironie
Accable, belle indolemment comme les fleurs,
Le poëte impuissant qui maudit son génie
A travers un désert stérile de Douleurs.

Fuyant, les yeux fermés, je le sens qui regarde
Avec l'intensité d'un remords atterrant,
Mon âme vide. Où fuir? Et quelle nuit hagarde
Jeter, lambeaux, jeter sur ce mépris navrant?

Brouillards, montez! Versez vos cendres monotones
Avec de longs haillons de brume dans les cieux
Qui noiera le marais livide des automnes,
Et bâtissez un grand plafond silencieux!

Et toi, sors des étangs léthéens et ramasse
En t'en venant la vase et les pâles roseaux,
Cher Ennui, pour boucher d'une main jamais lasse
Les grands trous bleus que font méchamment les oiseaux.

Encor! Que sans répit les tristes cheminées
Fument, et que de suie une errante prison
Éteigne dans l'horreur de ses noires traînées
Le soleil se mourant jaunâtre à l'horizon!

—Le Ciel est mort.—Vers toi, j'accours! donne, ô matière,
L'oubli de l'Idéal cruel et du Péché
A ce martyr qui vient partager la litière
Où le bétail heureux des hommes est couché,

Car j'y veux, puisque enfin ma cervelle, vidée
Comme le pot de fard gisant au pied d'un mur,
N'a plus l'art d'attifer la sanglotante idée,
Lugubrement bâiller vers un trépas obscur . . .

En vain! L'Azur triomphe, et je l'entends qui chante
Dans les cloches. Mon âme, il se fait voix pour plus

Nous faire peur avec sa victoire méchante,
Et du métal vivant sort en bleus angelus!

Il roule par la brume, ancien et traverse
Ta native agonie ainsi qu'un glaive sûr;
Où fuir dans la révolte inutile et perverse?
Je suis hanté. L'Azur! L'Azur! L'Azur! L'Azur!

(The eternal Azure's serene irony
Overwhelms, as indolently lovely as the flowers,
The impotent poet who curses his genius
Through a sterile desert of Sorrows.

Fleeing, with closed eyes, I feel it watching,
With the intensity of a prostrating remorse,
My empty soul. Where can I flee? And what haggard night
Can I throw, in shreds, throw on that distressing scorn?

Fogs, arise! Cast your monotonous ashes
With long rags of mist into the skies
As they drown in the ashen marsh of autumns,
And build a great and silent ceiling!

And thou, rise from the Lethean ponds and gather
As you come the mud and the pale reeds,
Dear Boredom, to block with tireless hand
The great blue holes that the birds wickedly drill.

Again! Let the sad paths without respite
Smoke, and let the soot of a wandering prison
Stifle in the horror of its black trails
The yellowish sun dying on the horizon!

—Heaven is dead.—To you I run! Give, o matter!
Oblivion of the cruel Ideal and of the Sin
To this martyr who comes to share the bedding
Where the happy cattle of men are lying,

For there, since at last my brain, emptied
Like the pot of make-up lying at a wall's foot,
No longer has the art of decking out the sobbing idea,
I want to yawn lugubriously toward an obscure death . . .

In vain! The Azure triumphs and I hear it singing
In the bells. My soul, it becomes voice to fill us
With more fear through its wicked victory,
And from the living metal it comes as a blue Angelus!

Ancient, it rolls along the fog, and penetrates
Your inborn agony like a sure blade;
Where can I flee in my useless and perverse revolt?
I am haunted. Azure! Azure! Azure! Azure!) (*OC*, 37–38)

The most Baudelairean of Mallarmé's poems, this early work reveals the figure of the impotent poet, despairing of ever capturing the world's beauty, here epitomized in the term *azure,* and attempting instead, like Lear in the wilderness, to summon up fogs and storm clouds, representatives of Matter that will blot out the splendor of the Ideal. Because the later Mallarmé rarely talks about his work in much detail, it is worth quoting from this revealing letter at some length. The poem, he confesses,

> gave me a lot of trouble, because in banishing a thousand lyrical flourishes and fine lines which constantly haunt my brain, I wanted to remain implacably within my subject. I swear to you that there's not a single word which hasn't cost me several hours of research, and the first word, which contains the first idea, not only helps create the general effect of the poem, but also serves to prepare the last word. (*CC*, 160)

The poem's opening words, preparing the last despairing cry, are "De l'éternel azur la sereine ironie / Accable" (The eternal azure's serene irony / overwhelms) (*OC*, 36). That stress on effect is a direct reference to the writer mentioned in this letter as Mallarmé's great master, Edgar Allan Poe, whose explanation of the importance of a poem's total effect dominates his *Philosophy of Composition,* which Baudelaire had translated as *Genèse d'un poème.* While "L'Azur" is far from being Mallarmé's finest poem, this image of the creative process, in which the flow of inspiration is held severely in check in order to create a whole, every part of which contributes to a carefully controlled overall effect, illuminates our reading of the later verse. But Mallarmé was eager to ensure not only that the poem produced the desired effect but also that it contained "a reflection of the Beautiful" (*CC*, 160), as he puts it in terms whose Platonic overtones recall the influence of Baudelaire even more than Poe. Mallarmé gives Cazalis a reader's tour of his verse, urging his friend to "follow [his] thought through the poem" to see if, as in Poe's "The Raven," "the reader's soul takes pleasure *exactly* as the poet wanted it to":

> To OPEN ON A BROADER SCALE and to deepen the whole, I myself do not appear in the first verse. The azure tortures the impotent in general. In the second verse, the reader begins to suspect, because of my flight before the possessive sky, that I suffer from this cruel malady. In this verse I also prepare, by means of a piece of boastful blaspheming, *And what haggard night,* the strange idea of invoking the mists. The prayer to "the beloved tedium" confirms my powerlessness. In the third verse, I'm as frenzied as the man who has seen his

relentless vow come to fruition. The fourth begins by the sort of grotesque exclamation one expects from a schoolboy who's been set free: "Heaven is dead!" And suddenly, armed with this admirable certainty, I implore Matter. That's precisely what fills the Impotent with joy. Weary of the ill that gnaws at me, I want to savor the common happiness of the herd, and await an un-sung death. . . . I say "I want." But my enemy is a specter, the dead sky haunts me, and I hear it singing in the azure bells. It passes by, indolent and all-conquering, without soiling itself on the mists, and, quite simply, it pierces me through and through. At this I cry out, full of pride and failing to see in this a just punishment for my cowardice, that I am suffering an *immense agony*. Again I seek to flee, but feel I am wrong and admit that *I am haunted*. That entire poignant revelation was needed to motivate the sincere and bizarre cry of the conclusion, *the azure*. (*CC,* 161–62)

It was that bizarre cry that Mallarmé's pupils mockingly chalked on the classroom blackboard. Mallarmé justifies the emphasis given in this summary to the thematic content, by saying that readers like Des Essarts and Cazalis himself, who seek in poetry a dramatic structure in addition to "the music of the verse," will find in it a real drama. His assertion that drama is intrinsically hostile to the idea of pure poetry, opposing its tensions and turbulence to the calm of real poetry, not only justifies his complaint about how difficult it was to combine the two aspects in this poem but also acts as a kind of warning to Cazalis, and to us, about the relative value of these elements. It's also quite possible that Mallarmé is pulling Cazalis's leg, trying to goad him into a deeper reading by making so plain to him both the poem's dramatic line and the inadequacy of any reading that is satisfied with that line. The undertone of mockery is certainly present in this letter, although it's directed primarily at the "I" of the poem, impotent, possessed of a schoolboy mentality, longing for the joys of the common herd, falsely proud and basely craven. There's a certain puckish humor about the letter that suggests it shouldn't be taken too seriously and that draws our attention to the slippery nature of language, especially the kind of language friends use in informal letters such as this. I don't mean by this that none of it can be taken seriously, just that it needs to be approached with some degree of caution.

Occasionally letters to his friends ask for help with his poetry. Thus in May 1868, when he was at work on the poem that would become "Ses purs ongles" (Her pure nails), which has only two rhymes, *or* and *ix*, he turned to both Lefébure and Cazalis for suggestions: "I may write a sonnet," he explains,

and as I have only three rhymes in -ix, do your best to send me the true meaning of the word ptyx, for I'm told it doesn't exist in any language, something I'd much prefer, for that would give me the joy of creating it through the magic of rhyme. This, Bour and Cazalis, dear dictionaries of all lovely things, as quickly as possible, I beg you to send with the impatience of "a poet in search of a rhyme." (*CC*, 386)

The quotation recalls Baudelaire's poem "Le Soleil," with its depiction of the poet "flairant dans tous les coins les hasards de la rime" (sniffing out in corners chance rhymes).[14] The request itself, more important, suggests that just as in his essay on the experiments surrounding *vers libre*, "Crise de vers," Mallarmé will affirm that each line of poetry creates a new word, produced by the juxtapositions and bonds of the words within the line, so words can be created by the exigencies of the poetic form itself, and in particular the need for rhyme.

A similar insistence on the self-contained nature of poetry can be found in a letter to Cazalis that provides a commentary on—or rather a reader's guide to—"Ses purs ongles." Because Mallarmé is rarely so helpful, it's worth quoting the sonnet here:

Ses purs ongles très haut dédiant leur onyx,
L'Angoisse, ce minuit, soutient, lampadophore,
Maint rêve vespéral brûlée par le Phénix
Que ne recueille pas de cinéraire amphore

Sur les crédences, au salon vide: nul ptyx,
Aboli bibelot d'inanité sonore,
(Car le Maître est allé puiser des pleurs au Styx
Avec ce seul objet dont le Néant s'honore).

Mais proche la croisée au nord vacante, un or
Agonise selon peut-être le décor
Des licornes ruant du feu contre une nixe,

Elle, défunte nue en le miroir, encor
Que, dans l'oubli fermé par le cadre, se fixe
De scintillations sitôt le septuor.

(Her pure nails held far aloft to dedicate their onyx,
Anguish, this midnight, supports, lamp-bearer,
Many a vesperal dream burnt by the Phoenix,
Dreams no funeral amphora encloses.

On the credenzas, in the empty room: no ptyx,
Abolished trinket of sonorous inanity,
(For the Master has gone to gather tears in the Styx
With this object from which alone the Void takes honor).

But near the window on the empty North, a gleam of gold
Dies according perhaps to the scenery
Of unicorns kicking fire at a water-nymph,

She, the naked corpse in the mirror, while
In the closed oblivion created by the frame, takes form
Immediately in scintillations a constellation of seven stars.) (*OC*, 68)

In his letter Mallarmé explains that the sonnet is "inverted, by which [he] implies that its meaning [. . .] is evoked by an internal mirage created by the words themselves." He presents his poem as a sonnet that is "empty and reflects itself in all possible ways" (*CBM*, 392), both phonetically, through the internal mirage mentioned earlier, and thematically, in its evocation of the dream and the void. Cazalis's response was diplomatic rather than enthusiastic: "Your sonnet is truly bizarre. Will it please? Certainly not, but it's all to your credit to flee popular taste."[15] Mallarmé's allegorical sonnet, in the form in which he sent it to Cazalis, is irregular, in that the quatrains rhyme *a-b-a-b* instead of *a-b-b-a*, and unusual, in that the tercets, instead of opening up a new series of rhymes, continue with the two rhymes of the quatrains. Moreover, whereas the tercets of a regular sonnet would provide a couplet in the first two rhymes, followed by crossed rhymes, these tercets rhyme *b-a-a-b-b-a*, with an internal assonance on the *b* rhyme appearing in the last line of the first tercet (*licorne*), thus providing yet further examples of the internal reflections Mallarmé mentions in his letter.

There are also moments when the letters provde the opportunity not just to try out ideas but also to explore rhetorical possibilities. Thus Mallarmé's letter of November 14, 1869, opens with an extraordinary passage in which studied spontaneity produces a series of rhythms and images reminiscent of some the prose poems written in Tournon during 1864:

B ECAUSE YOU DID NOT COME, filling the dark stairway with your well-known footstep, to tell us as you opened the door: "It's me," because I'm all alone as I close my book on my Sunday, I'll light the lamp before dinner, I won't listen to Marie or Vève telling me about their walk when they get home, and I'll put this sheet of paper between the two of us. Breaking the spell of your permanent presence, it will at least initiate you into what the invisible do not see, the minute detail of my days: it's thanks to that agreeable compensation that I've reached this decision. (*CC*, 450–51)

The images of the dark stair that forms the link, the corridor even, between two minds, of the lamp that illuminates silent conversations, and of the blank sheet of paper that interrupts one form of communication in order to create another by providing the small details of everyday life—all these are part of Mallarmé's imaginary universe, and their presence in this letter reveals the extent to which for him prose, even when used for the most banal of purposes, should always avoid the clichéd. The rhythms here are also arrestingly beautiful, building up to the two high points: "between the two of us" and "I've reached this decision." There is indeed the sense of an act of will here, a determination to overcome, for a brief interval, a bout of inhibiting depression. The letter is short, but it offers a fine demonstration of Mallarmé's growing powers of concision, already revealed in letters to Lefébure. The evocation of the tiny details of everyday life, for instance, is as much a finger exercise as it is a bridge between minds: "By getting up very early, I've been able to work several hours each morning; but in the evening it wasn't long, after those thankless days, before I fell asleep over a book of poetry: an autumnal Pan-like stroll at dusk: and there you have my days" (*CC*, 451). Whereas Carl Barbier and Lawrence Joseph draw attention to the similarities between the image of the closed book and that which opens the poem "Mes bouquins refermés sur le nom de Paphos" (My Books closed again on the name of Paphos; possibly written in 1869), I would argue that not just the phrasing but, more important, the entire rhetorical nature of the letter is closely linked to Mallarmé's creative writing in general. Moreover, the subtle transition between the clock that presides over the family's suppers and Mallarmé's work on his poetic tale *Igitur* shows both the obsessional nature of inspiration and, more pragmatically, the ways in which this epistolary bridging of minds allows experimentation with structure and connections.

The letters between Cazalis and Mallarmé illustrate another element of this kind of bridging of minds, in that Cazalis's familiarity with many of Mallarmé's other friends makes it possible for his letters to include their comments on his poetry, or more generally on aesthetic matters. Thus a letter written in April 1870 shows Cazalis using the gifted composer Augusta Holmès as a mirror through which he reveals not just her response but also his own reaction to their friend's cryptic, demanding, and complex poetry. Having asserted that the musician was intoxicated with Mallarmé's image of Herodiade in his version of the Salomé legend ("now she's asked me for your address so she can write to you, or so she can cut off your head, I'm not sure," says Cazalis wittily [*HC*, 436]), he adds a significant "but," which other passages in his letters suggest is at least in part ventriloquy:

> *B*UT, SHE DOESN'T LIKE, or likes less, your other poems,—and since nothing is beyond you, she asks you not to neglect, as you too often do, to give your mind to making the form clear and the expression simple. She doesn't want you to be common: she wants you, if it's possible, to be *human*: she wants you to speak the *human* tongue; and not an exquisite and angelic tongue that no mortal can decipher or read. (*HC*, 436)

Regardless of whether Augusta Holmès made any such statement, the fact that Cazalis passes it on without commentary reveals that he agrees with its basic premises. Yet throughout his work and in his letters Mallarmé insists on the essential nature of that "exquisite language" to the extent that it is difficult to believe that Cazalis has not yet understood his friend's meaning. Indeed, within a few months their friendship was to become less important at least to Mallarmé, and such comments, even conveyed indirectly, suggest part of the reason why. However difficult it may have been for Cazalis to understand fully his friend's image of poetry, he did provide intelligent and often enthusiastic support, responding most importantly with emotion, sincerity, and generosity to Mallarmé's extraordinary (and frequently quoted) letter of May 14, 1867, in which he asserts: "My Thought has thought itself": "You are the greatest poet of your time, Stéphane, you can be sure of that; and however high you may be, let this homage, my poor friend whose life has been so painful, so holy, and so sad, let this homage console whatever remains human in you" (*HC*, 354). (In Interlude 2 I return to the letter that sparked this generous response from Cazalis.)

Mallarmé's letters to both Lefébure and Cazalis contain tantalizingly brief reflections of what he was writing. Thus in October 1864 when he was embarking on his transformation of the Salomé story so popular in these decades, he announces to Cazalis, "I have at last begun *Hérodiade*. In terror, because I am inventing a language which must necessarily burst forth from a very new poetics that could be defined in a couple of words: *Paint, not the thing, but the effect it produces*" (*CC*, 206). In terms that, as Bertrand Marchal argues, continue the aesthetic argument of Poe as seen through the lens of Baudelaire, Mallarmé here prepares the way for his long meditation on poetry that culminates, analytically, in the essay "Crise de vers." The importance placed in that study on the bonds between words—"The line of poetry [. . .] creates from several terms a total, new word, unknown to the language and as it were incantatory" (*OC*, 368)—is already adumbrated here in Mallarmé's assertion that "the line of poetry in such a case should be composed not of words, but of intentions, and all the words should fade away before the sensation" (*CC*, 206). Several months later, again to Cazalis, he spoke once more of "Hérodiade" and of the vision of poetry it contained:

IF ONLY I'D CHOSEN AN EASY WORK! But, precisely, I, who am sterile and crepuscular, have chosen a terrifying subject, whose sensations, if they are strong, reach the point of atrocity, and if they are vague, have the strange attitude of mystery. And my Verse hurts me at times, and wounds as if it were of iron! I have, moreover, found an intimate and unique way of painting and noting down the very fleeting impressions. I should add, which is even more terrifying, that all these *impressions* follow on one another as in a symphony, and I often have entire days when I ask myself if this impression can accompany that one, what is their relationship and what their effect. . . . You can guess that I write few lines in a week (*CC*, 220).

The semantic and phonetic games that the mature Mallarmé plays with words in his poetry are already clearly envisaged here, as he struggles to master and convey what

W. B. Yeats was later to call "the fascination of what's difficult."[16] What's more, just as the poem is made of impressions rather than individual words, so it is set free from the kinds of historical or mythological matrices that dominate Romantic and Parnassian verse. This is the point Mallarmé makes to Lefébure in February 1865, when the latter had sent him information from Michelet's *Bible de l'humanité* that he thought might be useful for "Hérodiade." Mallarmé's response shows how sharply he has broken away from a form of poetry dominated by narrative and theme, and how firmly he is aiming at a poetry of impressions and words:

THANKS FOR THE DETAIL YOU PROVIDED about *Hérodiade,* but I won't use it. The most beautiful page of my book will be that which contains only the divine name of Hérodiade. The small amount of inspiration I have had is entirely owing to that name and I believe that if my heroine had been called Salomé, I would have invented that sombre name, as red as an open pomegranate, Hérodiade. Besides, I want to make of her a being purely of dream and utterly independent of history. (*CC,* 226)

Although Mallarmé had originally conceived of the work as a play, we find him writing to Théodore Aubanel in October 1865 and explaining that he now saw it as a poem, "above all because in this way I gain the attitudes, costumes, décor and furnishing, not to mention the element of mystery" (*CC,* 253). However much he would later admire the theater, and especially mime and ballet, he seems always to have preferred what he refers to as "the sole theater of ourselves" (*OC,* 300), the reconstruction of the scene within the imagination.

The overture to "Hérodiade" is first mentioned in a letter to Cazalis in December 1865, as a cause of despair, a poem that sang within him but that he could not write down (*CC,* 259). One of the reasons for the difficulty he encountered in writing the poem, apart from the general fact that, as he remarked to Catulle Mendès, he envisaged it as possessing an almost unattainable perfection, was that he seems to have consistently set himself in writing it extraordinary prosodic and rhetorical challenges: "I had reached a sentence that was 22 lines long, turning on a single verb, and even then the verb had to seem subdued when at last it did appear" (*CC,* 295). Although Mallarmé would publish a fragment of "Hérodiade" in the *Parnasse* of 1870 and would continue to dream of completing it, he did not really return to the poem he had abandoned after the crisis of 1867 until a few months before his death, when he began revising it so intensely that the manuscript version now seems very close at last to being completed.

"Hérodiade," at least in its early version, was conceived as a winter task, possessing and reflecting the icy perfection of that season. Another major project he undertook while in the provinces was the poem that eventually became "L'Après-midi d'un faune" (The afternoon of a faun), a work initially written for the theater and further shaped by Mallarmé's conception of it as a summer task. In this poem the narrator, who is a faun—half-man, half-goat, wholly adolescent—tries to decide whether, earlier on, he had in fact stumbled on two nymphs whom he attempted to ravish, or whether he had merely dreamed it. The poem becomes an exploration of sexuality, of the sublimation of erotic desires into music, of the artistic transposition of the world's beauty, and of the existential question of whether we have any proof that the external world exists.

In June 1865, a letter to Cazalis contains the first allusion to a "heroic interlude, whose hero is a Faun." Mallarmé makes it clear from the outset that, while this poem was to be allied with summer, it was no less demanding than "Hérodiade," since, as he argues in this letter, "it contains a very lofty and beautiful idea, but the lines are horribly difficult to create, for I am making them absolutely theatrical, not just *possible on the stage,* but *demanding the stage*" (*CC,* 242). Yet, despite that "horrible" difficulty, Mallarmé was confident enough to add, in his letter to Cazalis, that he planned to present it to the Théâtre Français that August. Cazalis's amazement is understandable and leads to a lapse of memory or the pen: "What! an act on the drawing board and it'll be finished in the month of April [*sic*]!"[17] In fact, Mallarmé for once was as good as his word and sent what was then called the "Monologue of a Faun" to the theater in August. Constant Coquelin, one of the leading actors of the day, was to have performed it, but as Mallarmé dryly reported to Théodore Aubanel in October 1865, the reading committee, consisting of the poet Théodore de Banville and Coquelin, while admiring the verse, reported that it lacked the "necessary anecdote the public demands" and affirmed that "it would be of interest only to poets" (*CC,* 253). Banville, as Bertrand Marchal points out, had already warned his younger friend, as politely and firmly as he could, to keep the general public in mind when writing for the stage:

I CAN'T CONGRATULATE YOU TOO WARMLY, dear friend, on your excellent idea of writing a Herodiade, for the Théâtre Français has exactly what's needed in terms of scenery to perform it, and that would be a strong reason for accepting it. What generally provides an obstacle for poetic plays is the fear of spending money on a dubious venture. Try to ensure that it contains dramatic interest, together with the poetry, for you'll do more for your cause by writing a play that will be accepted and performed than in making it more poetic and less performable! (Quoted in *CC,* 253)

Nine years later Mallarmé was to send a revised version of his poem, now entitled "Improvisation of a Faun," to the judges of the *Troisième Parnasse contemporain,* where it was again turned down.[18] It was not until 1876 that the eclogue as we know it appeared, published by Alphonse Derenne, with a frontispiece and ex libris by Manet and the famous ribbons in pink and black silk so admired by Huysmans's character

Des Esseintes in *A rebours*. By that time Mallarmé's friendship with Cazalis was a thing of the past.

One of the reasons for the importance scholars have placed on Mallarmé's correspondence with Lefébure and Cazalis lies in the chance fact that we possess so many of the letters they exchanged, and especially those of Mallarmé himself. At this stage we do not know the whereabouts of another very important series of letters—those Mallarmé wrote to the painter Henri Regnault. Regnault died in the closing moments of the Franco-Prussian War, recklessly firing off his last bullets after the command to retreat had been given. Portions of his letters were published the following year by his friend Arthur Duparc, who used them to illustrate his biography of Regnault.[19] What is instantly clear from reading these letters is, first, the wonderful epistolary gifts of the young painter and, second, the depth of the sympathy and friendship between Regnault and Mallarmé. There is no doubt that what we can glimpse through this fragmentary and deficient record is a meeting of minds at least as important as that found in any of Mallarmé's other early friendships. Regnault, who had met Mallarmé through their mutual friend Emmanuel Des Essarts, seems to have begun writing to him in September 1862. The first letter already reveals the easy intimacy that unites the two men: "I'm distressed that, although I haven't left you since Fontainebleau, I haven't proved it to you every time I thought of you" (*DSM*, 7: 417). A letter written late in 1864 affirms that friendship and shows even more importantly their affinity of interests and purpose:

I'M UNDERTAKING A GIGANTIC WORK, but I think I can reach my goal; I feel within me an ardor and a vigor that makes me consider that nothing is too bold. I can see my painting in my head and what I see is *superb*. So my hand must just correspond to my head. I won't show it in public unless I'm completely satisfied with it. It's my conviction that you should never expose to the criticism of others anything you yourself judge to be bad. As long as you can see weak spots in something, you should correct them and not leave anything that isn't as you dreamed it. I won't rush, so I can give my judgement the time to make more progress than my hand, since it's the head that's got to lead, and I believe it's impossible to climb and soar when you don't think you're a long way below where you ought to be. I live in a perpetual struggle with the clock: it's sad to say, but I'm often defeated. (*DSM*, 7: 421–22)

The emphasis on the idea of perfection, of showing only that which the artist believed to be beyond improvement, the stress on the domination of the intellect over inspiration or emotion, and the inexorable sense of the swift passage of time are all, of course, common to Mallarmé's thinking at this time, too. Regnault, moreover, reveals an emotional maturity of outlook in regard to their friendship—an outlook quite different from that of either Lefébure or Cazalis, recalling more Jean-Paul Sartre in its tranquil acceptance of camaraderie without the need to receive frequent affirmations of it. Writing on January 2, 1865, Regnault reassures his friend in the following terms: "Rest assured, I don't bear you any grudge for your silence. What punishment would I inflict on you, given that I, who have no class to teach, no dramatic poem to write, no child to raise, let whole months go past without writing to you? But what point would there be to our friendship if we were obliged to send each other cards for New Year? The very word *card* produces the same effect on me as the name of *Rome* did on Hannibal" (*DSM,* 7: 421–22). This appealing rejection of conventions in favor of spontaneous gestures of friendship is typical of Regnault, and even though the later Mallarmé clearly took a certain pleasure in composing brief rhymes for official holidays—those feast days that he considers especially important in the cultural life of a community—there can be little doubt that he would have been touched by the easy acceptance of a friendship that did not rely on such external triggers and traces to confirm it.

The fine letter Regnault wrote to Mallarmé after the sudden and unexpected death of the painter's mother indicates the considerable depth of that friendship and reveals why it did not need the formalities of mere politeness: "It was a joy to me to think that one day, when you'd be settled in Paris, you and your wife would find in her a second mother. She already loved you, because you loved me, and I was just waiting for the moment when we could find a half a day to spend together to introduce you to her. But what becomes of our plans? They turn into regrets and tears" (*DSM,* 7: 428).

Regnault's letters also indicate from the outset a desire to test his ideas on Mallarmé, a delight in hearing his friend's views that did not prevent him from making clear his own: "If the poet loves winter, with its evenings by the fireside," he asserts in January 1865, "we painters detest all that is not light, beautiful light, the beautiful sun, the beautiful warmth that lets us work in shirt sleeves and slippers" (*DSM,* 7: 423). As Bertrand Marchal has shown, in *La Religion de Mallarmé,* it was Lefébure who was to reveal to Mallarmé all the importance that warmth, light, and color had for him, however much he might find winter a more lucid time for working. It was a revelation for which Regnault had already prepared him.

After Regnault's departure for Rome and his residency in the Medici palace that the prestigious Prix de Rome made possible, the letters Duparc quotes in his biography of the painter are mainly those written to his father, with an occasional note to Cazalis. Yet there is no reason to think that his friendship with Mallarmé had lost anything of its easy intimacy.[20] On Regnault's death in 1870, Mallarmé's grief was profound. It was partly in tribute to Mallarmé's friendship with Regnault that the painter's fiancée, Geneviève Bréton, and her family brought pressure to bear on the minister for education, Jules Simon, to appoint the poet to one of the recently created positions as teacher of English in Paris, and subsequently to increase his annual salary from 1,700 francs to 3,800 francs.[21]

While what we have here is merely scraps of bone and hide from which the whole animal cannot with any certainty be reconstructed, these letters point to a reward-ing and enriching friendship, and the calm, unquestioning terms in which their ca-maraderie finds expression sheds a different light on the youthful Mallarmé—one less imperious in demands for letters than the exchanges with Cazalis and Lefébure, taken alone, would suggest. Moreover, the understated rhetoric of Regnault's letters seems to point forward to the more mature poet who would offer us in his sonnet "Dame, sans trop d'ardeur" (Lady, without too much ardor) that most powerfully understated image of a meeting of hearts: the "simple jour le jour très vrai du senti-ment" (the simple day by day nature of true feeling) (*OC,* 60).

Early letters such as these, and the phantoms of those known to exist but as yet undiscovered, demand a constant leap of the imagination, a continual awareness that the past is another country. What, for instance, could the young Mallarmé have seen in a poet who was almost exactly his contemporary, who enjoyed great popularity during his lifetime and achieved the kinds of honors denied to Mallarmé himself, but who now is remembered, if at all, only for a few anthology pieces and for the judg-ment made of him by another of Mallarmé's friends, Laurent Tailhade, who said he was "ass enough to eat hay" ("bête à manger du foin")?[22] The early poetry of François Coppée nonetheless seems to have struck a chord with Mallarmé, and the letters he wrote to him from the provinces contain some of the most potent of his images of friendship and of the mind. It was while on vacation in Paris in December 1865 that Mallarmé met Coppée at the home of that crusty doyen of Parnassian poets, Leconte de Lisle.[23] Mallarmé's unwavering love of art and beauty no doubt helps explain the fact that he could describe a series of Coppée's poems as "simplement *réussie*" (simply successful) (*CC,* 381), praise that appears to have been given "totally with-out irony" as Bertrand Marchal argues,[24] although the adverb "simply" might give one pause for thought.

His first letter to Coppée, written at the end of 1866, when the Mallarmés had just moved from Tournon to Besançon, uses yet again the richly evocative image of the poet's room as symbol for the mind:

> So FAR I HAVE ONLY HALF MY ROOM, and won't come to life until I have my own room, alone, full of my thoughts, its windows bulging with inner Dreams like the drawers of precious stones in a rich piece of furniture, and tap-estries falling into their familiar folds. I would love, even in writing this letter to you, to write a few lines of verse in the temporary corridor I'm inhabiting, just as one burns perfume in a vase, or to wait a full year until my solitude has been recompensed within these walls. Ah! the old mirror of Silence has been broken! (*CBM,* 328)

Two weeks later, as we have seen,[25] Mallarmé sent Verlaine a letter with a similar image. Not surprisingly, this is a device he used fairly frequently, putting his letters to work to try out various tropes. Most noticeable here, however, is the way in which, in the letter to Coppée, the image not only arises from Mallarmé's personality but also, and this I think is crucial to an understanding both of his social persona and his poetic voice, responds to his recipient's personal imagery. This letter is motivated by the arrival of what Mallarmé terms a "charming invitation to abandon [his] torpor" (*CC*, 328), Coppée's gift of his volume *Le Reliquaire* (The reliquary). Mallarmé singles out two poems in particular: "Le Lys" (The lily) and "Ferrum est quod amant" (Iron is what they love). The first of these evokes a domestic scene of the static, impersonal richness much in vogue among the contributors to *Le Parnasse contemporain:*

> Hors du coffre de laque aux clous d'argent, parmi
> Les fleurs du tapis jaune aux nuances calmées,
> Le riche et lourd collier, qu'agrafent deux camées,
> Ruisselle et se répand sur la table à demi.
>
> Un oblique rayon l'atteint. L'or a frémi.
> L'étincelle s'attache aux perles parsemées,
> Et midi darde moins de flèches enflammées
> Sur le dos somptueux d'un reptile endormi.
>
> Cette splendeur rayonne et fait pâlir des bagues
> Eparses, où l'onyx a mis ses reflets vagues
> Et le froid diamant sa claire goutte d'eau;
>
> Et, comme dédaigneux du contraste et du groupe,
> Plus loin, et sous la pourpre ombreuse du rideau,
> Noble et pur, un grand lys se meurt dans une coupe.

> (From the lacquer chest with its silver nails, amidst
> The flowers of the yellow carpet with their calmed shades,
> Streams the rich, heavy necklace, closed with cameo clasps,
> Half of it spreading out over the table.
>
> A slanting sunray strikes it. The gold quivers.
> The spark clings to the scattered pearls,
> And noon shoots fewer flaming arrows
> On the sumptuous back of a sleeping reptile.
>
> The shining splendor dims the scattered rings
> Where onyx has set its vague reflections
> And the cold diamond its clear drop of water;
>
> And, as if disdainful of the contrast and the group,
> Farther off, under the curtain's shadowy crimson,
> Noble and pure, a great lily is dying in a vase.)

Mallarmé's analysis of Coppée's style points forward to many of his later comments on poetry in general:

> CHANCE HASN'T PLAYED A ROLE in a single line, that's the important thing. Several of us have achieved that feat and I believe that with lines that are so perfectly delineated, what we should aim for above all is the situation in which, in the poem, the words—which are already sufficiently individual not to receive any further impression from outside—cast reflections on each other to the point where they no longer have their own color but are all just transitions in a gamut. Although there is no space between them, and although they touch each other wonderfully, I think that sometimes your words draw life from a mosaic of jewels. (*CC,* 329–30)

What is striking here is that while Mallarmé's imagery is derived directly from Coppée's poem, his formulation of poetic principles points forward both to his comment on his "sonnet en yx" that "reflects itself in all possible ways" (*CC,* 392) and to the frequently-quoted sentence he was to write more than twenty years later in "Crise de vers": "The work of pure poetry implies the elocutionary disappearance of the poet, who yields the initiative to words, set in motion through the clash of their inequalities; they shed light on each other through their reciprocal reflections, like a virtual trail of fire on gemstones, replacing the detectable respiration in the old lyric beat, or the personal enthusiasm that directs the sentence" (*OC,* 366). Equally, the stress on the refusal of chance reflects a frequently reiterated conviction in Mallarmé's later writing, a belief he also expresses in "Crise de vers": "The order of a book of poems breaks through, innate or universal, eliminating chance" (*OC,* 366). Indeed, the correspondence is particularly revealing of the ways in which Mallarmé uses the works of others as testing grounds for his own beliefs and theories, rather as Baudelaire's literary criticism helped hone and refine his aesthetic thinking.[26]

The letter to Coppée is not just significant in showing the young Mallarmé developing personal metaphors by quarrying the works of his contemporaries. It also suggests that the strong spatial imagery typical of his thinking throughout his adult life may well be largely responsible for his admiration of Coppée, who in this sonnet creates the kind of contained space that Mallarmé himself produces in such poems as "Ses purs ongles" (Her pure nails) and "Une dentelle s'abolit" (Lace abolishes itself). Coppée's "Le Lys," however, with its explicit statements and its lack of enigma, can be seen as typical of the poems against which Mallarmé is writing in his poem "Surgi de la croupe" (Surging from the croup), in which the dying lily is replaced by the spectral "rose dans les ténèbres" (rose in the darkness) (*OC,* 74), or in his homage to the poet Théophile Gautier, where the master is depicted as the one who can awaken for the rose and the lily the mystery of a name (*OC,* 55).[27] What is at issue in great poetry, for Mallarmé, is the powers not of description but of evocation: "I say: 'A flower!' and out of the oblivion to which my voice relegates any contour, as something other than the well-known calyces, musically arises, the perfect, suave idea, the flower never found in any bouquet" (*OC,* 368).

This does not mean that Mallarmé's professions of admiration for Coppée in his letters to the poet cannot be taken at face value. Rather, as in later years when, a sympathetic and intelligent bystander, he watched the development of free verse, it seems that he is eager to respond to what his correspondent is attempting, rather than reveal what he himself would have endeavored to do. It's a rare gift, and one to value. Neither Hugo nor Baudelaire truly possessed it, although Flaubert may have. We see it again in an 1868 letter written in response to Coppée's volume *Intimités,* when Mallarmé suggests the gap between his own impossibly difficult image of an *œuvre pure* and what Coppée has achieved, but he goes on to affirm,

YOUR VOLUME, SO WELL-BEHAVED in its limited frame, accompanied the voices that reproach me for my error. Believe me, I loved it all the more for that! I was thrilled with it before that particular coincidence: its melody is a fine line, as if drawn in Chinese ink, and its apparent fixity has so much charm only because it's made of an extreme vibration. But why should I tell you what you yourself set out to do? The only word that will bring you pleasure, if you're not already more aware of it than I am myself, is that this series of poems is simply *successful.* I would give the magnificent vespers of Dream, with all their virgin gold, for a quatrain, written for a tomb or a candy wrapper, that was *successful.* (*CC,* 380–81)

Two of Mallarmé's own poems (as well as the many pieces of occasional verse he did indeed write for the equivalent of candy wrappers) are suggested by the imagery that he uses here. The contrast between apparent motionlessness and extreme vibration recalls the early piece "Sainte" which dates from 1865 and which explores the power of an angel depicted in stained glass to suggest the motion and sounds of the harp she is playing:

A la fenêtre recelant
Le santal vieux qui se dédore
De sa viole étincelant
Jadis avec flûte ou mandore,

Est la Sainte pâle, étalant
Le livre vieux qui se déplie
Du Magnificat ruisselant
Jadis selon vêpre et complie:

A ce vitrage d'ostensoir
Que frôle une harpe par l'Ange

Formée avec son vol du soir
Pour la délicate phalange

Du doigt que, sans le vieux santal
Ni le vieux livre, elle balance
Sur le plumage instrumental,
Musicienne du silence.

(On the window hiding
The old sandal wood with the gold flaking
From its viol glittering
In years gone by with flute or lute,

Is the pale Saint, displaying
The old book which unfolds
From the streaming Magnificat
In years gone by at Vespers and Compline:

At this monstrance window
Touched by a harp the Angel
Forms with her evening flight
For the delicate phalanx

Of her finger which, without the old sandalwood
Or the old book, she balances
On the instrumental plumage,
Musician of silence.) (*OC*, 53–54)

"Sainte," in its elliptical depictions and its suggestion of the power of darkness and silence to evoke colors and music, seems to exemplify the contrasts that Mallarmé alludes to in his letter to Coppée, just as the reference to the fine ink line evokes the Chinese drawing in "Las de l'amer repos" (Weary of the bitter rest), a February 1864 poem in which the poet yearns to turn away from the fascination with the difficult toward the apparent simplicity and vast evocative power of Chinese brush paintings:

Las de l'amer repos où ma paresse offense
Une gloire pour qui jadis j'ai fui l'enfance
Adorable des bois de roses sous l'azur
Naturel, et plus las sept fois du pacte dur
De creuser par veillée une fosse nouvelle
Dans le terrain avare et froid de ma cervelle,
Fossoyeur sans pitié pour la stérilité,
—Que dire à cette Aurore, ô Rêves, visité

Par les roses, quand, peur de ses roses livides,
Le vaste cimetière unira les trous vides?—

Je veux délaisser l'Art vorace d'un pays
Cruel, et, souriant au repoches vieillis
Que me font mes amis, le passé, le génie,
Et ma lampe qui sait pourtant mon agonie,
Imiter le Chinois au cœur limpide et fin
De qui l'extase pure est de peindre la fin
Sur ses tasses de neige à la lune ravie
D'une bizarre fleur qui parfume sa vie
Transparente, la fleur qu'il a sentie, enfant,
Au filigrane bleu de l'âme se greffant.
Et, la mort telle avec le seul rêve du sage,
Serein, je vais choisir un jeune paysage
Que je peindrais encor sur les tasses, distrait.
Une ligne d'azur mince et pâle serait
Un lac, parmi le ciel de porcelaine nue,
Un clair croissant perdu par une blanche nue
Trempe sa corne calme en la glace des eaux,
Non loin de trois grands cils d'émeraude, roseaux.

(Weary of the bitter rest where my sloth offends
A glory for which in years gone by I fled from the adorable childhood
Of woods of roses under the natural azure,
And seven times more weary of the hard pact
To spend the watches of the night digging
A new grave in the cold, ungiving terrain of my brain,
Gravedigger whom sterility moves not to pity,
—What can I say to that Dawn, o Dreams, visited
By the roses, when, to the fear of its livid roses,
The vast cemetery will unite the empty holes?—

I wish to leave behind the voracious Art of a cruel country,
And, smiling at the time-worn reproaches
Leveled at me by my friends, the past, genius,
And my lamp, although it knows my agony,
And imitate the Chinese with his limpid, delicate heart
Whose pure ecstasy lies in painting the end
On plates of snow stolen from the moon
Of a bizarre flower which perfumes his transparent life,
The flower that he felt as a child

Grafting itself to the blue filigree of his soul.
And, like death with only the sage's dream,
Serene, I will choose a youthful landscape
Which I would paint again on the plates, withdrawn.
A thin azure line, pale, would be
A lake, amidst the sky of naked porcelain,
A clear crescent lost behind a white cloud
Dips its calm tip in the ice of waters,
Not far from three great emerald eye-lashes, reeds.) (*OC*, 35–36)

What Mallarmé seems to be suggesting, therefore, to himself if not directly to Coppée, is that by making what he calls in "Las de l'amer repos" "the hard pact to spend the watches of the night digging a new grave in the cold, ungiving terrain of [his] brain" (*OC*, 35), he has made it infinitely tougher for himself to succeed even in the apparently simple task of perfecting a quatrain for a tombstone or a box of sweets. Coppée has, so this argument runs (and if Bertrand Marchal is right to detect no trace of irony here), achieved success in his poetry by setting his sights somewhat lower. The final sentence in this passage is particularly potent in its symbolism, with the suggestion of virgin gold harking back to the opulence of Coppée's "Le Lys," while the magnificent vespers sets up yet more echoes with "Sainte," as well as with passages in the prose piece "Offices."

Now, while it might be true at least to some extent that what is being revealed here is a continuity of interests and images that runs through all Mallarmé's work, published or private, despite his frequent protests that letter writing is a burden because it is less central to his interests as a poet than creative writing,[28] there is nevertheless a sense that in his letters he is working toward a universal image of the mind. This image draws on his private, imaginary constructions, but it also incorporates the metaphors of other poets, and in this case particularly those of Coppée. In other words, there is striking evidence in these letters that Mallarmé's rhetoric is at once highly personal and also part of a more wide-reaching effort to construct the universal book, the impersonal language that the younger Mallarmé, at least, strove for such a long time to create.

Over the years Coppée regularly sent Mallarmé copies of his publications, and Mallarmé continued to reply with his habitual punctilious politeness and with the warmth typical of a long friendship. There is, I think, a clear diminution of interest on Mallarmé's part, a sense, too, that nothing he could say would alter Coppée's intractably Parnassian and somewhat pedestrian poetic standards. There is something prophetic in his early warning that the longer poems were too reminiscent of Hugo (and not the best Hugo by any means), a warning expressed with all the politeness and comprehension that Mallarmé could muster—"Since I'm playing the pedant, let me tell you I like your long pieces less than your short ones, because in them you have something of the tone of Hugo, which doesn't seem to me to belong to you. (But I imagine that you did these just as studies?)" (*CC,* 330).

His last letter sums up this complex attitude, the fact that Coppée was an old friend, that he had done much to try to help Mallarmé find a position as a librarian, and that his regular columns in the newspaper *La Patrie,* especially from 1880 to 1884, had consistently stressed beauty and the intrinsic value of art. On November 15, 1896, Mallarmé wrote,

THANKS, DEAR COPPÉE, for letting me read *Le Coupable,* the first book I've read this year by the great fire of the evenings; above all, the book, even when I'd closed it, brought with it—friendship. I greatly enjoyed its vehemence expressed through so much charm, and the way your terrible and pitiable story, drawn with the large strokes of medieval print-makers, remains secretly that of a man of letters, and doesn't distort the sentences: you've visualized it and it seems imprinted in the good sense of the word, because you've also thought it through.

But, give me your hand, I think I was on the point of talking literature with you. (*Corr.,* VIII: 287)

From our vantage point at the end of a century that has seen the rise of Mallarmé's reputation and the fading of Coppée's, it is tempting to disregard the friendship's importance and easy to misinterpret Mallarmé's words of praise as somewhat empty flattery. Friendship rather than shared aesthetic aims seems to be the clue to this relationship, but clearly in the early years there was a sense of community in their intellectual interests and poetic goals.

Friendship, as I've shown in the Introduction, together with a far greater intellectual and aesthetic sympathy, also lies at the heart of Mallarmé's relationship with Verlaine. That intimation of a close camaraderie that is present in Mallarmé's first letter to the author of *Poèmes saturniens* quickly became a calm acceptance of an unchanging truth, so that by May 1887 Mallarmé was able to assert, "My good friend, You know very well that the desire to show you anything other than an old and unchangeable friendship has never bothered me: it's really bad enough that my deplorable existence doesn't allow me to prove that affection from closer by" (*Corr.,* III: 107). This, too, was how he saw Verlaine's essay collection *Les Poètes maudits,* the critical work that, more than any other, brought Mallarmé to the attention of the wider reading public: "So here it is at last, this delicious little book, in which so much friendship bursts forth! I believe it's the first time anything of this sort has been seen" (*Corr.,* 2: 257). While part of this wording derives from modesty, the intimation that friendship alone motivates Verlaine's high opinion of his poetry, clearly there is more at issue here: an affirmation of earlier statements concerning the central intellectual as well as emotional value of this kind of relationship.

Two images in the letters to Verlaine attract particular attention. First, apologizing for his late response to *Sagesse* (a work that, as a letter to the dandy and poet Robert de Montesquiou-Fezensac suggests, appealed to Mallarmé considerably less than Verlaine's earlier poetry—"it's very religious and in it he repents of past masterpieces" [*Corr.,* IV; 464]), he draws on imagery that shows how much more important nature has become for him since his discovery of the Mediterranean in visiting Lefébure: "the absurd gust of lost hours which blows away the first leaves of the entire coming year" (*Corr.,* 2: 220). While the earlier image of the room of the poet's mind recalls several of his sonnets, this image is closer to poems such as "Sur les bois oubliés" (Over the forgotten woods) or "Mes bouquins refermés" (My books closed once more), with its chillingly unforgettable line "Coure le froid avec ses silences de faux" (Let the wind speed by with its silence of sickles) (*OC,* 76). This sense of time passing without leaving the opportunity for the poet to stamp his imprint on the world is also central to the second image I wish to mention: "I've been very unwell this winter, without an hour's sleep; and that deprived me of sufficient spiritual ink to make a really good season of work" (*Corr.,* II: 257). "Sufficient spiritual ink"—this wonderfully suggestive and elliptical expression points forward to a passage written more than ten years later. Mallarmé's theoretical writing, while it evolves and becomes richer with the passage of time, nevertheless maintains a remarkable consistency of terms. The passage in question appears in "Quant au livre" (As for the book):

To write—
    The inkwell, the crystal of conscience, with its drop, in the depths, of blackness, a drop essential if something is to come into being: then, set aside the lamp. (*OC,* 370)

Writing to Verlaine on January 17, 1881, in reference to his friend's publication of *Sagesse,* whose vague religiosity disquieted him even while he sought to understand what Verlaine was attempting to do in the volume, Mallarmé steers a judicious middle course between expressing disappointment and urging Verlaine on to greater things. In doing so he makes masterful use of subtle and tactful rhetorical ploys:

Here's a book that it's good you wrote, as one loves the white curtains of a dormitory in which new dreams circulate, simple and perfect. But if it were only for your preface which I consider monstrously exquisite, you mustn't forget, you no more than any one else, the Verlaine of days gone by, whom we cherish; my dear, the *Fêtes galantes* are an eternal jewel. . . . Do you know yourself by heart? I mean, not the books already published, but the future poet you will continue to carry? I'm not sure you do, I think you nibble a little at whim the quills of your imagination, which, after all, needs only quills to be an angel, under whatever skies that may be. (*Corr.,* II: 220)

This triple movement is skillfully orchestrated and recurs frequently in the later correspondence. Yes, this book represents a significant challenge squarely faced (the dreams are described as new and perfect, recalling again the importance Mallarmé placed in a previously quoted letter to Coppée on perfection, even if what is perfect is something quite minor), but past achievements suggest that other directions might be more fruitful for you, and, moreover, have you meditated closely enough on where you as poet are going, on what your trajectory will be? Both in this emphasis on the need to keep constantly in view the poet who is to be and in the ready assumption that his correspondent does indeed have this image always before him, we can find something that is part of the quintessential Mallarmé. The sandwiching of criticism between expressions of praise is of course a familiar and widespread technique, but the ability to transform implicit criticism into a sense of commonly held goals and to translate that sense in a metaphor of quite unexpected intensity is typical of him. Not that intensity need preclude either humor or an indication of difference: Verlaine as angel, wearing his feathers threadbare by putting them through extraordinary gymnastics, is an image witty enough to allow Mallarmé to slip in that brief pinprick of "under whatever skies," in which he implies that Verlaine's sojourn in the Christian heavens need not be a permanent move, and that other, perhaps more stormy skies remain to be explored. For Verlaine, however, touchy and insecure as he was, that pinprick may well have gone deeper than Mallarmé intended. In 1883, as Verlaine prepared the Mallarmé section of his *Poètes maudits,* his references in letters to Charles Morice to what he termed his friend's "épatarouflances"[29] seem lighthearted enough but reveal an incomprehension that leads to a compensating desire to mock: "I'm swotting up Mallarmé's *Faun* and his *Toast* [to Gautier]. Explain the *Faun* a bit to me, could you? I don't understand it very well, and how I'm to talk about it I don't know! I have the prose poems, including the death of that Pppénultième [sic]."[30]

Mallarmé's concept of the future poet contained within the present one, known to him or her "by heart" and ready to burst forth, is not just a passing fancy on his part. In the letter responding to Verlaine's *Les Poètes maudits,* which included studies of Arthur Rimbaud and Tristan Corbière, he suggests a similar idea, expressed this time in all the rhetoric of personal modesty:

IT'S ABSOLUTELY FORTUNATE THAT YOU'VE SAVED from utter loss a few leaves of Rimbaud's work, and extracted from libraries the poems of that astonishing Corbière. As far as I'm concerned, you know what I think! Perhaps there is within me, waiting to emerge one day something deserving of what you're saying already, and it's in that vein that I accept your kind words, with a courage that's totally fresh. But I have behind me nothing that is worth anything, except insofar as it has been superbly thrown into relief by your sympathy, my dear Verlaine, nothing, or almost nothing, truly. (*Corr.,* II: 257)

Mallarmé's generosity is instantly clear in his brief reference to Rimbaud (whose personality could hardly be further removed from his own but whose genius he brilliantly evokes in an article published in the periodical *Chap Book* in April 1896) and to the exceptional, idiosyncratic gifts of Corbière. That generosity is also evident from his suggestion that it is Verlaine's judgment in Les *Poètes maudits* that will give Mallarmé the courage to become what Verlaine claims he already is. What really strikes the reader, however, is the reference to the way in which Verlaine's sympathy has thrown into relief the "nothing, or almost nothing" of what Mallarmé has actually produced so far. A similar sense of productive fraternity marks his well-known sonnet "Salut" (Greeting), in which he offers a toast to the brotherhood of poets: "Rien, cette écume, vierge vers / A ne désigner que la coupe" (Nothing, this foam, a virgin verse / Merely designating the cup) (*OC*, 27). The opening line, like Verlaine's praise, merely designates, traces, suggests as a possibility the poetic work that is to follow, or the thirteen lines that will complete the sonnet.

Curiously, while Mallarmé seems to regard their friendship as unshakable, Verlaine's perception was sometimes rather different. In a cantankerous letter to Charles Morice in 1887, for instance, Verlaine professed that he had "fallen out with 'Décadisme'": "At bottom, I'm not pleased with either Mallarmé or Ghil, or any of that lot. Little old ladytudes, perfiditudes, insinuationettes and so forth."[31] A few days later, he went further:

MY REASONS FOR BEING ANGRY WITH MALLARMÉ? Here they are in a nutshell. A certain Wyzewa in the *Revue indépendante* spends his life repeating things that are obviously uttered rue de Rome 87 or 89 (for is it 89 or 87?) by the Master of the place: Verlaine bores us with his *perpetual* fêtes galantes, his prose (which flows, moreover, and it's true it's not for des Esseintes!) focuses on subjects that have no interest. Why should we bother about his Louise and his Pierre [Louise Leclercq and Pierre Duchatelet] and with his personal adventures! His Ghil, too, takes the liberty of subdividing me, and classing me, *risum ténéas! [sic]* with the commercial classes, getting in on the Decadent school out of pure speculation, in complicity with Baju, and God knows what else. And when I talk about it to his disciples, they just say: "It's Vanier who feeds you that!" And then, between the two of us, now that the blow has been struck, that the hole has been made, I'm happy to be done with the faunish, toastish puns, and with Arsène and Virginie, and Anastase and Pulchérie.[32]

This outburst of venom, sparked off principally by envy of the Polish-born critic and theorist Teodor de Wyzewa and his apparently favored position, passed quickly and seems to have left no further trace in the relationship between the two men. Mallarmé may well indeed have had no inkling of Verlaine's wrath, as he consistently refers to their unchanging friendship. In any case, his letters to James McNeill Whistler show him remarkably quick to understand the sensibilities of the touchy and the irascible, and equally remarkably slow to take offense.

Certainly the "old and unchangeable friendship" (*Corr.*, III: 107) informs Mallarmé's delighted response to Verlaine's autobiography, a gentle evocation of his childhood following his soldier father from garrison to garrison. It is significant that Mallarmé, for whom the contemporary tendency toward biographical criticism, made popular by Sainte-Beuve, revealed interests that were "nothing less than impertinent" (*OC*, 517), barely touches on the substance of the autobiography. His own autobiographical notes, written in response to one of Verlaine's wonderfully idiosyncratic letters, present the bare bones of his life, stripped of anecdotes, "quite the opposite of what the newspapers have for so long been churning out, making me seem very odd," as he himself puts it (*OC*, 664). What delights him about Verlaine's *Confessions* is the manner in which the tale is told:

A H! VERLAINE, WHAT A DELICIOUS BOOK, when it growls, once or twice and how furious in its calm, and, above all, supremely elegant, your natural and witty *Confessions, Notes autobiographiques*. I, who love you dearly, but who also dearly love sentences when they go infinitely far, however that may be, in imagination within the text, find there are certain sentences here that I've followed with anxiety and charm right to their imperturbable conclusion. Dear grammarian, I'll say: you truly control your syntax. (*Corr.*, VII: 246–47)

There is a sense of joyous delight in that penultimate sentence, with its lucid and ludic mirroring of tenor and vehicle, holding his intended reader poised on a cliff ledge of possible syntactical disasters before gently setting him down at the imperturbable conclusion. We shouldn't, of course, see in this reference to grammar and syntax any kind of ironic intention, any hint of damning with faint praise. Grammar as *grimoire*, as book of magic spells, and as a safety net, appears as a constant in Mallarmé's theoretical and creative writing. Take, for instance, the following passage from "Quant au livre," written in the same year as his letter about *Confessions*:

W HAT PIVOT IS THERE, I MEAN, in these contrasts, from unintelligibility. We need a guarantee—
Syntax—
Not its impulsive tricks, which, alone, are included in conversational facility; although artifice excels in convincing. A language, French, retains a certain elegance when it appears in négligé and the past bears witness to that quality, which first established itself as the gift of a race that's basically exquisite: but our literature goes beyond the genres of letters or memoirs. The abrupt, high wing beats find their reflection there, too: whoever controls them perceives

an extraordinary appropriation of the limpid structure belonging to the first thunderbolts of logic. (*OC*, 385–86)

The parallelism between his thinking in his correspondence and that in his theoretical writing seems particularly evident here.

While Mallarmé's years of exile were obviously felt as that—as a period of isolation and deep depression—his letters reveal that it was also a time of self-creation. The very fact of his separation from friends and from other writers forced on him not only that solitude crucial to his development as a poet, but also the need to find self-expression through letters. And it formed the basis for several long-lasting and profoundly satisfying friendships. Looking back at it through the somewhat rose-tinted and misty lens of time, Mallarmé was to present it to the young Paul Valéry, who had written from his own provincial isolation in the town of Sète, as a particularly productive and significant stage in his development. Thus does exile become Elysium.

Depression

La chair est triste, hélas! et j'ai lu tous les livres.
—Œuvres complètes, 39

The deep depression into which Mallarmé fell around the beginning of 1866 and that colored almost all his time in the provinces—certainly in his evocation of it at the time and probably in the way in which he lived it—has been variously analyzed. Some critics have used medical theories to conclude that the poet suffered from "cyclothymie," manic-depressive illness, now known as bipolar affective disorder. Others have pointed to some kind of seasonally affected depression syndrome. That it was chemically determined, however, seems unlikely, as Mallarmé's return to Paris apparently cured him once and for all. He himself asserted in February 1869 that he had put his depression firmly behind him and that the first part of his life had finished (CC, 425). While his desire for control is clearly illustrated in such a statement, the longing to dominate his depression would not in itself have been enough had he really been suffering from either bipolar disorder or a seasonally affected depression syndrome. It seems more likely, from the evidence of the letters and other written records, that numerous factors combined to contribute to that long slide into depression, precipitated, as Bertrand Marchal has so seductively and convincingly argued, by the visit to Cannes and the discovery of an intense earthly beauty, that simultaneously revealed to him the existence of the void and plunged him into a metaphysical crisis.[1]

One factor leading to Mallarmé's depression must have been the sense of being trapped in a career and a marriage, neither of which was particularly satisfying. His choice of teaching as a career, selected so as to leave him free time for writing poetry, had had numerous unforeseen consequences. While he initially looked to teaching as a means to escape the brutish state, the "abrutissement" that he feared would result from the career his family wanted him to pursue in the records office, he must soon have realized that his lack of commitment to it made him, if not a bad, at least a weak teacher, with results he had not predicted. Probably he would never have been able to convince his family to let him continue his studies at university.

This was, in any case, not necessarily an expectation for the majority of those in his social class at that time in France. But going almost straight into teaching from secondary school, with a command of English that would always be faulty and with no dedication to the career, hobbled him intellectually and harmed him emotionally. Although there is something ridiculous about Enid Starkie's suggestion that had the eighteen-year-old Baudelaire been English he would have gone up to Oxford or Cambridge and there under careful tutorial supervision grown out of his greensickness,[2] it is hard not to compare Mallarmé with Proust, whose postsecondary education may have been dilatory and dilettante but who acquired through it an unquenchable curiosity and an unparalleled ability to listen.[3] Mallarmé, by contrast, certainly after his return to Paris and to a large degree even before then, is above all a monologuist, drawing his material from himself. He did not share Rimbaud's passionate interest in new discoveries. He was neither unaware of them nor indifferent to them, but they would never be for him the source of his inspiration. The Mardistes tend to depict him as the one who did most of the talking at their gatherings while the others listened, and although there is evidence that, in private, he did indeed listen and respond to his younger friends at this stage, the set of his mind is introverted, wanting to control and dominate his material rather than let it overwhelm him with excitement or enthusiasm. When he listens to others it is almost invariably to help them, not because he thinks he himself might benefit from what he hears. At one point his lack of further education or at least of further qualifications does seem to have spurred him to consider writing a thesis on a linguistic topic, and to ask Henri Cazalis for recommendations of books to read, but he soon abandoned the project, overcome by lack of time and of energy (*CC,* 473).

The demands of the schools at which he taught inevitably—and to our eyes predictably—ended by taking far more time than he had imagined. As is so often the case in Mallarmé's writing, silence is significant. At no point in the correspondence does he mention his teaching in any but negative terms. It is seen as something that devours time that might otherwise be devoted to writing, that forces him to conform to patterns of behavior he finds alien. It threatened to gag him as a poet when his pupils' scandalized parents complained that they were being taught by someone who published poetry. Most forcefully, he comments to Cazalis in 1866 that he would only make his friend suffer were he to describe the extent to which he was exhausted by classes "full of halooing boys and flying stones" (*CC,* 298). Nowhere is there even a fleeting reference to a sense of achievement in the classroom, not even a discussion of what he might try to teach. He does not practice his English with his friends across the channel, using the language only when he felt that his correspondent didn't understand French. He does not ask them about questions of grammar or vocabulary, or ways of conveying English language and culture to schoolchildren. The textbook he wrote is whimsical, a reverie on sounds and shapes of letters, "Mythology as much as Philology" as he himself states in another context (*OC,* 997), while the translation sentences in his *Thèmes anglais* (Passages for translation into English) are a compilation of revealing clichés—"girls should be seen and not heard" (*OC,* 1116), "misfortunes rarely come singly" (*OC,* 1119)—into which slip here and there sentences that seem curiously to comment on Mallarmé himself: "a man must plow with the ox he has" (*OC,* 1067), "he who swindles one schoolboy, swindles twenty men" (*OC,* 1082). And his list of a thousand English idioms to learn by heart must have been as consistently depressing for the schoolchild as they are occasionally disconcerting for the English speaker: "As tall as May-Pole" or "she is as quiet as a wasp in one's nose" (*OC,* 1134). His career hangs in the correspondence like a black backdrop against which the few hours he can devote to poetry offer a brilliant but fleeting meteor shower of pleasure and light.

There is every indication, too, that he felt trapped by the marriage he had so hastily entered into. The most telling image we have of the young couple is of Stéphane looking in amusement at the stockings Marie has negligently draped across his copy of *Les Fleurs du mal* (*CC,* 151). While there is nothing intrinsically philistine about such an act, there is a sense in which this can be read as Marie's attempt to turn her husband's eyes away from literature and to her. And the implicit pun in the word "bas," meaning both stockings and low, tugs at our attention when we read this, as a threat Mallarmé himself may not consciously be acknowledging but that had slipped from him in a moment when language took over. Marie is said to have commented to another poet's wife that she felt her lack of familiarity with the French language alienated her from her husband's poems, which she failed to understand. There would have been little comfort in knowing how many native French speakers also failed to understand her husband's verse. As a woman and as a German in France in the second half of the nineteenth century when the two countries were so hostile to each other, Marie must have felt herself doubly distanced from Stéphane's cultural and educational inheritance.

The images of Marie that Mallarmé incorporates into his poetry focus on her physical presence, and especially on her maternal role. She is "the young wife nursing her child" (*OC,* 38) (not even "nursing *our* child"), the "calm sister" (*OC,* 39), the "berceuse" with her daughter and her cold feet (*OC,* 40). All these terms define her in relation to the other—husband, brother, child—never as an individual in her own right. In his prose poem "Le Phénomène futur" (The future phenomenon) of 1864 he speaks revealingly of an "unhappy crowd of men beside their sickly accomplices, bearing in their wombs miserable offspring with which the world will perish" (*OC,* 269), and while this suggests an imagined future rather than the present, there is a strong indication that the disgust it conveys is not merely literary but personal. In another prose poem written during this period of exile, "Frisson d'hiver" (Winter shiver), Mallarmé gives us a gentler picture of her, as a German woman sensitive to the "grace of faded objects" (*OC,* 272). In that prose poem the narrative persona depicts a domestic contentment that is curiously bloodless, and fails in any case to hold the attention of the woman:

> COME, CLOSE YOUR OLD GERMAN ALMANAC which you read attentively even though it came out more than a hundred years ago, and the kings it announces are all dead, and, lying on the antique rug, with my head resting on your charitable knees in your faded dress, oh calm child, I'll talk to you for hours on end; there are no more fields and the streets are empty, I'll talk to you of our furniture. . . . But your attention is wandering? (*OC*, 272)

Well, perhaps women don't always want to listen "for hours on end" while someone talks, even of furniture.

"La Pipe," a prose poem that also dates from 1864, leaves us with a melancholy little vignette that draws on lived experience (the separation of the two lovers when Marie briefly abandoned Stéphane in London before their wedding) but transforms it into a telling symbol of their relationship: "my poor wandering beloved, clad in travel clothes, a long dull dress the color of the dust of the roads, a cloak that clung wetly to her cold shoulders, one of those straw hats without a feather and almost without ribbons, that rich ladies throw away when they arrive, so torn are they by the sea air, and that poor beloveds refurbish for many more seasons. Around her neck was looped the terrible handkerchief one waves when saying farewell for ever" (*OC*, 275–76). There is no real sense here of a meeting of minds. While this is a question we need to return to later, it appears at this point that Mallarmé's depression in the mid-1860s is intimately connected with a perceived sterility that was both marital and poetic.

To some extent, where poetry was concerned that sterility was a voluntary and self-inflicted state of mind, resembling in far less verbose terms the first chapter of Alfred de Musset's *Confession d'un enfant du siècle* (1836), with its lengthy outburst against the impossibility in the post-Napoleonic era of young men finding a suitable outlet for their gifts and interests. Mallarmé at this stage is engaged in writing difficult poetry—difficult because of its themes, its language, and its structures—and given what he consciously perceived as the need to break away from easy forms, the subject of difficulty, and of sterility in the face of that difficulty, offered itself as a quintessential part of the whole endeavor. The poem "Brise marine" (Sea breeze) offers a particularly forceful example of this situation:

> La chair est triste, hélas! et j'ai lu tous les livres.
> Fuir! Là-bas fuir! Je sens que des oiseaux sont ivres
> D'être parmi l'écume inconnue et les cieux!
> Rien, ni les vieux jardins reflétés par les yeux

Ne retiendra ce cœur que dans la mer se trempe
O nuits! ni la clarté déserte de ma lampe
Sur le vide paper que la blancheur défend
Et ni la jeune femme allaitant son enfant.
Je partirai! Steamer, balançant ta mâture
Lève l'ancre pour une exotique nature!

Un Ennui, désolé par les cruels espoirs,
Croit encore à l'adieu suprême des mouchoirs!
Et, peut-être, les mâts, invitant les orages
Sont-ils de ceux qu'un vent penche sur les naufrages
Perdus, sans mâts, sans mâts, ni fertiles îlots . . .
Mais, ô mon cœur, entends le chant des matelots!

(The flesh is sorrowful, alas! And I've read all the books.
Flee! Flee over there! I sense that birds are intoxicated
With being between the unknown foam and the skies!
Nothing, not the old gardens reflected in the eyes,
Will hold back this heart which plunges in the sea
O nights! and not the deserted brightness of my lamp
On the empty paper defended by its whiteness,
Nor the young woman feeding her child.
I will leave! Steamer swaying your masts
Raise your anchor for an exotic nature!

A Boredom, saddened by cruel hopes,
Still believes in the final farewell of the handkerchiefs!
And, perhaps, the masts, inviting storms
Are among those that a wind leans over lost wrecks,
Without masts, without masts, and no fertile islets . . .
But, o my heart, listen to the song of the sailors!) (*OC,* 38)

The world-weary claim that he—or at least his poetic persona—had read "all the books" is clearly a pose, part of the image he was creating for himself of being the victim of the "modern Muse of Impotence" (OC, 261). But when he writes "the flesh is sorrowful, alas!" is he being merely Byronic or is this a cri de cœur? The theme of sterility that runs through the poems first written during this period refers primarily to a dearth of inspiration, but the sense of unhappiness in the marriage may well also have resulted in physical impotence. The poem "A une putain" (To a whore), written early in 1864, seems to indicate a fastidious dislike of sexuality, transposed, as was often the case in this second half of the nineteenth century, into misogyny, allowing the feelings of self-disgust to find expression in a professed sense that women were repugnant. Of course it is also an exercise in Baudelairean strategies and vocabulary, a finger exercise of the sort that marks the apprentice poet's writing in the previous decade and that may have little to do with any lived reality.

Nevertheless, the sense of nausea that life causes spills over into his letters of this time. In a bitter response to Emmanuel Des Essarts's rather fatuous *Poésies parisiennes,* which he had recently reviewed in the embarrassed tones of someone having to support a friend's work (*OC,* 249–52), Mallarmé wrote to Cazalis in June 1863, "Earthly happiness is ignoble—you'd have to have truly calloused hands to pick it up. Saying 'I'm happy' is saying 'I'm a coward'—and more often 'I'm an ass.' For you must see above this ceiling of happiness the sky of the Ideal, or deliberately close your eyes" (*CC,* 144). His poem "Les Fenêtres" (The windows) is, as he goes on to claim, an exploration of these ideas. In it he reviles the "homme à l'âme dure / Vautré dans le bonheur" (the hard-souled man / wallowing in happiness) and concludes despairingly that "ici-bas est maître" (this earthly life is master):

> Est-il moyen, mon Dieu qui voyez l'amertume,
> D'enfoncer le cristal par le monstre insulté
> Et de m'enfuir, avec mes deux ailes sans plume
> —Au risque de tomber pendant l'éternité?

> (Is there a way, oh God who sees the bitterness,
> to break through the crystal insulted by the monster
> and to flee, with my two featherless wings
> —at the risk of falling for all eternity?)[4]

The imagery here—the reference to flight, to wings, to mirrors ("Je me mire et me vois Ange!" [I gaze into the mirror and see myself as Angel!]), to death, and to a rebirth in the ideal—point forward curiously to the seminal letter he wrote to Cazalis in 1867. It's as if he has been so absorbed in a Baudelairean universe of acedia and despair that he has created a linguistic web from which he broke free only after an immense struggle.

When "Brise marine" presents a longing to leave, to go to new places, there is little doubt about the intensity of the poet's feelings, for all they may be couched in the borrowed terms of Romanticism's longings for the exotic. What he had in mind was just as inaccessible to him at that point, however familiar it may have been. The life he led in the provinces—enclosed, lonely, and impecunious—filled him with longings for Paris. Writing to Cazalis in the early spring of 1865, he both explores the germ of the poem and touches on a familiar grouping of themes:

I'M SAD. A BLACK, GLACIAL WIND prevents me from taking a walk, and I don't know what to do with myself in the house when my weak brain forbids me to work. And then, I disgust myself, I fall back from mirrors, when I see how degraded and dull my face is, and weep when I feel myself empty and can't write a single word on my implacably white sheet of paper. [. . .] Everything has conspired to annihilate me. My brain is weak, and I needed all the stimulus I could get, especially that of friends whose voices set you ablaze, that of paintings and music, noise and life. If there was one thing on this earth that I should have avoided, it was solitude, which gives strength only to the strong. (*CC*, 235)

Later in his life he would not allow himself such revealing statements. Indeed, according to Régnier, he would stress to the Mardistes that solitude was what taught the poet most about his craft. Painting, music, conversation: These were what he longed for in the cold and damp of Tournon or Besançon, in what he perceived as a philistine and hostile society. Marie is brushed aside impatiently as merely an extension of himself, an image of his own alienation: "Marie, but she's myself, and I see myself reflected in her German eyes" (*CC*, 235).

If much of the poetry Mallarmé wrote during the mid-1860s bears the stamp of Baudelaire, both in terms of its rhetoric and in regard to the dominant mood of boredom and suffering, his often-quoted letter to Cazalis of May 14, 1867, reveals a melancholy that seems more genuinely felt, a determination to find a more individual form of expression, and a desire to articulate his despair in terms that are often associated with Hegel. While Hegel's influence on several of Mallarmé's friends, and on Villiers de l'Isle-Adam in particular, is well documented, Mallarmé's own response to the German philosopher seems far more questionable. He owned a copy of Hegel's works, but on his death these volumes were found to be uncut. He claimed that he lacked the mind of a philosopher, yet in letters such as this to Cazalis he appears to have made use of Hegel's terminology to give sharper expression to his intellectual experiences of the last few years. I suspect that at a time when he was desperately trying to break free from the influence of Baudelaire, he was reluctant to adhere too closely to the thinking of anyone else, but that he drew on a Hegelian vocabulary that was part of the common, if superficial, knowledge of his times to put in writing, and thereby to come to terms with the memory of months of despair that had come close to resulting in his destruction as a poet.

Mallarmé's letter of May 14, 1867, has been probed for philosophical and psychological insights, ransacked for religious implications, pored over for clues to his reading and his thinking, and all too frequently seen as occupying a pivotal place in his theoretical statements about poetry. Seen in the context first of the letters written during his years in the provinces and then more specifically in that of his correspondence with Cazalis, the letter acquires somewhat different contours; its expressions become part of a familiar lexicon, and while it remains a powerful indication of a time of deep depression, it takes up a less vital position in the record of Mallarmé's thought. There is certainly a degree to which Mallarmé echoes and makes his own certain expressions that had become current coin or that are remnants of Romanticism, more redolent of Chateaubriand and Musset than of Baudelaire and Gautier. But there is also a sense in which Cazalis's bemoaning of his fate appears to have combined with Mallarmé's own sharp awareness of the way in which decisions he had made in late adolescence—his choice of career, his marriage—had imposed on him unforeseen limitations and restrictions that would henceforth curtail many of his ambitions. Cazalis may be longing to find a woman he could marry, but Mallarmé was increasingly aware of the loneliness of his own marriage, and while Lefébure was painstakingly preparing himself for the career of his choice, Mallarmé was contemplating a future in which he had no choice but to continue in teaching—a future, moreover, in which he would have to struggle continuously to make space for what he really wanted to do, which was to write poetry. Because much of this could not be openly confessed, not even or perhaps especially not to so close a friend as Cazalis, he couched it in terms that have more to do with the kind of philosophical clichés of the time than with the careful avoidance of cliché that marks his later letters:

I'VE JUST SPENT A TERRIFYING YEAR: my Thought has thought itself and reached a pure Concept. All that my being has suffered as a result during that long death cannot be told, but, fortunately, I am utterly dead, and the least pure region where my Spirit can venture is Eternity. My Spirit, that recluse accustomed to dwelling in its own Purity, is no longer darkened even by the reflection of Time.

Unfortunately, I've reached this point through a dreadful sensitivity and it's high time I wrapped it in an outward indifference, which will replace my lost strength. After a final synthesis I have reached the stage of slowly acquiring that strength—you can see I am unable to distract myself. But this was even more the case a few months ago, firstly in my terrible struggle with that old and evil plumage, which is not, happily, vanquished: God. But as that struggle had taken place on his bony wing which, in death throes more vigorous than I would have suspected him capable of, had carried me into the Shadows, I fell, victorious, desperately and infinitely,—until at last I saw myself again in my Venetian mirror, such as I was when I forgot myself several months before.

I confess, moreover, but to you alone, that the torments inflicted by my triumph were so great, I still need to look at myself in that mirror in order to think and that, if it were not in front of this desk on which I'm writing to you, I would become the void once again. That will let you know that I am now impersonal and no longer the Stéphane you knew—but a capacity possessed by the spiritual Universe to see itself and develop itself, through what was once me. (*CC*, 342)

These last lines are a reworking that is nevertheless central to Mallarmé's personal conviction of the long tradition that presents the poet as a vehicle through which the universe speaks, as the sibyls of antiquity allowed the god to speak through them and as mystics and prophets permit the divine to address the populace. That Cazalis, on reading this letter, felt in some way that Mallarmé had gone beyond him and that their friendship would never be quite the same again, is, I think, clear from his reply (see p. 48). What we might notice above all, reading through the histrionics, is the determination to regain control, to wrap himself as he puts it in an outward indifference. While it took him some years to achieve that control, the desire to do so and the determination to withdraw from confessions begin to dominate his letters from this point on, and even in his letters to those who were later very close to him, there is none of this outpouring of emotion, none of the exploration of ideas that marks these early letters.

When Mallarmé confesses that "my Thought has thought itself, and has reached a Pure conception" (*CC*, 342), he is clearly striving to give expression to an experience that demanded translation into a language that would adequately convey its intensity. As the notes to Bertrand Marchal's edition reveal, his first thought here had been to describe that conception as divine. The correction underpins a movement away from any form of religion other than that of poetry itself. Reaching such a state of intellectual purity, of freedom from the material and physical world, has been achieved only at the expense of his own death, he claims, meaning by that his death as individual ego rather than poetic voice. As Marchal suggests, this statement harks back to an earlier letter, written to Cazalis just over a year before in April 1866 and confessing that his meditation on poetry had led him to a discovery of *le Néant,* the Void. At that stage his response to the realization that there was no truth apart from the void was to sing of the triumph of the soul, the power of the imagination, and the glorious lies that humanity had created to deny the reality of that sole truth (*CC*, 298).

By 1867, however, this sense of grim exhilaration has given way to a feeling of desolation, at the final loss of religious belief, now replaced by a bleak determination to allow himself to become the mouthpiece for what he calls "the spiritual universe." Part of what goads him on at this point is the sense, already mentioned in the April 1866 letter, that his lungs had been weakened by the terrible winters of Besançon and the fear that he might not live to complete the "three verse poems" and "four poems in prose, on the spiritual conception of the Void" (*CC*, 343). Integral to this experience is the sense that he has lost his identity, has been forced to lose it in order to accommodate the spiritual universe—"I am now impersonal, and no longer the Stéphane that you knew" (*CC*, 343) as he puts it, rather melodramatically, to Cazalis. Only by staring at himself in the Venetian mirror can he cling to his identity. While this letter has often been seen as Mallarmé's definitive statement on his poetic task and on his vision of poetry, it would be more exact to regard it as part of a constant search for a sharper conception of what modern poetry might be. Mallarmé's later work shows him moving beyond this initial, somewhat bloodless and ethereal vision to allow a far more sensual and often frankly erotic poetry. Roger Pearson is surely right when he argues that "if one looks at the internal, textual evidence, [. . .] there is every reason to suppose that Mallarmé's career was one long, sustained, and graduated assault upon the summit of poetic perfection."[5] As Pearson contends, we can see Mallarmé moving from the group of poems published in *Le Parnasse contemporain* in May 1866, to the photolithographed manuscript collection of 1887, to those in the posthumously published Deman *Poésies* of 1899, and on to the extraordinary mastery of *Un coup de dés*. The 1867 letter to Cazalis is an important milestone along that path, but, as subsequent letters reveal, it does not mark the poet's final destination. The presiding divinity here is not Terme but Janus.

By May of the following year Mallarmé was able to write to Lefébure that the deep depression he had suffered in the two years since visiting him in Cannes was beginning to dissipate. He admits that his suffering has marked him, but adds that he wants to make of that experience "un Sacre" (a consecration) (*CC*, 385). Here again we find Mallarmé's willpower taking over, his fate determined by his desire, rather than being left to the whims and winds of chance. The void and the absolute, he adds, in a tone that sounds much closer to the older Mallarmé, will not form the basis of his poetry, as they have in his friend Villiers's writing: "I am descending back into my Self, abandoned for two years; after all, even poems which are merely tinged with the Absolute, are already beautiful, and they are rare—and what is more, reading them might awaken in the future the poet of whom I dreamed" (*CC*, 385). The impersonality of the poet allowing the universe to speak through him is abandoned: not without sorrow, but with a sense that there is still much to do in exploiting the self. It's not that Mallarmé will henceforth indulge in the egotism of some of his predecessors and contemporaries, but that he realizes that poetry, even poetry that bears the traces of the absolute, needs a fixed point in human experience.

A year later, in February 1869, Mallarmé was able to write to Cazalis that the first phase of his life was over. There is, in these confident statements to friends, a sense of wanting to convince himself above all, but there is also a feeling that he wants the depression to end, that it can no longer serve his artistic objectives. The writing of *Igitur,* coinciding with his short-lived interest in linguistics, reflects that determination to heal himself of a melancholy that he had come to see as quintessentially destructive. *Igitur,* an exploration and analysis of the incapacity to write, or indeed to act at all, was to be a vigorous attack on the old monster of impotence, a kind of homeopathic cure. His first allusion to it is in a letter to Cazalis of July 1869, in which he refers to "a fine tale" he hopes to create. He returns to it in another letter to Cazalis, dated November 14, 1869: "I'll just say a word about my work, the one I'll bring you next summer. It's a tale, through which I hope to conquer the old monster of Impotence, which is moreover its subject, in order to cloister myself in my great task which I have already begun to study anew" (*CC*, 451). The letters are frustratingly sparse in allusions to the tale, yet these comments indicate the extent to which Mallarmé sought, through his analysis and the artistic transposition of his apparent inability to write, not merely to create something that would in itself be beautiful but that would free him to pursue a far more beautiful artistic production. The story of his reading *Igitur* to his uncomprehending friends Catulle Mendès and Villiers de l'Isle-Adam has often been told. When, at the end of his life, he was to read *Un coup de dés* to an intelligently appreciative Paul Valéry, he had succeeded in creating the kind of audience his works needed, through a reeducation of his readers, or at least of those he cared about. And that reeducation took place partly through his letters, partly through his journalism, and partly through the long conversations he held with friends in his house in Paris on Tuesday evenings.

CHAPTER TWO

Finding a Voice

I don't know if it's possible to convey what Symbolism was for
those who *lived* it. A climate of the mind, a ravishing place of
exile, or better of repatriation, a paradise. All those images and
allegories that, for the most part, now dangle limp and dried out,
spoke to us in those days, enveloped us, helped us, ineffably. We
strolled along those "terraces," plunged our hands in the "pools,"
and the perpetual autumn of that poetry shed a delicious yellow
light even on the fronds of our thoughts.

—*Jacques Rivière*, Miracles

When Mallarmé returned to Paris after France's defeat in the Franco-Prussian War
and the fall of the Commune in 1871, the political situation in France was under-
standably and predictably tense, but art, music, and letters were flourishing. The
rate of technological and medical advances also increased, and the work of Jean-
Baptiste Lamarque and Charles Darwin was beginning to filter through to a broader
populace to change humanity's conception of its beginnings. This was the year in
which Darwin, whose *Origin of Species* had appeared in 1859, published *The Descent
of Man*. This was also the year that saw Arthur Rimbaud's superbly imaginative poem
"Le Bateau ivre," Jules Verne's *Une ville flottante,* Lewis Carroll's *Through the Looking
Glass,* George Eliot's *Middlemarch,* and Fyodor Dostoyevsky's *The Devils.* Giuseppe
Verdi completed *Aïda,* Richard Wagner produced *Siegfried,* and Anton Bruckner
wrote his second symphony. In 1871 one of the most influential political thinkers of
the 1830s and 1840s, Pierre Leroux, died, and Jules Vallès's left-wing newspaper, *Le
Cri du peuple,* was founded. It was in that year that Paris began installing the drinking
fountains that Richard Wallace gave the city and that are still so much a part of it.
This was a time in which writers and artists were intensely involved in exploring
contemporary society. In 1872, the year in which Friedrich Nietzsche's *Birth of Tragedy* was published and the Remington typewriter invented, Emile Zola produced *La
Curée,* his study of the sexual and financial greed that he saw as marking the Second
Empire; Victor Hugo turned his attention to the empire's collapse and military defeat

in *L'Année terrible;* and Alphonse Daudet responded by creating his Don Quixote–like figure, Tartarin of Tarascon. Edgar Degas focused on the bourgeoisie at play, in such paintings as *Le Foyer de danse,* and Pierre-Auguste Renoir depicted the working class relaxing in *Les Canotiers à Chatou.*

Over the next decade and a half, the United Kingdom went through its strongest imperialistic and colonial phase, while France turned its attention to Indochina. These were the years that saw the rise and fall of the monarchist movement in France. In 1873 the movement was strong enough to campaign successfully for a seven-year period of office for the president of the republic, but the refusal of their candidate, the Comte de Paris, to abandon the white flag of the monarchy for the red, white, and blue of the postrevolution era precipitated their decline. It was, however, not until 1879 that there came to power the group most closely associated with the Third Re-public—a group that was lower–middle class, anticapitalist, anticlerical, antimili-taristic, and above all committed to education as a means of liberating the masses. Elsewhere in the world the question of women's education was becoming a pressing issue, with the University of Adelaide in South Australia and the University of Lon-don in England both deciding to grant women diplomas in 1874. Women's educa-tion was not to receive serious attention in France until the law of 1880 provided secondary education for girls. The 1880s saw the promulgation of laws concerning freedom of the press and making primary education free, secular, and compulsory.

In 1874, the year Wagner's opera *Götterdämmerung* made its debut, the first Impressionist exhibition was held in the studio of the photographer Félix Nadar. The following year, Alexander Fleming discovered chromosomes, Amédée Bollée invented his steam-driven automobile, and Georges Bizet's light opera *Carmen* pro-voked a scandal at the Opéra Comique in Paris. With the phylloxera virus devastat-ing the vineyards throughout the decade, peaking in 1876, emigration from France reached its highest level. In that same year, 1876, Wagner opened his Festspielhaus in Bayreuth, and Mallarmé published his evocative and very beautiful "L'Après-midi d'un faune" (Afternoon of a faun). This was also the year in which Leo Tolstoy pub-lished *Anna Karenina* and Mark Twain gave permanent form to the dreams of Amer-ican childhood in *The Adventures of Tom Sawyer.* The following years saw the grow-ing success of the Impressionist painters, the rise and fall of the charismatic but enigmatic politician Léon Gambetta, and the invention of the phonograph. *La Plume,* probably the most influential artistic and literary review of the time, was founded in 1877, and French children began to discover more about their French heritage, both physical and intellectual, through Mme Brunet's novel *Le Tour de France de deux enfants.*

The face of Paris was changing, too, with the construction of the Trocadéro pal-ace, while Thomas Edison's invention of the electric lightbulb in 1879 heralded yet greater changes. While Auguste Rodin was creating his statue of the thinker and his intricately sculpted Gates of Hell, the metropolitan opera was being built in New

York, and Berlin saw the first electric trams. The first years of the new decade were productive, too, in terms of painting and literature. Zola continued publishing his volumes in the *Rougon-Macquart* series and formulated his theories, somewhat tongue-in-cheek, in *Le Roman expérimental;* Jules Vallès's *Le Bachelier* presented a stinging indictment of the inadequacy of current education curricula in preparing young men for the workplace; and Louise Michel revealed the suffering of the very poor in *La Misère.* Gabriel Fauré, César Franck, and Jules Massenet were revitalizing French music, while Henri Toulouse-Lautrec, Paul Signet, and Gustave Moreau opened up new directions in painting, using and expanding the potential of Impressionism. Elsewhere, Henrik Ibsen was writing *An Enemy of the People* and *Ghosts,* Henry James's intricate tales of morals and manners intensified the possibilities of the psychological novel, and Johannes Brahms, Bedrich Smetana, Antonin Dvorák, and Gustav Mahler were changing the image of the symphony. These were years of change, excitement, and opportunity for anyone living in so cosmopolitan a city as Paris, and Mallarmé was far from being unaffected by what they had to offer and by the challenges they posed.

Not surprisingly, despite the decade's energy and innovations, Mallarmé's move to Paris did not bring the sudden and abrupt transformation in his situation that he had imagined during his years of exile. Nevertheless, living in Paris meant that he was able to become more rapidly aware of changes in the artistic world than he had in the provinces, and the move also led to a series of important friendships. Some of the most valuable of these were with the young artists of the burgeoning Impressionist movement (friendships that form the subject of Chapter 3).

Looking at Mallarmé's activities and plans from 1871 to 1884, especially as he discusses them in his letters, the reader is struck by the poet's comparative energy and the variety of what he set out to do. If he was revitalized by his return to the capital, he was nevertheless looking beyond it for other sources of inspiration. Several trips to London reinforced his growing friendships with English writers, artists, and journalists and led, among other projects, to the series of "Gossips," as they were quaintly called, that he provided for the London review the *Athenaeum.* Indeed, in many ways this was the decade in which England and the English language played its most important role in his life. He wrote his curious language manual, *Les Mots anglais;* translated a not particularly good short story, Mrs C. W. Elphinstone Hope's "The Star of the Fairies"; produced a study of myth that is largely a translation and reworking of George Cox's mythology of Aryan nations and the same writer's *Manual of Mythology in the Form of Question and Answer;* penned an introduction for William Beckford's Gothic masterpiece *Vathek,* which had first been published in French; dreamed of writing a detailed study of Algernon Swinburne; and worked on complementing Baudelaire's translation of Edgar Allan Poe's prose writing by turning his hand to the poems.

Friendships that had originated through an exchange of letters with poets living in Paris now began to strengthen. Mallarmé had already begun writing to the Parnassian poet José-Maria de Heredia in 1865, and despite the enormous differences between their conceptions of poetry, this friendship lasted throughout Mallarmé's life. It was, for example, to Heredia that he wrote in April 1872, seeking his friend's moral support for a "beautiful, luxury review" (*Corr.,* II: 26), the thought of which was currently obsessing him. Indeed, we misunderstand Mallarmé if we think of him as uniquely devoted to poetry. His correspondence abounds in references and allusions to plans such as this—dreams, usually impractical, of making money and gaining fame by quite different forms of publication. This review, *L'Art décoratif,* was to remain an attractive obsession. It suggests the extent to which Mallarmé was aware of both the artistic life of the day and its leading exponents, and it foreshadows his review, *La Dernière Mode.* Indeed, the importance of the decorative, of the art of embellishing in order to lead reader or viewer into the heart of the matter, is central not only to Mallarmé's work but also to Symbolism more generally. Heredia was a friend of the artist Claudius Popelin, whose work Mallarmé wanted to use on the letterhead and cover page of his projected review. In addition, Heredia must have seemed an ideal person to help promote the periodical because of the decorative nature of his own poetry. While harder-headed friends dissuaded Mallarmé from a venture whose financial future seemed to them distinctly rocky, this interest in decorative art and the role it played in his own concept of poetry functions as a filigree running through Mallarmé's thinking, and it doubtless formed a particular bond with a poet whose Parnassian vision of poetry was in many other ways at odds with his own but who shared the value Mallarmé placed on ornamentation.

Mallarmé's relationship with Anatole France was more complex and, at least briefly, more agitated. This urbane, prolific novelist, who enjoyed widespread popularity in his lifetime but whose themes and style speak less directly to a modern audience, was part of the larger circle of Mallarmé's acquaintances in those early years back in Paris. They could have met through Charles Marie Leconte de Lisle, through Catulle Mendès, or at the home of Nina de Gaillard, whose salon offered throughout the 1870s a congenial and relaxed gathering place for writers, artists, journalists, and musicians. More important, France was among those who contributed to the memorial volume for Théophile Gautier for which Mallarmé wrote his masterly threnody "Toast funèbre." While the relations between the two men seem at first, and were again to become, cordial if not friendly, a letter to Mendès of late July 1875 reveals Mallarmé in the kind of rage he was later to find so disquieting in his friend Degas. For the third volume of the poetry anthology, *Le Parnasse contemporain,* Mallarmé had offered a version of the poem that was to become "L'Après-midi d'un faune," on which he had been working since June 1865. The editorial board of Le *Parnasse contemporain,* consisting of Théodore de Banville, François Coppée, and Anatole France, found themselves more than perplexed by this demanding and beautiful work. The urbane and open-minded Banville felt it should be accepted, despite its "lack of clarity," because of what he termed "the rare harmonic and musical qualities of the poem,"[1] but Coppée and France rejected it, the latter going so far as to write in the reasons he supplied to the publisher, Lemerre, "No, we'd become a laughing stock!"[2] And this reaction came at a time when Mallarmé's financial position was so bad that he had to pawn his gold watch, "condemn it to prison for a month," as he puts it in a September 1875 letter to his wife (*Corr., IV*: 410).

Mallarmé's remark to Mendès reflects a side of his character that appears from time to time, expressed in sudden moments of sarcasm or in quiet, rapier-sharp condemnation:

MY POEM HAS BEEN REFUSED by the Parnasse committee; but don't mention it to Lemerre except with a smile and in terms of a ridiculous possibility, because that's how I myself received the announcement of this deed. If I'd taken a different response and if it proved to be true, I'd believe myself obliged to go and slap the three judges, whoever they may be. And I'm so tired, oh! far too weary to put anything in motion. (*Corr., II*: 65)

Although the names of the judges were meant to be a secret, as this letter reveals, it seems likely that Mallarmé did discover fairly soon who they were. While this brief spurt of anger is part of Mallarmé's character, in both its intensity and brevity, it's also typical of him that he was less concerned for himself than for another poet, who, together with Paul Verlaine, risked having his offering rejected: Leconte de Lisle. When it looked as if the elder poet's poor relationships with the volume's publisher, Lemerre, threatened to lead to his exclusion from a volume that was to contain many names now completely forgotten, Mallarmé and Léon Dierx did their utmost to smooth matters over. While "L'Improvisation d'un faune," as Mallarmé's poem was then titled, does not grace the third *Parnasse contemporain,* Leconte de Lisle's "L'Epopée du moine," or more precisely the first part of it, was eventually accepted.

Mallarmé continued to exchange letters and publications from time to time with Anatole France, who, while he was later to denounce the Parnassian movement, never showed the slightest comprehension of the Symbolists. A year after the Parnasse affair, Mallarmé was to write his most revealing letter to "the sweet singer," as Proust calls him when he transforms him into Bergotte. Belatedly responding to the gift of France's collection of poems, *Les Noces corinthiennes (The Corinthian Weddings)*, Mallarmé may indeed be yielding to some desire for revenge, as he declares his opposition to all but lyric poetry in terms that are unusually categoric for one who more often indicated that his own preferences were not necessarily what he demanded from everyone:

WHERE THE *NOCES* ARE CONCERNED, I want to express an opinion which for me has the force of a law, with respect to the mold in which you've cast them: the dramatic poem fills me with despair, for if I have any kind of principle, where criticism is concerned, it's that one must, above all, maintain the purity of genres. Theater on the one side and poetry on the other: but I'm willing to accept, and I do indeed want it to be the case, that if one distributed the techniques of the two genres very skillfully, one might, like all our masters and those of all the ages, insert a discussion in the middle of descriptions, or indeed of outbursts of the soul. Moreover, as the innovation revealed in Mendès's latest poem demonstrates, one can simply juxtapose backdrop and dialogue, and allow to float between them an atmosphere that truly becomes that of the work itself. Don't you think that doing anything else creates an inconvenience in the absence of the coming and going of characters amidst the visible scenic enchantment, lighting and stage sets of the theater? (*Corr.*, II: 116)

While Mallarmé may conclude with some words of praise, this sharply focused attack on the genre and in particular on France's use of it must have hit home, at least in revealing Mallarmé's wrath if not in changing France's aesthetic convictions.

One of the other judges for Le *Parnasse contemporain* was a man of a very different nature from that of France, a poet who was in many ways central to Mallarmé's self-definition as he moved ever closer toward an image of poetry far removed from the mimetic and the descriptive. Théodore de Banville, who had leapt to precocious fame with his first volume of verse, *Les Cariatides,* published before his twentieth birthday, was above all a master of virtuoso rhyme and inventive rhythms, a poet whose themes seek to fuse Greco-Roman mythology and modern urban life. Amiable and courteous, he was far more approachable than either Hugo or Leconte de Lisle, and his nature made him seek out company, especially among the young. Since as early as 1860 Mallarmé had been an admirer of Banville's supple, witty verse, exemplified especially in his collection of 1857, *Odes funambulesques.* Soon after Mallarmé's return to Paris he began to seek Banville out. Their families became close friends, and the friendship that linked the two poets continued throughout Banville's life. Mallarmé's obituary for Banville, first published in London's *National Observer* and then revised for the inauguration of the older poet's monument, reflects the cult he admitted to devoting to him, one reflected in Henri de Régnier's diary, where he reports Mallarmé's response to Banville's death: "I've had tears in my eyes for two days now. I adored that man" (*Annales,* notebook of November 1, 1890, to May 1, 1891).

If Banville's star has waned, it is in part because of the power of poets who have come after him, but it is also because until very recently, scholars did not possess a first-class edition of his works. Now that such an edition exists,[3] Mallarmé's enthusiasm is less surprising. He analyzes the work of Banville, along with that of Baudelaire and Gautier, in his creative critical piece of 1866, *Symphonie littéraire.* What Banville had to offer Mallarmé was partly the model of a poet determined to be first and foremost just that, a poet. But it was also the image of a great manipulator of words, rhymes, and rhythms. While Rimbaud, in the muscular and inventive poem

"Ce qu'on dit au poète à propos des fleurs" (What one says to the poet regarding flowers) that he sent to Banville, might urge him to do much more than he already did with the wonderful, intoxicating inspiration of the modern world, Banville was nevertheless one of the most technically gifted and innovative French poets of the century. In his obituary of Banville, Mallarmé establishes the poet firmly, if with characteristic linguistic play, in that light:

POETRY, OR WHAT PAST AGES DEMAND that poetry should be, clings to the soil, with faith, to the dust that all remains. For that reason it demands deep foundations, whose deep shadow increases the underpinning, combines with it, and fixes it. This cry of stone finds its unity as it soars up to the sky through its uninterrupted pillars, its arches drawing from prayer the boldness of their upward surge. But not without some immobility. I'm waiting for the dazzling bat, which seems to transform gravity itself into wind, suddenly, with a tip of its aboriginal wing, mad, adamantine, enraged, wheeling, a genius, to strike the ruin and break free, in the whirlwind that it alone is.

Théodore de Banville sometimes becomes that supreme sylph. (*OC*, 521)

If in Mallarmé's eyes Banville has defied gravity (in part through his lack of gravity) and, through his witty, innovative poetry, has broken free from the massive structure built up through centuries of accretions around the notion of poetry, it is above all because he unites the genius, madness, anger, and adamantine integrity necessary to incarnate flight itself. For all the playfulness of the trope Mallarmé uses here, there is a serious purpose. Like his clown figures, especially the protagonist of one of his most famous poems, "Le Saut du tremplin" (The leap from the springboard), Banville breaks free, if only occasionally, from the relative immobility of French prosody, just as Mallarmé himself sought both to retain the echoes, mirrors, and suggestions inherent in a long-established tradition and to go beyond, soar above, interrupt a continuity that stultified. To the young Mallarmé, exploring the possibilities offered by the very restrictions of the alexandrine and perhaps aware of a fact that Baudelaire formulates in a private letter, that "because the form is restricting, the idea bursts forth all the more intensely,"[4] there must have been something quite extraordinarily liberating about Banville's experiments. In a letter of June 1865 to Eugène Lefébure, for example, we find him searching in vain for Banville's volume, *Les Améthystes*, which he qualifies as "simple rhythmical studies" (*CC*, 246). By mid-1866 we find him on several occasions asking to be remembered to Banville (*CC*, 288, 296), whom he "adores more and more," as he claims in a letter to Villiers de l'Isle-Adam (*CC*, 370).

Their friendship was strengthened by their mutual acquaintance with the English poet John Payne, who dedicated to Banville a poem Mallarmé translated from the English for Banville's benefit. (In 1880 Banville published in his periodical *Le Na-*

tional Mallarmé's review of Payne's collection *New Poems [Corr.,* IV: 462n].) Because he was able to visit him, Mallarmé wrote less often to Banville than to friends who were geographically more distant. Moreover, many of the letters seem to have been lost, existing only as frustrating phantoms attested to by Banville's brief responses. Nevertheless, Mallarmé's references to him in letters to others and the tone of the letters to Banville that we do possess show a relationship of friendship and trust that was based, to a considerable degree, on Mallarmé's enjoyment of what Banville had succeeded in doing.

While Mallarmé continued to develop friendships with writers such as Heredia and Dierx, whose convictions and practice are closer to Parnassianism than his own suggestive and elliptical Symbolism, and with such older poets as Banville, his openness to the new literary world he was discovering in Paris led to a friendship with a very different writer, the novelist Emile Zola, whom he may well have met through their mutual friend Edouard Manet. Certainly Zola's defense of the painter would have been attractive to Mallarmé, but his letters to the writer reveal more than a sense of gratitude for the support of a mutual friend or even for the support of an approach to art. Léon Deffoux, who was the first to publish nineteen of the poet's letters to Zola, argues that they constitute both a testimony to Mallarmé's serene artistic judgment and an incomparable lesson in critical intelligence.[5] That intelligence is already clearly discernible in a letter Mallarmé wrote on November 6, 1874, after attending a performance of Zola's play *Les Héritiers Rabourdin,* which had opened a few days before at the Cluny theater. The critical response to this play was so fierce that, as his most recent biographer, Frederick Brown, argues, Zola was in considerable need of moral support from his friends.[6] While acerbic critics such as Auguste Vitu and Francisque Sarcey railed against the play's bleakness, Mallarmé saw it as a "bitter farce" (*Corr.,* II: 50) whose depths the critics, with their "utter dearth of reflection," had simply failed to plumb. That failure, Mallarmé suggests in a sentence that admirably portrays both his intellectual curiosity and his rejection of artistic prejudice, stems from a stultifying conviction that art can only be highbrow, that it can project no "popular illumination." Mallarmé himself, as he states here, "admires a poster, colored and drawn as so many posters are, just as much as he admires a ceiling or an apotheosis, and does not admit that any viewpoint in art is inferior to any other" (*Corr.,* II: 51). This is the kind of conviction that sustains his study of fashion, that explains the time he spent on the rhyming addresses, and that enables him to respond so intensely and so intelligently to such a range of works of art and culture.

If such letters reveal the breadth of Mallarmé's aesthetic interests, they also show the degree to which he sought to analyze a work's reception. The letter to Zola in March 1876, when he had just read his "dear colleague's" new novel, *Son Excellence Eugène Rougon,* becomes an opportunity to explore two very different modes of reading—the breathless dash through the narrative and the slow analysis of each aspect. According to Mallarmé, Zola's novel lends itself to both approaches, for, he argues, "a deep interest is admirably dissimulated under the chance folds and cracks, with which today's novelist is forced to bulk out his conception" (*Corr.,* II: 107). The apparently haphazard folds and cracks of the modern narrative, the twists and turns of plot as the narrative voice charts the difficult progress of the politician Rougon, have their interest for Mallarmé but are not the central attraction. It is the novel's deeper purpose, hidden under this rough surface, that demands that slow analytical reading. In one sinuous sentence Mallarmé sums up what for him are Zola's highest achievements in his novel—the creation of the great political force represented by the two contrasting characters, Rougon and Clorinde, and the swift, transparent style that possesses the lightness and impersonality of the modern gaze. If critics don't appreciate this achievement, he claims, it is because the current critical mode lacks lucidity and looks only for fantasy. It would, of course, be easy to read hidden criticisms into this comment, especially in regard to the transparency of style, given Mallarmé's refusal of such transparency and his tendency to force his reader to pay attention to the surface and nature of the sign itself as well as to what it may signify. But that is not really what is at issue here, I believe. Mallarmé begins this summary with an assertion that his own point of view, that of a poet, is not the right one when it comes to a different genre, the novel. Moreover, his castigation of critics who seek only the fantastic reveals clearly enough that he decries all who read from only one point of view, who lack the flexibility to enter into what the writer or artist has attempted to do. There is a further point to stress here, one that shows Mallarmé appreciating both the individual novel and that novel's position in the development of the genre. Referring to the "attractive evolution" of contemporary fiction, Mallarmé raises the question of the function of history, and especially of the novel's role in delineating contemporary history. Given that Zola's novel captures with acerbic brilliance the self-seeking nature of the Second Empire, the fragility of power, and the sordid side of politics, Mallarmé's interest in these "fatal chaps who believed they were better than bearers of principles" (*Corr.,* II: 107) reveals a sharper awareness of contemporary power struggles than might have been guessed. In Interlude 5 I examine the relationships that existed between Mallarmé and some of his anarchist friends, but it's worth stressing that already in the mid-1870s the poet reveals an attitude that is far from the ivory-tower remoteness that certain critics have attempted to foist on him.

Equally, the antipopularist Mallarmé created by those who place too much weight on the early work "L'Art pour tous" (Art for everyone) is very far from the man who read Zola's *L'Assommoir* with such insight and such interest. It was in February 1877 that Mallarmé wrote to Zola about this novel of urban poverty and the destruction of the individual less by alcohol than by the indifference of modern industrial life. Like many readers after him, Mallarmé is struck by the descriptions of people at work, performing humble tasks. The Homeric quality that Zola brings to the depiction of Gervaise's laundry or to Coupeau's roof-repairing, the awareness of the value of work, has its predecessors in realist painting—one thinks of Gustave Courbet's winnowers or stone breakers, for instance—but it is true of French literature that Zola's presentation of that value is indeed, as Mallarmé claims, "something utterly new." The novelty springs partly from the subject matter and partly from the rhythms, created by both description and plot. When Mallarmé refers to "these pages that are so tranquil and that turn like all the days of a life" (*Corr.,* II: 146), he is paying tribute to skills and ambitions very different from his own desire to seize and distill the significant moment. What is striking, however, is what one might call an intellectual determination to remain open to other possibilities and a keen sense of the direction in which the novel as genre is headed.

Paradoxically, the point at which Zola and Mallarmé seem closest, where *L'Assommoir* is concerned, occurs in the novel's linguistic experiments, its attempt to capture the forms, rhythms, and idiosyncrasies of working-class speech. However far removed this focus may be from Mallarmé's poetic language, the underlying aim, the desire to break away from what was considered the rhetoric of literature, is identical for both writers. Mallarmé's earlier ambition to write a thesis on linguistics, his determination to forge a poetic language that demanded from his reader an active decoding rather than a passive absorption, and his refusal of the hackneyed all seem to underlie his response to Zola's interest in capturing colloquial language. That interest is in itself part of a growing nineteenth-century tradition, continuing Honoré de Balzac's delight in thieves' cant in, for example, *Le Père Goriot,* or Victor Hugo's fascination with street jargon in *Les Misérables.* Zola, however, typically pursues it with an intensity and a wholeheartedness that goes well beyond the more sporadic use of such language in earlier writers. What it recalls most strongly is not these works with their literary aspirations but rather novels written merely to amuse and delight, especially perhaps such page-turners as Ponson du Terrail's *Rocambole.*

That Mallarmé considers Zola's novel as quite different in quality from works written merely to entertain is clear from the two reproaches he makes in passing. He points first to the way in which the battle in the laundry, for all its magnificence, is somewhat extraneous to the work, out of character with Gervaise's generally passive temperament and more in the nature of a splendid but somewhat otiose set piece. The second criticism concerns the swift change in the young girl Nana, although here, with the benefit of hindsight, readers familiar with the novel *Nana* might be more willing to leave Zola space to develop her elsewhere and merely sketch rapidly her early progress in a novel that is, after all, devoted to her parents.

Both the letters Mallarmé sent to Zola and the highly condensed study of his play *Renée* that the poet published in the late 1880s reveal that one of the reasons Mallarmé so admired a writer who seems so different from him is that he considered Zola quintessentially modern, uniquely able to transform contemporary mores and convictions into works that corresponded with particular skill to contemporary modes of thinking and reading. Mallarmé, shaped and conditioned by Baudelaire as he was, and fully aware of the master's injunction to blend the modern and the timeless, might have sought to place more emphasis on the second element than the first, but there can be no doubting his awareness of Zola's skill in perceiving and capturing exactly those attitudes and enthusiasms that typify Second Empire France.

In discussing *Une page d'amour* with its author in April 1878, Mallarmé enters into a sustained meditation on what it is that makes this novel so strikingly modern. And in doing so he suggests—not dogmatically, perhaps not even in ways that Zola perceived, but as though he were marking a personal difference—what separates his vision of art from that of his colleague. Both poem and novel, *Une page d'amour,* so Mallarmé argues, throws into question the notion of separate genres for which he had argued so fiercely in his letter to Anatole France, or rather it indicates that a single work can combine the achievements of each genre—the novel's task of depicting contemporary life blending perfectly here with the poem's task of transforming that depiction by metaphor and metonymy into an exploration of timeless realities. The impression conveyed by this blending of genres is so intense, Mallarmé argues, that on closing the book the reader feels not so much that this intuition has been mediated by a rapid transcription but rather that it has been relayed directly, leaving the reader with the sense of having experienced a "profound and limpid vision" (*Corr.,* II: 172).

In responding to the novel's effect, Mallarmé stresses particularly the absence of a clearly detectable authorial position, the illusion of having read an autonomous text. Clearly he is reacting here to an appreciable difference between, on the one hand, the novels of Balzac, for instance, with their frequent voice-over commentaries, and on the other those of the more impersonal Zola. Ceding the initiative to words, that central tenet of Mallarmé's creed, is clearly a novelistic as well as a poetic skill, and I see no reason to doubt the sincerity of his praise in this regard. But Lloyd Austin is surely right to detect in what follows a subtle criticism that is also, I would argue, a personal *mise en garde:* What if impersonality is such that it convinces the reader that the work is perfectly self-contained, enclosed within itself and therefore allowing no loophole through which the reader can enter and dream? Balzac's novels, precisely because of that insistent voice-over of the omniscient narrator, constantly provoke and frequently invite readerly rebellion or at least readerly independence: Paradoxically, Zola's white-noise narration can leave the sense that all has been said, that no chink allows access to the reader's reverie. The strength of that criticism, however subtle, can be seen when Mallarmé, although quick to insist that the novels nevertheless create the impression of life itself (*Corr.,* II: 173) and to draw attention to particular instances of that re-creation of life, still allows a glimpse of his claws. Of course, as many critics have stressed, Mallarmé turns away from the mimetic function of art, demanding of his reader the personalized and internal response that transforms the imprecise reference, say, to a flower into a particular significant and highly personalized memory of an individual violet or rose. As a result, there is a certain ambivalence in Mallarmé's allusion to the beauty of Zola's Paris skies:

> WHAT MAKES THEM ESPECIALLY BEAUTIFUL, in addition to the incomparable variety and lucidity of the description, is that they never allow the reader to leave your universe for a moment, since you provide him or her with the horizons and the distant views. And at those points where normally one lifts one's eyes after an episode of the tale, to think one's own thoughts and relax a little, you appear with superb tyranny and provide the backdrop to our reverie. (*Corr.*, II: 173)

And he sharpens that criticism when he asserts that he cannot see the moral link between those skies and the subject itself. Clearly for him the descriptive can be justified only by its ability to externalize or otherwise reflect and comment on the moral or psychological. It is not, of course, that the intrinsic poetry of such descriptions is lost on Mallarmé: it's rather that here he seems, more so than in his earlier letters to Zola, to be placing higher demands on those fine gifts for description and urging the writer on to a different kind of novel, one that I suspect Huysmans comes closer to achieving in, for example, *Là-Bas* than Zola ever did.

There is something poignantly ironic in the fact that even Mallarmé's reference to the fourth in Zola's *Rougon-Macquart* series, *La Conquête de Plassans (The Conquest of Plassans)*, as a "masterly work" (*Corr.*, II: 51) was not enough to inspire in the novelist the same openness to difference. His own published response to Mallarmé's poetry reveals an inability to accept a vision of art different from his own: "His poems contain only words set side by side, not for the clarity of the sentence but for the harmony of each piece."[7] There is also something disturbing in the fact that those of Zola's letters to Mallarmé that have been discovered are all somewhat perfunctory, even superficial, none of them attempting to enter into the kind of intellectual debate that Mallarmé's letters propose. The two men seem to have met quite regularly, either at Mallarmé's "Tuesdays" or Zola's "Thursdays," and Zola, in a brief letter of 1876, claims that he would be "charmed" to see his "dear colleague," yet none of that charm, none of the delight in intellectual exchange, is conveyed in the novelist's letters. Looking at what Mallarmé wrote to Zola, set in the context of the novelist's apparently sterile responses, I would suggest that Mallarmé writes in large measure to explore, sharpen, and refine his own responses, even to a genre to which he would never himself creatively contribute. Zola's apparent lack of enthusiasm for such a process had little bearing on Mallarmé's explorations. Again, one could argue that Mallarmé's desire for control was such that he would allow no amount of cold water that Zola could pour to dampen his enthusiasm for analyzing the *Rougon-Macquart* series in particular and the novel form more generally.

That exploration is also evident in letters to the lesser-known novelists Léon Hennique and Léon Cladel. Hennique was one of the contributors to the collection of short prose pieces known as Les *Soirées de Médan* (The Médan evenings), works that indicated the intellectual and aesthetic preoccupations of the new school, known as Naturalism. In 1878 he sent Mallarmé a copy of his novel *Les Héros modernes* and received a detailed if somewhat tardy response. One of the aspects of the genre that seems most to appeal to Mallarmé, or at least to demand much of his attention, is the ability to re-create an atmosphere, to represent a reality so palpably that it is completely convincing. Mallarmé praises Hennique's novel for evoking "the air, the true and breathable air" and for allowing the majority of the characters to "step out of the book, once you've closed it, and become part of your existence" (*Corr.,* II: 181). But even here there are hesitations, modestly expressed, exceptions and queries that Mallarmé puts forward as a kind of agenda for discussion when they next meet. Above all, Mallarmé seems to indicate that this kind of novel reflects primarily an external vision, and while he praises Hennique's skills in re-creating that vision, the stress on that epithet undoubtedly carries with it the implication that internal vision, as well as the ability to suggest it rather than to evoke it in all its clarity, is of greater importance to him. Later, in 1884, when Hennique sent him another novel in the series *Les Héros modernes,* Mallarmé wrote in more enthusiastic terms, describing it as "something as attractive as a poem" (*Corr.,* II: 257). Yet for all the pleasure he claims to have experienced in reading it, there are some hesitations and doubts. After all, when Mallarmé writes somewhat formulaically, "this work is of interest to all readers and bound to achieve the greatest success," one can't fail to hear a hint of irony, a suggestion that writing for everyone and in view of a public triumph is not necessarily an attitude that results in the highest of achievements in the long term or in the abstract. And when he describes the book's characters as being "just like what we see in the real world day after day" one can't help wondering how much he would have preferred the exceptional to the typical.

Léon Cladel, whose early short stories had benefited from the suggestions of Baudelaire, was much closer to Mallarmé. They exchanged many letters, and whereas the correspondence with Hennique suggests merely a professional exchange of views, those to Cladel indicate that theirs was primarily a relationship based on shared interests and experiences. When his regional novel *L'Homme de la Croix-aux-bœufs* appeared in 1878, Cladel received the following enthusiastic response from his poet friend: "Now there's a book! As a novel this work is situated in the very terrain of the novel, beyond the reach of all social powers. He to whom the law has not given justice, avenges himself, setting the law aside" (*Corr.,* II: 177). Mallarmé's earlier statement to France about the need to keep genres separate helps illuminate this expression; it also suggests that one of the functions of the novel as a genre is to investigate the great themes of human emotions and behavior without the restrictions of legal and social conventions. Cladel's style also attracts enthusiastic praise: "So many new aspects of language, miraculously thrown into relief, appear emphasized for the first and last time. [. . .] At every moment there's a new note drawn from an instrument that seemed to have given almost all its notes already." But there is an indication— in addition to the predictable points of disagreement or unease about the plot—of Mallarmé's belief that novels are written for an audience different from that of po- etry, demanding of their writers a series of clues and guidelines that poetry is not only able but obliged to avoid: "I even consider essential to the total effect the few exaggerations which give the uninitiated the key to your art" (*Corr.*, II: 177). Mal- larmé's response to the evolution of the novel, and especially to the appropriation of the form by the Naturalists, is clearly far from being simply one of enthusiasm. He frequently points to problems and limitations in the genre, and while he remains re- ceptive to it, it seems undeniable that what he seeks from the novel as from other works of literature and art is the ability not to build a complete and enclosed uni- verse but to inspire and permit dream, a parallel rather than a mimetic universe.

That lively intellectual response to the novel found a far more receptive reader in Joris-Karl Huysmans, whose ironic portrayal of decadence in *A rebours* (*Against the Grain*), with its account of the protagonist's meditations on Mallarmé, did so much to draw the poet to the attention of the reading public. From the early 1880s, the two men entered into a probing discussion of the possibilities and limitations of the novel form in the age in which they lived. Indeed, a letter of October 1882 sets the stage for *A rebours,* with its discussion of Huysmans's plan to produce a "singu- lar short story" in which the last scion of a great race would seek refuge in solitude, driven there by his disgust with the growing "Americanization" of contemporary ex- istence and by his desire to avenge himself and his friends on the "wet blankets who've never understood anything about the very penetrating language we are at- tempting to write."[8] Mallarmé's response was both rapid (Huysmans's letter is dated 27 October; Mallarmé wrote his on the 29th) and enthusiastic. Referring to Huys- mans's "magnificent project," he went on to affirm, in terms that show how deeply he had been thinking about the evolution of the novel as genre in fin-de-siècle France, that "our age could not come to an end without this novel's being written." (It is sig- nificant that whereas Huysmans spoke of a short story, Mallarmé implied that such a theme required the elbow room of a novel.) Mallarmé's excitement is all the more intense in that he is convinced he already knows the living prototype of Huysmans's protagonist: the eccentric poet Robert de Montesquiou, who also played a role in in- spiring Proust's character Charlus (*Corr.,* II: 234–35). Huysmans's reply to this let- ter was equally rapid, written in a white heat of enthusiasm for his project and rage against the great majority of the reading public. One comment in particular merits attention, in light of Mallarmé's view of the explosive potential of creative writing: "It is true that more than poetry, perhaps, the prose poem terrifies the Homais who make up the great majority of the public."[9] The allusion to Flaubert's archetypal bourgeois figure is significant, indicating the extent to which creative writers of this period sought their parallels less with the world of business or politics than with works of the imagination.

When Huysmans's novel appeared in 1884, Mallarmé's response was characteristic of him:

> TRULY, CLOSED AS I SEE IT ON MY TABLE, while under my gaze the entire treasure of its knowledge meditates, I cannot imagine it other than it is. You know, in that hour of reverie that follows a reading, a different book almost always substitutes itself even for a book we admire. No! not in this case, nothing is missing, perfumes, music, liqueurs and the old or almost future books; and those flowers! It's an absolute vision of all that can open, to an individual placed before a barbaric or modern pleasure, a paradise of pure sensation. What's admirable in all this and what gives your work its strength (which will be described as coming from an insane imagination and so forth) is that there's not an atom of fantasy in it. You have succeeded, by this refined tasting of all essences, in showing yourself as more strictly documentary than anyone, and in using only facts, or reports, that are true, that exist just as much as do vulgar ones. Those you have chosen are subtle and demand a princely eye, that's all. But as pleasure demands a constant refinement of the sources of pleasure, anyone who is intense and delicate will certainly reach the same conclusions as you. They'll reach that point, and no further and in exactly the same way; stopping at the point you have decreed. Thus your work assumes in the mind a terrifying aspect, for it sets down something that is definitive. (*Corr.,* II: 261)

This is really the kind of work he admires, regardless of the genre—the book that allows for, indeed enables, reverie, the kind he evokes in his sonnet "Mes bouquins refermés." And Mallarmé clearly differentiates between the novel that allows such reverie merely by virtue of its reliance on fantasy and what Huysmans has achieved in a work that is "more documentary than that of any other writer." There can be little doubt that Mallarmé is here setting up a comparison between the detailed and painstaking realism of Zola and that revealed in *A rebours*. Later, in his 1893 piece "Magie" (Magic), which takes as its starting point Huysmans's novel *Là-Bas,* he gives even more weight to the transformation of documentation into work of art when he refers to this novel as "a work whose impact is infinitely different from the fact of providing documents, however extraordinary they may be" (*OC*, 399).

Mallarmé's delight in Huysmans's friendship, and the very different quality of his letters to him as compared with those to Zola, may also derive from the fact that Huysmans's powerful, idiosyncratic, and perceptive art criticism showed him to be inspired by aesthetic convictions close to Mallarmé's. Responding to Huysmans's *L'Art moderne,* which brings together his accounts of the annual art Salons of 1879, 1880, and 1881, as well as his review of the Impressionist exhibitions of 1880 and

1881, Mallarmé reveals his delight, politely suggests two points of disagreement or at least two areas where he would like further discussion, and closes with a warmly encouraging word inquiring into the state of the projected novel. One of the points he raises touches on Manet's art, implying that the paintings Huysmans mentions, the product of the artist's sad last years, are perhaps not the most characteristic of him, rendering Huysmans's criticisms less valid than would otherwise be the case. The second is perhaps more controversial: Mallarmé seems to take issue with Huysmans's anger at the contemporary artist Bouguereau's naked women, plunged incongruously into a landscape.[10] (Huysmans, whose appreciation of erotic art is forcefully expressed in his criticism, was no prude. His censure here derives from the prurience and incongruity of Bouguereau's techniques.) Mallarmé writes, "Perhaps there might be the possibility when we meet to chat a little about nudity, since from now on for the next thousand years we are going to see popular, more or less official palaces, the sort that draw for their decoration on classical art, treating nudity in a lively but allegorical fashion" (*Corr.,* II: 242). Obviously Mallarmé did not foresee a time—though nor I suspect did Huysmans—when such allegorical transpositions of women's naked bodies would be called into question, making their use in public buildings at least open to serious criticism. Clearly for Mallarmé, at this stage at least, the allegorical function outweighs the representative, so that for him the presence of the naked woman in a naturalistic landscape does not pose the kind of problems that it may for Huysmans and that it does for many members of a modern audience.

Mallarmé's friendships with Zola and Huysmans draw primarily, it seems, on the poet's profound respect for the commitment each writer had to his own vision of art. While Huysmans's rage against the philistine is very different from Zola's sharp awareness of the commercial possibilities of art, Mallarmé appears to have found in both writers a testing ground for his own ideas, and, even more important perhaps, images of commitment to an ideal that he may not have shared but that was pursued with an intensity that helped to strengthen his resolve. This was especially important in these years when his return to Paris was posing a series of problems different in nature from those he had encountered in the provinces but equally dispiriting.

One important feature of these difficulties concerns his identity not so much as a teacher of English but as a reader of English, and the use to which he could put that skill. In purely pragmatic terms, his ability enabled him to supplement his meager finances through the publication of his *Les Mots anglais* in 1876, at a time when he was desperately short of money.[11] If he also foresaw the possibility of acting as a commentator and spokesperson who could enable the French and the English to discover recent trends and experiments in each other's literature, he was moved only in part by financial reasons. At least since his encounters with the Félibrige, the group attempting to revive Provençale as a literary language, Mallarmé had been drawn to the idea of an international society of writers, together with the creation of a reading public eager to go beyond national boundaries. It is in this context that we should see his attempts to build up strong relationships with English critics and writers in the 1870s and early 1880s.

Mallarmé's growing friendship with the gentle and witty poet Théodore de Banville led directly to one of his closest English friendships, that with John Payne. Poet and translator, Payne had dedicated a volume of sonnets, *Intaglios,* to Banville, whose poor command of English had led him to seek a translator in Mallarmé. Through Banville's introduction, Mallarmé met Payne during his brief visit to London in 1871 to gather information for a proposed article on the Great Exhibition there.[12] A man of singular charm, broad linguistic gifts, and considerable eccentricity—he wrote his entire translation of *Thousand and One Nights,* according to his biographer, while riding in the upper deck of buses[13]—Payne was eventually to become a recluse, living almost entirely for literature. Such eccentricity would hardly tell against him in Mallarmé's eyes, of course. At the time Mallarmé first met him, however, Payne appears to have formed friendships quickly and easily, soon using the informal "tu" in his letters to the French poet. An ardent Wagnerite, credited with playing a leading role in introducing Wagner to the British public, Payne had written a poem dedicated to the German master in his collection *Songs of Life and Death.* Mallarmé offered to have the poem conveyed to Wagner by the intermediary of Catulle Mendès, who knew the composer well. Theirs seems to have been above all a friendship inspired by mutual friends, especially Banville and Leconte de Lisle. We find Mallarmé willingly delivering copies of Payne's books to his French friends and asking his advice on how best to procure good quality stout for Banville, whose poor health obliged him to drink it. Payne visited Mallarmé in France on various occasions, and they developed mutual friendships. The letter Mallarmé mailed to Payne hours before his son Anatole's death reveals in its moving simplicity the depth of their personal friendship: "I have often felt from afar your sympathy with our tears, since these evil days began, as if you'd been fully aware of our anguish; for I know you love us" (*Corr.,* II: 201). It seems fairly clear that he appreciated Payne less as a poet than as a translator, although when he published his collected poems in 1902, Payne dedicated them to the memory of "my very dear and most bitterly lamented Stéphane Mallarmé, an exquisite spirit and a heart of gold," who, according to Payne, loved these poems "nevertheless."[14] The French poet's enthusiastic response to Payne's translation of *Thousand and One Nights,* for example, reflects his own concerns as translator of Poe: "What excellent turns of phrase you've found to translate the repeated formulas: you've made some truly felicitous efforts there. I'm not sure that I wouldn't embrace you even more warmly for having written this book in a delicious English than for having succeeded in that monstrous feat of knowing Arabic" (*Corr.,* II: 232). Payne, for his part, certainly seems to have admired Mallarmé as a poet, writing to him, at a time when "L'Après-midi d'un faune" was attracting sneers from the Parisian press, that he found in the poem "lines of pentelic marble, translucid and glowing golden in an age-old sun" (*VM,* 385).

It was through Payne that Mallarmé met a group of writers with whom he was to form close ties. Payne's closest friend, apart from the artist and mystic John Trivett Nettleship, whom Mallarmé seems not to have met, was the poet Arthur O'Shaugnessy, thought to be the illegitimate son of the novelist Lord Lytton. Payne had gathered around him a literary circle, known as the Fetherstone Club, after the hotel at which their meetings took place. According to Payne's biographer, Thomas Wright, the mysterious letters that can be found on the club's programs, P.B.Y.O.B., meant nothing more than "please bring your own bloater."[15] However difficult it might be to associate Mallarmé and soused herrings, the intellectual interests of this group would certainly have struck an echo in his mind, and he and O'Shaugnessy exchanged several letters.

A follower of Swinburne, O'Shaugnessy had published several poetry collections by the time Mallarmé met him in 1875; among these were the collection *Lays of France,* which adapted poems by the twelfth-century poet Marie de France. Well aware of current literary trends in France, O'Shaugnessy frequently wrote articles for the *Athenaeum,* bringing French writers to the attention of the English public. He was also the English correspondent for the French periodical *Le Livre.* In responding in September 1875 to O'Shaugnessy's gift of his poetry collection *Music and Moonlight,* Mallarmé would have been well aware of the role the author could play in introducing him as poet and critic to English readers. Indeed, the letter accompanying the poems talks of O'Shaugnessy's intention to write a "nice paragraph" for the *Athenaeum* on *Vathek,* at a time when Mallarmé was working on his projected preface to the book. The paragraph, qualified by Mallarmé as "charming," appeared on September 4, 1875. O'Shaugnessy, after announcing that this deluxe edition of *Vathek* would appear in the original French, added, "The interest attaching to this celebrated work, well known to most Englishmen, will, we think, still be strong enough to attract many to make an acquaintance with it in the original language and form."[16]

The degree to which O'Shaugnessy's poetry struck Mallarmé as so many variations on such poets as Walt Whitman and Swinburne is suggested in the letter in which he thanks his friend for the gift of *Music and Moonlight.* Mallarmé, I think, considered much modern English poetry as derivative and repetitious, but here he is clearly attempting to understand what his new friend is attempting, or at the very least he is avoiding offending him. Moreover, Mallarmé singles out as his favorite poems at least some that do possess a particular beauty. The opening "Ode" has become, and deservedly so, an anthology piece:

We are the music makers,
We are the dreamers of dreams,
Wandering by lone sea-breakers,
And sitting by desolate streams;—
World-losers and world-forsakers,

On whom the pale moon gleams;
Yet we are the movers and shakers
Of the world for ever, it seems.[17]

While one might regret the banal makeweight of "it seems," and while the nostalgic Romanticism and simple clarity of these lines are far from the thickness and complexity of Mallarmé's own verse, their beauty and their image of the poet as both dreamer and changer of the world are undeniably powerful. In another of Mallarmé's favorites, "Song of the Palms," however, not only are the central theme and the way in which it is presented reminiscent of Banville's evocation of the palms of Bordighera, first published in *La Mer de Nice* in 1860, but the rhymes also strike a native English speaker's ear as not merely forced but bordering on the downright embarrassing:

And its long luxuriant thought
Lofty palm to palm hath taught,
    While a single vast liana
All one brotherhood hath wrought,
Crossing forest and savannah,
Binding fern and coco-tree,
Fig-tree, buttree-tree, banana,
Dwarf cane and tall mariti.[18]

Summing up O'Shaugnessy's *Music and Moonlight* in a judgment that Lloyd Austin finds suspicious, Mallarmé affirms, "Always a marvelous song, but always a beginning, a middle, and an end; nothing but what is simultaneously lyrical and cunningly composed: that's the supreme goal and you achieve it almost at every attempt" (*Corr.*, II: 73). Ten years earlier, as Austin reminds us, Mallarmé had written in a letter to Cazalis, "Let me close with a recipe that I've invented and that I follow: you should always cut the beginning and the end from what you write. No introduction and no finale" (*Corr.*, 1: 117). There is something slippery and disturbing in the combination of the song and the firm structure, a potential warning in the use of the word "but" that can be read as either indicating that songs are normally written without such structure, (yet O'Shaugnessy has succeeded in creating a strong formal structure while remaining lyrical) or that there is a jarring contrast of vehicle and tenor. But of course there are conventions in thank-you letters, especially when the volume is sent less in search of advice than as a pledge of friendship, and Mallarmé is not so much being duplicitous here as indicating that O'Shaugnessy's "supreme goal" has been met, even if he himself doesn't share it. What is beyond doubt is Mallarmé's awareness of contemporary poetry and his familiarity with the Anglophone tradition.

Another letter to O'Shaugnessy sent in October of that same year reveals both Mallarmé's kindness and his interest in promoting French literature in England, as he attempted to facilitate his friend's task in obtaining copies of books to review. For his own part, Mallarmé seems to have relied to some extent on O'Shaugnessy to edit his "Gossips" for the *Athenaeum.* Not knowing how familiar his readership would be with contemporary French literature, he included details that could if necessary be cut—surely one of the very rare examples of Mallarmé giving more rather than less than was needed.

In this autumn when Mallarmé strove to publish "L'Après-midi d'un faune" and sought a possible English publishing house to handle distribution of the volume on the other side of the Channel, he drew heavily on O'Shaugnessy's advice, and while his friend's best collection of poems, *Epic of Women,* languished with Manet, from whom Mallarmé was supposed to collect it, he must have been sufficiently confident in his friendship not to feel obliged to read and comment on it with any alacrity. Yet O'Shaugnessy was also attracted to the Herodiade theme, and while his presentation of Salomé is indistinguishable from the many fin-de-siècle versions on both sides of the Channel, his Saint John is somewhat closer to Mallarmé's. One stanza of the Salomé section should suffice, even if its fascination with jewels finds parallels with Mallarmé's presentation:

> The veils fell round her like thin coiling mists
> Shot through by topaz suns, and amethysts,
> > And rubies she had on;
> And out of them her jeweled body came,
> And seemed to all quite like a slender flame
> That curled and glided, and that burnt and shone
> > Most fair to look upon.[19]

Saint John receives rather better treatment:

> And often, while the sacred darkness trailed
> Along the mountains smitten and unveiled
> > By rending lightnings,—over all the noise
> Of thunder and the earth that quaked and bowed
> > From its foundations—he could hear the voice
> Of great Elias prophesying loud
> To Him whose face was covered with a cloud.[20]

The frequent messages Mallarmé sent O'Shaugnessy at this time, together with a variety of different "Gossips," reflect the breadth of Mallarmé's interest in the intellectual and cultural life of Paris as well as a growing financial worry. There were other anxieties, too: Mallarmé's letter of early February 1876 responds to O'Shaugnessy's concerns about his wife, whose fragile health was to lead to her death some three years later.

Meanwhile, O'Shaugnessy worked tirelessly to promote the publication of *Vathek,* an act of friendship for which Mallarmé was especially grateful, for, as he claims in a letter of May 1876, the preface was one of the prose pieces on which he had lavished most care, distilling into it the quintessential aspects of Beckford's career and genius (*Corr.,* II: 118). In this preface he sets out above all to "seduce the dreamer" (*OC,* 549), and he certainly succeeds in creating a shimmering image of a tale whose structure is not only masterly, to use Mallarmé's term, but that finds an external referent in the protagonist's translation from the top of a tower from which he read the firmament to the depths of an enchanted cavern. This great dream that has surged up from the narrator's mind is presented as marked by fleeting impressions, a richness of local color, and above all a poetry of melancholy, fear, and remorse. Many have seen the tale as providing the initial inspiration for the sonnet "Quand l'ombre menaça" (When the shadow threatened), and certainly much of the preface's language recalls that of the poem, suggesting that the tale provided a fertile source for Mallarmé's imagination. More important, perhaps, the preface reveals some of his finest writing and indicates the extent to which the challenge of pieces such as this and the "Gossips" he was writing for O'Shaugnessy sharpened and refined his techniques. We could take, for example, the following passage (even if making such a choice poses for us the same problem as Mallarmé himself encountered in choosing examples from *Vathek:* "How can anything be extracted without rendering it an empty shred?" [*OC,* 565]):

A FORM OF POETRY (even if its origin is neither alien to us nor yet part of our own habits), linked in truly unforgettable fashion to the book, reveals itself in some strange juxtaposition of almost idyllic innocence and the vast or vain solemnities of magic. That moment of revelation brings color or life, like the black vibrations of a planet, to the natural scenes, and does so to the point of unease; but not without creating at this approach of the dream something simpler and more extraordinary. (*OC,* 550–51)

Much of this judgment applies directly to Mallarmé's own poetry, with its alienating, uncanny (*unheimlich* in Freud's polyvalent use of the term) effect on the reader and its ability both to intensify our awareness of the world and to create something at once very different from the world, something oneiric yet so simple as to clarify that everyday world.

Mallarmé's preoccupation with Beckford's novel clearly has another cause—one that is centrally related to his friendships with Anglophone writers and his own perception of himself as a speaker and reader of English. The very act of writing in a foreign language brings the writer closer to the heart of creative language:

> MANY A PASSAGE, VEILED OR INTENSE, calm and mighty, owes its multiple nature to the ever-watchful vigilance of the writer. [. . .] Everything flows naturally, with an intense limpidity, with a broad swell of sentences; and the brightness tends to melt in the general purity of the flow, which carries with it many riches of diction that at first are unnoticed, as is perfectly natural in a foreigner worried that an overly bold expression might betray him by arresting the reader's attention. (*OC,* 565)

Coming to terms with a passage written in a foreign language, exploring and exploiting an alien tongue, becomes therefore a metaphor for Mallarmé's own perception of the poetic language, and although he never perfected his English, one is tempted to believe that the gap between an English text and his comprehension of it stimulated in him the kind of productive reverie that he himself strove to inspire and re-create in readers of his poetry.

O'Shaugnessy continued to promote Mallarmé's reputation in England with articles in the *Athenaeum* and the *Morning Post,* and by helping him to publish his article on Manet and the Impressionists in *The Art Monthly Review.*[21] Moreover, O'Shaugnessy introduced Mallarmé to Louise Chandler Moulton, whose enthusiasm for the works of Edgar Allan Poe played a role in inspiring Mallarmé's tribute to the American poet, the "Tombeau d'Edgar Poe" (Tomb of Edgar Poe). With the years the friendship between the two men and their families became increasingly strong, so that in July 1877 Mallarmé was able to write to O'Shaugnessy in terms that recall the warmth and confidence of his earlier letters to Cazalis: "In my view, there are no letters except business letters; for the only friends we have are those on whose confidence we can count, even in the most unbroken silence, the sort one loves to live in, in order to work" (*Corr.,* II: 153). O'Shaugnessy and his wife sent the Mallarmés a pudding for Christmas 1877, together with the poet's *Epic of Women.* When O'Shaugnessy's wife died in 1879, Mallarmé's letter of condolence reveals his distress, together with the warmth of his friendship. It also speaks of the role of conjugal love in the life of both the individual and the poet, in terms that Mallarmé's later relationship with Méry Laurent has led commentators to overlook: "I sympathize with your grief, my friend, doubly, for I know the price any sensitive man places on a charming and good companion; and as a poet I also know all you may have put of your divine and infinite self in the chosen and beloved woman, in the hours of youth when she became your fiancée" (*Corr.,* II: 188).

It seems that no letters from Mallarmé to his friend have been found between this one and O'Shaugnessy's own death a mere two years later, when he succumbed to an inflammation of the lungs caused by walking home in a violent snowstorm in January 1881. John Payne leaves us with a poetic account of that death in his threnody "A Christmas Vigil," depicting O'Shaugnessy dying with François Rabelais's great phrase on his lips: "Je vais quérir le grand Peut-être" (I go to seek the great Perhaps).[22] In addition to the role he played in making Mallarmé's name known in England (if only to the happy few), and in his promotion of *Vathek*, O'Shaugnessy, through his encouragement of the "Gossips," may well have given a particular impetus to that concise and powerful expression of the questioning of contemporary cultural life that Mallarmé elevated to such a refined art over the next two decades.

Nevertheless, Mallarmé's preoccupation with such matters of the mind was not likely to attract the benevolent support of his superiors at the Lycée Fontanes, at which he was currently teaching. The principal, indeed, wrote a ferocious report on this unconventional English master:

> THIS TEACHER IS BUSY WITH MATTERS other than his teaching and his pupils. He is in search of fame, and no doubt, of commercial gain, too, through publications that have no connection with the nature of his functions at the lycée Fontanes. These are *insane productions,* in prose and in verse. Those who read these bizarre lucubrations of M. Mallarmé's mind must be astonished that he occupies a post at the lycée. (Quoted in *VM,* 377)

Although Mallarmé must, given his financial situation, have been dismayed by so violent an attack, and indeed was to publish little more for another six years or so, he did respond positively to a request to write yet another poem in this busy and depressing year of 1876. Sara Sigourney Rice, president of the Baltimore citizens' committee, which in late 1875 had inaugurated a memorial monument to Edgar Allan Poe (rather belatedly, since the poet had died some twenty-five years earlier, in 1849), was also the driving force behind a memorial volume for him. Having invited all the principal American poets to the ceremony (as Lloyd Austin succinctly remarks, the only one who bothered to come was the greatest of them, Walt Whitman [Corr., II: 109–10n. 2]), Rice also sent information to the English poets, notably Tennyson and Swinburne. It was Swinburne who wrote to her in early November of that year in terms that can only have delighted her:

> I HAVE HEARD WITH MUCH PLEASURE of the memorial at length raised to your illustrious fellow-citizen. The genius of Edgar Poe has won on this side of the Atlantic such wide and warm recognition that the sympathy which I cannot hope fitly or fully to express in adequate words is undoubtedly shared at this moment by hundreds as far as the news may have spread through not England only but France as well; where as I need not remind you the most beautiful and durable of monuments has been reared to the genius of Poe by the laborious devotion of a genius equal and akin to his own [Baudelaire]; and

where the admirable translation of his prose works by a fellow-poet, whom also we have now to lament before his time, is even now being perfected by a careful and exquisite version of his poems, with illustrations full of the subtle and tragic force of fancy which impelled and molded the original song; a double homage due to the loyal and loving cooperation of one of the most remarkable younger poets and one of the most powerful leading painters in France—M. Mallarmé and M. Manet.[23]

It was Swinburne, too, who sent Mallarmé's address to Rice,[24] thus enabling her to invite him to contribute to the memorial volume she was preparing. While Mallarmé's reply suggests that he is certainly enthusiastic about her project, it remains somewhat disquieting, first for the awkwardness of its expression and then for the image it conveys of his sense of women's role in such intellectual endeavors, an image that doesn't appear in his letters to Rice's colleague, Sarah Helen Whitman. For a man whose mastery of language and its nuances was considerable, and many of whose letters reveal a beautiful simplicity and freshness, there is something disconcertingly pompous and hackneyed in this reply, written in French:

> YOUR TASK, ONE OF THOSE that bring most honor to a woman in the world, for through all the ages women have assumed the fine role of those who bury the most noble remains, has long conquered for you my sympathy and admiration; and that's not all: now you want a handsome book to perform the task of glorifying your poet of predilection. Piously I, for my humble part, shall carry out your wish by sending you, by whatever date you care to name, a few lines written, Madame, in your honor: I mean in commemoration of the great ceremony of last autumn. (*Corr.*, II: 110)

What had Mallarmé known or read of Sara Sigourney Rice before this letter? Had he really been filled with sympathy and admiration for the elocution teacher who is known, in addition to her memorial volume, for compilations from classical texts of America, England, and the rest of the world? Why raise the question of her gender at all, except to indicate a limit beyond which nice girls don't go? There is also something uncomfortably stilted in the style, which may just possibly reflect the influence of Swinburne's prose and thus correspond to a particular notion of formality that Mallarmé may have felt an English speaker required from someone barely known. However that may be, the poem Mallarmé wrote, the "Tombeau d'Edgar Poe," was, as is well known, not merely a beautiful threnody for Poe as an individual but also a meditation on the relationship of poetry and fame, the artist and the public. Moreover, the extent to which he had thought about what such a volume should contain is clear from the two suggestions he made in his letter of April 4, 1876. He proposed that Rice include an engraving or etching by Manet, and "one of the magnificent prose passages written by our late great poet and my master, Charles Baudelaire, as a preface to his immortal translation of the *Tales*" (*Corr.,* II: 111). Neither suggestion was taken up, since, as Mallarmé was soon to realize, Rice's notion of the memorial volume was quite different from his own.

When he received his copy of the text, Mallarmé wrote to Rice in terms that clearly indicate his surprise at the nature of the collection and, typically, the importance he placed on the physical appearance of a book or a poem: "The *Memorial for Poe* is very good, typographically, and I would like the cover were it not for the gilded portrait and cottage which don't seem to me to belong to decorative art. Had he seen the book, that, I believe, would be Manet's opinion, which you asked me to convey to you" (*Corr.,* II: 141). The stress on the value of decorative art reinforces the image of a Mallarmé immersed in the thinking of the avant-garde, convinced of the need for new publications to reveal the way to the future even if they are conceived as memorial volumes, and responsive first of all to the physical appearance of a work. He was even more forthright about the nature of the enterprise, informing Rice that he had imagined it would consist exclusively of poems, as that would constitute the "offering *par excellence.*" Had he known that there were to be so few poems in a collection given over mainly to prose, he claims, he would have preferred to show his solidarity with the spirit of the undertaking by means of a simple letter.

The shadow cast by Poe, already lengthened by Mallarmé's preoccupation with his translation of "The Raven," was further intensified by his growing acquaintance with two other women, Sarah Helen Whitman and Louise Chandler Moulton. Whitman was engaged to Poe in 1848 and claimed she was the inspiration for several of his poems, including "Annabel Lee." She wrote a spirited defense of his work in her study *E. A. Poe and His Critics,* first published in 1860. The stirring conclusion of this brief tribute makes it easy to understand why Whitman responded so warmly to Mallarmé's letters:

> HAVING RECORDED OUR EARNEST PROTEST against the misapprehension of his critics and the mis-statements of his biographists, we leave the subject for the present, in the belief that a more impartial memoir of the poet will yet be given to the world, and the story of his sad, strange life, when contemplated from a new point of view, be found—like the shield of bronze whose color was so long contested by the knights of fable—to present at least a silver lining.[25]

It was through Poe's biographer, John Ingram, with whom Mallarmé had been corresponding since mid-1875, that he came in contact with Whitman. His first letter to her is radically different in tone and style from that to Rice, as though her presence as the Helen of Poe's poems had long since made him familiar with her. In that first letter, written on the same day as the letter to Rice, he remarks, "As I have been fascinated since my childhood with the works of Poe, your name has long been linked with his in my earliest and most intimate sympathies" (*Corr.,* II: 112). It is in this letter, too, that he states his desire to translate those works of Poe that "our great Baudelaire" left untranslated—that is, "the poems and many of the critical pieces" (*Corr.,* II: 112).

The ease with which Mallarmé writes to Whitman bears out his affirmation that she, at least in the form in which Poe has immortalized her in his verse, has become part of his mental horizons, intimately connected with his desire to carry on from Baudelaire the task of making known both in France and more widely the man whom he argues may have been "the intellectual genius of our century" (*Corr.,* II: 131). Although Mallarmé refers to his hopes of publishing the complete translation of Poe's poems in the near future, the volume was not to appear until 1888, by which time his enthusiasm may well have waned somewhat.[26] Certainly in the letters to Whitman he was full of an almost missionary zeal on Poe's behalf, addressing the poet's former fiancée as if she were the high priestess of his cult: "However noble and touching a guardian of his memory you are, you who today represent for all those who loved him one of the most magnificent beings ever to have honored this earth, one of the monarchs of Thought and of Human Love, you ought truly to live much longer still, before you are seen, you and he, only in the ideal glory of a double immortality avenging evil destiny" (*Corr.,* II; 136). Poe fuses with Baudelaire here to form the archetypal image of the *poète maudit,* and Sarah Helen Whitman comes to represent the mediator between poet and reader, a position to which Mallarmé as translator and critic also implicitly aspires. It is hardly surprising that Whitman reported to Ingram that she had received "an exquisitely beautiful letter from Mallarmé, who is in truth a 'prose poet' in his letters."[27]

The role of critic, of enthusiastic and impassioned guide who leads the reader through the poet's thought, is evoked in the letter Mallarmé wrote to Whitman in January 1877. He had by then received her volume, *Poe and His Critics,* which he described as "pages which, however great the interest long since inspired by their title and your name, still surprise through an unexpected charm and a penetrating beauty, far from bringing the disappointment we sometimes get from works from which we've expected a great deal before knowing them" (*Corr.,* II: 144–45). Whitman's beautifully written study, in addition to a sturdy defense of the poet against what Mallarmé, in his sonnet, calls the "noirs vols du Blasphème" (the black flights of Blasphemy) (*OC,* 70), contains an exploration of the deep melancholy that pervades Poe's work. She sees this melancholy as being prompted partly by the skepticism of the age and partly by a more deeply rooted personal fear of death: "Nothing so solitary, nothing so hopeless, nothing so desolate, as his spirit in its darker moods, has been instanced in the literary history of the nineteenth century."[28] That profound depression, pinpointed so sharply here by Whitman, may well have touched a particular and personal chord in Mallarmé.

Critics have argued at length about Poe's impact on the thinking of both Baudelaire and Mallarmé and the reasons underlying the cult that both professed for him. Whatever the motivation, whatever the extent to which Poe became for Mallarmé the archetype of the scorned genius, it is clear that in these years when he was searching for a personal voice in the cultural hubbub of Third Republic Paris, the act of translating, as well as that of encapsulating the quintessential poet in his memorial poem for Poe, played a crucial role. He must, therefore, have been particularly touched by Whitman's letter of February 6, 1877, in which she says of his translation of "The Raven," "Since I wrote you, the 'Corbeau' has become my fireside companion—a presence as real for me as any dream while you are dreaming it." She concludes by affirming, "Your translation is wonderfully true." This praise must have meant even more to him in that she added a (fully justifiable) query about his translation of the raven's "stock and store" as "son fond et son bagage." That sensitive remark moves her eulogium out of the domain of mere politeness in the same way that many of Mallarmé's letters to fellow poets home in on a flaw or a moment of awkwardness. And yet, for all their skill, Mallarmé's translations of Poe's poems justify Baudelaire's decision not to translate them, not to submit to the ensuing loss of what he terms the "voluptés [. . .] du rythme et de la rhyme" (the intense pleasures of rhythm and rhyme).[29] Nevertheless, the cluster of correspondences, in both senses of the word, that gather around the memory of Poe reveal the vital role that he, or at least that his image transformed by fate, time, and Baudelaire, played in Mallarmé's intellectual life in his first decade back in Paris.

One area in which that search for a voice was sharpened and refined in his letters to Whitman was that of his concept of a new form of theater. His letter of 28 May, 1877, responds to her invitation to tell her more about his plans for a play, and in doing so reveals an aspect of his creative endeavors that is not initially revealed to anyone reading Mallarmé's *Poésies* in isolation. It is in this letter that he makes clear the vast ambitions he has, in ways that illuminate above all *Igitur* and "L'Après-midi d'un faune":

THE GREAT ATTEMPT TO CREATE an entirely new form of theater, to which I'm devoting myself, will take me several years before I can show any external result. Very ambitious, it's not just one genre I'm changing, but all those that in my view are theatrical: magic drama, popular and lyric drama. And it's only when the work has been completed for all three that I will make them all public, more or less simultaneously. Like Nero in Rome, I shall set fire to three corners of Paris. (*Corr.,* II: 151)

The importance of the interest he reveals in popular theater both here and in such prose poems as "Le Spectacle interrompu" (The interrupted spectacle) should not be overlooked. As Evlyn Gould and Mary Shaw have both revealed,[30] Mallarmé's fascination with popular festivals, poster art, and street or lowbrow spectacle is far removed from the ivory-tower image we have all too often been given of him.

In this letter to Whitman, Mallarmé appears to be talking above all to himself, working through the difficulties that lie ahead of him, the "mountains to move" (*Corr.,* II: 155), before returning to his awareness of her presence to ask if she can help him find work on an American periodical to which he could contribute anonymously (obviously wanting to avoid the anger of his employers in the department of education). After she died in December 1878, Mallarmé received through her executrix a portrait that, so he remarks in his thank-you letter, recalled Poe's lines from "To Helen": "How daring an ambition! yet how deep / How fathomless a capacity for love" (*Corr.,* II: 215).

While Sarah Helen Whitman was thus one of the most important mediators Mallarmé found between himself and Poe, she was not the only one. The second such mediator was an American writer whose works included children's tales,[31] novels, poems and, in 1894, the first biography of Mallarmé's friend O'Shaugnessy. Indeed, it was through this mutual friend that Mallarmé met Louise Chandler Moulton (*Corr.,* II: 134). Moulton, who translated Mallarmé's tribute to Poe into English and who was to write an obituary for Sarah Helen Whitman, was living in Paris in 1876. Her comments on their meeting in her book *Lazy Tours in Spain and Elsewhere* are both illuminating in their information about Mallarmé's assessment of his Impressionist friends[32] and amusing in their reflections on his English. Remarking on how strange it was that English was so rarely spoken by the French, in comparison with educated Russians, Germans, Swedes, and Norwegians, she states that an English poet (Payne) gave her introductions to "a large group of the French poets and novelists of the day" but warned her that only one spoke English: "Monsieur M., you will find, speaks very well. In fact, he is professor of English in a French college."[33] While later she refers specifically to Mallarmé, using his full name, it seems more than likely that Monsieur M. is also Mallarmé:

> MONSIEUR M. WAS A GREAT COMFORT and pleasure to me that winter, and his English was such, at least, as I could readily understand; but he always made three syllables of "themselves" [. . .] and he used to say "lov-ed" and "wish-ed." He talked of things as "unuseful" instead of "useless," and he usually put his objects before his verbs instead of after them. And *he* spoke better English than I have heard from any other Frenchman above the rank of a valet or a courier.[34]

She did, however, send him a copy of these memoirs (see *Corr.,* IV: 425n3), so if Monsieur M. is indeed Mallarmé, we can assume that their relationship was strong enough to withstand some teasing.

In fact, Mallarmé's friendship with Moulton drew on more than their shared interest in Poe. She, too, was a writer, and in January 1878 Mallarmé sent her an enthusiastic thank-you letter for the volume of *Poems* she had given him, referring to it as an "admirable collection of lyric poems" (*Corr.,* IV: 425). He even professed such admiration for the sonnets included in the volume that he promised to translate them one day, although it was a promise he never carried out.

Mallarmé's interest in Poe is not just a product of his veneration for Baudelaire. As Marshall Olds points out, the "line of internationalism runs through much of the disparate activity undertaken by Mallarmé during the 1870s."[35] In November 1873 Mallarmé wrote to the Félibrige poet Frédéric Mistral, whom he had come to know during his years in the provinces, proposing something that he mistakenly thought would appeal to his fellow poet—the foundation of an international society of poets. If such a thing is necessary, he argues, in terms that prepare the memorial poem for Poe, it's because "a certain number of us love a thing that is abhorred, and so it's good that we should know how many we are, that's all, and get to know one another, that the members read each other and that those who travel should see one another" (*CC,* 543). Mistral's response was unenthusiastic—indeed, it verged on the choleric: "The Provençal poets," he snorted, "are the natural friends of poets of all countries and they've proved it for over twenty years, with regard to the poets of Paris, England, Spain and Germany, indeed all those poets who've been willing to come to Avignon and shake hands with us. For that to happen there's no need of written or sworn obligations: sympathy is the best of constitutions" (*VM,* 352). Nevertheless, a French branch of the society did indeed come into existence, as the weekly paper *La Semaine parisienne* reveals: "*The International Society of Poets* (French branch) held its second general meeting last Saturday evening in M. Carjat's studio" (*Corr.,* II: 41). Mallarmé's name appears among those voted onto the committee. Indeed, as Olds points out, the seeds of this movement were already sown in Mallarmé's mind at the time of the memorial volume to Gautier, which, he argues in his letter to Mistral, could have been made more international. In much of his subsequent behavior can be seen this desire to break down the barriers between writers. His friendship with the Belgian Symbolists, the lectures he gave in Oxford and Cambridge, and his moral support of writers from many different countries all point to an extension of this conviction.

It is above all, perhaps, that desire to break down linguistic barriers and recognize poetry in all languages that underpins Mallarmé's letters to Swinburne. The English poet is closely associated with yet another of Mallarmé's ventures in the 1870s: the founding of the periodical *La République des lettres,* to be edited by Catulle Mendès. This venture was made possible, at least on one level, by an encounter with Alphonse Derenne, described by one of the associate editors of *La République des lettres,* Henri Roujon, as "a temperamentally nostalgic bookseller, who published books on obstetrics but preferred spending his time in cafés."[36]

Writing to Swinburne at the end of December 1875, Mallarmé makes that international connection quite clear: "We, by that I mean the contemporary poets and writers belonging to a group who admire you as one of our Masters, are founding a review, the *République des lettres:* the chief editor is M. Catulle Mendès. Such are the bonds of friendship or enthusiasm that today unite the poets of Paris and of England, that those of us over here immediately decided to ask for the kind collaboration of someone over there: and before anyone else we of course dreamed of possessing your name" (*Corr.,* II: 90). Indeed, as he goes on to confess, the first number of the review, which by that stage was already in print, contained Augusta Holmès's translation of Swinburne's poem "The Pilgrims."

The choice of Swinburne should come as no surprise, for, as Ruth Temple points out in *The Critic's Alchemy,* her study of the introduction of French Symbolism into England, Swinburne had already established a name for himself as an enthusiastic supporter of such poets as Gautier and Baudelaire. He was, moreover, in correspondence with such French writers as Auguste Vacquerie, the brother of Hugo's son-in-law and a fervent Hugolian, and Leconte de Lisle, to whom he sent a copy of his poem *Erectheus* when it was published in early 1876. His threnodies, "Memorial Verses on the Death of Théophile Gautier" and "Ave atque Vale," the latter written for Baudelaire, reveal the openness of mind with which he approached a poetic school that most of his compatriots at that time derided. That openness is also evident in his letters to Mallarmé, all of which, as Temple argues, "are remarkable not only for the excellence of his French prose but for his courteous deference to a younger poet who was, for almost ten years to come, to remain practically unknown." [37]

Swinburne had already written to Mallarmé earlier in the year, responding warmly to the gift of "Le Corbeau," the joint production of Mallarmé as translator and Manet as illustrator of Poe's work. His letter of July 7, 1875, must have delighted Mallarmé for its enthusiastic judgment that in "those wonderful pages" the leading American poet "twice finds himself so perfectly translated, thanks to the collaboration of two great artists." [38] Swinburne was not just flattering his correspondent in writing this judgment, as he repeats, in a letter to his future biographer, Edmond Gosse, written a few weeks later, his belief that the translation is "very exquisite." [39] Apart from his poems on Gautier and Baudelaire, Swinburne had two further claims to Mallarmé's interest. He had visited Manet in the company of his friends James McNeill Whistler and Henri Fantin-Latour some twelve years earlier and recognized the painter's genius; he also shared the scorn that Poe enthusiasts felt for "that infamous Griswold," the critic whom Baudelaire had termed the "vampire-pedagogue" and whose "lies and calumnies" had now been laid low by John Ingram. [40]

In his reply to Mallarmé's invitation to participate in the *République des lettres,* Swinburne reveals the extent to which he delighted in experimenting with the fixed-form verse popular in the Renaissance and re-introduced into French prosody by such writers as Hugo and Banville. In sending Mallarmé his *sizaine,* a poem of six-line stanzas, he also revealed his desire to avoid any error of French, having in the past been accused by a French critic of writing verse that seemed the "efforts of a barbaric giant"[41]—a judgment that might indeed give anyone pause. Mallarmé took him at his word, thanking him for his "cordial contribution," expressing admiration for the poet's boldness in choosing a rhythm (the ten-syllable line later so triumphantly used by Valéry in "Le Cimetière marin") that "no one anywhere approaches without trembling" (*Corr.,* II: 98), and raising a question about his line "Pour recueillir rien qu'un souffle d'amour" (to gather nothing but a breath of love), which for reasons of euphony he advised him to change to "Pour y cueillir rien qu'un souffle d'amour." He raised a further query in regard to the fifth verse of Swinburne's poem, in which the English writer, momentarily confusing Italian *orma* (trace or track) and French *orme* (elm tree), had posed his readers an unintentional enigma that doesn't bode well for internationalism.

In addition to their mutual interest in Poe, Mallarmé and Swinburne each reveal a devotion to earlier poets whose works they strove to make better known. In Swinburne's case, this was especially true of William Blake, whom he felt would be of interest to the French poets. He seized on the existence of the *République des lettres* to further this aim. In his letter to Mallarmé of February 1876, he wrote,

I'VE BEGUN A LITTLE STUDY that I'm planning to offer to the *République des lettres,* on the great painter-poet William Blake, whom I believe to be all but unknown in France. Seven years ago, I published a fairly long essay on him, and I think I could give a shortened version of his life, with some extracts from his poems that would perhaps not be without interest for the French poets. But since we've lost Baudelaire, you are the only one who would be worthy of undertaking this glorious task, which I hardly dare assume myself, but of which I hope to send you in the near future a few samples.[42]

Writing to his colleague Theodore Watts a few days later, Swinburne clarified his plan by explaining that the Blake study would "include versions (in prose of course) of some of his lyrics and perhaps other fragmentary excerpts."[43] Mallarmé, as his reply reveals, had already read Swinburne's *William Blake: A Critical Essay,* which he describes as "one of the best aesthetical readings made by a poet" (*Corr.,* II: 105) and which some Swinburne critics regard as his best longer prose work.

While they shared other interests—the use of figures from Greco-Roman mythology adapted to a contemporary purpose, for instance, in both "L'Après-midi d'un faune" and "A Nympholept" (although the latter dates from 1894)—and while Mallarmé told Swinburne that each line in his poem "The Last Oracle" was "interminably beautiful" (*Corr.,* II: 115), a modern reader is far more likely to be struck by their differences. Indeed, I would argue that between the English poet and his French contemporary lies all the dissimilarity in perspective and practice that separates the pre-

Raphaelites from the Symbolists. The pounding rhythms and relentless alliterations, the archaic language, and the prevalence of description over evocation make a poem such as "The Last Oracle" a work far removed from "L'Après-midi d'un faune"; still, however, the English press decried "The Last Oracle" with the same fervor as the French press derided Mallarmé's eclogue. Characteristic of both poets is the desire to cross those differences, to recognize and respect the genius of the other, and to encourage what may not have been understood. Swinburne certainly seems to have attempted to respond favorably to the gift of "L'Après-midi," even if what he stressed above all was the physical beauty of the volume.[44] One senses between the two writers not so much friendship as respect: If they ceased to be regular correspondents after 1876, the reasons are to be found less in any intellectual and poetic differences than in changes in interest for both of them. What their exchange reveals, at least where Mallarmé is concerned, is an ongoing openness of spirit and a much more short-lived desire to forge links with English writers.

As the years went by, it became increasingly clear that for all his internationalism of outlook, Mallarmé's real sympathies were less with poets of other countries than with artists working in different media. England became less important to him as his attention was captured more and more strongly by Paris's theaters, by the ballet, and by Impressionist art. Increasingly the 1880s would see him turning his energies to an exploration of these other arts.

Figure 1. Portrait of Stéphane Mallarmé by Edouard Manet. Courtesy Musée d'Orsay. Photo © RMN.

Figure 2. Portrait Paul Verlaine by Louis Anquetin, from the frontispiece to Verlaine's Confessions, 1895. Courtesy the Lilly Library, Indiana University, Bloomington.

Figure 3. Drawing of Villiers de l'Isle-Adam by Paterne Berrichon. Courtesy © Roger-Viollet.

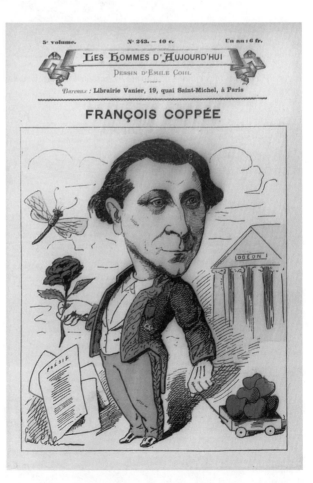

Figure 4. Caricature of François Coppée from Les Hommes d'aujourd'hui. Courtesy the Lilly Library, Indiana University, Bloomington.

Figure 5. Illustration from Le Corbeau, *1875. Courtesy the Lilly Library, Indiana University, Bloomington.*

Figure 6. Cover of La Plume *for 1893. Mallarmé frequently contributed to this periodical. Courtesy the Lilly Library, Indiana University, Bloomington.*

Figure 7. *Drawing of Stuart Merrill from the* frontispiece *to* Les Fastes, *1891. Courtesy the Lilly Library, Indiana University, Bloomington.*

Figure 8. *Caricature of the publisher Léon Vanier from* Les Hommes d'aujourd'hui. *Courtesy the Lilly Library, Indiana University, Bloomington.*

Figure 9. *Drawing of Georges Rodenbach from the frontispiece to* Du silence, *1888. Courtesy the Lilly Library, Indiana University, Bloomington.*

Figure 10. Paul Nadar photograph of Stéphane Mallarmé toward the end of his life. Courtesy © Roger-Viollet.

Figure 11. Drawing of Henri Cazalis. Courtesy © Roger-Viollet.

Figure 12. Drawing of Henri de Régnier from
the frontispiece to Les Lendemains, 1886.
Courtesy the Lilly Library, Indiana University,
Bloomington.

Figure 13. Painting of Méry
Laurent by Edouard Manet.
Courtesy Musée des Beaux-
Arts, Nancy. Photo © RMN.

Figure 14. Photograph of Geneviève Mallarmé. Courtesy Mme Stanislas.

Figure 15. Fan signed by Stéphane Mallarmé, together with the writers Leconte de Lisle, Judith Gautier, Pierre Loti, Juliette Adam, and Jean Aicard; the painters Raphaël Collin, Paul Baudoüin, Paul Dubois, A. Mercié, Gustave Courtois, Paul Laurens, Luc Olivier Merson, and Louis-Maurice Boutet de Monvel; the actors Mounet-Sully and Paul Mounet; and the musician Richard Hammer. Photograph by Paul B. Riley. Private collection.

Figure 16. Saxony clock. Courtesy Musée Mallarmé.

Father and Daughter

O rêveuse
—Œuvres complètes, 58

In one of his more unusual photographs, Edgar Degas depicts Stéphane Mallarmé and Pierre-Auguste Renoir against a mirror in which are reflected not merely the photographer himself, partially obliterated by the dazzle of the flash, but also the poet's wife and daughter, sitting in the same place in which they themselves feature in another of his photos. Stiff and formal in their Sunday best, they gaze mutely at the photograph's two protagonists. Barely visible in the mirror, her presence and her gaze depending on the personality of her husband, Marie Gerhard remains a shadowy figure, yet to understand Mallarmé's vital relationship with his daughter, we need to understand something about his relationship with his wife. Odd fragments from her long letters enter the Mallarmé correspondence here and there, and we hear echoes of her voice in the young Mallarmé's letters in the days before they married, but she is largely hidden from our sight, effaced from the public record. From Mallarmé's desperate sense of isolation and loneliness in those years in the provinces that were also the first years of their marriage, we can deduce that his wife was not an intellectual companion to him. The contrasting images of the passionate faun and the ice-cold Hérodiade that above all dominate and symbolize the poetic production of those years may well be less the result of some degree of bipolar affective disorder than a complex and distorted reflection of Mallarmé's sexual personality and, by extension, a mirror that also allows a glimpse of his wife's personality.

We can guess from his absence during the last stages of her pregnancy with Anatole in July of 1871, and perhaps also from the fact that the couple had only two children, that the marriage had lost much of its charm by the end of the decade. Anatole's conception may in itself indicate a desire to try once more to make the marriage work, but if it was that, Mallarmé's absence during the child's birth indicates that the attempt was connected more with Marie's wishes than with Stéphane's. Of course it can be argued that men at that time did not interest themselves in the late stages of pregnancy, in the act of giving birth, or in the care of the very young infant, who was in many cases, and certainly in the Mallarmé household, farmed out to a wet nurse (see *Corr.,* IV: 364). But the husband's absence from the scene during the final stages of his wife's pregnancy was far from being widespread by this late date. Other models are set down for us in very different modes by, among others, Jules Michelet's *La Femme* and Gustave Droz's *Monsieur, Madame, et bébé,* indicating that educated and intelligent men were beginning to see their role as father in a different light from that of their parents. Marie Mallarmé herself wrote to her husband, who had gone to Paris, that she hoped he could be present for the child's birth, although she added that, financially speaking, she believed it would be better for him to stay in Paris so as not to lose a moment (see *Corr.,* IV: 360). It's not hard to read between these lines a plea for him to return, couched in terms of sympathy for his own needs. But in this case Mallarmé clearly could not or would not read between the lines.

What was it that was so important to Mallarmé that he ignored his wife's plea and left her to her own devices for the weeks leading up to Anatole's birth? And what does his absence tell us about him as individual and as head of a family? Part of the answer lies in his disgust with teaching as a career. While Marie was in the final stages of pregnancy, Mallarmé was in Paris, staying with Catulle Mendès and attempting to locate part-time employment in museums, libraries, or printing presses. After his son's birth he had time only for a brief visit with his family before dashing off to London, where he planned to write pieces for several newspapers on the Great Exhibition there. Yet it is indicative of Mallarmé's financial naiveté and symptomatic of his lack of insight into the world of journalism that he made the trip so late that most of the newspapers no longer wanted articles on an event that had ceased to be topical. He was soon to realize that he would have to stay with teaching. Although the reasons for his absence and especially for his desire to abandon a hated career are clear enough, the timing of his search for an alternative career remains problematic. As it happened, his request for a teaching position in Paris rather than the provinces was granted, and the family was able to move to the capital that year.

Just as he didn't share his son's birth, so, when he knew that Anatole was dying, Mallarmé bore that knowledge alone, allowing his wife to continue in her state of denial rather than treating her as an equal by revealing the facts to her. Courteous in all his public conduct, he behaved toward his wife in the later years of their marriage, according to observers, with gentle charm. But charm and courtesy are not the same as sharing, and they can indicate condescension rather than any notion of equality. There seems little reasonable doubt that the marriage, made in haste and against Mallarmé's better judgment, offered little in the way of intellectual or emotional companionship. After Anatole's death, a very close bond formed between Geneviève and her mother. Indeed, it is only to her daughter and not to her husband that Mme Mallarmé wrote any letters at all after her son's death. When Mallarmé was away from them he wrote to them collectively. The way in which his letters address both his wife and his daughter as his "petits enfants" (*Corr.,* III: 241 and passim) suggests affection but not equality, a relationship that was warm but limited, although we cannot tell from this distance which of the two imposed the limits. Lloyd Austin raises the question concerning this mode of address, but leaves it unanswered (see *Corr.,* IV: 476).

Geneviève's letters to her father, and Mallarmé's to her when she was away from home, depict Mme Mallarmé as someone frequently ill and of increasingly feeble mind. In 1881 Mallarmé was to exclaim to Jean Marras, "Why is it that my wife's health, which in the past was so robust, has now reached the point where the slightest disruption to her monotonous existence puts the poor creature beside herself for several days!" (*Corr.,* V: 253). The answer seems clear enough, yet in his biography of Mallarmé, Gordon Millan, following in the misogynistic legacy of Mondor, relegates her suffering, apparently unquestioningly, to a lower order of magnitude than that of her husband: "The impact of Anatole's death upon Mallarmé and his wife was profound and long-lasting. From now on, Marie Mallarmé became almost continually unwell, suffering from stomach cramps either real or imagined and from nervous dyspepsia. She never fully recovered. As for Mallarmé himself, he was quite simply devastated."[1] I would argue that there is little doubt that Marie's stomach cramps relive a difficult pregnancy, one that may well have been initiated in a vain attempt to revive a marriage in difficulties, and that she, too, and with less possibility than her husband to direct herself either socially or intellectually outside her own sufferings, was "quite simply devastated."

Realizing the intensity with which both responded to this tragedy is essential to our understanding of Mallarmé's behavior in the last twenty years of his life. Jean-Paul Sartre certainly presents an uncompromisingly bleak picture of the relationship and its results when he depicts Mme Mallarmé in the following terms:

> LATER ON, DECEIVED, UNWELL, A bit of a whinger, a very slightly abusive wife, tyrannizing her daughter as a means of getting her own back, she can sometimes be seen at concerts. A very subtle and very criminal ruse effected the non-violent assassination of this woman. Without ever giving her reason to complain, her very gentle and very charming husband stripped her of her flesh and spirit. All that remained was a shadow. But that's what the poet needed: a phantom wife, devoured by abstraction and regrets, and inspiring in him only abstract feelings.[2]

The acid nature of this attack may have more to do with Sartre's own feelings of guilt or his rejection of the poet's apparently apolitical stance than with any real truth about the Mallarmé marriage, but it does offer a vision that we cannot simply refuse to confront. There is a degree to which charm, a condescending kind of charm that most women, even now, have experienced often enough in their lives to recognize instantly, can gag women's wit, brush aside female ability, deny any suggestion of sexual equality.

With his marriage increasingly less important to his emotional life, Mallarmé turned to his daughter to fill part of the void. Geneviève was remarkably close to both her parents, no doubt torn between them in ways that increased her dependence on them. While he may not consciously have colluded with his wife in condemning his daughter to a long spinsterhood, Mallarmé did little to help her step out of his shadow. Undoubtedly she loved him, and equally undoubtedly she saw herself as essential to him, writing letters to his dictation, copying his poems for him, acting as a secretary during his absences. Their relationship was vitally important to the last two decades of his life, yet it has often been occluded, overshadowed by the teasing ambiguity of his relationship with Méry Laurent.

Mallarmé's German biographer Kurt Wais refers to Geneviève as "a true poet's daughter, gentle, as Whistler painted her, gray and pink and in an arm chair."[3] Yet whereas this picture presents her as the physical and silent manifestation of the true daughter of a poet, she also fulfilled other, more cerebral aspects of that function, and she frequently left the armchair to lead an active physical and cultural life. While Marie Gerhard moves out of the center stage with the return to Paris, Geneviève comes to play an increasingly important role in her father's intellectual and affective life. The letters they exchanged when one or the other of them was away from home, together with the recollections of various Mardistes and of Geneviève herself, reveal the poet in a different, more complex, and richer light. Over the years she often accompanied him in place of her mother to dinners and receptions. That they were very close is beyond dispute. That this relationship inhibited her development as an adult woman (her first vacation away from her parents took place when she was twenty-seven, and despite numerous suitors she did not marry until after her father's death) is also a fact to be kept in mind in reading the remarkable exchange of letters between the two and in seeing reflections of Geneviève not just in Degas's mirror or Whistler's canvas but also in her own and her father's letters. It should of course be added that in her recollections of her father she depicted him not as someone who had in any way circumscribed her existence but as "the older comrade, gay and fraternal—and so kind."[4]

In a brief article written for Camille Mauclair and published in La *Nouvelle Revue française* in November 1926, Geneviève presents her father in the following terms:

AS FAR BACK AS THE EYES of my childhood can see, the dear figure remains unchanged in my memories: the one who always does what should be done. In all life's circumstances, be they serious or happy, he had the right gesture, good, upright, sure or charming. And I assure you, C—, that it's not just my filial admiration speaking here: I say it because it's true. Goodness, tenderness, these words so often used in their humdrum or vague sense seem to me to have been created for him. And another word: serenity. A serenity obtained by the clarity of his soul.[5]

While the deep affection these words convey pervades her letters to him, the rather stilted phraseology and the reverence, fortunately, do not. Their correspondence, more than that of Mallarmé and any other correspondent, suggests something of the nature of their conversation—witty, irreverent, and sparkling.

From her early infancy, Geneviève (frequently referred to by the pet name Vève) appears in her father's letters to others as a rhetorical device for strengthening friendships and for making invitations and requests warmer and more natural than they might otherwise be. Such phrases as "Kisses from children to children" (*Corr.,* II: 157), "I wanted to leave you this note, which comes equally from my little girl and her mother" (*Corr.,* II: 36), and "Those around me, wife and children, say hello to you" (*Corr.,* II: 42) are scattered through his letters; these terms of affection also help build his consciously created image as a family man. We find him somewhat boastfully professing concern that Geneviève reads too many novels (*Corr.,* II: 244), voting for the bellicose politician General Boulanger because his unenfranchised daughter is a Boulangiste (*Corr.,* III: 126–27, 291), and helping her build up her collection of autographs of writers and artists (*Corr.,* III: 215). And when he goes to Royat, a spa town in the Puy-du-Dôme, to visit Méry Laurent, his letter, while addressed to "Mesdames Mallarmé," is clearly written for the young woman whom he asks to act as his secretary. Describing their drives through the countryside near Royat, for instance, he evokes the "green, cool heights, the horizon sometimes masked by mountains and sometimes wildly free. Here the wheat is tiny and they turn it into toy stooks. The peasant women wear on their heads frilly chamber pots" (*Corr.,* III: 243).

It was not until 1891, when she was twenty-seven, that Geneviève Mallarmé took her first vacation away from her parents, traveling to the seaside to stay with family friends, the Ponsots. Mallarmé's first letter to her at this time begins, revealingly enough, with the sentence "So you're fleeing from us, at this very hour" (*Corr.,* IV: 260). Their almost daily exchange of letters shows that Geneviève possessed excellent epistolary skills, producing long, chatty, affectionate letters that transform the banality of her everyday experiences into wit or drama. Mallarmé's delight in these letters is clear in his replies and suggests a father-daughter bond of warmth and mutual respect. Geneviève's enthusiastic depiction of the sun setting into the sea, for instance—"I don't think I've ever dreamed anything as lovely as the sea yesterday evening, around 8 o'clock, at sunset" (*Corr.,* IV: 262)—brought this response: "Little cat, your letter is awaited as eagerly as people await their daily newspaper, and becomes the subject of our conversation for the rest of the day" (*Corr.,* IV: 263).

Sharing her father's friendships and tastes in terms of literature and art, Geneviève portrays the coast in Impressionist terms, especially in telling her father that

Whistler, who had been expected to stay in the vicinity, had not yet appeared: "Not so much as the echo of Whistler's laugh. The Stevens, with whom he'll be staying, isn't that right?, have only been there for a few days, at most. What admirable work he'll do! The other evening I thought of him, in the fog with the sea like a lake and in the half-light all the sails of the little fishing craft, fifty of them, motionless, as if frozen to the spot, it really was an astonishing sight, and exactly in Whistler's manner" (*Corr.*, IV: 275). A few days later she lamented Whistler's absence again, extolling the beauty of the moon that seemed as much in the sea as in the sky, creating an effect that Whistler alone could reproduce. Later vacations by the sea inspire similarly descriptive letters, some of which in turn inspired her father to write the witty little couplets and quatrains now included in the collection of his occasional verse. When she related, for example, that Willy Ponsot had given up drinking and smoking but had replaced these sins with that of chewing tobacco, Mallarmé wrote, "Willy's replaced his propensities Bacchic / With the delights of a cud tobaccic" (*OC*, 166). Similarly, a passage about the Hève lighthouse, to which she refers as the twin diamond eyes, provoked the following couplet: "I see my daughter Vève / And the cape of the Hève" (*OC*, 175). Mallarmé as lighthouse, looking at both the cape and his daughter, is a revealing image, implicitly phallic and explicitly custodial of the "Eve" the rhyme reveals.

Geneviève's letters indicate a lively interest in the written word as well as in art. In July 1892, for instance, she speaks with admiration of Auguste Rodin's letter to her father, in which the sculptor, who had just received the Légion d'Honneur, wrote with charming modesty, "We are both being spoken of by the public voice, and it's always a pleasure for me when your name catches my eye in the newspaper or a periodical; where, dear poet, you reign as a demigod, and I rise in my own esteem when I think I'm your friend and when I can say boastfully that I am indeed your friend" (*Corr.*, V: 98). In the same letter she tells her parents that she'll read "attentively" the speech Emile Zola delivered at the novelist Léon Cladel's funeral. Her cousin Paul Margueritte, moreover, has left a moving record of her skill as an actress in the plays performed at Valvins, in which she took on such roles as Nérine in Banville's play of that name, Guillemette in the medieval farce *Maître Pierre Pathelin*, and Colombine in the mime *Pierrot l'héritier*.

We also find her sharing her father's interest in theatrical performances, judging one of Jules Richepin's plays, for instance, as "interesting, lots of things to look at and some pretty lines" (*DSM*, 2: 266), and apparently more enthusiastic about Richard Wagner than her father was, attending a performance of *Die Meistersinger*, for instance (see *DSM*, 2: 230). While her father was in Oxford, delivering his lecture on music and literature, Geneviève Mallarmé attended a performance of Villiers de l'Isle-Adam's *Axël*, which she described for her father in terms that illuminate more sharply the degree to which they shared aesthetic tastes and judgments:

Y GOODNESS! HOW BEAUTIFUL IT WAS. Too beautiful, because when you leave the theater you're irritated at seeing real streets again and at having to take the tram again. Something like that should go on forever. [. . .] The staging was entirely satisfactory, the scenery for every act was perfectly chosen, and so were the costumes. Axël was made up to look like poor Villiers, which I found deeply moving. He acted very well, even if he was a little too human for my taste. I don't know if you'll understand this, I'm not expressing it well, but it may be, as you said, impossible. Mlle Camée seemed to me to have the same defect. But I'm only too aware that it's not their fault, and they did the best they could. (*DSM*, 3: 237–38)

Geneviève's ability to understand a play that many rejected as boring or unintelligible (as her letter reveals) must have touched her father, as it was clearly meant to do.

Mallarmé in turn teased his daughter if she mixed her metaphors, in ways that indicate a shared delight in language and its intelligent manipulation, even in letter writing. Thus in a letter from Honfleur in which she claims to have regained all her lost strength, she writes, "The first few days I was completely dazed and really tired but now I'm made of iron, no longer anything like the fly I used to be" (*Corr.*, IV: 275). Because her letter of the previous day had claimed, "I'm just lazy when it comes to working or moving about, so that everyone calls me: 'Slug,'" her father teased her for the changed metaphor by pointing out, "If you're of iron, you can't be a slug" (*Corr.*, IV: 275). She seems to have shared his pleasure in the physical appearance of a book, as her response to his edition of *Vathek*, sent to her while she was in Honfleur, indicates: "What a charming book, father, and what a pretty edition it is, what a delight for the eyes. I love the type face, and I'm licking my lips at the thought of the wonderful day I'll spend reading it" (*Corr.*, IV: 127). I suspect that Geneviève enjoyed art exhibitions more for her father's commentaries on the works of art than for the art itself, as in one letter she recounts receiving tickets for a *vernissage* but declining them because Mallarmé can't accompany her. In another letter her account of Odilon Redon's exhibition is entirely social:

ESTERDAY AFTERNOON WE PLAYED THE PARISIANS and went to see the opening of Redon's exhibition at Vollard's. There were pastels as well as some monsters from his Temptation [of Saint Anthony]. The three Redons were there, and Bougrelas, furnished with a pile of labels he'd nicked from goodness knows where, was sticking them on all the paintings, with the message: "Sold." Saint Redon and his wife very friendly; they're relying on the sale to get them through the summer and won't go to Samois until June. I also saw Mlle Duret, the good Vuillard, everyone spoke nicely about you, father, Duret seizing his hair in his effort to understand why you'd fled. I forget to mention Gallimard, whose glowing youth you haven't stressed enough, it was beyond belief (*DSM*, 2: 252).

And she certainly wasn't overawed by the talented young men who paid tribute to her father. Of Edvard Munch's portrait of Mallarmé, for instance, she wryly comments, "It's pretty enough, but it's like one of those heads of Christ imprinted on a saint's handkerchief and under which you find written: 'if you look at for a long time, you'll see the eyes close'" (*Corr.*, IX: 198).

While the article Geneviève wrote for Mauclair indicates that she enjoyed the Mardis, she could be irreverent and gently mocking of the Mardistes, as in her letter of November 12, 1896, when she tells her father about an evening party she attended: "I met, guess who, I was expecting to see them, the new couple of Paul and Victor Margueritte, both dressed in the same way, from hat to shoes, in a severe black. They were surrounded by old men, bald and decorated, and were doing their utmost to be gracious. They really made laugh! Then Mauclair, very kind. He spoke to me of Mother in a friendly way, much more friendly in fact than my complicated cousins" (*DSM*, 2: 137). A little later we find her recounting for her father's delectation the gossip about an adulterous relationship between the painter Odilon Redon and a Samois neighbor: "We were really amused, mother and I, to learn that the story of Saint Redon's temptation by Blanche [the wife of Mallarmé's cousin Paul Margueritte] is true, in all its details. That wretched man, ever since they arrived in Samois six years ago, has been passionately attached to my cousin, to the point of confessing everything to his wife who would have torn out both parties' eyes" (*DSM*, 2: 147). There may be a coded warning here to Mallarmé himself, whose adulterous relationship with Méry Laurent seems to have inspired in Geneviève a jealousy that she kept carefully under control—no scratching out of eyes for the daughter of Stéphane Mallarmé—but that she nevertheless revealed from time to time.

The relationship between father and daughter created a world from which some of their less close friends must have felt excluded. Leconte de Lisle, for example, clearly let Mallarmé pull his leg on occasion, as we can see in an entry in Edmond de Goncourt's diary, in which he notes, "Talking of Mallarmé, Leconte de Lisle affirmed that the symbolist had some mad quirks, and that he'd met him once, carrying a letter in his hand, written by his daughter and addressed to Prince Azure, and that he was taking it, in all seriousness, to be mailed."[6]

In his letters to his daughter, especially those written during his visit to Oxford and Cambridge in 1894, or when he was at Valvins and his two "ladies" were in Paris, Mallarmé reveals sides of his character that rarely appear either in his published writing or in his letters to friends and colleagues. His love of the autumn leaves he could see from his house at Valvins is, of course, reflected elsewhere, finding its most notable reverberation perhaps in the beautiful sonnet that the Australian poet Christopher Brennan wrote in his memory—"Red autumn in Valvins around thy bed"—but it is also present in an exchange with his daughter in 1896. In a letter composed in late September of that year, Mallarmé wrote, "The curtain has risen on the season in an admirable and deliberate way. Here at least there reigns a sun that we had long forgotten" (*Corr.*, VIII: 238). Geneviève replied from Honfleur, "The autumn is very beautiful, perhaps more so than summer, although the terrible storm we had on Friday that broke so many trees, grilled or froze the leaves without allowing them to pass through the shades of autumn" (*DSM*, 2: 122). Writing in early November, Mallarmé replied: "Yesterday [. . .] we took a carriage ride through the valley, where the colors are amazing just now. [. . .] The leaves are falling vertiginously, since you left, ladies, and the forest opposite reveals its denuded summits. The water is dropping and is once again becoming transparent. Only two little green leaves remain, the budgerigars which kindly keep me company" (*Corr.*, VIII: 262).

These exchanges are dominated by allusions to the family's cats, especially Lillith and La Mine, whose reactions to the absence of one or the other human are charted minutely. Letters include bits of information especially for them. Writing about their behavior and commenting on their bad manners or their concern or lack thereof for the absent master or mistress clearly provided both father and daughter with an endlessly enjoyable trope. In May 1897, for example, Mallarmé set off for Valvins accompanied by Lilith, and obviously enjoyed reporting her shameless behavior on arrival:

A S FOR MY COMPANION, coming here just added fuel to the flames. No sooner had I let her go than she abandoned her nice piece of liver, and took herself off to the orchard with the Lover in person, following him and cuffing him, her eyes like two flowering buttercups. All the same, she slept in the kitchen and performed a thousand functions there, but this morning it was impossible to keep her in, she kept standing up against the doors, thinner than ever. We're not going to see much of each other. I seized her by main force, by the scruff of her neck, last night, on the stairway as she howled. (*Corr.*, IX: 162)

Again, Geneviève's memories suggest that the love of pets was deep-seated in her family: "The house," she tells us, "was never without some little animal or other":

H E NEEDED THESE SMALL LIVING PRESENCES, with all their naïveté. I'll list them, to make you smile, and in chronological order: the bluebird and the waxbill, the white angora cat we called Snow, and her white son, Fog; the greyhound bitch, Yseult, and the Russian greyhound dog, Saladin, the owl, Clairde-lune, the black cat Lilith; an unbroken succession of little green parrots, whose descendents are still with us, and whom we irrevently called: the little academicians.[7]

"These small living presences, with all their naïveté"—at times Geneviève must have felt relegated to such a function herself.

The letters to Geneviève also let us see the poet as gardener, and quite knowledgeable gardener at that. Her recollections in the *Nouvelle Revue française* article indicate that the love of flowers found in his poems is no mere rhetorical gesture but part of his nature. "The house," his daughter remarks, "was always full of flowers."[8] We know, moreover, from the correspondence that when Geneviève and her mother wanted Stéphane to understand that it was time to return from Valvins to Paris, they conveyed the hint by not renewing the flowers in the vases. In May 1898, a few months before he died, he wrote an exuberant letter, cataloging with a joy that only a gardener who also loves language can fully share:

THE ARTIST CAME, AFTER HIS DAY'S WORK, to plant half the flowers. We kept the rest for tomorrow as night falls so fast just now. There are some indeterminate dahlias from Charles Lecoq, we'll see the result in three weeks, and there'll still be time to start again with new corms. In the big bed we planted 4 snapdragons, 4 phlox, 4 or 5 forty-day stocks, and there are 5 hollyhocks there already. In the middle bed we put 3 chrysanthemums, 5 or 6 arbor vitae, 3 verbenas, and there are 4 hollyhocks. In both beds we put both single and double dahlias. The lilac bed received 3 big low daisies and 2 pyrethrums. All these plants cost between two and five sous each: they're my humble follies. Against the wall I planted a standard rose to replace the one that died, and some pansies. There are a few hollyhocks there, too. When you come, absolutely all you'll need to do is plant some balsams and some China asters. The chestnuts are in flower, the lilacs are in flower; everything's setting off in an astonishing way. I believe, without guessing what the slugs may do, that the ensemble will be pretty. (*Corr.*, X: 169–70)

A few weeks later came another, equally ecstatic list: "The garden, peonies, roses, false ebony, lilac, is in one of its great moments. How disappointing that you're not here! Much of all this will have gone by next week" (*Corr.*, X: 205).

Mallarmé's love for his daughter is present in all the letters he wrote to her, and there is no doubt that she reciprocated it, providing him with the warm, unchallenging, and supportive atmosphere he needed. The one poem he dedicated to her (apart from the occasional verse), "Autre Eventail, de Mademoiselle Mallarmé" (Another fan, for Mademoiselle Mallarmé), first published in 1884 and set to music after the poet's death by Claude Debussy, suggests certain of Geneviève's attributes that were especially attractive to him:

O rêveuse, pour que je plonge
Au pur délice sans chemin,
Sache, par un subtil mensonge,
Garder mon aile dans ta main.

Une fraîcheur de crépuscule
Te vient à chaque battement

Dont le coup prisonnier recule
L'horizon délicatement.

Vertige! Voici que frissonne
L'espace comme un grand baiser
Qui, fou de naître pour personne,
Ne peut jaillir ni s'apaiser.

Sens-tu le paradis farouche
Ainsi qu'un rire enseveli
Se couler du coin de ta bouche
Au fond de l'unanime pli!

Le sceptre des rivages roses
Stagnants sur les soirs d'or, ce l'est,
Ce blanc vol fermé que tu poses
Contre le feu d'un bracelet.

(O dreamer, if I'm to plunge
Into the pure delight that needs no path,
Know, by a subtle lie,
To hold my wing within your hand.

The coolness of evening
Comes to you at each beat
Whose imprisoned movement drives back
The horizon, delicately.

Vertigo! Now space
Shivers like a great kiss
That, maddened at being born for no one,
Can neither burst forth nor fade away.

Do you feel the wild paradise
Like a hidden laugh
Flow from the corner of your mouth
To the depths of the unanimous fold!

The scepter from the rosy banks
Stagnant under the golden skies, that's what it is
This white flight closed so that you can place it
Against the fire of a bracelet.) (*OC*, 58)

Whatever literary allusions critics may have detected in the opening words "O rêveuse" (see *OC*, 1475), there can be little disputing the fact that Mallarmé's most important inspiration here was, uncomplicatedly, his daughter's capacity for dream and reverie, a capacity reflected in her letters. Equally, her propensity to laugh, frequently recorded in her letters, is emphasized in the poem's penultimate stanza, with its mention of the "hidden laugh, flowing from the corner of your mouth," while her love of flowers and sunsets, together with the beauty of her young womanhood, are captured in the last strophe. The fan's white, closed flight encapsulates its latent potential, the way in which it is capable of putting air to flight and suggestive of the flight of birds; reading the verse from this distance, however, it's hard not to feel a sense of sorrow for Geneviève's own "closed flight," the life so long controlled by an invalid mother and a father who couldn't let go. The poem's central stanza finds yet another conceit for the fan, whose gentle breath sets the air around it trembling like a great kiss, maddened to find that it has been born for no one. Unable either to burst forth or to find peace, the kiss trembles on the edge of existence, as Geneviève must at times have appeared to her father to tremble on the brink of an awakened adulthood that neither of them could quite resolve to let her enter.

When her father died, Geneviève Mallarmé found on his desk an unfinished note to her, urging her to burn his papers. It remains unclear how many of them she did commit to the flames, torn as she was between filial duty and the desire to preserve her father's heritage, despite himself. Certainly the injunction was at most only partially obeyed. The enigmatic nature of this response to a request that she may well have felt was not, after all, the true expression of his last wishes provides a fitting climax for a relationship that was in its own way constantly enigmatic. Two years later, as if to recapture something of the relationship she had had with her father, she was to marry one of the Mardistes, Edmond Bonniot. She died, childless, in 1929.

CHAPTER THREE

Forging an Aesthetic

> Poetry speaks for [. . .] what is deeply felt and might otherwise
> go unrecorded: all those unique and repeatable events, the little
> sacraments of daily existence, movements of the heart and intima-
> tions of the close but inexpressible grandeur and terror of things,
> that is *our* history, the one that goes on, in a quiet way, under
> the noise and chatter of events and is the major part of what hap-
> pens each day in the life of the planet, and has been from the
> very beginning.
>
> —*David Malouf,* The Great World

A few years after he returned to Paris, early in 1875, Mallarmé wrote to the English writer Richard Hengist Horne. This colorful figure, whose sale of his first volume of poetry at a quarter of a penny per copy had earned him the sobriquet of "The Far-thing Poet," had recently stayed with Mallarmé in Paris. While there, he had dis-cussed with Mallarmé and Catulle Mendès his project of publishing in England an anthology of French poets. Mallarmé's letter reassures Horne that he is consulting a range of poets about the anthology and then raises the possibility of a project of his own: "A letter on the literary movement sent from Paris regularly once a week (a let-ter or notes), and that could be edited in London to suit the Magazine, do you think it would find a place and would it bring in any money? I'm living in exactly the right milieu here to let nothing that's important and even just curious escape me; and you could find in the thousands of revelations or criticisms that I'd send you on the cur-rent works and their authors the text of a very exact and very attractive chronicle of French arts and letters" (*Corr.*, II: 58). This was the germ of a series of brief articles, known, somewhat oddly, as "Gossips," that Mallarmé was to publish over the next year or so in the London journal *The Athenaeum*. While the desire to make the idea as seductive as possible may have intensified the colors in Mallarmé's letter, it remains true that, over the next two decades, the poet did remain close to the center of all that was at the forefront of Parisian cultural life, and that he responded to it with an openness of mind and a lively enthusiasm that transform his correspondence into the "very attractive chronicle" he envisaged in this letter. This chapter, therefore, charts some of his friendships with the artists and musicians who were part of that avant-garde and whose conversation as well as their works allowed Mallarmé, if not to develop, at least to refine, to expand, and to justify his own aesthetics.

On Sunday July 13, 1890, Mallarmé, accompanied by Berthe Morisot and her husband, Eugène Manet, spent an afternoon with Claude Monet at Giverny. Their host, contrite at not having produced the illustration he had promised for Mallarmé's prose poem "La Gloire," offered him the painting of his choice. Returning home with his booty, *Le Train à Jeufosse,* on his knees, a radiant Mallarmé announced that one thing that made him truly happy was his luck in living at the same time as Monet.[1] The art critic Gustave Geffroy was later to say of this canvas, in terms that sketch the close links between Mallarmé's art and that of Impressionism, that it was "a landscape presented as if only glimpsed and yet deliciously precise, a meander in the river, an arabesque of water running through the countryside, that Mallarmé used to compare to the smile of the Mona Lisa" (*Corr.,* III: 212). The train is represented only by its smoke, evoked rather than described, to use the terms Mallarmé himself favored in indicating what a work of art should do. Mallarmé's delight in the visual arts, his eclecticism in responding to the art of his time, and his extraordinary ability to create lasting friendships with talented people whose suspicions and jealousies he was adroit enough to defuse allowed him to enjoy the company of numerous painters, sculptors, and musicians, even when they behaved with considerably less courtesy than did Monet.

When the artist James McNeill Whistler was working on his portrait of Mallarmé, for instance, he kept the poet standing motionless for so long in front of a blazing fire, screaming at him if he ventured to move, that when Mallarmé eventually escaped, he found he had real burns on his legs. Whistler's response on hearing this tale was, characteristically, to burst into a gale of laughter. Mallarmé's response was even more characteristic: he wrote a playful poem about the incident:

Ce me va hormis l'y taire
Que je sente du foyer
Un pantalon militaire
A ma jambe rougeoyer

(I don't mind—provided I can speak of it—
that the fire
is painting a pair of red military trousers
on my leg) (*OC,* 67)

It was Mallarmé's puckish sense of humor, his tact, and above all his love of beauty that allowed him to establish lasting friendships with many artists, even those as irascible, dictatorial, and demanding as Whistler.

His friendships with artists have left many traces, in addition to this playful poem.[2] Edouard Manet, Auguste Renoir, James McNeill Whistler, Paul Gauguin, Edvard Munch, and Félix Valotton all made portraits of him; Degas took his photo with Renoir, at the same time capturing his own image in the mirror behind the two men; Mallarmé himself dashed off rhymed addresses for Berthe Morisot, Degas, Monet, Renoir and Redon, among others, and penned medallions for Whistler and Morisot, wrote a sonnet for the fresco painter Pierre Puvis de Chavannes, and translated Whistler's so-called Ten o'clock lecture. His friendships with painters also find their reflection in the diaries of Henri de Régnier and Julie Manet, in Manet's illustrations for "L'Après-midi d'un faune" and for Mallarmé's translation of "The Raven," and in Mallarmé's own articles on art. And the poet was not associated merely with the Impressionists. A fan signed by a range of establishment figures reveals Mallarmé's signature accompanied by those of several academy painters.[3] We find his signature linked with that of Puvis de Chavannes and Whistler on Mme Rodenbach's fan; his collaboration with Jean-François Raffaelli is reflected in his *Chansons bas;* and on his death Auguste Rodin exclaimed, "How long will it take for Nature to mold another mind like his?" (*VM,* 803).

Mallarmé's early friendship with Henri Regnault and the brief article he published on the first anniversary of the young painter's death in no way really prepare us for the quite remarkable articles in defense of Manet that appeared in 1874 and 1876. The first of these protests against the rejection by the jury of two of the three paintings Manet submitted for that year's Salon, one of the many rejections that prompted the first exhibition of Impressionist paintings, held in the studio of the photographer Félix Nadar on April 15, 1874. Mallarmé's 1874 article was written in a particularly creative and productive year, not just for art but also for literature and music. In that year Degas was working on his powerful, disturbing, and enigmatic canvas, *Le Viol* (The rape); Manet, under the influence of his younger colleagues, Renoir and Monet, was transforming his palette in ways that gave birth to such luminous scenes as *Les Canotiers d'Argenteuil* (Rowers at Argenteuil); Monet produced the beautiful *L'Eté* (Summer); and Renoir revealed how profound a change had taken place in both subject matter and perspective with *La Loge* (The box). Zola, at work on his monumental exploration of the Second Empire, published his novelistic study of the 1848 revolution, *La Conquête de Plassans* (*The Conquest of Plassans*), while Verlaine was further loosening the confines of prosodic structure with his volume of poetry, *Romances sans paroles.* Abroad, Whistler's *Portrait of Carlyle* disproved the sitter's fear that the artist's main interest lay in representing his coat, by showing a penetrating physiological exploration of the historian's face; Bedrich Smetana completed his paean to the beauty of his native Czechoslovakia in *The Moldau;* Giuseppe Verdi wrote his moving *Requiem;* and Richard Wagner had begun the Ring Cycle with *Götterdämmerung.*

In his article on Manet's rejection from that year's Salon, Mallarmé, playing ironically on the conceit that the jury's action was prompted by a wish to protect members of the public from losing their capacity to value the eternal when faced with the power of the modern, explores the two rejected canvasses, *Le Bal de l'Opéra* (The opera ball) and *Les Hirondelles* (The swallows). Mallarmé's ability to see the technical problems posed especially by the choice of subject for the first of these, with its milling crowd and its lack of single focus, suggests both his delight in confronting difficulties and his awareness that the real subject is less the modern crowd than the color black. Similarly, he depicts the central theme of *Les Hirondelles* as the harmony of gray dresses and a September afternoon. And he concludes by reminding the jury, in a warning that would have been particularly potent with the 1870–71 Commune still so fresh in everyone's memory, that the real arbiters of taste, the real jury, is the people, over whom no single group can hold permanent jurisdiction.

The article that most modern readers see as being of primary importance in charting Mallarmé's aesthetic development is "The Impressionists and Edouard Manet" published in an English translation (the original is lost) in *The Art Monthly Review and Photographic Folio* in September 1876.[4] These were heady days for anyone interested in the avant-garde. The previous year had seen the inauguration of Paris's new opera theater, with a performance of Georges Bizet's *Carmen* that had provoked a scandal, while in 1876 itself Bayreuth's Festspielhaus had been opened with a performance of Wagner's Ring Cycle. The continuing refusal of the Salon's jury to accept the Impressionists must have made Mallarmé, now in his mid-thirties, feel that the time had truly come to take a stand against the growing philistinism of the French middle classes.

Conveying the essence of Manet's "brilliant" conversation in terms that clearly echo his own convictions, Mallarmé insists that the real artist never paints to a formula but makes each work a "new creation of the mind" (*DSM*, 1: 69). But if the public is to learn to appreciate these new creations, it will only be as a result of an education brought about through the artist himself or herself, and if the artist is to succeed in producing those new creations, it will be by denying subjectivity and allowing what Mallarmé calls "nature" to speak through the artist. Of course Mallarmé is in part using this article to explore and express his own convictions, but he is also intensely aware of the importance of a new aesthetic that is unique to this form to painting, that of *pleinairism*. Taking as his example the painting *Le Linge* (The washing), Mallarmé shows how it is "deluged with air":

EVERYWHERE THE LUMINOUS AND TRANSPARENT atmosphere struggles with the figures, the dresses, and the foliage, and seems to take to itself some of their substance and solidity; whilst their contours, consumed by the hidden sun and wasted by space, tremble, melt, and evaporate into the surrounding atmosphere, which plunders reality from the figures, yet seems to do so in order to preserve their truthful aspect. Air reigns supreme and real, as if it held an enchanted life conferred by the witchery of art. (*DSM*, 1: 75)

If Mallarmé is able to grasp with such certainty what it was that Impressionism sought, it is partly through his conversations with Manet, to whom he was particularly close in these years, and partly because there are points of similarity between avant-garde painting and his own art. Mallarmé's insistence that lines of poetry exist as newly invented words, in which each element confers some of its intellectual and sonorous content onto the surrounding elements, is indeed very close to his vision of open-air painting, and his attempt to convey the quality of light in such poems as "Victorieusement fui" and "L'Après-midi d'un faune" has much in common with the specifically painterly search for truth he outlines in this seminal article.

The influence of Japanese prints[5] is also emphasized as Mallarmé insists on the way in which eyes veiled by convention can be shown new truths by changes in perspective, by cropping, and by using the frame to bring the viewer into the scene, just as Mallarmé in all his writing, his prose as much as his poetry, refuses conventional ways of presentation and forces his readers to consider the familiar with minds freed, however momentarily, from the blinders of convention. His early poem "Las de l'amer repos" (Weary of the bitter rest), probably written while he was in Tournon in 1862 (*OC,* 1427), expresses a longing to imitate the simplicity and suggestive power of Chinese art (see Chapter 1).[6] The European fascination with Asian art in the second half of the nineteenth century (when the terms "Chinese" and "Japanese" were often used interchangeably) can be seen in many of the period's great works of literature and art, and it is not surprising to find Mallarmé taking an interest in it so early, just as it is not surprising that it should be one of the many points of contact between him and the Impressionists. The suggestive power of Asian art offers a forceful parallel to Mallarmé's desire to paint not the object, but the effect the object produces, in ways similar to those in which Manet's depiction of the woman and child in *Le Linge* is less concerned with precision than with evocation. This is not to claim that Mallarmé entirely shared Manet's aesthetics. It is rather that, as with so many of the experiments he intelligently and sympathetically observed, Mallarmé had the rare skill of perceiving what the other was trying to do, appreciating what had been achieved, and extracting from that attempt elements that extended, sharpened, or merely confirmed his own vision. As in many other cases, at issue is not whether each man fully understood the other's work but how open they remained to different viewpoints. Thus, while Mallarmé strove for perfection, endlessly polishing his sonnets, Manet seems more interested in seizing a fleeting moment and revealing the imperfection and transience of art.

Just as Manet the painter exemplified for Mallarmé "the steadfast gaze of a vision restored to its simplest perfection" (*DSM,* 1: 86), as he puts it in the 1876 article, so Manet the individual was one of his closest friends in the early years of his return to Paris. If, as Harry Rand argues, "Manet looms over his times as an intensely private man,"[7] and, as Françoise Cachin asserts, "Manet remains one of the most enigmatic, least classifiable artists in the history of painting,"[8] Mallarmé must have been in a better position than most not only to appreciate that elusive and enigmatic mask but also to penetrate it. In his "autobiographical" letter to Verlaine of November 1885, he states that for ten years he saw his "dear Manet" daily and finds his absence in death "invraisemblable" (improbable) (*Corr.,* II: 303). Both presented to the public a life stripped of anecdotes, as Mallarmé puts it in the same letter (*OC,* 664). In the early 1870s they lived on the same street, the rue de Moscou, near the Gare Saint-Lazare, which is wittily absent from Manet's *Le Chemin de fer* (The railway line), a painting he began in 1872, the year the friendship may have started. Returning home from the Lycée Fontanes (now Condorcet), where he was teaching, Mallarmé would drop in at the studio to enjoy those conversations mentioned so temptingly and so fleetingly in his 1876 article. Manet, after all, represented not only an artist whose search for truth paralleled his own but also a vibrant link with Baudelaire, who had written to reassure the artist in bracing terms early in his career:

So I MUST TALK TO YOU about yourself once again. I must knuckle down and show you what you're worth. It's really silly what you demand of me. "People are mocking us"; the "jokes" irritate you, etc. etc. Do you think you're the first to be put in such a position? Do you have more genius than Chateaubriand or Wagner? But people mocked them pretty roundly, didn't they? It didn't kill them. And so as not to make you too proud, I'll tell you that those men are models, each in his own way, and in a very rich world, and that you are *merely the first in the decrepitude of your art.* I hope you won't mind my treating you in such a cavalier way. You know what friendship I feel for you.[9]

Mallarmé's biographer, Henri Mondor, makes the following claim for the exchanges that took place between Impressionist painter and Symbolist poet:

THEIR DIALOGUE, SPREAD OUT OVER 8 to 10 years, benefiting from their almost daily meetings, and consisting on the one side, of ingenious remarks full of imagery, and on the other, of energetic, sarcastic replies, must be considered one of the moments in which French art, which was currently scintillating and would continue to scintillate for twenty years, with an exceptional luster, found ways of understanding and expressing itself as it ripened in the intimate familiarity of two creative spirits. (*VM,* 411)

Because of this close daily contact, few letters survive: a letter from Mallarmé written in September 1882, when Manet, suffering from an inflammation of the leg, had gone to convalesce at Rueil, and a handful of letters from Manet or members of his family to the poet. Those that have been found reflect the warmth and the openness of their friendship, especially in Manet's rueful change of mind after he had initially rejected the suggestion that he produce a series of lithographs to illustrate Mallarmé's translation of Poe's "The Raven."[10] In 1875, the year that saw this marvelous but at the time misunderstood collaboration, Manet also did his frontispiece and ex libris for "L'Après-midi d'un faune," with their sinuous allusions to the text's core images.[11]

It was in 1876 that Manet produced one of his most remarkable works, his portrait of Mallarmé. In it, as Harry Rand argues, he "fashioned a concise motif for those considerations that bound him to Mallarmé."[12] Seated on a divan and leaning into the center of the painting, the poet gazes neither at the spectator nor at the book on which his hand is resting. He is not reading but meditating on what he has read. This deflected gaze can be read as representing the refusal of Sainte-Beuve's promotion of the link between art and the individual who created that art. In Mallarmé's aesthetic, what counts is the relationship not of reader and individual poet but of reader and text. In the hand that rests on the book, he holds a cigar from which rises a spiral of smoke, in the form of a question mark. The Japanese screen behind him, with its mere suggestion of flowers and butterflies; the transubstantiation of text into smoke; and the poet's rapt contemplation all combine to suggest the blend of intellect and sensuality, the quiet understatement of the essential point that united the two friends.

If it is hardly surprising that Manet chose to depict a poet, if not reading, at least meditating over a book, it remains true that many of Manet's paintings do show people reading: his 1861 *Lecteur* (Reader); *A la plage* (At the seaside) of 1873; *La Liseuse* (The reader), produced somewhere around 1862–65; the 1868 *La Lecture* (Reading); *La Gare Saint-Lazare* (Saint-Lazare Station); and so forth. Manet's letters to Mallarmé suggest that books and writing were a central element in their discussions. In a letter dated June 23, 1880, the painter asks a convalescing Mallarmé. "Have you read Zola's articles that appeared in the *Voltaire,* entitled *Naturalisme au Salon* [Naturalism at the Salon]? If so, let me know what you thought of them. If you don't have them, I'll send them to you and you can tell me what effect they had on you and what effect you think they might have on the public" (*VM,* 411). And in September 1882 Mallarmé indicates the vital role reading played in their conversation when he writes, "I reread, thinking of you, who read it last year, Jean-Jacques [Rousseau's] *Confessions:* yes, it's a fine book" (*Corr.,* II: 231). Manet, in his reply to this letter, turned to a quite different kind of literature, the racy adventure tale: "I've just read *Rocambole* by Ponson du Terrail, it's extraordinary" (*Corr.,* II: 230).

Further light on Manet's seductive charm is shed by Henri de Régnier, who, commenting secondhand on the man's great personal charm, writes rather maliciously, "I suspect Manet of being so charming that he fascinated his friends into admiring him for his painting" (*Annales,* January 11, 1887). But then elsewhere Régnier comments, "When I think of the effect painting really has on me, I'm obliged to acknowledge that this art is incapable of charming me and I have to confess the profound scorn I feel for it. [. . .] Manet fills me with horror" (*Annales,* notebook of March–April 1888).

It was also through Manet that Mallarmé came to know the woman who would be so important to him in his last two decades of life: Méry Laurent. According to Mondor, Manet first encountered her when she came to see the paintings that the jury of the 1876 Salon had rejected and that he had put on display in his own studio. Standing in front of *Le Linge,* she exclaimed in a cry that brought Manet hurrying from another room, "But that one's really good!" (*VM,* 381). In 1881 she was to model for him for his painting *Autumn* (Figure 13), wearing a pelisse, about which an enraptured Manet wrote to Mallarmé: "She's had a pelisse made. What a pelisse, dear friend, in a yellowish brown with a lining in old gold. I was mesmerized. I left Méry Laurent, saying to her: 'When you've worn that pelisse out, give it to me.' She promised me she would, it'll make a terrific background for projects I have in mind" (*VM,* 416). There is in such letters a tantalizing glimpse—no more than a curl of smoke from an unseen cigar—of conversations in which the two men talked about the things they each dreamed of creating.

Manet died on May 7, 1883. In October of that year his widow, Suzanne, remarked in a letter to Mallarmé: "You really were his best friend, and he loved you dearly." [13] Over ten years after Manet's early death, Mallarmé wrote his extraordinary "medallion" of the painter, which he sent originally to a publication edited by Edmond Girard, *Portraits du prochain siècle,* which folded before Mallarmé's contribution could be published (*Corr.,* VII: 160). The medallion subsequently appeared in Mallarmé's collection of prose pieces *Divagations.* In two brief, dense paragraphs the piece sums Manet up as an intense, superbly gifted painter struggling against the incomprehension of the crowd and the malignancy of fate. Recalling Manet's own elliptical statement that the hand was an eye, Mallarmé evokes the artist's handshake as though it contained within it a key to his genius: "The clear, ready pressure you felt announced the mystery into which the limpid gaze descended, to bring order to the new and French masterpiece, lively, washed, deep, sharp or haunted by the certainty of blackness" (*OC,* 532–33). There can be no doubt that Mallarmé's portrait of Manet is also a portrait of the ideal artist and therefore of what Mallarmé himself sought to be.

In his 1876 article on the Impressionists, Mallarmé insisted that Manet's "influence as from friend to friend is wider spread than that which a master exercises over a pupil, and sways all the painters of the day" (*DSM,* 1: 79). The central role of friendship in the growth of Impressionism cannot, indeed, be overstated, and Mallarmé goes on to evoke several other artist friends and their work in his study. In so doing he also suggests his own function within this loosely knit group of comrades.

Among those comrades, Mallarmé paid particular attention in his article to Manet's sister-in-law, the painter Berthe Morisot:

MORE GIVEN TO RENDER, AND VERY SUCCINCTLY, the aspect of things, but with a new charm infused into it by feminine vision, Mademoiselle Berthe Morizot [*sic:* a frequent spelling of her name] seizes wonderfully the familiar presence of a woman of the world, or a child in the pure atmosphere of the sea-shore, or green lawn. [. . .] The air of preoccupation, of mundane care of secret sorrows, so generally characteristic of the modern artist's sketches from contemporary life, were never more notably absent than here; one feels that the graceful lady and child are in perfect ignorance that the pose unconsciously adopted to gratify an innate sense of beauty is perpetuated in this charming water-color. (*DSM*, 1: 82–83)

For all its warmth and sympathy, for all the echoes of "L'Après-midi d'un faune" in the choice of the word "perpetuate" ("Those nymphs," asserts the faun, "I would perpetuate"), there is in this passage an air of condescension that recalls Baudelaire's review of Marceline Desbordes-Valmore's poetry and reinforces conventional views of what women could and should do, feel, and perceive. It is not surprising (though it is distressing) that in 1890, Morisot poignantly noted in her diary, "I don't think there has ever been a man who treated a woman as an equal, and that's all I would have asked, for I know I'm worth as much as they."[14] When Régnier came to write his series of poems devoted to artists, the poem for Morisot consists entirely of reminiscences about dining with her in the company of Mallarmé and the dog Laertes that Mallarmé had given to Morisot's daughter Julie. The degree to which women's gifts were consistently debased in these last decades of the century has permeated not just the thinking of Mallarmé and Régnier but of Morisot herself. As she regretfully wrote on the birth of her daughter Julie, "I regret that Bib isn't a boy; first, she has a boy's head, and then because she'd perpetuate a famous name, at bottom quite simply because all of us, men and women, love the masculine sex."[15] When, in the winter of 1893–94 Mallarmé invited her and her daughter to one of his Mardis, one at which he was to read the lecture he was preparing to give at Oxford and Cambridge, she clearly felt it was too masculine a gathering: "Certainly not," she wrote, with a frankness that is a further testament of friendship; "the bench full of students would intimidate us far too much."[16] Morisot's niece, the painter Paule Gobillard, was even blunter, according to Julie Manet. She insisted in a conversation with Renoir that Mallarmé disdained women. Renoir, with that form of gallantry that reveals the user's sense of his own superiority, asserted, "But women always think we disdain them, on the contrary, women are the only thing we think about, they're our only danger."[17] In all the photographs taken of her, Gobillard directs at the photographer a gaze that is little less than hostile: One doesn't feel she would have been placated by Renoir's glib answer.[18]

By the time Mallarmé wrote the introduction to the catalog of Morisot's works, compiled after her unexpected death in 1896, an introduction subsequently included in *Divagations*, poet and painter had enjoyed twenty years of a warm friendship, yet he still chose to refer to her as one of "the few dissidents among the female sex who present aesthetics other than by their own person" (*OC*, 534). While much of his Morisot medallion evokes the person—the beauty of her white hair, the intensity of her love for her daughter Julie, the wit and penetration of her conversation—it does include a passage making an essential link between poetry and painting: "Creating poetry, through the plastic arts, a means of direct prestige, seems the unmediated result of an atmosphere that awakens the luminous secret on the surface of things: or the rich analysis of life, done chastely, with the aim of restoring it, by means of a kind of alchemy—mobility and illusion" (*OC*, 536). Light, movement, atmosphere rather than anecdote, the mimesis of realism set aside for the allusive evocation of a more profound truth: Once again Mallarmé focuses most sharply on those elements that link his aesthetics with those of Morisot. It is not that he distorts her art—on the contrary—but rather that he enters it through doors and windows that are familiar to him, in order to appreciate fully its unique essence. And the Mallarmé who in his fashion journal lingered with such evident pleasure over feminine outfits (even if he later asserted to Verlaine that he did so only to make money) is also very much present in his ability to see that in her studies of women's clothes and jewelry there was a broader goal, that she studied them in order that "the intention behind the outfit should burst forth in harmony with the gardens and the beach, a hothouse or a gallery" (*OC*, 537).

Perhaps because of these qualities that he perceived in her, it was Berthe Morisot whom Mallarmé asked to provide an illustration for his prose poem "Le Nénuphar blanc" (The white water lily), which was to appear in his planned collection *Le Tiroir de laque* (The lacquer drawer). That she found difficulty locating windows and doors to enter his work is suggested in a letter she wrote in response to this request in December 1887: "Please come and dine on Thursday. Renoir and I are flabbergasted; we need some explanations for the illustrations." [19] While flabbergasted (*ahuris*) is a term that some might find offensive, Mallarmé knew exactly how to take it, replying, "I'm concerned to know you are flabbergasted: fortunately I can see your smile behind that" (*Corr.*, III: 151). And he adds that he's sending, "as an instrument of torture," the page he would like illustrated. In this beautiful and elusive poem, the narrator sets out by boat to greet an unknown woman (the friend of a woman friend). When he arrives at her riverside park he begins to dream about the close relationship between woman and setting, so that the expanse of water that borders her park becomes the calm mirror of her mind, and the slight mist silvering the willows represents "the limpidity of her gaze" (*OC*, 284). Transforming her entirely into a shining image, as he wonderfully puts it, the narrator predicts, but with a smile, that he will become enslaved by this potential woman. A sound he interprets as a footfall tears him from his reverie, but he can see no one. Rather than force his imagination to confront reality, he picks one of the white water lilies, drawn by its ability to "envelope in its hollow whiteness an absence" (*OC*, 286), and rows away, carrying with him this imaginary trophy, like "a noble swan's egg, from which no bird will ever fly" (*OC*, 286). Virginia Spate may very well be right to suggest that this poem would have been a better source of inspiration to Monet than the poem he was allocated, "La Gloire" (Glory),[20] but Mallarmé's prose poem is so evocative of Impressionism, so imbued with the painters' desire to capture the luminosity and mobility of water, so in tune with the imprecision of faces that allows such room for dream, that, were it not for the complexity of the syntax and the elliptical nature of the expression, one might have expected any of the Impressionists to jump at the chance to illustrate it. It seems that Morisot did indeed produce a chalk drawing, by which Mallarmé, rather blandly, professed himself "charmed," according to a letter written in February 1889 (*Corr.,* III: 290). Strangely enough, only Renoir's illustration appears in the volume, which was published under the title *Pages.*

Mallarmé was one of the small circle of friends, mainly painters—among them Degas, Renoir, and occasionally Monet—who gathered at Morisot's Thursday dinners during the 1880s. And in the summers he would invite her and her family to spend a few days at the house the Mallarmés rented in Valvins, on the Seine near Fontainebleau. In a letter to Monet dated March 14, 1888, Morisot referred to the poet as "one of our most faithful and your very great friend."[21] Later that year, in response to a bouquet of roses she had sent from where the family were staying in Cimiez, in the south of France, Mallarmé wrote one of those letters in which he seems, however banal the ostensible subject matter, to convey the essence of the friendship:

D EAR LADY, HERE'S A LITTLE MISSIVE from Valvins where we followed the roses, which are replacing on the chimneypiece the autumn that has failed us outside. It's raining, not leaves, but raindrops on windows we'd love to have wide open: for the temperature is more like that of late summer, despite the wintry landscape. So to some extent your flowers have let us visit Nice.

But as the papers speak of a new world of locomotion which will take us to Marseilles in 2 hours, I think I'm not going to make do for long with this belated hothouse temperature we have here, but will visit you this winter and even on the ordinary railway, why not! if I can find a way of doing it, dear friends. (*Corr.,* III: 274)

Delighted by this evocative response to her gift of flowers, Morisot promised that she would send more, and that Mallarmé could reciprocate with "a pretty piece of prose."[22] Mallarmé did better than that by sending a quatrain:

O fin de siècle, hiver! qui truques
Tout, excepté le sentiment,
J'aime quand tu mets gentiment
Aux camélias des perruques

(Oh winter! end of an age, you who rig
Everything, except my feelings,
How I like it when you come stealing
To adorn the camellia with its wig)[23]

And with a book to Julie Manet he included another quatrain of similar inspiration:

Ce poëme devenu prose,
Comme tout se passe à l'envers!
Moi qui devrais pour chaque rose
Ne vous envoyer que des vers

(This poem turned into prose,
How all goes from good to worse
In exchange for every rose
I should send you nothing but verse) (*Corr.,* III: 284)

The warmth of their friendship and the affectionate joy in her abilities at both painting light and bringing light into his existence are conveyed in a letter of April 1889: "Winter has dug its heels in here: take a brush of any color you like and change all that for us, you're the only one who can!" (*Corr.,* III: 306). When Eugène Manet's poor health forced the Manet family to leave Paris and find accommodations at Mézy, Mallarmé wrote one of his rhyming addresses:

Sans t'endormir dans l'herbe verte
Naïf distributeur, mets-y
Du tien: cours chez Mme Berthe
Manet, par Meulan, à Mézy

(Don't fall asleep in the green grass
Innocent postman, don't take it easy,
but run to Mme Berthe Manet,
via Meulan, at Mézy) (*OC,* 88)

It was from Mézy that they set out, with Mallarmé, to visit Monet at Giverny, on the famous Sunday during which Monet gave his friend the painting *Le Train à Jeufosse.* Eugène Manet's death in April 1892 made Mallarmé one of Julie's legal guardians, and the friendship was further strengthened when in the following summer Morisot and Julie stayed at Valvins. After they left, Mallarmé wrote, in a sentence that unpretentiously and beautifully evokes the nature of friendship itself: "Your visit was such a celebration for us, letting us appreciate a favorite walk in the neighborhood, and I savor all the value of its past charm: your presence here seemed so natural" (*Corr.,* V: 156). September saw them back in Valvins, from which they went to the nearby village of Moret, where Alfred Sisley, who had been living there since November 1889, was producing a series of paintings of the church. Julie Manet's diary notes, "Thursday 21 September. After a rainy morning, the day turned sunny, and we drove to Moret. It's very pretty; we went there through the open country and came back through the forest. We saw Sisley at Moret."[24] In early 1895 Mallarmé sent Morisot and her daughter a charming invitation to a theatrical performance at which Allys Arsel was to recite some of Mallarmé's poems:

> Je souhaite à ces jeux oraux
> Julie en chapeau Gainsborough
> pour me cacher, parce que vous serez en notre loge, s'il vous agrée, mesdames.

> (I wish for these oral games that
> Julie would wear a Gainsborough hat
> to hide me, because you'll be in our box, if that suits you, ladies.) (*Corr.*, VII: 129)

Morisot went on her own, leaving Julie at home in bed, with influenza. It was in caring for her daughter that Morisot herself caught flu, which turned to a pulmonary congestion that rapidly led to her death. Her last letter to Mallarmé was a brief note scrawled on February 27, 1895: "I'm ill, my dear friend. I won't ask you to come because it's impossible for me to talk."[25] She died on March 2. When Mallarmé wrote to him informing him of Morisot's death, Henri de Régnier, who had been a frequent visitor at her Thursday dinners, noted in his diary:

> MME MANET IS DEAD AND I SEE AGAIN that serious and exceptional woman, together with Mlle Julie and the greyhound Laertes,[26] their white, discreet home, the dinners I so often attended there, talking softly with Mallarmé, Renoir, and Degas, at first on the rue de Villejust and then rue Weber, the dinners in the dining room where Manet's paintings hung, together with those of Monnet [*sic*], and Renoir; all that is ended with the slender, energetic woman with her white hair, a little tense and delicate, haughty with something about her that was rather military and abrupt, and the deep gaze, black, almost haggard of her eyes, and the bearing of a mother of tragedy, and her smile with its hint of boredom or mischief, a kind of irritated melancholy. (Quoted in *Corr.*, VII: 174)

A year later, at the instigation of Mallarmé, Degas, Renoir, and Monet, there was an exhibition of Morisot's works, accompanied by a catalog for which Mallarmé had written the preface. The intensity of his feelings resulted in a prose of more than usual density and complexity that may not have best served his evident desire to make her works better known to the public. The musician Reynaldo Hahn, for instance, noted in his diary: "There are many things that should be said; Mallarmé probably said them in the preface he wrote for the catalogue, but unfortunately I couldn't understood a word of it" (quoted in *VM,* 725).[27]

Mallarmé's affection for Morisot continued after her death, not just through his eagerness to promote her posthumous fame but also in the seriousness with which he took his role as legal guardian to Julie Manet. Together with family members, he decided that the best course of action was for Julie to live with her two cousins, the daughters of Berthe's sister Yves, who had died a few years earlier. He helped choose a housekeeper to care for them, and he stayed in close contact with all three. When he died in September 1898, the three girls were staying with Renoir at Essoyes. Julie's despairing diary entry bears eloquent witness to the very deep affection in which she held Mallarmé and the extent to which she regarded him as a vital link with her dead parents:

> OH! WHAT A DREADFUL THING! A telegram tells us M. Mallarmé is dead, how can it be possible, what can have happened to him, it's awful! Poor Mme Mallarmé! Poor Geneviève! Ah! how unhappy I am at the death of that dear friend of papa and maman, whom they'd appointed my legal guardian! He was charming to us, he called us his "children" in such a fatherly way. He used to remind me of those truly delicious Thursday evenings at home. How atrocious it is to think that this man whom we saw in good health in July has now gone. Death is terrible. M. Renoir is very upset at this horrible news. He's leaving with us this evening for Valvins.[28]

As Julie Manet's comment makes clear, at the end of his life Mallarmé also counted Renoir among his close friends. In his 1876 article Mallarmé clearly delights in summing up Renoir's gifts in an evocative paragraph, in a style that may well draw inspiration from Baudelaire's art criticism:

> THE SHIFTING SHIMMER OF GLEAM AND SHADOW which the changing, reflected lights, themselves influenced by every neighboring thing, cast upon each advancing or departing figure, and the fleeting combinations in which these dissimilar reflections form one harmony or many, such are the favorite effects of Renoir—nor can we wonder that this infinite complexity of execution induces him to seek more hazardous success in things widely opposed to nature. A box at a theater, its gaily-dressed inmates, the women with their flesh tints heightened and displaced by rouge and rice powder, a complication of effects of light—the more so when this scene is fantastically illuminated by an incongruous day-light. Such are the subjects he delights in. (*DSM,* 1: 83)

While this passage offers a delicate echo of Baudelaire's exploration of color in his account of the Salon of 1846, it also suggests the correspondence that Mallarmé detected between his art and that of the Impressionism. The attention Renoir pays to the "shimmer of gleam and shadow" offers a direct parallel with Mallarmé's own conception of the interplay of words within the lines of poetry, a conception he explores in "Crise de vers." Words, he asserts, "illuminate each other through reciprocal reflections like a virtual trail of fire on precious stones" (*OC*, 366). It was probably through Morisot that Mallarmé's friendship with Renoir was established. While Jean Renoir, in his biography of his father, says little of this relationship, he does note that "of all the friends and companions who had been with him in their struggle for recognition [Morisot] was the one with whom he had kept most closely in touch." [29] Renoir had been a frequent guest at her Thursday dinners, which Mallarmé began attending on a regular basis toward the end of 1886. The following year saw Renoir agreeing to produce an illustration of the prose poem "Le Phénomène futur," in which Mallarmé plays with Baudelaire's concept of the beauty of the women of antiquity, a beauty far greater than can be found in the modern world. Although Renoir, as described earlier in this chapter, initially professed bewilderment when faced with the poem, there is little doubt that the description of this vital and exuberant young woman owes much to Renoir's own work, and it is hardly surprising that he should have responded with such a charming illustration of the following passage: "Some madness or other, original and naive, an ecstasy of gold, how can I put it? that she calls her hair, folds with the grace possessed by material around a face illuminated by the bloody nudity of her lips. Instead of vain clothing, she has a body; and her eyes, like rare gems, are less precious than the gaze that leaps from her joyous flesh: breasts raised as if full of an eternal milk, nipples to the sky, her smooth legs still marked by the salt of the first sea" (*OC*, 269). Who better than Renoir has depicted the "joyous flesh?" In a rhyming address Mallarmé captures his friend's delight in female beauty:

Villa des Arts, près l'Avenue
De Clichy, peint Monsieur Renoir,
Qui devant une épaule nue
Broie autre chose que du noir

(At the Villa des Arts, near the avenue
de Clichy, M. Renoir paints,
and when he gazes at a naked shoulder,
falls into something quite different from a brown study) (*OC*, 88)

The portrait Renoir made of his friend in 1892 was less to Mallarmé's liking. According to his future son-in-law Bonniot, he claimed it made him look like a "well-heeled financier" (*VM*, 654). Certainly the portrait has none of the evocative finesse of Manet's portrait. There is no equivalent of Manet's Japanese screen to suggest the sitter's interest in contemporary art, merely an indeterminate backdrop to set off the head; there's nothing to indicate what Mallarmé would consider the essential part of his personality, his existence as poet, nothing to allow a viewer to see him as possessing an individuality other than his physical presence. Facing us at three-quarters profile, with the slope of his shoulders and torso filling the lower third of the canvas and his head carefully centered, the three orderly parallels of hairline, eyebrows, and mustache emphasized rather than questioned by the exuberant cravat that breaks away from the pattern, the figure set before us seems curiously devoid of inner life. The broad brow draws on traditional concepts to suggest intelligence, but the mouth is hidden by the mustache, and the eyes could indeed be those of a person thinking merely of material gain. While this is recognizably the Mallarmé we see in photographs of the time, it clearly does little more than produce a physical likeness. This is mere statement, lacking the power of evocation that drew Mallarmé to the Impressionists.

Although, as this portrait suggests, it's likely that the painter did not truly understand the intelligence of his poet friend, Renoir was among those who attended Mallarmé's demanding lecture on Villiers de l'Isle-Adam in Morisot's studio (see *VM*, 571), and he and Mallarmé, both named legal guardians to Julie Manet, also worked together to ensure that after Morisot's death there was an exhibition of her paintings. It was probably in June 1894, at a dinner party in Degas's house, that Degas took his imaginative photograph of Renoir and Mallarmé, in which the photographer appears reflected by a large mirror that also allows us to see the forms of Mallarmé's wife and daughter. Mallarmé stands on Renoir's left, gazing down at his seated friend, who stares slightly obliquely at the camera: There is an uncanny suggestion in this wonderful photograph that Degas has captured the essence of their relationship, for as Mallarmé's focus on Renoir suggests, he seems to have understood the painter better than Renoir understood him. (A copy of this photo can, moreover, be seen in photographs of Morisot's studio.)[30]

While only two letters from Mallarmé to Renoir have been found, and six from the painter to the poet, the diaries of their contemporaries include tempting echoes and intimations of wonderful conversations between them: Régnier, referring to a dinner party in December 1893, asserts, "Truly, these two men said exquisite things to each other" (quoted *Corr.*, VI: 191). Julie Manet's diary also mentions "exquisite" conversations between the two men. On December 16 of 1897, for instance, the year in which it was discovered that the incriminating documents thought to have been written by Alfred Dreyfus were in fact in Esterhazy's handwriting, Julie asserts that "the conversation between these two intelligent men is always charming,"[31] although on March 17 of the following year, the fact that the two are discussing the topical question of the Dreyfus Affair provokes her into being considerably sharper: "They may well be very interesting, but really we have had enough of this affair."[32] Where the divisive Dreyfus Affair was concerned, Renoir, according to his son, sought to remain neutral: Mallarmé's position is less clear, as we see in a later chapter.[33] Whatever the exquisite or excessive things poet and painter said, however, neither Régnier nor Julie Manet is prepared to tell us about them in any detail.

In his brief comment on Monet in the 1876 article on the Impressionists, Mallarmé focuses on his love of water. This was the period when the artist was producing his wonderfully luminous studies of Argenteuil, often taken from the studio boat that Manet was also to depict and that he himself painted in an oil dating from the same year as Mallarmé's article, *Le Bateau-atelier* (The studio boat), now in the Barnes Collection. As the poet states, it is Monet's "especial gift to portray [water's] mobility and transparency, be it sea or river, grey and monotonous, or colored by the sky. I have never seen a boat poised more lightly on the water than in his pictures, or a veil more mobile and light than his moving atmosphere. It is in truth a marvel" (*DSM*, 1: 80).

Their friendship seems to have been fostered, as was often the case with Mallarmé and artists, by Morisot, whose Thursday dinners frequently winkled Monet away from his gardens at Vétheuil and later Giverny. He was among those who gathered to hear Mallarmé's "*causerie*" (chat) on Villiers de l'Isle Adam and seems to have responded to it with sympathetic understanding. The novelist Octave Mirbeau, apologizing to Mallarmé for his absence from the lecture, asserted that "Monet's enthusiasm gave my regrets a particular form: it made me detest these dreadful lands of the south for having deprived me of you" (*Corr.,* IV: 75). Mallarmé and Monet enjoyed a cordial and untroubled friendship, although, as Lloyd Austin affirms, it again seems to be that in general the poet understood the painter better than Monet understood Mallarmé (*Corr.,* III: 212). While more than twenty letters from Monet to Mallarmé have been preserved, Monet seems to have been less meticulous in keeping those of Mallarmé. Monet did, however, safeguard a letter to which the poet had attached the following delightful rhyming address, impossible to capture fully in English:

Monsieur Monet, que l'hiver ni
L'été sa vision ne leurre,
Habite, en peignant, Giverny
Sis auprès de Vernon, dans l'Eure

(M. Monet, whose gaze neither winter nor
Summer can deceive,
Lives where he likes to draw,
In the Ere, near Vernon, at Giverny) (*OC*, 88)

This is the only rhyming address so far found for Monet, although in a later letter, dated September 22, 1890, the artist thanked Mallarmé for his "kind address," while expressing an understandable degree of amazement that it hadn't been stolen by an "intelligent mailman" (*Corr.*, IV: 131). The letter itself contains an ecstatic response to Monet's exhibition of ten sea paintings he had made at Antibes. Mallarmé writes, "I've just left, dazzled, the work you did this winter; I've long placed what you do above everything else, but I believe that you are now in your finest hour. Oh, yes! as poor Edouard [Manet] loved to repeat, Monet is a genius" (*Corr.*, III: 212). Monet had traveled to the Mediterranean with Renoir in December 1883 but had returned after only a month, confiding to the art collector Paul Durand-Ruel, "I've always worked better in solitude and following my own impressions." [34] Part of what may well have attracted Mallarmé to Monet was the importance of a slowly developed imaginative response to external stimuli, since, as the artist insisted, again to Durand-Ruel, it took time for him to assimilate a new landscape. [35] But there is also a strong possibility that these intensely colorful canvasses, with their powerful evocation of the pink and gold light of the South, recalled Mallarmé's own joyous response to the beauty of the Mediterranean coastline encountered more than twenty years earlier.

Something of what Mallarmé saw as the essence of his friend's creative nature is conveyed in his choice of Monet to illustrate the prose poem "La Gloire" for *Le Tiroir de laque*. The prose poem suggests—narrate would be far too strong a term—a train trip to Fontainebleau, in which the poet finds himself the unwilling companion of a crowd of day-trippers. The theme of leisure, the motif of the train and the autumnal forest, the transformation of both the train conductor and the vehicle itself into mythological entities are all lightly and wittily adumbrated here, and if none of this seems to have fired Monet's imagination, the reason may lie primarily with the medium he was asked to use. As he explains in a letter of October 1889,

I'M REALLY ASHAMED OF MY BEHAVIOR and I deserve all your reproaches, but it's not ill will on my part as you could well think, the real truth is that I feel incapable of doing anything worthwhile for you, and perhaps there's too much vanity in that but truly as soon as I try to do the slightest thing with chalks what I produce is absurd and without any interest, as a result unworthy of accompanying your exquisite poems ("Glory" delighted me and I'm afraid I don't possess the talent I'd need to do you something that's any good) so don't think it's a vulgar defeat. That's alas the pure truth, so forgive me, and above all forgive me for having taken so much time to confess it to you. You know the sympathy and admiration I feel for you, well let me prove it to you by offering you as a memento of our friendship a little canvas, a sketch, that I'll bring you when I come to Paris one of these days and that you'll give me the pleasure of accepting just as simply as I offer it to you. (*Corr.,* III: 363)

Mallarmé's response to this fine (if breathless) letter indicates yet another parallel between his vision of art and that of Monet, for although he assures his friend that the sketches are no doubt far better than he fears, he goes on to affirm that he respects the painter's "solitary shyness" (Corr., III: 364): [36] Mallarmé himself, as countless of his letters to publishers and editors remind us, hated parting with any of his own works that he considered imperfect. In choosing as compensation what he was to describe to Régnier as "a magnificent Monet" (*Corr.,* IV: 137), *Le Train à Jeufosse,*[37] Mallarmé no doubt discovered some of the qualities he had hoped to find in the illustration he'd dreamed of for the prose poem, but the two men were clearly linked by much deeper similarities than those of mere subject matter and treatment. There is a hint in a letter dated July 9, 1890,[38] that Monet provided Mallarmé with a particularly powerful lens for looking at the external world: "You dazzled me recently with your haystacks, Monet, so much so that I catch myself looking at fields through the memory of your painting; or rather, they insist on being seen in that way" (*Corr.,* IV: 119). Here, in wonderfully concise and unpretentious language, Mallarmé suggests the essence of the great works of art, their power to change the ways in which we see things, however familiar those things may be.

In April 1892, in a letter to their mutual friend Octave Mirbeau, we find Mallarmé again expressing his intense delight in Monet's vision: "Where exhibitions are concerned, I for my own part have reached the point of looking at nothing but the Monet, hanging on my own wall, it delights me and that's enough. How lovely the poplars were; and now he's in front of a cathedral; the man is a true genius" (*Corr.,* V: 65). Monet's series of fifteen paintings of poplars on the river Epte had been on display in an exhibition in Durand-Ruel's gallery in March.[39] It was to be another three years before he put on view some of that masterly series of paintings of the cathedral at Rouen, mentioned in passing in Mallarmé's letter. Underlying this series is Monet's realization that, as he put it in a letter to his wife, "everything changes, even stone."[40] If Mallarmé wrote to Monet about that exhibition, the letter has not yet been found, but it's hard to imagine, given his love of the fleeting and the barely perceptible, that he would not have delighted in this amazing series of paintings.

Their friendship drew on other aspects of their personalities as well, of course. In one letter, for instance, Monet wrote reminding Mallarmé that he had promised to send some recipes for chanterelle mushrooms, which were growing abundantly in the Giverny area just then. While the gifted art critic Gustave Geffroy included part of Mallarmé's reply in the tribute to Monet that he published in 1924, he did not include the recipes, although a subsequent letter from Monet suggests they were indeed sent (*Corr.,* IV: 131). The winter of 1890–91 also saw Mallarmé striving to help his friend's son Jean, who had been seriously ill, get an extended period of leave from the army.

When Mallarmé died, Monet and his wife were in England, "in despair at being so far away," as Germaine Hoschédé, Mme Monet's daughter, wrote to Julie Manet (*Corr.,* X: 303). The friendship between Monet and Mallarmé had been long and calm, based on a deep conviction of each other's worth.

In Mallarmé's plans for a publication of the rhyming addresses he took such delight in writing, he initially drew up a list of artists, headed by the American-born painter James McNeill Whistler. When *Les Récréations postales* (Postal recreations) became *Les Loisirs de la poste* (The leisures of the post), Whistler's role in energetically promoting its publication was again acknowledged by Mallarmé's placing of his quatrain at the beginning of the section devoted to artists:

Leur rire avec la même gamme
Sonnera si tu te rendis
Chez Monsieur Whistler et Madame,
Rue antique du Bac 110

(The laugh, with its same scale, will ring out when
You go to the house of Mister
And Mrs. Whistler
On the antique rue du Bac, number 110) (*OC,* 88)

Whistler's laugh, so memorably captured here, also marked the review to which Whistler contributed, the *Whirlwind,* which claimed to be "eccentric, *original* and indiscreet,"[41] and which inspired Mallarmé's poem "Billet à Whistler" (Letter to Whistler):

Pas les rafales à propos
De rien comme occuper la rue
Sujette au noir vol de chapeaux;
Mais une danseuse apparue

Tourbillon de mousseline ou
Fureur éparse en écumes
Que soulève par son genou
Celle même dont nous vécûmes

Pour tout, hormis lui, rebattu
Spirituelle, ivre, immobile
Foudroyer avec le tutu,
Sans se faire autrement de bile

Sinon rieur que puisse l'air
De sa jupe éventer Whistler.

(Not the squalls whose sole task
Is to occupy the street
Subject to the black flight of hats,
But a ballerina who's appeared

A muslin whirlwind or
A fury scattered like foam

That lifts with her knee
The very muslin for whom we lived

To whip everything but him,
Once more, witty, drunk and motionless
With her tutu
and with no other sign of rage

Except a laugh that lets the air
Of her skirt fan Whistler.) (*OC,* 65)

While Whistler professed himself "delighted" with the sonnet and found the final couplet "superb, the work of a dandy,"[42] Mallarmé and Whistler rarely discussed each other's art at any length in their letters. They did not become friends, after all, until the mid-1880s, when each was already well established, if not in the mind of the public, at least in their own perceptions of art. Each, moreover, was more concerned with discussing his efforts to promote the other's work—Mallarmé, for instance, in encouraging the French government to buy the beautiful portrait of the artist's mother, and Whistler in finding an English publisher for Mallarmé's rhyming addresses. Whistler did, however, indicate the extent to which a book was for him, as it was for Mallarmé, a physical object to be admired and cherished for its appearance as well as for its intellectual contents. One can detect here clear parallels with his own interest in the framing and placing of his paintings, when he responds to the dedicated copy of Mallarmé's *Pages* that his friend had sent him: "What a fine book —first and foremost! Dear friend, what a pleasure to open it—to run one's hand over it—to feel with one's finger tips the coolness of the pages—the relief of the letters! And then the examination of the bold paper—perfect in weight and color! And now the joy—which also borders on the criminal—of slowly cutting the pages— and sweetly savoring as you turn the seductive morsels that sing for your eyes—just as it should be!—Yes—what a fine book!"[43] For his part, Mallarmé's most important appreciation of his friend's art seems to have been in a conversation during one of his Tuesday evening gatherings. Geneviève's future husband, Edmond Bonniot, recounts that Mallarmé presented Whistler as the artist who, above all others, wanted all the works he completed to be masterpieces, by which he meant not so much "perfect," whatever that might mean, but attaining the highest possible degree of impersonality. "Whistler," Bonniot reports that Mallarmé concluded, "is still the old style of painting, but in what hands!"[44] Such a statement clearly identifies Whistler as Mallarmé's painterly alter ego, separated from Impressionism to the same extent that Mallarmé himself remains separated from, yet sympathetic to, the Symbolist movement and especially those experimenting in *vers libre.* Where Mallarmé comes closest to an appreciation of Whistler's unique gifts, his wonderful ability to seize what John Walker has termed "all the indistinctness of failing illumination,"[45] is in a fleeting indication in a letter he wrote from the little seaport of Honfleur in the late summer of 1892: "Honfleur is in a wonderful region, nowhere else possesses so much greenery bordering the water, which, while it's not the ocean, is nevertheless enchanting. The little old Normandy port is a series of etchings. Whistler isn't here, he's washing his eyes in the grass of the rue du Bac."[46] What Mallarmé then does in a single sentence in this letter—and it's one of those that most clearly reveal his great talent for friendship—is to fill Honfleur with the presence not only of his absent friend but also of Whistler's much-loved wife, Trixie: "Madame Whistler, there are roses here that have so strong a perfume, at the Honfleur market, that I miss you; and everywhere there are blue China plates."[47]

One of the elements that played a central role in bonding these two men, to the amazement of their friends, was no doubt the image of art that Whistler expressed in his "Ten o'clock" lecture, translated by Mallarmé with the assistance of both George Moore and Francis Viélé-Griffin. Mallarmé must have been struck by Whistler's definition of the first artist as "that inventor of the beautiful—who perceived in the nature all about him, curious curves—as one sees faces in the fire—that solitary dreamer" (*OC,* 571–72). Rejecting mimetic art, Whistler places all his emphasis on the artist's power of transformation, his or her ability to perceive nature's hidden lessons of dignity and grace:

A ND WHEN THE EVENING MIST clothes the riverside with poetry, as with a veil, and the poor buildings lose themselves in the dim sky, and the tall chimneys become campanili, and the warehouses are palaces in the night, and the whole city hangs in the heavens, and fairy-land is before us—then the wayfarer hastens home; the working man and the cultured one, the wise man and the one of pleasure, cease to understand, as they have ceased to see, and Nature, who, for once has sung in tune, sings her exquisite song to the artist alone, her son and her master—her son in that he loves her, her master in that he knows her. [. . .] He does not confine himself to purposeless copying, without thought, each blade of grass as commended by the inconsequent, but, in the long curve of the narrow leaf, corrected by the straight tall stem, he learns how grace is wedded to dignity, how strength enhances sweetness, that elegance shall be the result. [. . .] In all that is dainty and loveable, he finds hints for his own combinations.[48]

This is very close to Mallarmé's own perception: "What is the point of that marvel which consists in transposing a fact of nature almost into its vibratory disappearance, according to the play of language, however; if it's not in order to set free from it, without the interference of a close or concrete reminder, the pure notion" (*OC,* 368). Mallarmé's medallion of Whistler sums him up in ways that suggest parallels if not between artistic goals then at least between the image each had of the artist: "the enchanter of a work of mystery, as tightly closed as perfection itself, which the mob would pass by without even feeling hostility toward it." And he closes his portrait with this astonishing description "a Dragon, battling, exulting, precious and worldly" (*OC*, 532).

While the friendship that united Mallarmé and Whistler is something of an oddity, less of a profound meeting of minds than a delicate balancing trick, another of Mallarmé's friendships with artists is both far more comprehensible and had a far greater impact on his writing. As Rosaline Bacou has so admirably put it, "The meeting of Mallarmé and Redon is one of the essential facts in the history of symbolism."[49] It was their mutual acquaintance, the novelist Joris-Karl Huysmans, who brought the two men together. In February 1885 Odilon Redon, responding to a suggestion from Huysmans, sent the poet a copy of the lithographs he had created in homage to Francisco José de Goya. Mallarmé answered with a delighted commentary that from the outset indicates a sense of wondering recognition: "A truly strange empathy made you portray in the delicious, mad hermit the poor little man who, in the depths of my soul, I would love to be" (*Corr.*, II: 280). Because the figure in the lithograph concerned is so indeterminate, what is stranger for us, looking at Mallarmé's reading of it, is his eagerness to suggest a meeting of minds so early in the relationship. Redon was to send him several books of his lithographs. On New Year's Day, 1888, for instance, we find Mallarmé beautifully responding to illustrations Redon had produced for Gustave Flaubert's *Temptation of Saint Anthony:* "It's an old and new joy to see again those inspired illustrations of many of our baffling dreams: that you've expressed here silently, with such subtlety and grief!" (*Corr.*, III: 158). Here, in one of his marvelously elliptical evocations, Mallarmé indicates how his correspondent has not only awoken old joys by triggering the suggestive power of memory, but has also created new ones, by making possible further discoveries and further interpretations. Baudelaire's admiration for Flaubert's novel,[50] which he had seen in an earlier version, may well have played a role in Mallarmé's fondness for the work, but there is no mistaking the fact that Redon has touched a very personal nerve here, as the expression "many of our baffling dreams" hints at, through both its message and its formulation.

In the summer of 1888 Redon became one of Mallarmé's neighbors, staying at Samois, the village next to Valvins. By December 1888 Redon had become "My good and dear Redon," and Mallarmé's delight in the second series of Saint Anthony lithographs[51] is, if anything, more strongly expressed than his joy in the first series: "But, my dear friend, here you've reflected for me a complete mystery, that no one else has glimpsed. I'm still stupefied by your image of Death, its upper body a skeleton, but below a powerful coil that one guesses never ends: I don't think any other artist has created or poet dreamed so absolute an image!" (*Corr.*, III: 279). The following month, it was through Mallarmé's good offices that Redon was invited to submit his work to an exhibition of painter-engravers at Durand-Ruel's gallery (*Corr.*, III: 281). When Redon's son, Ari, was born in April 1889, Mallarmé sent the following delighted note to his friend: "He'll be a little cabin boy for the Valvins boat, on which he has already sailed" (*Corr.,* III: 312). This was a promise Mallarmé renewed that summer in several notes inviting his friends to join him on the yacht that Paul Valéry was later unforgettably to describe as being "forever literary." Geneviève was subsequently to become godmother to Ari Redon. It was also when he was spending a summer near Samois, this time in 1890, that Redon fell in love with the wife of Mallarmé's cousin, the writer Paul Margueritte, a passion revealed six years later when the Marguerittes entered into a protracted divorce case (*Corr.,* VIII: 299). In telling her father about the affair, Geneviève wickedly refers to the painter as "Saint Redon," in a formula that both plays on his Saint Anthony series and hints at the difference between Redon's reputation and his real personality, but that also, I think, warns her father that his relationship with Méry Laurent risks earning him a similar sobriquet (*DSM,* 2: 252).

In 1890 the two friends set off together for Belgium, where Redon was to exhibit his work and Mallarmé was to give his lecture on Villiers. A brief and playful rhyming missive to Mme Redon assures her that her husband will be well looked after: "Je conduirai Redon / Jusqu'à son édredon" (which could be translated as "I'll see Redon is led / Safely to his cozy bed") (*Corr.,* IV: 45). Later letters continue to show Mallarmé helping his friend wherever possible. Just before setting out for England, for instance, he urged Durand-Ruel to look favorably on Redon's request for an exhibition in his gallery, a plea that helped set up the largest exhibition that had been held of the painter's work to that date. And in the last years of his life, Mallarmé dreamed of publishing his experimental *Un coup de dés* (A throw of the dice) with lithographs produced by Redon. A letter from the printer Ambroise Vollard to Redon in July 1897 sheds interesting light on this project and Mallarmé's vision of it:

As FAR AS THE *COSMOPOLIS* IS CONCERNED [this is the periodical that first published the Un *coup de dés*], I'll send it to you forthwith. In this regard I believe it important, if the work is to succeed, that the illustrations should be in black. I'm also very eager that the illustrations be *large,* given that I'll be selling the work at the price of *50 francs* per copy, and it will be bought to a very large extent for its *engravings,* since people can get the text in the *Cosmopolis* for about a franc. If the illustrations were not larger than in *The Haunted House* to give an example I'd run a great risk of getting my fingers burnt. If I remember correctly you told me earlier that you were afraid of weighing down the text if the engravings were too large, but the author considers, on the contrary, that it is vital to the success of his work that the engravings should indeed be very large—not that he's spoken to me about them specifically but it came up very simply in regard to a plate of the *Apocalypse* that I showed him, the one where there is a "character sitting down and holding a book, his animals at his feet," and Monsieur Mallarmé after saying how much he admired it added:

"Yes, but for the plates Redon makes me for my work, it's essential that the background be depicted: otherwise, if the illustration is on a white background, it will merely replicate the design of my text which is black and white." (*Corr.,* IX: 241n. 3)

Although Redon made four illustrations, the project eventually foundered when the publishers, the Didot house, faced with the unprecedented novelty of Mallarmé's poem, refused to publish the work of a man they considered insane.

Redon's last letter to Mallarmé was written in April 1898, full of the *Coup de dés* project and looking forward to meeting the "hermit," as he called the poet, in Valvins. On hearing of Mallarmé's death he sent a moving letter to Marie Mallarmé: "It was only yesterday, in the evening, that we learned of the terrible misfortune that has struck you and that fills us with grief. We wanted to send you our condolences as quickly as possible; believe them to be sincere and very tenderly affectionate and respectful in this great misfortune, and this void that such a death creates in me" (*Corr.,* X: 311).

Mallarmé and Redon, for all the differences in their techniques, are in many ways strikingly similar. That each should draw on a series of central and repeated images to re-create their own inner life is hardly surprising; what is astonishing is the similarity in the choice of images. Those that seem to me most central to the inner life of these two creative figures are the ships that in both convey the sense of spiritual journeys through life into the unknown; the flowers whose ability to suggest that they are both flora and fauna and whose refusal to be easily identified as belonging to a particular species break free from the late nineteenth century's mania for classification and thus argue in terms that are both personal and political the need for the indeterminate, the unclassifiable, the purely imaginary; and the bowl or vase that promises to body forth flowers never before seen, beauty never yet experienced, and thus symbolizes the free-wheeling world of fantasy. All three images carry an indeterminable weight of tradition and memory—individual, historical, and mythological—but all three also act as markers in a purely personal history, an autobiography, or at least a self-portrait that both Mallarmé and Redon invite us to perceive, however much they may turn away from the narcissistic reflections of self associated with conventional uses of the genre. Of all the painters whose company he enjoyed, and who in turn clearly delighted in his presence, Redon seems most to have accepted Mallarmé's genius on its own terms, to have perceived something of what he was doing, and to have valued him not just as a comrade but also as an intellect and an artist.

In exploring the friendships Mallarmé formed with artists, we can easily perceive what united him with some of those in his circle. There are strong similarities, for instance, between Mallarmé's personality and convictions, and the imaginative intensity of Redon, or the sensuality and the evocative nature of the art of Manet,

Monet, Morisot, and Renoir. Equally, Whistler's vision of art and fascination with seizing the transient, particularly in terms of light and weather, offer parallels with Mallarmé's exploration of these phenomena in his poetry. Yet there seems at first glance much less that binds the poet to Edgar Degas. Many Degas paintings, after all, create in the viewer a sense of indefinable but inescapable unease. One thinks, for instance, of the infinite gap between man and woman in *L'Intérieur* (*The Interior*) of 1868–69; the tensions and irritation expressed by the couple in *Bouderie* (*Sulking*) of 1869 to 1871; the 1865 *La Femme aux crysanthèmes* (*Woman with Chrysanthemums*), with its inexplicable balances and its opaque suggestions; and the many café and theater scenes that emphasize loneliness and isolation rather than the sharing of experience. It's an unease that seems far removed from the intellectual unease Mallarmé's poems may arouse, for in Degas's case the feeling is primarily social or experiential. Degas's crustiness and irascibility is beautifully evoked in Julie Manet's depiction of Mallarmé, Renoir, Monet, and Degas setting up the exhibition of Morisot's works after her death. Furious that his friends wanted to move a screen[52] from one room where he liked it to another, and to replace it with a seat for the benefit of weary viewers, Degas fulminated that *he* would be willing to stand for thirteen hours if necessary, contended that he didn't care a jot for the public, which would never learn to see in any case, and eventually stormed out of the room, barely shaking hands with his friends.[53] Among all those who gathered in Morisot's studio to hear Mallarmé talk about Villiers de l'Isle Adam, it was the cantankerous Degas who stormed out before the end, muttering that he couldn't understand a word of it. Indeed, Mallarmé, who sometimes found Degas's violence so disruptive as to border on the self-destructive, gave his friend the nickname of "the Rigorous One," and his bitterness and irony were such that even his best jokes froze the laughter on his hearers' lips (*VM*, 684). Although Degas took pleasure in writing poetry, a pleasure alluded to in the rhyming address for him—

Rue, au 23, Ballu.
          J'exprime
Sitôt Juin à Monsieur Degas
La satisfaction qu'il rime
Avec la fleur des syringas.

(23 rue Ballu. As soon as June
I say: "What a boon
Rhymes M. Degas
With a syringa.) (*OC*, 89)

—and studied assiduously Banville's treatise on French versification, which had been published in 1872, his conception of poetry was so far from that of Mallarmé that it was not in this common interest that their friendship was founded. After all, in one of Mallarmé's most famous epigrams, he responded to the painter's complaint that he'd wasted an entire day on a sonnet, even though he had plenty of ideas for it, with the dryly elliptical statement "It's not with ideas that one makes poetry, Degas, it's with words" (*VM*, 684). As Valéry puts it, "Nothing was more different from the *deliberately harsh* character, the directness that bordered on brutality, that you found in Degas, than the character that Mallarmé had *deliberately* created."[54] Nevertheless, something in Degas's vision appealed sufficiently to Mallarmé for him to invite the artist to contribute a drawing for the ill-fated *Tiroir de laque*. It may well be that Mallarmé was attracted to Degas because of the enthusiasm his friend, the art critic and novelist Huysmans, so energetically expressed for the painter. Michael Tilby, exploring this attraction Huysmans felt for Degas, offers a suggestion that would be equally true for Mallarmé: "Degas's art constantly surprises us. But above all he fascinates us through the way in which his works always appear to contain several possible representations, possibilities that one would often call incompatible with each other."[55] Perhaps, also, it was the representation of ballet that appealed to Mallarmé, or Degas's rejection of an easily interpretable anecdote in his painting. Certainly he would have been attracted to Degas's rejection of facility, his vision of the painting as "a series of operations,"[56] and his insistence on the artist's need at times simply to be alone: "You must immerse yourself in solitude," he wrote in his notebook in the spring of 1856. And, at least according to Valéry, "He could also be charming."[57] In the same way that Degas himself strikes many of us as "a formidable enigma," as his biographer Roy McMullen calls him,[58] so the relationship between painter and poet defies logic and reason. When Mallarmé had been able to persuade his friend Henri Roujon, whom the government had recently appointed director of fine arts, to offer to buy a Degas canvas for the Louvre, the painter flew into a rage, because, as he caustically explained to the writer and librettist Ludovic Halévy, "These people want to convince me I'm successful. Successful, what does that mean? You're always successful, and you're never successful—what do they mean, successful! It means being on a wall side by side with a lady by Bouguereau and a slave market by Toto Girod? I want none of it."[59]

The 1876 article on Manet and the Impressionists sheds some light on Mallarmé's vision of Degas's art: "A master of drawing, he has sought delicate lines and movements exquisite and grotesque, and of a strange new beauty" (*DSM*, 1: 82). The stress on newness and strangeness, on the blend of the exquisite and the grotesque, recalls Baudelaire's conviction that beauty was always bizarre and always composite.[60] A further clue to what he saw in Degas may be found when Mallarmé, in a brief article on ballet expanding on the initial statement "La Cornalba delights me" (*OC*, 303), affirms, "The ballerina is *not a woman who dances,* for these juxtaposed reasons that she *is not a woman,* but a metaphor resuming one of the elementary aspects of our form, a blade, cup, flower, etc., and because *she does not dance,* suggesting, by the miracle of shortcuts or leaps, with a corporeal writing what would take paragraphs in dialogued or descriptive prose: she's a poem set free from all the apparel of a scribe" (*OC,* 304). Degas's ballerinas, painted or sketched, do have the quality of metaphors, indications of femininity rather than depictions of women, and their movements, like the gestures of his singers and musicians, do suggest the body as hieroglyph.[61] Similarly, paintings such as *Bouderie* and *La Femme aux crysanthèmes* convey his belief (later abandoned) in the speaking power of expression and gesture. Just as the ballet, for Mallarmé, represented enigmatic art (*OC,* 306), much of Degas's painting may have appealed to him in the same way—as a series of signs inviting and always finally eluding interpretation.

It appears that no letter from Degas was sent to Geneviève and Mme Mallarmé on the poet's death. Perhaps the jingoism and anti-Semitism he revealed during the Dreyfus Affair had brought this surprising friendship to an end.

Throughout Mallarmé's writing, public or private, there can also be found references to other painters, at least one of whom had relatively little to do with the loosely knit group of artists we have just considered. Puvis de Chavannes was above all a painter of murals, portraying a vision closer to classicism than to the modernism of the Impressionists. While Manet represented a link with Baudelaire, who had recognized the painter's genius at an early stage and about whom he frequently talked, Mallarmé may have felt that through Puvis he was able to learn more about Théophile Gautier, who, in his role as art critic, claimed to have discovered him.[62] After all, as Kurt Wais points out in his biography, Gautier's *Italia* and *Le Roman de la momie* (The novel of the mummy) were among the first works in Mallarmé's boyhood library.[63] Puvis attended Morisot's dinners, and his signature joins that of Whistler and Mallarmé on Mme Rodenbach's fan, in a curious juxtaposition that implies something about the social life of fin-de-siècle Paris.

The correspondence, however, reveals little real enthusiasm for Puvis's neo-Hellenistic style. Indeed, in an 1896 letter to Whistler we find a postscript reporting that there is an exhibition of Puvis's work, but that Mallarmé hasn't yet seen it, and he didn't attend the banquet in Puvis's honor. By March of 1898 Mallarmé stated in a letter to Charles Morice that he was not in close or frequent contact with Puvis (*Corr.,* X: 124), yet he did write a sonnet in homage to the artist. Perhaps he was attracted merely by the possibility of the rhymes, as the first tercet of the sonnet runs as follows: "Par avance ainsi tu vis / O solitaire Puvis / de Chavannes jamais seul" (*OC,* 72). (Henry Weinfield renders this "Thus you come before the van / O solitary Puvis de Chavannes / never alone.)[64]

Although Mallarmé's love of painting offers a filigree running through all his adult existence, it wasn't the only art, by any means, that gave him pleasure. Edouard Dujardin, in his reminiscences of Mallarmé, asserts that "music revealed itself to Mallarmé and the symbolists, not as an art of virtuosity, piano or violin concerto, scales and acrobatics, but as the profound voice of things."[65] According to him, this Schopenhauerian concept was magnificently explored and extended in Richard Wagner's brilliant study of Beethoven, published in translation in the *Revue Wagnérienne*. Whether Dujardin, who after all was the editor of the review, is right in placing so much weight on Schopenhauerian and indeed Wagnerian ideas in the development of Mallarmé's musical sensitivity and knowledge, it remains true that many of the poet's friends were ardent Wagnerians, and that, according to his daughter, his interest in music was indeed a product of his maturity. Geneviève Mallarmé attests, "It was around 1885 that the magic of music opened up to my father. As a young man he disdained it."[66] Yet, as Suzanne Bernard points out,[67] Mallarmé's friend Eugène Lefébure had written to him as early as 1869, encouraging him to pursue his plan of studying music, although it is arguable that this reference may allude not so much to music in the common meaning of the word as to the musicality of poetry. In mid-October 1874, however, Mallarmé received a letter that seems to provide clearer evidence of an interest in music that predates the *Revue Wagnérienne:* J. Cressonnois, conductor of the Concert des Champs-Elysées, addressing the poet as "his dear friend," wrote assuring him of his assistance "where [his] profession is concerned," no doubt for the musical side of the fashion magazine Mallarmé was writing at that time, *La Dernière Mode (Corr.,* IV: 587). And while Mallarmé's writings frequently and rather truculently affirm the primacy of poetry over music, in what Valéry was to term "sublime jealousy,"[68] the younger poet, looking back in 1931 to the rise of pure poetry in France during the second half of the nineteenth century, is in no doubt that "any literary history of the end of the nineteenth century that does not speak of music will be of no avail."[69] He argues indeed that

> nothing can be understood of the poetic movement that developed from 1840 or 50 to the present day, if the profound and capital role that music played in that remarkable transformation is not revealed, elucidated, and clarified. The French public's musical education—and in particular that of a growing number of French writers—contributed more than all theoretical considerations to orient poetry towards a purer destiny and to eliminate from its works all that prose can render perfectly well. [. . .] This kind of re-education of poetry (considered in the period that runs from 1880 to 1890) had Lamoureux and the Lamoureux Concerts as agents of the highest importance. For Baudelaire it was the Pasdeloup Concerts, for Mallarmé and his followers it was the Lamoureux Concerts.[70]

Charles Lamoureux (1834–1899) was a violinist but owes his fame to his skills as a conductor and to the foundation of the series of concerts that he instituted in 1860 and that still bear his name. He and Mallarmé knew each other socially. Three visiting cards from the musician to Mallarmé have been preserved, and Mallarmé probably wrote to him quite often, requesting tickets for the concerts, which he faithfully attended through the winter months. In 1892 he wrote the only letter to Lamoureux that has been found so far, accompanied by the following rhyming address:

> Les poëtes n'ayant pour eux
> Que l'antique lyre bizarre
> Invoquent Monsieur Lamoureux
> Soixante-deux R. Saint-Lazare

> (Poets, who pluck the lyre bizarre
> In an antiquated purr
> Call on M. Lamoureux
> 62 rue Saint-Lazare.) (*Corr.*, V: 139)

Through these concerts Mallarmé discovered the works not just of the great composers of the past but also of such contemporaries as Vincent d'Indy, Camille Saint-Saëns, Emmanuel Chabrier, Ernest Amédée Chausson, Claude Debussy, and Edouard Lalo among others. The ambitious nature of these concerts can be gauged from a program of January 18, 1891: Felix Mendelssohn's *Ruy Blas* overture was followed by Robert Schumann's *Symphony in D Minor,* d'Indy's *The Enchanted Forest,* Saint-Saëns's *Danse macabre,* the funeral march from Wagner's *Götterdämmerung,* and Chabrier's *España.*

Scattered through Mallarmé's correspondence can be found echoes of these concerts, indications of how he responded to them, and a shadowy outline of his musical tastes. A letter written to Whistler in December 1892, for instance, confides that "there's a certain fragment of the choral symphony that haunts me; I've begun to write something about it" (*Corr.*, V: 171). If he did write an article on Beethoven's *Ninth Symphony,* it has, unfortunately, not been found, although, as Lloyd Austin suggests (*Corr.*, V: 171n1), a brief passage in the Oxford and Cambridge lecture on music and literature may well allude to that combination of choirs and orchestra.

Yet however important the Lamoureux concerts were in providing opportunities to hear music, Mallarmé's knowledge of contemporary music also resulted from a group of friends he had known since long before he started making his weekly pilgrimage to the Séances Populaires de Musique de Chambre. His friend Henri Cazalis had mentioned in a letter written in early 1864 that he had met a passionately musical young woman, to whom he was clearly sexually attracted. This was the highly gifted, ebullient, and very beautiful Augusta Holmès, who at the time Cazalis met her was not yet seventeen. She was to become the mistress of Mallarmé's friend Catulle Mendès, the reason that Gautier so opposed the latter's marriage to his daughter, and the cause of Mendès's and Judith Gautier's subsequent divorce. A talented composer, Holmès wrote several operas, set her own poetry (and that of others) to music, and achieved considerable fame during her lifetime, a fame rapidly destroyed after her death, when her charismatic presence was no longer able to override the voices of envy and prudery, who condemned her for what they would probably have unhesitatingly accepted in a man.[71] In 1870 Cazalis read "La Scène d'Hérodiade" to Mendès and Holmès, to the enormous enthusiasm of the young composer: "Have you received a dazzlingly enthusiastic letter from Augusta? I read her your Hérodiade. Your poetry intoxicated her for an entire evening" (*CC*, 472). After the fall of the Second Empire, Holmès, together with Mendès and Henri Regnault's fiancée, Geneviève Bréton, attempted to find work for Mallarmé with the publisher Hachette (*CC*, 492), and by July of 1871 the poet was addressing her in letters as his "dear friend." It was she who, at the end of that year, sent Mallarmé the news that he had been appointed to a Parisian lycée (*CC*, 532).

Cazalis, recalling this period of his youth later in life, spoke of the circle of artists and musicians who were his closest friends during these early years and draws attention to Holmès's role in revealing to them the music of Wagner, little appreciated in Paris at that time, as Baudelaire's study of *Tannhäuser* confirms and as anti-German sentiment makes in any case predictable. Like Judith Gautier, who published her study of Wagner in 1882, the young composer knew Wagner personally and drew inspiration from his concept of music in her own ambition, shared by many of the musicians who gathered around César Franck, to renew and enrich French music. An energetic and enthusiastic individual, she had chosen for her personal motto that of *Augusta per angusta*. An admirer of Manet, she was one of the few women to attend Mallarmé's Mardis, although she did so only occasionally, just as Mallarmé occasionally came to her Friday evening circle of artists and musicians, where he could meet, among others, his close friend Villiers de l'Isle Adam (*Corr.*, II: 57). Mallarmé's letters of the 1870s frequently mention her. She seems to have been close to Geneviève Mallarmé as well, as a typically impassioned letter of 1882 regretfully declines an invitation, explaining that she has just returned from Germany where "*Parsifal*, which is a wonder, the ascension of the Altkoenig, which is superb, and the 28 hours it took to return in the train, have somewhat shaken me" (*Corr.*, IV: 609). By the mid-1880s, however, although she still addressed Mallarmé as her "dear friend" (*Corr.*, IV: 615), we find him announcing the separation of Augusta and Catulle, with the laconic but telling comment "it was no longer charming between them" (*Corr.*, II: 297). A reconciliation took place, and at the end of the decade Mallarmé was responding warmly to an invitation to hear Holmès's music at one of the Colonne concerts at the Châtelet theater (*Corr.*, III: 300).

What did Mallarmé think of Holmès's compositions? The enthusiasm he expresses in letters to her suggests little more than common politeness, and while he may be entirely sincere, there is little indication that he responded with particular intensity to it, or applied to it the kind of intellectual questioning that he brought to literature, or the emotional delight he felt when looking at the paintings of his Impressionist friends. Régnier, never a neutral reporter where women were concerned, describes him making the following comment about her *Triumphal Ode:* "To give the people a celebration, which would demand so much preparation, and to improvise it in that way, would need the kind of shamelessness you find only in a woman" (*Annales,* notebook for August 1889 to March 1890).

Nevertheless, two address quatrains are included in Mallarmé's *Loisirs de la poste,* where they open the series to musicians, just as Whistler opens the series of those for artists. Other occasional verse was also addressed to her, together with new year's gifts of glacé fruits (*OC,* 117–18). Probably the most important role she played in the development of Mallarmé's thinking was in conveying to him, well before the appearance of the *Revue Wagnérienne,* the essence of Wagner's image of music, and her influence may well have been strongest in determining the rich ambivalences that mark his response to the *Gesamtkunstwerk* in his sonnet to Wagner and his *Reverie* devoted to the composer's work and ambitions. This ambivalence also marked his conversation, as we can see from the notes that one of the Mardistes, André Fontainas, took after a gathering in the rue de Rome on January 15, 1895:

> THE OTHER EVENING, MALLARMÉ WAS SAYING, and I think he's right, that the weak point in Wagner's theory lay in putting at the same rank poetry, music, and ballet. First, it seemed to him that Wagner nevertheless gave music an obvious predominance, such that poetry was subsumed into music, finding its starting point in music and returning to music,—whereas for Mallarmé the role of poetry was on the contrary the preponderant one.
>
> [. . .] But the serious objection is based on the nature of poetry and music on the one hand, and of ballet on the other. Ballet can no longer represent to a modern mind the traditional, regular, and plastic movement of the Ancients, and is in any case merely the materialized expression of what in the theater is conveyed by an author. It's a simple way of translating the meaning of musical and verbal sounds. Poetry and music, on the contrary, create the fiction, give it birth, and far from being a *means* of expression, they *are* what is expressed, or ought to be, by the scenic representation or even just by the imagination aroused by reading. Moreover Mallarmé hates the word poetry being used without distinction and so randomly that it is deprived of all meaning.[72]

Mallarmé's ambivalent response to Wagner, his realization of the man's genius, but his refusal to accept the composer's concept of art run through much of his thinking in the last decades of his life.

The possibility of hearing music performed was also part of the attraction of other social gatherings. In Belgium, for instance, Mallarmé attended a concert at which the Ysaÿe Quartet played, and his disciple Albert Mockel was also fond of inviting musicians to perform whenever Mallarmé or other Symbolist poets would be present. A few days before Christmas 1895, for instance, we finding him inviting André Gide and Stewart Merrill to a supper at his place, adding, "We'll probably make a little music, with Marcel Remy."[73] Mockel's enthusiasm for music is also evident in a reference to a performance of the first two acts of Wagner's *Tristan,* for which he particularly praised the orchestra for possessing "a limpidity and a power that dazzled and overwhelmed me."[74]

Musicians seem to have been even less careful about keeping Mallarmé's letters than were the artists. Tracing Mallarmé's friendships with composers through the correspondence is frequently frustrating, a series of brief encounters with ghosts and allusions. For instance, Mallarmé's friendship with Emmanuel Chabrier, who was almost his exact contemporary (1841–1894), is hinted at by a letter from the composer to the poet dated July, 18, 1888, the year in which Gustav Mahler wrote his first symphony, Richard Strauss finished *Don Juan,* and Friedrich Nietzsche published his study of Wagner. Mallarmé may, as Lloyd Austin suggests, have sent Chabrier a copy of his translation of Whistler's "Ten o'clock" lecture. Chabrier's response, whatever the cause, is warmly informal, indicative of a close friendship that has unfortunately left few other traces: "Affectionate embrace and sincere thanks given and sent to my friend Mallarmé by his colleague in rhythms" (*Corr.,* IV: 626). Chabrier's early death from tuberculosis in 1894 prompted Mallarmé to describe him, in a letter to his widow, as "a fervent and valiant man, and a superb artist cut short" (*Corr.,* VII: 57).

Mallarmé enjoyed a closer relationship with Ernest Chausson, whose wonderfully productive career was brought to an abrupt and premature end by a fatal bicycle accident in 1899 when the composer was only forty-four. From early in 1890, Chausson took English lessons from Mallarmé. Eleven cards and letters from the musician to the poet, the majority of them concerning the lessons, and fragments from a couple of letters—"I am, from afar, and from time immemorial, one of your fervent admirers" (*Corr.,* XI: 52; see also *Corr.,* XI: 99)—together with a witty address quatrain by Mallarmé are the only epistolary traces discovered so far of this relationship. In his quatrain, Mallarmé wrote,

> Arrête-toi porteur, au son
> Gémi par les violoncelles,
> C'est chez Monsieur Ernest Chausson,
> 21 Boulevard de Courcelles

> (At 21 Boulevard de Courcelles, oh
> Stop at the moaning cello.
> Bearer set your mind at rest:
> This is the home of Chasson, Ernest.) (*OC,* 91)

Chausson wrote to Mallarmé in 1892, asking how to subscribe to the monument for Baudelaire (*Corr.,* V: 129). In 1897, apologizing for having seen so little of him recently, Chausson invited his friend to dinner, with Odilon Redon, an invitation repeated in April of the following year. The musician was, moreover, a close friend of Camille Mauclair, whose novel *Le Soleil des morts* (The sun of the dead), with its admiring depiction of Mallarmé, is dedicated to "my friend, Ernest Chausson." On Mallarmé's death, Chausson wrote a brief but moving note to Mme Mallarmé: "I have just learned through the papers of the terrible news that sends all French literature into mourning" (*Corr.*, X: 281–82).

The contemporary musician most closely linked to Mallarmé's work is, no doubt, Claude Debussy, whose association with the Verlaine family—Verlaine's mother-in-law was Debussy's piano teacher, and her son Charles de Sivry played an important role in introducing him to the musicians, artists, and intellectuals who gathered at the nightclub known as Le Chat Noir—must also have played a role in his relationship with Mallarmé. As Paul Dukas was to claim, "The strongest influence that Debussy came under was that of the writers of his day, and not that of the musicians." [75] His aesthetic statements suggest a strong affinity with both Impressionist painting and Symbolist poetry. For him, music was "not confined to producing, more or less exactly, Nature, but the mysterious correspondences which link Nature with Imagination." [76] Although they exchanged few letters, Debussy attended the banquet given by the periodical *La Plume* in Mallarmé's honor, and by 1890, the year in which he was composing his settings of five poems by Baudelaire, he was to be found at the Mardis. [77] Indeed, the writer André-Ferdinand Herold claims to have introduced the two men, when he made it possible for Mallarmé to hear these settings of Baudelaire. [78] Late in 1894 Debussy invited Mallarmé to the first performance of his *Prélude à l'Après-midi d'un faune* (Prelude to the Afternoon of a Faun), referring to it as "the arabesques that a possibly blameworthy pride led me to believe were dictated by the Flute of your Faun" (*Corr.*, VII: 116n. 2). Although Mallarmé at first expressed surprise at such an enterprise, claiming that his poem had already put the theme to music, his letter of thanks after the performance was warm and sympathetic: "I've just left the concert and am deeply moved: what a marvel! your illustration of 'The Afternoon of a Faun' offers no dissonance with my text, except that it goes further, truly, in nostalgia and light, with finesse, uneasiness, and richness" (*CC*, 623). When he published the score in the following year, Debussy explained in his introduction that "the music in this Prelude is a very free illustration of Mallarmé's beautiful poem; it makes no claims to be a synthesis of the poem. It consists rather of a series of backdrops on which the desires and dreams of the faun move in the warmth of that afternoon" (*Corr.*, VII: 281). The quatrain Mallarmé included in the copy of the "Faune" he sent to Debussy in 1897 reflects a delicate desire to convey to the composer what Mallarmé saw as his greatest achievement in his *Prelude*:

Sylvain d'haleine première
Si ta flûte a réussi

Ouïs toute la lumière
Qu'y soufflera Debussy.

(Sylvain of ancient breath
If your flute succeeded
Listen to all the light
That Debussy will blow into it.) (*OC,* 114)

Henri de Régnier also leaves us a sharply etched image of Debussy and his transposition of Mallarmé's poem:

YESTERDAY AT THE HOME OF Debussy the musician, whom I found in a light,
sunny room at the top of a building on the rue Gustave Doré. He played
his "Afternoon of a faun" with a sort of quite exceptional languorous fury. He
looks Italian, with an intelligent face, black, almost frizzy hair. It's his stay at
the villa Médicis[79] that left on him the southern stamp. There's a kind of charm
in seeing him speak a little through his nose, something free and brusque
about him. There is in him a hint of the Calabrese shepherd mixed with an or-
chestral player. (*Annales,* Notebook 19)

In 1897 Debussy was present at the banquet given for Mallarmé at the restaurant
Père Lathuille (a popular eating place of which Degas has characteristically left a
somewhat disturbing picture). This banquet had originally been the brainchild of
Gide and Valéry, but it floundered in petty rivalries; indeed, some of Mallarmé's oldest and dearest friends had not been invited to it. Writing to his friend Pierre Louÿs,
Debussy claimed to have found the banquet prodigiously boring, a boredom he suspected that Mallarmé shared (quoted in *Corr.,* IX: 11). Debussy's letter to Mme Mallarmé and Geneviève after the poet's death is concise but poignant: "Allow me to join
my real and sharp pain to that which must be felt by all those who knew the admirable man who was Stéphane Mallarmé, and who have understood what a loss Art, in
all its manifestations, has just sustained" (*Corr.,* X: 283).

In light of the complexity of Mallarmé's relationships with artists and musicians,
it seems appropriate that 1898, the year of his death, was also that in which Emile
Zola was imprisoned for his courageous stand in the Dreyfus Affair, Oscar Wilde
wrote his "Ballad of Reading Jail," Richard Strauss composed *A Hero's Life,* and Auguste Rodin completed his portrayal of the power of the artist, his statue of the novelist Honoré de Balzac.

Love and Friendship

Tous de l'amitié. Sans ça l'on Ne saurait orner mon salon.
—Œuvres complètes, *171*

David Lodge, in his parodic novel *Small World,* has his French narratologist, Michel Tardieu, announce that each of us is a subject in search of an object.[1] Whether the object is the self or the other, letters provide a particular case of that search, as every letter constructs itself in relation to both the writer and a specific reader. Through their fragmentary, often one-sided nature, and through their creation of a private idiolect only partially penetrable by a modern reader, the epistolary exchanges of past centuries pose a particular challenge and offer a special fascination for the post-modern mind.[2] This idiolect, moreover, frequently depends in large part on an exploration of self and other in terms of a covert or overt sexual relationship. If it is true that Mallarmé's creative writing is a monument to beauty, it is perhaps even more true that many of his letters, poems, and occasional verse form a monument to love and friendship.[3] In this interlude I explore the ways in which Mallarmé's letters to Méry Laurent negotiate the creation of self and other within the late-nineteenth century's changing paradigms of gender-based expectations.

Mallarmé's letters to Méry Laurent (Figure 13) have long attracted the attention of scholars, not only because they cast a very different light on the intellectual nature of the man but also because, until very recently, many of them were not available for consultation. It has been argued that the 1996 publication of these letters leaves open the question of whether the poet of that paean to sublimated eroticism, "L'Après-midi d'un faune," was indeed Méry's lover or whether the two practiced a perfected form of the *amitié amoureuse*. Bertrand Marchal, who edited these letters, insists, for example, that they merely confirm convictions formed by the letters already published. Reading them as a group, separate from the other correspondence, however, lends them an intensity that makes it difficult to believe that in the late nineteenth century such expressions of fervor couched in those terms could be possible between people who were not lovers. Above all, a letter that seems to have been written in September 1891 contains a passage that it is difficult not to read as an expression of reciprocated erotic love:

I FEEL AT EVERY MINUTE that my place is wherever you are, and you already replace the landscapes. The feeling for you that I've sometimes stifled in favor of a true and good friendship easily becomes itself once more, you know it! and utterly invades me. I constantly [. . .] have you beside me, my friend: and am jealous of the instant when that will truly be the case. There's only you, you know. (*LML,* 78).

The feeling occasionally stifled in favor of friendship must, one feels, be that of erotic love. Both in the context of the time and in that of the other letters, it is all but impossible to read this passage merely as a statement of friendship, although it is also that.

What interests me more specifically in this set of letters, however, is the ways in which Mallarmé uses them to create an image of a perfect erotic friendship, especially through his use of the conventions, possibilities, and limitations of the letter form itself. The letter, as Bertrand Marchal points out in his introduction to this correspondence, becomes the kiss, given in the corners, "dans les coins," in secret but also in the corner of paper not yet covered with his writing. In addition, just as Edouard Manet's portraits of Méry create a certain vision of her, so do Mallarmé's letters create the Méry of this particular relationship, the Méry who is the delicious extract of vanity, warmth, and beauty of the poet's imagination. The trace she leaves—in the drawings of peacocks that embellish so many of the letters, in the rhetoric the two used, and in the network of echoes set up from letter to letter—is both palpable and fragmentary, all the more tantalizing for having so little connection with the personality detectable in the few letters and telegrams from her to Mallarmé that have been found.

Born Anne Rose Suzanne Louviot in 1849, Méry Laurent married at the age of fifteen, separated from her husband a few months later, and left Nancy for Paris in 1865. There she seems to have found some small roles on the stage and to have begun to establish herself as a courtesan. Bertrand Marchal, in his edition of Mallarmé's letters to Méry, suggests that, like Proust's Odette de Crécy, Méry Laurent was "an entire epoch," a summation of France's Third Republic. At some point, probably around 1874 or 1875, she met Thomas Evans, an American who had become the dentist and friend of Napoleon III and who continued to enjoy a powerful and comfortable existence under the new regime. Evans established Méry, around 1880, in a house on the rue de Rome, not far from Mallarmé's apartment. It was while living there that she became so close to the poet whose exploration of their friendship in letters and in poems has become such a monument to love and friendship. It seems likely that Mallarmé and Méry had first met long before that, however, as in 1873 both lived in the same apartment complex on the rue de Moscou (*LML,* 17), and

Méry's friendship with Manet probably meant that the two saw each other moderately often from 1876 on.

The long series of letters Mallarmé wrote to Méry are closely intertwined with the love poems inspired by her,[4] but they are also meditations on love itself. And to a considerable degree they re-create an idealized Méry who conforms to this image of love, in much the same way that Mallarmé re-created himself as child in his "autobiography" and in the anecdotes he told his friends about his childhood. Henri de Régnier's diary gives a rather different picture of the relationship. Of course it is not necessarily a more truthful account, as Régnier's own unhappy love life may have made him wish to transform the happiness of others into something distinctly less happy. The pervading melancholy in Régnier's poetry—the depiction of woman as unreliable, a physical representation of the transience of human relationships—suggests that the monocle through which he gazed at life was tinged with cynicism and encrusted with tears. Nevertheless, the diary entry deserves to be quoted as a further perspective on the relationship, especially because Mallarmé's reluctance to keep Méry's letters in case they were found by his wife or, worse still, by Geneviève means that Méry's voice is rarely heard. In July 1888 we find Régnier noting,

THE OTHER DAY AT MÉRY LAURENT'S. Champsaur, and Mallarmé, and Holmès. Still lovely despite her 40 years, Champsaur must surely be sleeping with her. In the middle of the living room stands an orchid, with metallic leaves and a single red flower, and Mallarmé the great explainer says: "What superb flesh, truly poisonous, and that flower, so red, wouldn't you say the feathers of a parrot's throat?" And when Méry tells him that when it reaches maturity the long red flower will weep, he adds, with that unique air of conviction which is his charm: "But it's a firework." (*Annales*, July 1888)

Régnier makes no comment on this curious exchange, and the phrase "Mallarmé the great explainer" offers itself to several, contradictory interpretations. Is it admiring or condemning or envious or a mixture of all of these descriptions? The two principal voices seem to be talking at odds—Méry about decay and old age, Mallarmé about the beauty of sudden destruction. And the expression "that unique air of conviction" suggests a charm that may be rather wearying over time. Moreover, the reference to the novelist and journalist Félicien Champsaur sleeping with Méry may possibly be innocent, or it may be mischievous, or it may simply indicate that the relationship between Mallarmé and Méry was not one of mutual fidelity. The couplet Mallarmé wrote for Champsaur takes on a particular light in this context: "quel chignon topaze ou saur / Subjugue à présent Champsaur?" (what hair, of topaz or icthyosaur, / currently subjugates Champsaur?) (*OC*, 171).

Two years later, in 1890, three passages in Régnier's diary shed a different light on matters. First we have a "singular conversation" in which Mallarmé considered the relationship between men and women: "The immodesty of showing oneself on a woman's arm—of the man's inferiority in this case and how it makes him look like a lackey. The woman's charity, her lack of disgust, which, when all's said and done, is nothing other than the long habit of receiving excrement in all its forms and even in the form of love. The woman's sex, an organ in a low and damp place. The man's sex a compliment, a kind of signature of living nature" (*Annales,* Notebook 13). Soon after this curious conversation we find Régnier again using the word "singulier": "Dined with Mallarmé at Méry L.'s. A singular situation developed. A delicious dinner, calm, with the windows open onto the evening and the trees as if mineralized against the night sky" (*Annales,* Notebook 13). Whatever it was that made Régnier detect a "singular situation"—the realization of the relationship between Méry and Mallarmé perhaps?—what strikes the reader of his diary is the way he turns away from it, to gaze out of the open window at the trees turned to mineral, as if some Ovidian metamorphosis has taken place amidst a happiness he doesn't share, or of a coming together of a male mind and female mind, a union that somehow excluded him. The hint of jealousy detectable here as Régnier refuses to acknowledge the possibility that someone else may be closer to Mallarmé than he himself takes a predictable form in the next entry that refers to Méry:

> I ARRIVE AT THE TALUS [Méry's home] around half past six. Méry Laurent clad in her cardinal's shawl and we strolled along the fortifications. In the grass I see my shoes lose the dust of the city. There's already something of the country about it, the evening comes softly, and there's a wind. We're chatting side by side and suddenly Mallarmé arrives unexpectedly and I see in the woman a little movement of pique at this surprise, at being spied on, perhaps a little irritation. We dine . . . with a hint of distance between us, a kind of difficulty in agreeing with one another, something a bit stiff which from time to time brought about a silence. Obviously there had been one of those mysterious little nothings that separate people and prevent a meal from being very harmonious, and you lose yourself in comments on the food. [. . .] On the avenue de Paris, once we two men were alone, in possession of our cigars, a rapprochement took place and I return listening to the admirable and sublime comments of Mallarmé. (*Annales,* Notebook 13)

There's something comic, something rather puerile, too, in this reconciliation of two men whom a woman (Méry loses her identity in the middle of this account to become merely "the woman") had temporarily separated, and worse, forced to talk about the food rather than enjoy the admirable and sublime conversation of men—or rather, the opportunity for one to speak and the other to listen. The cigars are a worry, too: What is Régnier suggesting here in terms of the physical relationship between the two men, given the earlier reference to the penis as a symbol of living nature? While Régnier's jealousy of his friendship with the Master pervades this account, and suggests that his interpretation of Méry's response may not be innocent, it nevertheless leaves open the possibility of a different Méry from that created by the letters Mallarmé wrote to her. At this distance in time, attempting to explore the differences between the Méry of the letters and the Méry others might have seen is much less rewarding than looking at how Mallarmé goes about constructing that chronicle of loving friendship.

The best known of these letters is doubtless that of September 11, 1889, which seems to transform an erotic relationship into one of friendship, although the tone of sensual and physical intimacy rapidly reappears. In this letter Mallarmé meditates on both love and friendship with a wholly remarkable depth to his understanding and warmth. He evokes love here as "an enchantment that seized his soul" (*LML*, 55). These are powerful terms—terms whose apparent simplicity and whose hackneyed use in everyday speech can't hide the fact that Mallarmé is reinvesting them with all the power they can command. In this sentence enchantment means a magical singing that takes control not just of the body but also, much more important, of the soul of whoever hears it. But unlike Circe, whose spells transformed men into beasts (or, more precisely, showed them as the beasts they were), Méry has had no such pernicious influence. Mallarmé is easily able to reject the role of suffering Byronic poet-lover and to replace it with an entirely different image of both poet and lover.

Everything about this letter suggests that Mallarmé worded it with a level of care that is exceptional even for him. It contains a degree of blackmail that he may not fully have recognized. We see this when he declares with apparent equanimity that "suffering on purpose is senseless." This statement sets up a telling dichotomy between his need as a poet to keep his nerves—the words he uses is "fibres"—constantly stretched taut and exposed and his apprehension of falling into the "vague" world of those whose fear of suffering makes them muffle their sensitivity to the point at which they no longer perceive anything. Having set up this image of the poet as a Marsyas who may be flayed but who decides which winds will blow on him, he softens the stoic mask to suggest that such an attitude can be maintained only in small doses, hence the need to space out his meetings with Méry.

This passage on himself as poet is followed by a paragraph on Méry and what she offers him that is a curious mixture of the loving and the condescending. "You are of a piece," he tells her, "and that is why I love you." But what does love mean for Mallarmé? He denies any knowledge of what the heart is. "The brain," he adds, "I use for enjoying art and with it I loved some of my friends." Mallarmé's use of the past tense is interesting here, for it perhaps suggests that his close friendships of the provincial years were vital to him but are now over. With a sudden turn of the screw he turns back to himself and Méry, adding to this implication that she is excluded from the friendships of the brain the statement that there is almost nothing in their individual ways of thinking that offers a common ground. What united them, and what therefore must constitute love, is the attraction she, *as a woman,* exerted over him. Much in this admission is disturbing and reflects a mind far more disturbed by the situation than Mallarmé is willing to admit openly. There is surely more here than "nothing but gratitude," as Mallarmé claims (*LML,* 57). But this is also a mind that takes control, and when the relationship resumed, it was on Mallarmé's terms. He is the one who announces that he'll be coming for lunch, or that he can't find time to visit her. The relationship during this period seems to have been just as intense, but the letters written after the 1889 letter suggest that the intensity is always under Mallarmé's control, especially his linguistic control.

A brief note written in May 1890 shows both the vibrancy of the emotion and the way in which Mallarmé has it firmly in check: "Delicious you, I have only enough time to send you your habitual kiss, on leaving: and I would have things to say, but will do so from there [Valvins]. How Méry you were and ideally perfect, yesterday evening, your shells of ears must have been burning, all the evening as we went home. I found five Reviews, I'll share them, you'll get three because you are the bigger. Farewell (ugly word) treasure and [drawing of a peacock]" (*LML,* 64). This is a remarkable letter: It contains an enormous sense of joy and excitement, together with an evident delight in conveying that pleasure in terms that have nothing of the hackneyed about them. But somehow this letter also reduces Méry's individuality—first by the masculine "délicieux" imposed by the grammatical gender of *toi* ("you"), then by transforming her name into an adjective, as though Méry were some unchanging category or essence to which she had to conform, and finally by eliding her name at the end and replacing it with a drawing of the bird whose vanity he presumes to recall her own. Below the unquestionable delight in her presence, there is also a need to reduce and control her, to define her in language as the punning use of the word *trésor* ("treasure" but also "thesaurus," "word-hoard") suggests.

Mallarmé's subsequent letters show him to be above all working to reinvent Méry, most obviously when he furnished her apartment, thus creating the ideal physical setting for her. Régnier's diaries suggest the extent to which this decorating experience was essentially erotic. In an entry written in 1892, the year Mallarmé was most involved in advising Méry on the decoration, we find Régnier noting that the poet has defined furniture as "man's true invention" (*Annales,* Notebook 14), and has talked to Régnier "deliciously" about the emotion that it causes him. In April 1893 we find the following curious entry: "Mallarmé speaks of the Louis XVI armchairs he's seen: Oh, he says, what wonders, it's enough to make you drop to your knees before them, yes; a woman sitting in them would have been a nuisance, on your knees because they have a form, a shape." The meticulous way in which he approached his task— the careful details set out in the letters, the precise instructions about where things should be placed ("the two armchairs can only go in the place of the two that were there before, there's no other place for them, and they're needed there" [*LML,* 88])—

suggests a degree of obsession and fetishism that seems to have less to do with the suggestions of the aesthete than with the needs of the controller.

That urge to dominate becomes most evident in Mallarmé's instructions about the mirror: "The cheval mirror [*psyché*] shouldn't have any particular place, but should look as if it's been set down randomly, here or there. I see it where the Louis XV wing chair is now, against the glass wall of the conservatory, near the chimney place, *diagonally—and above all never against a wall*. It should be put in the middle of the room, free-standing" (*LML*, 88). One can't help suspecting that Mallarmé here sees the mirror as Méry herself (the word *psyché* is, after all, heavily charged) and longs to be able to place her where he wants her.

Méry and Mallarmé frequently sent each other gifts of food. When he visited the seaside, Mallarmé would seize the opportunity to send her parcels of crabs, while she would send a ham or, choosing a gift that gave rise to the predictable puns, a tongue. In late August 1893 she contributed a cheese, provoking the following whimsical and multilayered response: "Here's to the cheese kiss. I can assure you that few people are as unctuous as it is. It's extraordinary and I can remember nothing like it. And so vast! I kiss you in consequence" (*LML*, 142). In an allusion that is equally full of double meanings, Mallarmé refers in 1894 to an anticipated gift of a Saint-Nectaire cheese: "The Saint-Nectaire has not yet put in an appearance and I'm devouring it in imagination, mingled with a little of your pâté, creamy lady" (*LML*, 174).

More seriously, the letters sometimes read like preliminary drafts for poems. In particular, one of the early letters paves the way for that beautiful paean to love, "O si chère de loin et proche":

O si chère de loin et proche et blanche, si
Délicieusement toi, Mary, que je songe
A quelque baume rare émané par mensonge
Sur aucun bouquetier de cristal obscurci.

Le sais-tu, oui! pour moi voici des ans, voici
Toujours que ton sourire éblouissant prolonge
La même rose avec son bel été qui plonge
Dans autrefois et puis dans le futur aussi.

Mon cœur qui dans les nuits parfois cherche à s'entendre
Ou de quel dernier mot t'appeler le plus tendre
S'exalte en celui rien que chuchoté de sœur.

N'était, très grand trésor et tête si petite,
Que tu m'enseignes bien toute une autre douceur
Tout bas par le baiser seul dans tes cheveux dite.

(Oh so dear from far and near and white, so
Deliciously you, Mary, that I dream

Of some rare balm emanating mendaciously
Over no stall of darkened crystal.

Do you know? Yes!, for me it's been years,
It's been forever, that your dazzling smile has prolonged
The same rose with its lovely summer that plunges
Into the past and then into the future too.

My heart, which at night sometimes seeks to understand
Or with which last, most tender word to name you
Delights in this, merely whispered, of sister.

Were it not that, very great treasure and head so small
You teach me an entirely different sweetness
Very low through the kiss alone in your hair spoken.) (*OC*, 61)

Because this poem was not published until a decade after Mallarmé's death, we do not know its date, but a letter mailed on June 2, 1888, is very close to it in sentiment and style:

> YOU, OR YOUR VOICE THAT sees me at the source of my being, your great presence with that dear handshake more mysterious and intimate and far away through its glove,—all the walk we took yesterday evening, my treasure,—that's what never leaves me and what I feel around me, as I throw back against the walls the shutters of an isolated room where for a long time nothing was thought; and as the daylight enters, it's you who fill it! Méry, how you know how to give, just in being the woman that you are, there, beside me, with a feeling so complete, so rich, young, simple, and serious, I had no inkling that such a thing could be. . . . A balm, you!, and a very good balm penetrates me. (*LML*, 40–41)

The poem's first quatrain in particular is clearly recognizable in the letter, with its suggestion of closeness and distance, of her "delicious" essence as the woman that she is, and of her transformation into a balm.

Other poems written for her also present close similarities with the poet's letters, setting up a complex system of echoes and quotations that reinforce Mallarmé's apparent determination not merely to avoid banality in his letters to Méry but also to make of them a work of art. A constant theme embroiders on the passing of time and how little it changes her, while adding immeasurably to the depth of their friendship. This theme is charmingly stated in the birthday poem he sent to her in April 1887:

Voici la date, tends un coin
De ta fraîche bouche étonnée

Où la nature prend le soin
De te rajeunir d'une année

(This is the day, give me a corner
of your fresh astonished mouth,
where nature is careful
to rejuvenate you by a year) (*LML*, 38)

It is further developed in the sonnet "Méry sans trop d'ardeur," sent in the closing days of 1887:

Ne te semble-t-il pas, Méry, que chaque année
D'où sur ton front renaît la grâce spontanée
Suffise selon tant de prodige et pour moi,

Comme un éventail seul dont la chambre s'étonne,
A rafraîchir du peu qu'il faut ici d'émoi
Toute notre native amitié monotone.

(Doesn't it seem to you, Méry, that every year,
when on your brow the spontaneous grace is born anew,
is enough, given such a miracle and for me,

as a fan alone that amazes a room
refreshes with the little emotion that we need
all our native unchanging friendship?) (*LML*, 39–40)

It reappears in a letter of May 1895: "You are the best and the most tender of friends, and to you, always born the day before, I can say—the oldest" (*LML*, 188).

The silence imposed on Méry by Mallarmé's destruction of her letters is, however, only partial. While reading Mallarmé's letters may leave us with a sense of his desire to control her, to invent her along the lines he sought, there are always cracks and fissures that let her shine through. In the "Rondel" he wrote for her, and for which she supplied the initial line—"Si tu veux, nous nous aimerons" (If you wish, we'll love each other) (*OC*, 62)—she provides him with a way of conveying love that has nothing to do with verbal exchanges:

Si tu veux nous nous aimerons,
Avec tes lèvres sans le dire
Cette rose ne l'interromps
Qu'à verser une silence pire

(If you wish, we'll love each other
With your lips without saying so

This rose you only interrupt
To shed a worse silence) (*OC, 62*)

That awareness of the language of touch and gesture is primarily, as Mallarmé suggests in "O si chère de loin," Méry's gift to him: "You teach me," he acknowledges in this powerful and erotic poem, "an entirely different sweetness / softly spoken in your hair by the kiss alone" (*OC*, 61). Her generosity, her easy goodwill, the practical help and emotional sympathy she gave him when Villiers was dying or when she heard of Banville's death—"I think of the pain you'll suffer and send you quickly this little note to let you know I share your sorrow" (*LML*, 71)—all point to a woman whose charms were exactly what Mallarmé needed when the death of his son brought his marriage to its emotional end. While she may not have possessed the kind of intellect needed to understand the more philosophical of his poems (but then, as we've seen, neither did Renoir, Monet, or Morisot), she did deploy an entirely different kind of intelligence, the sort that inspired him to write for her a series of multilayered love poems that are among the finest of his achievements. And she seems to have possessed the kind of tact and insight that allowed him in his letters to her to forge an image of Méry Laurent that may have little to do with any historically verifiable reality but that, because of the way she responded to it, is as much her creation as his.

CHAPTER FOUR

Becoming a Symbol

> M. Stéphane Mallarmé, his pipe in his mouth, talks to me in a
> soft voice, slightly teasing, and which from time to time adopts
> an ironic note—but vaguely, oh so vaguely!
> —*Georges Docqois,* Bêtes et gens de lettres *(1895)*
>
> Two marvelous hours, and the voice, the gaze, the familiar ges-
> tures of Mallarmé: I felt utterly comforted and *illuminated.*
> —*André Fontainas, December 22, 1897*

With the 1884 publication of Paul Verlaine's study of the century's ill-starred poets,
Les Poètes maudits, Mallarmé began to experience the pleasures and pitfalls of growing fame. While the increased attention brought him many friends and put him in
contact with creators and thinkers who increased his awareness of various aspects of
contemporary culture, it also brought with it countless duties. He was asked to serve
on the committee erecting a monument to Baudelaire, he was approached by impecunious poets requesting financial and practical assistance, and the number of books
he received from friends, acquaintances, and strangers rapidly increased, frequently
leaving him with the impression that he was forced to devote most of his time and
energy to responding to them rather than getting on with his own creative writing. Younger critics took up arms in Mallarmé's defense, often creating a degree of
half-ironic, half-wistful concern on the poet's part. It is indicative, moreover, of the
growing internationalism of the Symbolist movement that two of the most outspo-
ken young critics should be the Polish Teodor de Wyzewa and the Belgian Albert
Mockel. Wyzewa's *Nos Maîtres* (Our masters) is considered one of the most important contemporary documents on Symbolist theory, and the articles he wrote for such
periodicals as *La Vogue, La Revue indépendante,* and *La Revue wagnérienne* certainly
played a central role in building Mallarmé's image as "prince of poets," a title that still
exists in France today.[1] At one point, however, Wyzewa's enthusiasm is reported to
have provoked Mallarmé to remark, "Wyzewa is charming, but why must he expli-
cate my poems? It's enough to make people believe they're obscure" (*Corr.,* III: 23n).
Nevertheless, Wyzewa's intelligent interest in Mallarmé's beautiful but complex poem

"L'Après-midi d'un faune" cannot have failed to inspire many of his readers. In an issue of *La Vogue* published in mid-July 1886, for instance, he asserted that there is in the poem "a fluid lightness of syllables, a warm languor, an adorably ancient modulation, and an alternation of fleeting melodies and serious melodies, according to whether the illusion glitters or fades in the soul of that very subtle faun."[2]

Reading what Mallarmé wrote during these years leaves us with the conviction that many of the apparently lighthearted quatrains penned for feast days or to accompany the gift of a book reveal a testament to the nature of friendship itself, an exploration of one of the aspects of life that Mallarmé clearly found most deeply satisfying. Equally, many of his letters to friends seem to have as part of their underlying purpose the desire to meditate on and consolidate friendship, especially the bonds that exist between writers and readers. Understanding the nature of both Mallarmé's mind and the ties that united the Symbolist writers across time and space depends in part on an understanding of the ways in which these writers created and maintained their friendships.

Among the most important of Mallarmé's friendships were several formed with the growing numbers of Belgian Symbolists. As part of his Belgian lecture series to raise money for Villiers de l'Isle-Adams's wife and son,[3] Mallarmé visited that exquisite medieval city, Bruges. With its northern architecture, its narrow streets, and its pearly gray light reflected in the canals and waterways that run through it, this little city has a unique and unforgettable charm; its atmosphere was not likely to be overlooked by so sensual and sensitive an aesthete as Mallarmé. On his return to France he wrote one of his most beautiful poems of friendship, a poem that is at once a tribute to the city in which the friendships were formed, a transformation of that city into a symbol of the nature of friendship, and an evocation of how friendship comes into being:

A des heures et sans que tel souffle l'émeuve
Toute la vétusté presque couleur encens
Comme furtive d'elle et visible je sens
Que se dévêt pli selon pli la pierre veuve

Flotte ou semble par soi n'apporter une preuve
Sinon d'épandre pour baume antique le temps
Nous immémoriaux quelques-uns si contents
Sur la soudaineté de notre amitié neuve

O très chers rencontrés en le jamais banal
Bruges multipliant l'aube au défunt canal
Avec la promenade éparse de maint cygne

Quand solennellement cette cité m'apprit
Lesquels entre ses fils un autre vol désigne
A prompte irradier ainsi qu'aile l'esprit.

(At certain hours and with no breath to rouse it
All the dilapidation almost the color of incense
As if furtively and visibly I feel
The unveiling, fold by fold, of the widowed stone

Floats or seems to bring no proof on its own account
Except in scattering time by way of ancient balm
Upon us immemorial ones so happy
At the suddenness of our new friendship

O very dear friends met in the never banal
Bruges multiplying the dawn in the defunct canal
With here and there the promenade of many a swan

When solemnly this city taught me
Which among its sons another flight designates
To irradiate the spirit as swiftly as a wingbeat.) (*OC*, 60)

The poem begins by suggesting an imperceptible mist slowly rising to reveal the beauty of old stones and the complex architecture of a city and a friendship that has long been in existence, even if only recently discovered by those on whom the sonnet focuses, the "Nous immémoriaux si contents / Sur la soudaineté de notre amitié neuve" (Us immemorial ones so happy / At the suddenness of our new friendship) (*OC*, 60). The bracketing together of "immemorial" and "new" beautifully epitomizes the sense that love and friendship have always existed at some level, even if the lovers and friends have only just met. John Donne conveys it equally forcefully in his "Airs and Angels": "Twice or thrice have I loved thee, / Before I knew thy face or name."[4] As Emilie Noulet has remarked, moreover, "Written shortly after the death of Villiers and dedicated to a devoted group, who, in a far off and stultified Bruges, had had faith in him, the sonnet, occasional verse if ever there were, is eminently a poem of permanence. The permanence of memory, of friendship, of a town. The permanence above all of the glory that, according to Mallarmé, inevitably crowns the posthumous destiny of a poet."[5] Implicit in Mallarmé's wonderfully suggestive evocation of the way in which a friendship can seem to have existed forever is the value of common intellectual experiences that provide a substitute for the "ancient balm of time." Geographically and politically separated, these poets enjoyed a common heritage, and in Symbolism they found a common aesthetic that bound them together as the canals of Bruges bind together separate sections of the city.

Bruges becomes, in Mallarmé's sonnet, not just the arbitrary city where the meeting took place but the very embodiment of friendship and of poetry, exemplified by its swans, symbols of poets, reflected in the city's canals as the friends found their interests reflected in one another. These sluggish canals—in themselves "defunct," as Mallarmé puts it—give life to multiple sunrises, multiple discoveries of new beginnings. The sunrise becomes the symbol of both the dawn of friendship and the upward flight to glory of the Belgian poets, whose works are destined to fill their readers' minds with light.

Two poets who were central to the growth of the Symbolist movement in Belgium were Georges Rodenbach and Emile Verhaeren, both of whom corresponded with Mallarmé. Rodenbach was thirteen years younger than Mallarmé but died in the same year he did. They met around 1878, through Théodore de Banville, and became close friends after Rodenbach returned to Paris to live in 1887. A photograph of the Belgian poet in the living room of his Paris apartment on the rue Gounod reveals something of the complexity of fin-de-siècle taste, a complexity that a hundred years later strikes the viewer as cluttered to the point of inducing claustrophobia.[6] The multiplicity of patterns on the carpet, drapes, and tablecloths; the numerous orna-ments on the mantlepiece and the paintings on the walls; the intricate chandelier; and the large mirror that repeats that complexity all seem to some degree an exten-sion of Rodenbach's intricate character. He himself stands in a corner of the room, elegantly dressed and nonchalantly leaning against a table cluttered with ornaments and vases. Other depictions of him—the illustration reproduced in his 1888 volume *Du silence,* for instance (Figure 9)—show a somewhat delicate man with fine regu-lar features, a clean-shaven face (apart from a drooping mustache), and thoughtful deep-set eyes.[7]

In his letters to Rodenbach, Mallarmé displays a gently intelligent courtesy, con-veying an intellectual pleasure in what the Belgian poet was achieving, rather than any sense of deep excitement. What is more important than the degree to which the two men really shared an aesthetic program is the delicate determination both re-veal to build and maintain a friendship that was in some way equally important to both.[8] Mallarmé's response to *Du silence* is typical of this determination. Writing on March 25, 1888, he begins, characteristically, with a meditation on the title:

> YOUR TITLE [*Du silence*], even before one opens the volume, stems from some-one who is initiated into the meaning of poetry which indeed has only to speak on behalf of everything that talks to us tacitly and directly and arouses reverie. And that art, which is supreme, consists, isn't this true? in never as one sings stripping the subtle objects under our gaze of the veil, exactly, of Silence under which they seduce us, the veil which now lets us divine the Secret of their Significance. That's why one needs delicate fingers, made for indicating without touching, because no reality remains; it evaporates in writing!
>
> This is what haunted me between those poems that count among the most pure and miraculous that I've read: soon we'll chat about them line by line, for each is a rare bow stroke. (*Corr.,* III: 177)

The opening sentences suggest an ongoing meditation that was to reappear when his response to Paul Margueritte's mime *Pierrot assassin de sa femme* (Pierrot assassin of his wife) was included in *Pages* three years later. There the article "Mimique" began with this pregnant statement, "Silence, the sole luxury after rhymes, an orchestra creating with its gold, its strokes of thought and evening, merely the outline of its meaning, like an unspoken ode which the poet, aroused by a challenge, must translate! The silence of musical afternoons" (*OC*, 310). The allusion to the orchestra is already present in the letter to Rodenbach, through the reference to the violinist's bow stroke, an image that appears in various guises throughout Mallarmé's mature work. More important, Mallarmé repeats here, in beautifully elliptical form, the central credo of his kind of Symbolism, the need to maintain the enigmatic quality of things, the veil that seduces us as readers into trying to penetrate their significance.

When Rodenbach's story of unhappy love, *L'Art en exil,* appeared in late April of 1889, Mallarmé's reply was just as warm in its friendship, even though we might detect a suggestion that for him prose was a lesser vehicle for the Belgian writer's true talents:

I T'S YOUR QUALITIES, ALL OF THEM, that create this book, with a perfect dosage, from the savory to the poignant: a poem, and the few motifs that compose it never break and the soul's song never stops. With what care you avoid the make-weights and all the bad habits of what is strictly speaking termed a novel; and the narration occurs spontaneously, as air circulates through your landscape. I place *L'Art en exil* among those books one sees again, and whose glistening and rare text doesn't vanish after a first reading. (*Corr.,* III: 316)

Although he indicates that there is a suggestive correspondence between the landscape evoked in the narrative and the narration itself, there is something more conventional in Mallarmé's response, a hint of courtesy rather than enthusiasm, an indication that this "glistening and rare text" may, despite what he says, rapidly lose its power.

Two years later, in 1891, Rodenbach's new work *Le Règne du silence* (The reign of silence) inspired a complex and intricately formulated expression of enthusiasm and friendship. Typical of his thinking, especially perhaps at this point in his career, is Mallarmé's insistence on the value of analysis in art, when that analysis is intrinsic to the work and not just added on, a filigree not a veneer, together with his emphasis on the transformation of the most humble apartment into something regal, once it becomes the site of meditation. As he puts it,

I FINISH, RAVISHED. I DON'T BELIEVE that anyone has begun with such subtlety and gone further and more deliciously in threading the analysis; as at times you incorporate everything in a touch which is full and vibratory. And that's not to mention this divination of apartments where the humblest can become a prince through the fact that there the dream bursts forth, your soul always gives this high, luxurious impression that it *has enough time*—may that prove to be the case—not to lose a single spiral but to unfold each in its turn, line by whispered, singing line. *Le Règne du silence,* "a poem" in truth, I understand; and, for the first time, the motif of a work is composed, together with its mysterious link, almost of that which is not said, but purely; soars, haunted; that's very fine and very Poe, that [c'est très beau et très Poe, cela]. (*Corr.,* IV: 225)

In similar ways Mallarmé seems to be trying to permeate his letters with his sense of friendship for Rodenbach, so that, all but unstated, it can soar above them, unifying them.

This carefully developed skill of forging a language of friendship, not just appropriate to the stylistic characteristics of each individual but reflecting those characteristics as a proof of friendship's ability to enter into the mind of the other, is one of Mallarmé's great personal discoveries. It doesn't seem to have been automatic but rather something he worked on, particularly after his return from the provinces, when the bulk of his letters were written. He sought not to express his own longings, doubts, ambitions, and fears but to respond to those of others, either openly stated or suggested in the works sent to him. We can see this effort in his letters to the Belgian writer Emile Verhaeren, whom Mallarmé seems to have respected more than he did Rodenbach but perhaps liked somewhat less. It might be fairer to say that, compared with the correspondence with Rodenbach, the letters to Verhaeren convey less of a sense of sympathy and more of a sense of equality. Mallarmé's response to Verhaeren's 1888 collection *Les Soirs* (Evenings) gives a wonderful if elliptical impression of the French poet being deeply engrossed in the book, or rather engrossed in his meditations after reading: "You know what reading you means for me: it's a great pleasure, and then a prolonged study amidst the lamp" (*Corr.,* III: 162). There's something very Baudelairean about this reference to delight followed by study, a determination to transform pleasure into knowledge,[9] but it is also typical of Mallarmé to find a way of making his letter proclaim something about the specific pleasure and nature of reading. We can detect a faint image of the older Mallarmé looking back (sympathetically, but with a touch of amusement) at his younger self, the self who wrote "Brise marine" (Sea breeze), in which he deplores the "clarté déserte de ma lampe / Sur le vide papier que sa blancheur défend" (the deserted brightness of my lamp / on the empty paper its whiteness defends) (*OC,* 38).

The act of reading—the joy followed by the analysis and exploration—leads to two comments, both typical of Mallarmé's response to a book of poetry. He responds fully to his friend's prosodic experiments, recognizing them for what they are and separating them from those of so many lesser poets who seek novelty merely for its own sake: "Because you are not unaware, and echo, although it normally repeats so stupidly what I say, may have whispered to you, that whenever I speak of you, I say this, in particular: that among the poets of the current generation either here or over there [that is, in France or Belgium] you are the one from whom can be expected the greatest innovation! Yes, you're the one who is best renewing poetry, and you're doing so without recourse to passing fads" (*Corr.*, III: 162). The judgment concisely summed up, Mallarmé again typically avoids the need to explain and justify by alluding to a time in the near future when all this can be talked over: "I won't explain this, since I'll have the opportunity to be explicit in the course of the coming week, and will give you a very exact account of my impression of the *Soirs.*"

Clearly, however, that opportunity didn't arise, as he wrote again, a week later, with a more detailed appreciation. He opens with a brilliantly concise indication of the way in which a symbol needs to be both allusive and grounded in reality. In this case the evenings of Verhaeren's title suggest both death and more general endings, and at the same time they evoke physical evenings, saving them from the fate of many minor Symbolist works—that of having no anchor in external nature: "After your subject, the evenings, one of the themes of soul and beauty, where you go as far as possible into personal divination and luxury, but always juxtaposing that with some aspect or other of nature, with the result that these are the evenings, both in the skies and in us! in a word, according to the precise spiritual situation of Poetry" (*Corr.*, III: 166). This complex and somewhat clotted formula, whose syntactical structure reflects the tight braiding of inner and outer worlds, reveals the extent to which Mallarmé was aware of the fatal flaw of much Symbolist poetry and invited a double reading of his own poems, such that the swan trapped in ice is always present, both as a natural object and as a sign of a spiritual, inner universe in which it exists in metamorphosed form.

Mallarmé is also highly sensitive to what Verhaeren is doing in moving the traditional alexandrine toward free verse while avoiding the pitfall of transforming it into mere prose: "What I find no less interesting is your treatment of verse, which in you more than in anyone else has reached a crucial point. You have taken it out of the old forge, in fusion and in all its aspects, to the point of stretching it even at the end of the strophe beyond its strict measure, and yet it is still verse" (*Corr.*, III: 162). Here one can see Mallarmé putting down his pen, meditating on the role of the individual poet in this surge away from fixed forms, and pondering the need to hide the strings and pulleys used to move the line of poetry out of a groove that had been a central part of French everyday thought since Racine. He writes, "In this I congratulate you on possessing a special sense," but he realizes that the phrasing of that sentence is too personal, puts too much emphasis on Verhaeren as craftsman, and he adds,

O R RATHER THE WORKER DISAPPEARS (for that is absolutely the discovery of our time) and the poetry acts alone: a feeling with its leaps or its delight creates its own rhythm and becomes poetry, without anyone imposing it brutally and from outside! And that's what takes place marvelously here, such light and music happens along and clothes the poem, and are entirely contained in the interval of a sentence, like a forgotten sunset cloud; or other pieces so torn apart by their own inner storm and constantly starting anew, loftily and noisily, a dream. (*Corr.,* III: 162)

The disappearance of the craftsman to give way to the pure work of art is essential to his "Crise de vers," a first version of which he had been writing in the previous year: "The pure work implies the elocutionary disappearance of the poet, who yields the initiative to words, mobilized by the shock of their inequalities" (*OC,* 366). The reference to the leaps and somersaults that provide the rhythms of the new form of verse also suggests that Mallarmé had been meditating on Baudelaire's preface to his prose poems: "Who among us has not, in days of ambition, dreamed of the miracle of a poetic prose, musical without rhythm and rhyme, sufficiently supple and sufficiently disjointed to adapt itself to the lyrical movements of the soul, the undulations of reverie, the leaps of conscience?"[10] Baudelaire had found his miracle in prose poetry: Mallarmé clearly believes it can be found in verse. But I think this letter also suggests that Mallarmé had in mind not just a theoretical but a poetic statement. In several ways, his evocation of Verhaeren's verse as fragments of sunset or flotsam from a wreck both recall "Victorieusement fui" (Victoriously fled), published in 1885, and point forward to the later sonnet "A la nue accablante tu" (Unspoken to the crushing cloud). Of course I do not mean to suggest that these poems have as their sole subject the current debates about poetry, but rather that Mallarmé makes it possible here to read them in that light. He has, after all, cleared the way by insisting to Verhaeren on the need for a symbol to be rooted in reality if it is truly to be able to convey a higher meaning.

Later letters to the Belgian poet reinforce this suggestion that he was one of those who most enabled Mallarmé to refine his vision of poetry. His response to *Les Flambeaux noirs* (The black torches), written on April 14, 1891, for example, takes up yet again themes found in "Crise de vers" and states even more forcibly than the previous letter the need for a reader to transform passive pleasure into active understanding:

I DON'T KNOW THAT IT'S NOT the most extraordinary of the three, this book, *Les Flambeaux noirs.* I've lived with it for several days, to really make sense of an hallucination, which is truly the supreme hallucination where reading is concerned and which has now become my conscious and admitted mode of enjoyment here: the Line, which is admittedly borrowed from speech, has so reimmersed itself, in accordance with the fury of your instinct, and other things, that it becomes, I'm sure of this because I recite you in my head, a new element unmediated and individual, naked and devouring its own words. And I'm starting to think that this is what, throughout the ages, had to be done.— I'm very happy for you for I'm so fond of you,—but we ought to talk about this. (*Corr.,* IV: 223)

Yet while we get a sense of delight in the hallucinatory power of Verhaeren's writing, there is clearly also both approval and hesitation concerning the means of creating that hallucination. The transformation of the line of poetry into something unique, sui generis, drawing on but breaking free from the words that make it up, is again very close to a frequently quoted passage from the "Crise de vers":

T HE LINE THAT, WITH SEVERAL SOUNDS, recreates a complete word, new, un-known to the language and so to speak incantatory, achieves this isolation of the word: denying with a sovereign stroke the elements of chance which has clung to the terms despite the artifice of their alternating immersion in sense and sonority, and causes you that feeling of surprise at never having heard such an ordinary fragment of speech, at the same time as the reminiscence of the named object bathes in a new atmosphere. (*OC*, 368)

But how do we interpret the instigating factor in Verhaeren's case: "the fury of your instinct"? Mallarmé adds "and other things," but one can't help sensing both in the formulation of the first expression and the vague addendum a significant difference between Mallarmé's method and what he perceives to be Verhaeren's. Mallarmé does not argue that the poet has to be in control all the time. He urges that the initiative be handed over to language. But between that kind of external, impersonal force and the drive of instinct there is still a considerable difference. It doesn't appear that by "instinct" Mallarmé means a sense of what is poetically right. *Instinct* isn't a word he often uses in connection with poetry. He's more likely to use a term like *toucher* (touch) or *doigté* (fingering). And "furie" strikes a further discordant note, quickly muffled by the emphasis in the second half of the sentence on what is nevertheless achieved. That he admired Verhaeren's accomplishments is, I think, beyond doubt, but that he wanted to suggest differences and concerns seems very likely.

Later letters to Verhaeren can at first glance appear far more perfunctory, indicat-ing that where Mallarmé was looking for progress, movement forward, and perhaps away from the fury of instinct, he found more of the same. In January 1892, for in-stance, he sent the following thank-you note for *Les Apparus dans mes chemins* (Those who have crossed my path), a volume that had come out the previous year: 'Thank you, Verhaeren, belatedly; but I am incapable of talking of poems like yours at the mo-ment when they still reecho, so vibrant, within me, some with such fury and others so calm, each being the complete and necessary line from which it seems the entire poem, in its rapidity, is suspended. Ah! it's not made of language, but a song almost pure of any writing, in which the word scintillates. Your dream is more poignant than ever and even unique" (*Corr.*, IV: 29). This doesn't give the impression of a col-lection carefully read and savored, but rather an attempt to find a formula that is elastic enough to cover a variety of possibilities. The words that stand out are "fury," "rapidity," and "scintillates," leaving the impression that, for Mallarmé, this collection is more about verbal pyrotechnics than the kind of crafted reverie he himself is seeking.

There is, however, another reason for the lack of precision in these later letters to Verhaeren, in addition to any doubts Mallarmé may have had, and of course the sheer practicalities of replying to so many gifts of books: Verhaeren, so Mallarmé suggests in a letter of May 14, 1893, has reached the point at which he has discovered his own personality in his writing, found what is unique to him, and all that remains is to go on mining that lode. Suggestions, criticisms, and even commentaries are no longer what is required between friends. In this letter, responding to one of Verhaeren's best-known and most beautiful collections, *Les Campagnes hallucinées* (The hallucinated countrysides), Mallarmé seems more concerned with exploring an image of a mature poet than with encapsulating his response. Besides, as he adds, between friends, it's in conversation that poems are best discussed:

> I FIND—LATE, NO, you can be sure I was immediately enchanted, but replying!—your book admirable: and besides it's by you; and Verhaeren speaks in it, not just the verse! You have reached the hour in an artist's life which is the perfect hour, where what he does and he himself are one and the same; no more magnificent effort in one direction or another, everything is established and simple. After so many studies that bordered on miracles, your work now becomes your way of existing, naively; something other than literature. This is what I see, by way of an intimate handshake, now I've read the collection of *Campagnes hallucinées;* but what if we talked side by side, what if we went into details! (*Corr.,* VI: 91)

The perfect union of poet and poetry, the sense of immediacy without any awareness of effort or manipulation, the ease the reader feels on exploring the poems—these are clearly what Mallarmé sees as hallmarks of the mature poet, elements he himself is attempting to achieve. We might note here the use of "literature," with a meaning very similar to that given it by Verlaine in "Art poétique": "Et tout le reste est littérature" (And everything else is literature).[11] The result of such maturity, moreover, is to transform the volume of poetry into an intimate handshake from one friend to another. What's interesting in this suave appreciation is partly what it leaves out and partly the way it changes subject. Verhaeren's volume is above all remarkable for its nightmarish transformation of nature. Neither the theme nor its treatment is of great interest to Mallarmé, whose love of the autumnal woods around Valvins never finds direct expression in his verse, and whose mind is far more shaped by the concision of Baudelaire than the expansion of Hugo, who was clearly a central influence for the Belgian poet. Mallarmé's silence about this major thematic aspect of the volume and his decision to focus on the nuts and bolts of its transformation into poetic form may well have been made up for in discussions, as he suggests, but in the letter it leaves us with a sense of an admiration that may also be relief. Verhaeren's interests and aims were, after all, so unlike Mallarmé's that there could be no question of true rivalry. This is what enables the double reading of the letter in terms of both *Les Campagnes hallucinées* and the friendship between the poets, itself at that easy mature stage that requires no major work to keep it running.

When Verhaeren turned from the hallucinatory forms of the country to those of the villages, Mallarmé's response to him intensified earlier comments but also provided a further brief insight into how he perceived the nature of reading. Again he insists on the way in which Verhaeren's poetry contains a unique voice, again he uses the word "fury" and emphasizes the apparent spontaneity that results from careful orchestration, and again he underlines the sense of speed that the poems convey:

VERHAEREN IT'S PRODIGIOUS. You've brought the line of poetry to the point where, although it lasts, it's no longer anything but the verbal, intimate, spontaneous form that bursts from you; it's what your abundant, controlled fury limits itself to. Never, I'm rambling because of you who make me say it for at least the third time, never, dear friend, has there been so obvious a demonstration as in *Villages illusoires,* your latest work and as always the most striking, of what you have wanted, invented, produced. These lines that rush along, in all their primal silence, to some unknown lair they've dug out, I hear them with the hearing of the multitude (there are a thousand of us reading them alone): so infinite is their voice! (*Corr.,* VII: 149)

What is new, and what is only rarely encountered in Mallarmé's writing, is that tantalizingly brief suggestion of the nature of reading. The "hearing of the multitude," with the explanatory parenthesis "(there are a thousand of us reading them alone)," suggests a community of minds, an imaginary city of readers, the band of dreamers Mallarmé invokes in his prose poem "Un spectacle interrompu." There are echoes here of Baudelaire's multitude and solitude, so often evoked in his prose poems, but there is also something miraculously modern about that perception and above all the image itself. The poems' movement from their initial silence toward the lair they themselves hollow out seems to move poetry away from the Platonic cave and into an entirely new space created by both modern art and writing, and by a modern awareness of the crowd. What Mallarmé is also suggesting here, in addition to that fleeting reference to the nature of reading, is the vital importance of literature in overcoming the solitude to which humanity is condemned. Verhaeren, in other words, is not just a personal friend but also an embodiment of the nature of friendship as it is contained in the act of writing literature.

This point is emphasized again when Mallarmé writes to congratulate Verhaeren privately on the banquet held in his honor by *La Plume:*

I DON'T KNOW WHY, VERHAEREN, but after the celebrations, after the unanimous and fine acclamation of some great Someone, I feel an old desire to shake your hand on my own account; and to tell you how I also love, in a corner, *Les Villes Tentaculaires* [The tentacular towns]. Your voice, dear friend, has often been very powerful in intensity and solitude; here I find it vast, swollen with the multitude, an eternal echo that seems transmitted from very massive walls, with clashes of the crowd. I'll soon take off with me, in the coming spring and leisure, to Valvins, in order to read them again, your *Poëmes*. (*Corr.*, VIII: 81)

There is a hint here that Mallarmé is transforming Verhaeren into the Hugo of his generation through the depiction of a voice that is powerful in solitude, as Hugo spoke for so long from exile in the Channel Islands. Nevertheless, there is also a very real sense that Mallarmé is not being merely polite and perfunctory. He doesn't hide their differences, as the juxtaposition of Verhaeren's powerful voice and Mallarmé's quiet praise spoken from a corner makes perfectly clear. The letter stands out as part of a much broader meditation on the relationship between poets and their readers, an attempt to distinguish between the individual voice and the eternal echo. Mallarmé seems to be suggesting in this elliptical sentence that modern poetry and above all urban poetry gains much of its force by exploiting the vast walls of previous poems, and building on the linguistic energies of the crowd. In part, Mallarmé's imagery is determined by Verhaeren's choice of subject matter—the spreading, tentacular nature of modern cities—but it's not merely an attempt to flatter by copying. The images here, drawing energy from their elliptical and enigmatic nature, have a power far removed from the voice of common civility we can detect in some of Mallarmé's thank-you letters.

The meditation on reading and in particular on the relationship between the solitary reader and the crowds of other equally solitary readers continues through the letters Mallarmé wrote to his Belgian friend. The last letter, dated a few months before Mallarmé's death, shows him still meditating on this subject, as if something about Verhaeren particularly prompted it:

ADMIRABLE VERHAEREN, I WAS THINKING that I'd see *Les Aubes* [The dawns] on a stage in Paris, this winter. How little I grieve that until now the performance has been reserved for the sole theater of ourselves, which demands, to give it in all its prodigiousness, the flow of all our vital sumptuosities and magnificent watches of thought: only there where we are tragic in the face of destiny, at our most pure, our most bitter, our most glorious, can we house, even for an artistic pleasure, this superior and grandiose exchange of human cries traversed by an extraordinary beating of the Verse, of which you alone are capable, for you were the first to launch it with such terror! (*Corr.*, X: 133)

Mallarmé's central interest here lies in the radical difference between a theatrical representation on the stage and the act of private reading, the "sole theater of ourselves" (compare *OC,* 300). The passivity of the theater audience is sharply contrasted with the reader's need to bring to bear all his or her "vital sumptuosities," as Mallarmé characteristically puts it, together with the power of thought. To us, knowing he has only a few more months to live, there is in the formulation, especially in its intensity, a premonition of early death, yet Mallarmé's point here is more generally that human life is intrinsically tragic and that reading allows us to transform the solitude and isolation of that tragedy into an exchange between minds.

Through his letters to Verhaeren, perhaps more than to any of his other friends, Mallarmé was thus able to explore the nature of what might seem the least social of activities—private reading—recast through Mallarmé's meditation into a uniquely direct communication between minds and across time. But relationships maintained above all through letters were only part of the rapidly increasing network of acquaintances that Mallarmé was enjoying in these years. Even more important to him as a forum for developing his ideas in the company of friends were his Tuesday evening gatherings at his home on the rue de Rome.

The year 1885 marks the beginning of what Edouard Dujardin was to call the "heroic period" of the Mardis.[12] These gatherings of writers, artists, and intellectuals have been described by several of those who attended them at various times, and they leave their trace in the correspondence of those who attended them. Dujardin's study, Mauclair's novel *Le Soleil des morts,* Geneviève Mallarmé's brief evocation, Bonniot's article, and above all Régnier's diaries (among many others) all bear vivid testimony to the importance of these meetings, not merely for Mallarmé himself, who seized the opportunity to work through central preoccupations that were later to appear in written form, but also for the many aspiring writers who attended and who found in Mallarmé a sympathetic supporter of their ambitions. The beguiling charm of Mallarmé's conversation is noted even by the relatively hostile Edmond de Goncourt, who writes in a diary entry of January 7, 1895, "That Mallarmé has a truly seductive way with words, with a form of wit that's never cruel, but that's supported by a dash of malice."[13] Régnier evokes all the bewitching appeal of the Mardis in a comment jotted down in his diary in November 1890: "Nothing will replace for me those evenings at Mallarmé's house where in addition to the delicious, perfect presence of the master of the house, you have the chance to meet an intelligent company." The fame of these gatherings not unexpectedly provoked envy in several of Mallarmé's contemporaries, notably Goncourt, who snidely remarks in a diary entry for August 7, 1895, "That glory before which the younger generation is kneeling on all fours! That glory fabricated solely with 'L'Après-midi d'un faune,' a poem whose meaning, even after 20 years, has still not been established by the critics, and which the crafty sphinx who wrote it is very careful not to reveal, hasn't that hoax gone on rather too long? Oh this age, with its insane enthusiasms, Mallarmé, Villiers de l'Isle-

Adam, the great men of today's youth!"[14] We might note in passing that although Gordon Millan claims in his biography that women as well as men attended the Mardis,[15] his contention is substantiated by only a single reference to one woman, Tola Dorian. Although we know that Juliette Adam also attended the gatherings at a certain period, it seems more accurate, on the basis of the descriptions we have and on the remarks of Morisot,[16] to say that the Mardis reflected the general views of contemporary male society where the role of woman was concerned.

Most important, perhaps, is that the nature of these meetings reveals much about the nature of Mallarmé's mind. While several Mardistes have argued that they were not merely devoted to listening to Mallarmé speak, and that he did encourage the participation of others in his meditations on art, society, and life more generally, it remains the case, as his letters reveal, that he was above all interested in exploring his own mind and intellectual and emotional responses. When he invites comment from others, it's not out of the sense of driving and intelligent curiosity that so marks the personality of Marcel Proust, for example, whose appetite for knowledge and information was vast and eclectic. Mallarmé is not narcissistic in the sense that Robert de Montesquiou, for example, indubitably was, but everything in his letters and in the reflections of the Mardis that have come down to us makes it clear that while he may have taken pleasure in letting others explore their thoughts aloud to him, his primary focus of curiosity was his own intellect. It is this attitude, this tendency to place paramount importance on the inner world rather than any aspects of the outer world, that informs the complexity of his language. He uses it not to convey information but to seek out ways of making language correspond in its beauty and complexity to the convolutions of thought and emotion. It is not that his mind was closed to contemporary events; on the contrary. The point is more that those external events—cultural, social, or political—were of interest to him primarily if not exclusively as triggers to his own meditations on the nature of thought and language itself. While he claimed in his response to the journalist Jules Huret that "what made [him] seem a leader of a school, is first that [he'd] always been interested in the ideas of the young" (*OC,* 869), that interest was not fueled by a desire to make any personal use of those ideas, as Proust's interest was, but more by a courteous desire to allow others to explore their own thoughts in a receptive atmosphere, as Mallarmé himself was doing. André Gide, looking back at the Mardis in his autobiography, evokes their "almost religious atmosphere" and describes Mallarmé's conversation in the following terms:

CERTAINLY MALLARMÉ PREPARED HIS CONVERSATIONS, which were often not much different from his most polished "divagations;"[17] but he spoke with such art and in a tone that had so little of the doctrinal about it that it seemed as if he had just that instant invented each new proposition, which he didn't affirm so much as seem to submit it for your consideration, almost interrogatively, with raised index finger, as if to say: "Couldn't we put it like that? . . . perhaps. . ." and almost always ending his sentence with a "Isn't that so?" and it was doubtless that which enabled him to hold such sway over certain minds.[18]

The Mardis did, of course, also provide an ideal focus for discussing the cultural and political events of the time. In the last fifteen years of his life Mallarmé was able to participate far more than in earlier years in the concerts, ballet, and theater that the capital had to offer. The country's growing, if complex, interest in the music of Wagner, for instance, together with the urgently felt need to find a French response to his concepts of opera, finds a clear reflection in Mallarmé's writing of the time, and it is echoed in accounts of the Mardis. The role of experimental ballet and of mime is also a recurrent theme. But as Régnier's diary reveals, Mallarmé's meditation on such matters was idiosyncratic and highly personal, not so much a study of what was happening, although it is also that, as fioriture on the eternal nature of art and artistic production.

Tantalizing evocations of all these themes can be found in Régnier's as yet un-published diaries. That Régnier was fully aware of how important those accounts were to prove is suggested in his comment in the notebook he kept between May and December 1891, in which he draws an implicit parallel between himself and the famous diarist of the age, Edmond de Goncourt: "Of the necessity of a Goncourt. A man who keeps a diary is as necessary to an age as the police or the brothel." It was, moreover, to Régnier and his burgeoning career as poet, novelist, and critic that Mallarmé devoted over these years some of the richest and most suggestive of all his letters. Photos of Régnier at the time Mallarmé first met him, in the mid-1880s, show a rather gaunt young man, slightly balding under his side-parted hair, his mustache carefully trimmed and his deep-set eyes suggesting an equally deep-seated melancholy (Figure 12). Dapper in his high-collar and beautifully cut waistcoat and over-coat, he is a far cry from some of the more bohemian of Mallarmé's friends, yet he is also typical of a large group of intellectuals, whose transformation of the central tenets of Romanticism did so much to make fin-de-siècle France what it was. Henri Mazel, in his exuberant reminiscences of Symbolism, describes him in the following terms:

A STRANGE CHARM EMANATED FROM his haughty and melancholy personality. Very tall and lithe, he had an undulating walk, or, if he was sitting, he would seem to be lost in some vast armchair. He struck you as one of those thoughtful creatures of distinction that we would love to be able to place in the palaces of a Florence or Venice of days gone by. His voice was very soft, a bit toneless, with catlike inflections when he came out of those long silences in which thought seemed to fade away behind the spirals of tobacco in which he loved to envelop himself. And his physiognomy was in harmony with that voice, or his attitude or his walk was in harmony with his aristocratic face, which seemed one disdainful descent accentuated by two long blond mustaches falling on either side of a chin that went on and on, his gaze deeply veiled, one eye half shut, the other watching you from on high through a crooked monocle, the very broad brow revealed by a rapid baldness, and all that—the pensive brow, the melancholy gaze, the falling moustaches of a northern warrior—created the strange and almost contradictory ensemble of a barbarian king turned monk to illuminate manuscripts that sing of the glory of the old Vikings who were his ancestors.[19]

Goncourt depicts him as a "charming man, easy to get on with, and a witty talker,"[20] although others found him cold and aloof. Paul Reboux's memoirs describe him as "a lofty gentleman, with narrow drooping moustaches in the Chinese style, long hands, a long nose, a long chin, looking profoundly bored and so cold behind his monocle that when you were near him you wanted to put on your hat to avoid catching a cold. But how could you put your hat on in front of a man as correct and courtly as Régnier? You went away sneezing and blowing your nose."[21] Gide, who knew him rather better, asserts that "under the manners of a charming although somewhat haughty cordiality, he hid the constant but discreet belief in his own superiority." But he adds that Régnier's conversation, when alone with a friend, was "exquisite."[22] Régnier's ill-judged and unhappy marriage to one of the daughters of the poet José de Heredia—a marriage forced on the young bride by her father, who sought relief from his gambling debts in the pockets of his son-in-law—further exacerbated the deep unhappiness that profoundly marks both his poetry and his private journal. Highly regarded in his lifetime, this prolific poet, novelist, and critic fell rapidly into oblivion after his death. No doubt the yawning gulf between his personal concerns and poetic techniques on the one hand and, on the other, the changing social climate, the brutality of the war, and the sudden shift in educational patterns added to posterity's forgetfulness. The conservative nature of his subject matter, if not his treatment of it, also makes it difficult for him to compete with such personalities and talents as those who worked for the *Nouvelle Revue française* in its heyday at the beginning of the twentieth century.[23]

Régnier lacks the instantly perceptible charm of some of the friends of Mallarmé's youth—a Henri Cazalis or a Eugène Lefébure, for instance. As his diary reveals, his mind follows more established routes than theirs, reveling in creating the kind of maxim that turns less on the pithiness its writer no doubt perceives in it than on the desire to reduce and thus control the difference of the other, especially the female other. The essentialism of these aphorisms—with their dual pretension of understanding a characteristic, imaginary, female mind and their patent inability to understand real women—while initially arousing a reader's pity for a man so palpably lonely, quickly become tedious. Nevertheless, the relationship between the two poets and the traces we find of it in the diaries and letters reveal a great deal about the Mallarmé of the last decade or so of his life. Certainly Régnier's journal, as has long been realized, sheds an interesting if sporadic light on the Mardis, on many of Mallarmé's artist friends, and more generally on his increasingly important role as mentor to several generations of poets and artists. Régnier's diary is studded with reminiscences about what Mallarmé had said at a certain Tuesday gathering, or what he is described as habitually saying: "Mallarmé was saying the other evening: I love Dickens for his astonishing maniacs" (*Annales,* April 25, 1888); "You see, Régnier, our souls are lovely ladies who want to be richly maintained and who give us nothing in return" (*Annales,* June 1, 1888); "Maxim: the sole inspiration and safeguard is solitude—from others you take nothing—Mallarmé often said that to me" (*Annales,* Notebook 8); "Mallarmé had found this title for a book: On Human Incompetence" (*Annales,* March 1889). These entries give us glimpses of the way in which Mallarmé worked and insights into the way in which conversations with others helped to shape his critical articles devoted to art, music, theater, and ballet.

Moreover, the letters Mallarmé wrote to Régnier in response to his publications are so rich, dense, and generous that they in themselves re-create our image of Régnier, send us back to him and his creative writing curious to see what it was that Mallarmé found there. The first letter responds to Régnier's poetry collection *Les Lendemains* (Tomorrows):

> THAT'S AN EXCELLENT BEGINNING, or if I don't have here you first real poems, at least it's a charming way for me to get to know you. It's more than a pamphlet, almost a slim volume, given the variety of techniques and subjects on which you touch, exercising your fingers as if on a very complete keyboard. Your poetic form is very clear, in its half-tones that endow it with reverie (to use comparisons taken from all the arts, but then Poetry subsumes them all, and you prove that to be the case with very different gifts) and your language strikes me as capable of fullness and delicacy. So now you can go forward and work at acquiring an "individual voice" that's absolutely necessary today. When it comes down to it, everyone has such a voice, latent in them, and all you have to do to produce it is listen to yourself. (*Corr.,* II: 305–306)

The letter is dated November 26, 1885, a mere week after the "pamphlet" was published, on November 19. These poems initially appeared in the periodical *Lutèce* under Régnier's pseudonym, Hugues Vignix, with its clear double tribute to Victor Hugo and Alfred de Vigny. Mallarmé's letter to Régnier is distinctly different from those he wrote to his earlier friends or to those he regarded as contemporaries and equals. For the first time we find him advising someone on how to proceed rather than simply encouraging him in what he is doing. He draws attention to the young poet's need to break free from the poets who have influenced him, urging him to work at acquiring his own voice. There is in this statement both comprehension and urgency; Mallarmé himself, of course, struggled in his twenties to break free from just such crushing influences, mentioning their effect in a letter to Cazalis, in which he says, "Dierx's book [*Les Lèvres closes* (The closed lips)] is a fine development of Leconte de Lisle. Will he break free from him as I did from Baudelaire?" (*CC*, 346). How does one, after all, in the very year that Hugo died, avoid echoing the great voices of the immediate past—the voices of the French Romantics, who did so much to revitalize poetry; of Hugo, whose influence was pervasive and almost inescapable, both poetically and politically; and of Baudelaire, whose importance was really only beginning to dawn on the younger generation of intellectuals while still being rejected by the larger reading public? Mallarmé here, typically for him, chooses to raise an issue that is vital not just for his correspondent but also for poetry in general and himself in particular. It is the conviction that each writer has his or her own voice— and needs only to listen to find it—that allows him to continue with his own manipulation of metrics within the constraints of traditional forms, while others, especially in the next few years, were increasingly turning to *vers libre,* in which the line length and the placing of the rhymes is infinitely variable, the product of the individual poet and the subject chosen.[24] It is also Mallarmé's belief that each poet needs to hear and reproduce his or her own voice that enables him to follow the debate about *vers libre* with enthusiasm and equanimity, freed from both the urge to defend classical verse and the desire to follow others along this new path. Mallarmé has realized and is here sharing the importance of each poet discovering a means of personal expression. However impersonal he may urge the poet to be, that impersonality obviously concerns themes rather than technique. The individual voice does emerge, if set free, but what it proclaims is the universal predicaments and joys of humanity.

Just as Mallarmé uses the young poet's verse to meditate on the need for a personal voice, so he also finds in it an opportunity to explore the interrelationship of the arts. Increasingly, and perhaps above all because of the growing importance of Wagner and his concept of the *Gesamtkunstwerk* (the work that unites all branches of the arts), a concept that is predicated on the primacy of music, Mallarmé will stress the centrality and primacy of poetry. In writing to Régnier, he chooses metaphors drawn from the visual arts and recalling the Impressionist techniques he defended in his remarkable article on Manet, but he also depicts poetry as music, and words and rhythms as a kind of keyboard each poet has to create. The image of poetry as music stays with him throughout his life. In one of his last letters, a response to a journalist, he ends with a slightly ironic coda: "Never has a thought presented itself to me detached, I don't have such thoughts and this leaves me in an awkward position; my thoughts form the line, musically placed, of an ensemble, and if I isolate any of them I feel them lose everything, even their truth, and that makes them ring false; but after all, this avowal may perhaps constitute such a detached thought, suitable for the white sheet of an album" (*CC*, 641).

What is so striking in his brief letter to Régnier is the way in which it draws on so much of Mallarmé's personal and long-standing meditations while also responding specifically to the volume that ostensibly inspired it. Because *Les Lendemains* is certainly rich in echoes of ancestors, especially Baudelaire, reading it must have stimulated Mallarmé to think about the complex relationship of influence, inspiration, and creativity. As recent studies have shown, his own poetry, for all the often startling originality it reveals, can be read as an inspired and determined reworking of such predecessors as Baudelaire, Hugo, and Banville. Listening to that inner voice, the personal voice, as Mallarmé suggests in his letter, seems to be a process enhanced, if not enabled, by listening to the great conversation of centuries of poets.

One further sentence in the letter demands attention: "Your poetic form is very clear, in its half-tones that endow it with reverie (to use comparisons taken from all the arts, but then Poetry subsumes them all, and you prove that to be the case with very different gifts) and your language strikes me as capable of fullness and delicacy." The clarity of the verse I take to mean the metrical structure, the overall form, to which the words and images add the essential wash of halftones that promotes reverie. Regardless of its applicability to Régnier, this is very much self-referential, focusing on Mallarmé's own attempts to use the alexandrine in ways that would, as he remarks in "Crise de vers," "loosen from within that rigid and puerile mechanism" (*OC*, 362) while continuing to maintain the indispensable enigma. Mallarmé's delight in drawing on the terminology and possibilities of all the arts—a delight he shares with many of the poets of nineteenth-century France—is obvious in this letter. Régnier's diaries suggest that he himself had a greater love and understanding of music than of the plastic arts. He admits liking very few contemporary painters, apart from Pierre Puvis de Chavannes, whose flat washes and mythologized figures offer a visual parallel with his own poetry, but later in his life he would devote many poems to painstaking and somewhat mechanical transpositions of the works of painters. It is perhaps not too fanciful to suggest that it was Mallarmé's conversation rather than the influence of Wagner that sparked Régnier's attempt at this series of works that reveal the interrelationship of all the arts.

A year later, on November 15, 1886, Mallarmé wrote to congratulate Régnier on another publication:

IT WAS ONLY BECAUSE I WAS OVERTAKEN by the unexpected need to return to an interrupted task, over the last few days, that I was prevented from writing to you immediately on closing your book [*Apaisement* (Calm)], to describe the exquisite and almost unanticipated impression it made on me: how far you've come from your first poems, which nevertheless had plenty of charm! The subtler fingering you needed, you now possess, retaining the art of the old unchangeable verse while mingling it with the delicious discoveries of the present, with the result that your reverie, at once precise and remote, possesses an exact instrument. I congratulate you warmly, and that's apart from all my friendship for you, flattered by one of your rare dedications preceding the sonnet "The Island," one of my favorites. (*Corr.,* III: 70)

Apaisement is certainly a more mature work than Les *Lendemains,* richer in its range of theme and in the techniques it deploys, less evocative of earlier writers, and more aware of the possibilities of experimentation. "Idylle" reveals some of this complexity in the play of internal rhymes and in the flexibility of the alexandrines:

> Au treillis du berceau grimpait un chèvrefeuille . . .
> L'heure était langoureuse, et j'avais espéré
> Que le calme et la paix de ce lieu rétiré
> Attendriraient son cœur assez pour qu'elle veuille
> Accueillir en faveur l'aveu réitéré.[25]

> (On the trellis a honey suckle climbed . . .
> The hour was languorous, and I had hoped
> that the calm and peace of that remote spot
> would soften her heart enough for her to be willing
> to accept favorably the reiterated confession.)

Here the theme of repetition is captured in both the rhyme patterns and the assonantal echoes in ways that suggest a far greater control of what Mallarmé calls the "doigté" (fingering) than had previously been the case. Régnier's fondness for the villanelle, with its haunting suggestions of incompleteness and a longing for fulfillment, is still evident in this collection, where it is used above all to evoke the uncertainties of love and the fear of loneliness. Four ten-line villanelles grouped under the heading "Toute une année" (An entire year) reveal some of the complexities Régnier extracts from the form, as can be seen here:

> Et, dans la grotte où rit le satyre cornu
> Qui regarde couler l'eau des claires fontaines
> Sentant le même mot à nos lèvres venu,
>
> Nous joindrons d'un baiser nos bouches incertaines.

> (And in the grotto where the horned satyr laughs
> As he watches the water flow from the clear springs
> Feeling the same word on our lips,
>
> We will join with a kiss our uncertain mouths.)[26]

The poem dedicated to Mallarmé, "L'Ile" (The isle), may in many ways be more reminiscent of Baudelaire, but it does reveal a certain relationship between reverie and poetic execution:

Avec son chant clameur qui soulage les âmes
Par l'assoupissement des moroses pensers,
La mer s'en vient mourir en rythmes cadencés,
Berçant de vieux espoirs dont longtemps nous rêvâmes.

Et le désir nous prend de voguer sur les lames
Au roulis vagabond des vaisseaux balancés,
Par des pays brûlants et des climats glacés,
En de frigides nuits et des midis de flammes,

Pour voir (ô rêve inné soudainement éclos)
Sur cette immensité frissonnante des flots,
Aux confins de la mer brumeuse et matinale,

Surgir à l'horizon s'ouvrant comme un décor
Dans le magique éclat d'une aube virginale
L'Ile des fleurs de pourpre et des feuillages d'or.

(With its clamorous cry that brings relief to the soul
By softening somber thoughts,
The sea comes to die in cadenced rhythms,
Rocking old hopes that have long been our dreams.

And we are seized with the longing to sail on the seas
Rocked on the wandering roll of the ships,
Through burning lands and frozen climes,
Through frigid nights and noons of flame,

To see (oh innate dream formed suddenly)
On that shivering immensity of the waters,
On the edge of the misty morning sea,

Ascend on the horizon opening like a stage set
In the magic glow of a virginal dawn
The Isle of purple flowers amidst their golden leaves.)[27]

Despite Mallarmé's fondness for river sailing, it is hard to imagine that this poem would have been singled out for attention and listed as one of his favorites had it not been dedicated to him. The limpidity of its images and the banality of much of its vocabulary establish it far more in the territory of such Parnassians as José Maria de Heredia and François Coppée than in the domain of Symbolism. What such discrepancies reveal is that Mallarmé was far less interested in establishing a certain school of poetry than in encouraging the development of an individual voice in his younger friends, and that his open-minded reading accepted as axiomatic the individuality of poetic diction. The banality of that final image, with the virginal dawn illuminating the crimson flowers and golden foliage, nevertheless suggests that when Mallarmé speaks of Régnier's achievement of a personal touch and technical skill, he was deliberately sidestepping the whole vexed question of content. In so doing he was himself following the path established in Hugo's 1829 preface to *Les Orientales,* which orders the critic to focus not on the subject, as all subjects are acceptable in modern poetry, but on the subject's treatment. Moreover, Mallarmé's own art of suggestion and evocation, his insistence on the need not to describe the forest but to evoke the movement of leaves and the play of light, or, as he puts it, "a chord all but stripped of any reminiscence of the hunt" (*OC,* 522), seems here to have been set aside, disregarded, in the desire simply to explore the poems from Régnier's point of view.

Six months later, the publication of Régnier's next volume, *Sites,* inspired the following letter from Mallarmé: "Your poetry has become very ample and has taken on a hint of the gesture that gives without counting: indeed, the profusion of precious characteristics of passion or reverie reveal that there is in you a state of intense imagination and I rejoice in a poetry that is so spacious and so rich. There is not one of your sonnets that is not a complete poem: that's very fine" (*Corr.,* III: 116–17). "That gives without counting": in this phrase it is hard not to detect a note of irony on the part of a poet who published so little poetry, and then only when he believed a poem had reached near perfection. While Mallarmé's expression implies generosity, the subtext suggests a prolixity that suffers from insufficient revision. Nevertheless, Mallarmé's sympathetic assessment of Régnier's poetry as "spacious and rich" intimates that it does open up for him possibilities of meditation and reverie, and that his generosity in creating so rich a network of potential and allusion appeals to the older poet despite its occasionally slapdash or vacuous nature.

By this time Régnier was noting in his diary frequent visits to Mallarmé's Mardis, and the increasing warmth of their relationship is evident in the letters. The nature of the letters changes, too, now that they could draw on a collective memory of discussions about the nature and function of poetry. Mallarmé's response to *Episodes,* Régnier's volume published early in 1888, is exceptionally revealing in the light it sheds on his reaction to contemporary poetry:

YOU KNOW THE LIFE I LEAD and how little it favors letter-writing; and besides I can say aloud and everywhere what I think of a work, before talking on paper about it to the author.

I want to stop making you wait and sum up my feelings directly to you.

Episodes is a book that ranks you. It occupies its position among the first in the very turbulent poetry of this end of an epoch. It reveals itself to be essentially protected with an armor of certainty and evidence.

I don't believe that the new combinations of the poetic line, since it was restructured, are infinite; and you have had the opportunity and the honor of having fashioned a number of unforgettable ones, truly delicious lines, of the kind that the alexandrine hasn't yet given us. Yes, as I've repeated several times to myself, in reading you and closing you to think about it, this volume marks a stage not only in your literary life, but also more generally in the current poetic efforts; and it contains devices that people will borrow from you but which date from you.

Now, as concerns the poetic matter itself, you deserve just as much praise, for I knew all the subtleness of your atmosphere, but here you add much more richness. There is in the course of these pages some very precious music, where everything, even the subject itself to start with, the feelings and the reverie, plays and swings in a clearly-delineated atmosphere, and with what lightness! It has all the transparency of a high fresco or of an orchestra that cannot bear to pack up and go home.

And all this is full of substance, to the extent that the sonnet seems to have been selected as an initial departure point with a certain degree of mischief. (*Corr.*, III: 190–91)

Mallarmé, like many of his contemporaries, was to give much thought over the ensuing decade to the possibilities and limitations of fixed-form poetry, traditional line structures, and free verse. The experiments of such poets as Gustave Kahn, Marie Krysinska, and Henri de Régnier himself were leading to a vision of poetry quite different from that which had dominated French literature from the Renaissance, a new vision that Mallarmé was to announce with excitement and a sense of disquiet to his audiences in Oxford and Cambridge in 1894. The source of his disquiet and the limitations to his concept of free verse are made clear in this letter to Régnier when he indicates that he believes the number of permutations to be strictly limited. As a poet for whom the alexandrine was always the explicit or implicit starting point, he considered the new form as inalterably tied to the twelve-syllable line, existing less in its own right than as a variation on that line. This is what leads Mallarmé to consider that Régnier's inclusion of impeccably regular sonnets among the free verse acts as a somewhat ironic reminder of what should be seen as the standard. Hence, too, his belief that Régnier's free-verse lines were in some way templates to which other poets would be forced to return. The idea that the free-verse form was entirely unlimited in its possibilities, or limited only by the individual poet and his or her concept of the subject matter, Mallarmé seems unwilling to accept, at least when he wrote the letter. There's also a strong suggestion that some of the effects Régnier had achieved with free verse, although they had indeed not yet been realized using the alexandrine, were not necessarily beyond the possibilities of the twelve-syllable line. If Régnier has thrown down the gauntlet, the letter seems to imply, Mallarmé is only too eager to accept the challenge.

The intensity of his evocation of Régnier's subject matter here, together with the use of an image that is a favorite of his—that of the orchestra tuning up or, as in this instance, being reluctant to acknowledge that the concert has ended—suggests that here Mallarmé is happier dealing with this aspect of the volume. Nevertheless, as his Oxford and Cambridge lecture reveals, he was fully aware that French literature had reached a decisive point in its development, one that for all his doubts he had no intention of underestimating. And, at the same time as he was writing such letters as these, we can find him already working toward the formulations in that lecture, a revised version of which was published in 1894 as "La Musique et les lettres." One obvious example is the reference in the Régnier letter to the time in which they lived, which points forward to Mallarmé's assertion in "Crise de vers" that a manifest turning point had been reached in the evolution of French poetry, one that marked, strictly speaking, the end of an epoch.[28]

To understand Mallarmé's perception of free verse when he wrote the letter to Régnier, we need to bear in mind that it was only in the middle of 1887 that he had first really begun to come to terms with this development. In a letter to Gustave Kahn, one of the more vociferous of the poets who claimed to have created *vers libre,* Mallarmé wrote in response to the volume *Les Palais nomades* (Nomad palaces):

YOU MUST INDEED BE PROUD! This is the first time in our literature and I think in any literature, that a Gentleman, opposing the official rhythm of a language, our old Verse, has created one all by himself, a rhythm that's perfect or rather simultaneously exact and enchanting: that's an entirely novel adventure! The result of adopting this new point of view is that anyone who is at all musical can, by listening to the special arabesque that commands him, provided he succeeds in noting it, create his own personal and unique metrics, different from the general kind (the kind that had become a public monument at least in our own city). What delightful freedom! For take good note that I don't consider you've put your finger on a new form in the face of which the old one must withdraw: for the former line will remain, impersonal, for anyone and everyone who wishes to seek a different isolation, that will be their choice. But you open up one of the paths, your own: and what's no less important, you have done it in such a way that thousands can be created. The very clear laws can quickly be perceived in reading you, and you've recognized their existence within the language, for they were there already, like many others no doubt that a different ear will perceive. The charm is considerable, independently of the very subtle qualities that are yours alone, and those that arise exquisitely from poetry: there is here in addition to the established musical forms something that appears vitally rejuvenated in the word that offers itself less supported and with less preparation, just as there may also be some loss of the complex fire of the facets, a loss incurred by not incrusting itself in an age-old melodic mold which the reader has already totally absorbed. (*Corr.,* III: 120)

What arises from this generous and complex response is that Mallarmé, for all his originality, for all his rejection of the clichéd in terms of imagery and vocabulary, nevertheless found in the established mold of fixed form and especially of the alexandrine line an essential template. What he implies is that the experimentation in free verse is valid only insofar as it takes the standard forms as an implicit point of reference. Even within the alexandrine the complex and multiple possibilities suggested by the experimentation of the Romantics and those who came after them draw their force from the reader's memory and expectation of the classic line with its standard caesura after the sixth syllable. By its very insistence on this belief, Mallarmé's letter to Kahn suggests that he suspected his correspondent did not share it. Régnier's diaries tend to bear this out, although occasionally one glimpses a degree of professional and personal jealousy on Régnier's part that may have interfered with his exact reporting of his master's voice. At one point Régnier asserts, "Mallarmé gives an admirable definition of Kahn's poetry as the immediate and unmediated consumption of thought" (*Annales,* Notebook for April 1 to August 7, 1889). While this is hardly an attitude Mallarmé was likely to support, it may be that what was really said paid more attention to the effect of spontaneity that the poetry produced, a nuance the envious Régnier may well have chosen to gloss over. Régnier himself, in an entry in the ninth notebook of his diaries (December 1, 1888, to April 1, 1889), evades the whole question of Kahn's role in the development of French poetry by saying, "In brief, Kahn is not in my eyes a French poet; he's a kind of oriental or Persian." (This is a standard accusation leveled at the early users of *vers libre* and ironically one that Kahn used against Marie Krysinska, whose claim for inventing it is in direct competition with his own.) Whatever Mallarmé really thought about the ultimate value of Kahn's experiments, he certainly saw them as both central to and characteristic of what was happening in contemporary poetry. His letter to Kahn reveals above all a sense of heady freedom, of individuality (not necessarily a virtue for a poet to whom impersonality was a watchword), and of the rejuvenation of language. Of all these, the last is by far the most important and the only aspect that is entirely positive.

Mallarmé's letter to Kahn, together with several of his letters to Régnier, can be seen as a starting point for the famous lecture he gave in Oxford and Cambridge some six years later, by which time he had been able to watch the development of free verse in the hands of many of the country's younger poets. "La Musique et les Lettres," the title he subsequently gave to the article based in part on that lecture, together with his article "Crise de vers," teases out many of the implications of his letter to Kahn and of similar explorations in letters to others, notably, indeed, to Régnier. Mallarmé's discussions with younger poets—in private, during the Mardis, and through letters—underpin, for instance, his affirmation that "our phase, which is the most recent, if it isn't closing, at least takes a breather or perhaps takes note; a certain attention sets free the creative and relatively sure will power" (*OC,* 360). What he terms the exquisite and fundamental crisis that he and others detected in contemporary literature derives in large part from the removal of the overwhelming shadow cast by Hugo, whose vast influence and unquenchable ambition seemed almost, as Mallarmé puts it, to forbid all late-comers to speak at all. Of course Mallarmé is far from being the first to make such a claim: Baudelaire used something very similar both in his critical articles on Hugo and in his defense of the 1857 edition of *Les Fleurs du mal* when he claims that his predecessors, and especially Hugo, have ranged so widely as to leave only a small field open to newcomers. But Baudelaire was referring above all to subject matter, whereas Mallarmé's attention is focused more on the possibilities of the poetic form. In "Crise de vers" he asserts that it was soon after 1885 that language, having waited for the master's death, began to escape: "The entire language, adjusted to fit our metrics, discovering in metrics its vital pauses, breaks away, shatters into a free disjunction of a thousand simple elements; and, as I'll show, does so in a way that recalls the multiple cries of an orchestra, but an orchestra that uses language" (*OC,* 361). The influence of Wagner and his assertion of the primacy of music over poetry is evident in the images that Mallarmé uses in both his letters and his lectures as the poet struggles to reveal what for him is the primacy of poetry over music.

In finding examples to illustrate his presentation of the change taking place, Mallarmé focuses first, not on Kahn, but on Régnier and Jules Laforgue. Specifically, he again takes up in the lecture the suggestion that Régnier has discovered some of the viable alternatives to the alexandrine. His letter to Régnier of April 1888 had asserted his conviction that the variations free verse could offer "were not without limit" (*Corr.,* III: 190). Two years later we find a more developed form of the argument:

THE EXQUISITE TISSUE OF YOUR POEMS yields only to the delicacy of the line, this line that you manipulate only with the most exemplary prudishness; bringing it, as if fearfully, through all the subtleties of approximation, producing it only as something that is at once evident and fleeting, and only for the length of time necessary to fix it before it disappears. I don't know how you've achieved that! But it is one of the finest poetic results and an utterly supreme phase of the art . . . little by little you managed it, through a special sense, that's what it must be. (*Corr.,* IV: 86–87)

Moreover, in "Crise de vers" he uses a word that frequently recurs in the letters to Régnier, *doigté,* which I've translated as "fingering." In a powerful paragraph signaling both the resources and the limits of *vers libre,* he claims,

THE POET WHO HAS ACUTE TACT always considers this alexandrine as the definitive gem, which should be brought out, blade, flower, only rarely and for some premeditated motive. He touches it modestly, or merely plays around it, granting it neighboring chords, before producing it superb and naked: letting his fingering falter against the eleventh syllable or extending it to the thir-

teenth, on many occasions. M. Henri de Régnier excels at these accompaniments which he has invented, an invention I know to be as discreet and proud
as the genius who established it and which is indicative of the passing trouble
of those who perform poetry when faced with this hereditary instrument.
Something different, or simply contrary, is the deliberate rebellion that can be
detected, when the weary old mold is set aside, when, for instance, Jules Laforgue, right at the beginning, initiated us into the certain charm of the irregular verse. (*OC,* 363)

Laforgue, whose influence on T. S. Eliot is so well known, was not among Mallarmé's
correspondents, but his name does appear among the Mardistes listed by Dujardin,
and it has been suggested that Mallarmé's title "Divagations" (Wanderings) stems
from Laforgue's aphorism "Mallarmé est un sage qui divague" (Mallarmé is a wandering sage). Laforgue was among those whose poems were published in the periodical
called the cradle of Symbolism, *Lutèce* (*VM,* 424), and in various other journals in
which Mallarmé himself published poems. The central point Mallarmé is making
here is that *vers libre* reveals either a continuous expectation of the alexandrine or a
temporary dismissal (a vacation rather than a retirement) of the old mold. Just as in
his letters to Régnier, therefore, Mallarmé does not present the new development as
opening the floodgates to total freedom but as a form that can function only if both
poets and readers retain firmly in their active memory the rhythms of the alexandrine, that "national cadence" (*OC,* 362). His lecture on Villiers de l'Isle-Adam, written around the same time, makes a similar point:

THE SOMEWHAT RUSTY SIGN OF *Le Parnasse contemporain,* traditional as it was,
has been blown down by a wind that has come from no one knows where,
but which cannot be denied; the old French metric (I dare not add, poetry) is
undergoing, at this moment, a wonderful crisis, unknown at any other age
or in any other nation, where among the most zealous changes to all literary
genres, prosody is left untouched. Nevertheless, the Parnassian precautions
shouldn't be seen as useless, for they have provided a marker between the
highly audacious renovations of Romanticism, and freedom; and they delineate (before versification dissolves away into something that's indistinguishable
from the primitive keyboard of speech) a game that is official, or submitted to
a fixed rhythm. (*OC,* 491)

Clearly, throughout his writing at this time, published and private, Mallarmé was
meditating on the values of tradition and change, and his was an important voice in
determining the nature of the experimentation.

The importance of Mallarmé's letters to Régnier in helping to formulate the argument and the language of "Crise de vers" is also obvious when one considers the

vital sentence that reveals that while this "national cadence" is the basic language, each poet creates within it his or her own idiom: "Each soul is a melody, and all you have to do is start it up again; and for that all that's needed is each poet's flute or viol" (*OC*, 363). Similarly, in the 1885 letter to Régnier, Mallarmé had urged him to establish "his own particular sound" (*Corr.*, II: 306).

Kahn, however, is not forgotten in "Crise de vers" but is credited with adding to the richness of *vers libre* through his "erudite notation of the tonal value of words" (*OC*, 363). This expression recalls Mallarmé's letter to Kahn, in which he praises the younger poet for his perception of "the very clear laws [that] can quickly be perceived in reading you, and you've recognized their existence within the language, for they were there already, like many others no doubt that a different ear will perceive. The charm is considerable, independently of the very subtle qualities that are yours alone, and those that arise exquisitely from poetry" (*Corr.*, III: 120).

Kahn's prickly personality made him a much more difficult correspondent than the more urbane Régnier. In 1893, for instance, Kahn was to write a furious letter to Mallarmé about an anecdote that the latter is supposed to have recounted. Kahn's letter reveals the kind of irascible egotism that gives little weight to prior proofs of friendship:

I HAVE LEARNED FROM AN IMPECCABLE SOURCE that one evening (it would be a year or a year and a half ago) you recounted the following anecdote: "Being intoxicated, after a dinner I'd given to the Young Belgium movement, I'm supposed to have got up during a literary discussion and thrown a bottle at my wife's head with the words: 'There's only one great poet, and that poet is Kahn! Kahn! Kahn!'" I'm not writing to thank you for concerning yourself about me and my drinks, but to forbid you to represent my wife as having bottles thrown at her head, and you will no doubt prefer to tell me who betrayed you rather than leave me to think that this infamy was a mere improvisation. (Corr., VI: 55)

Mallarmé's letter, dripping an icy civility, disclaims all memory of such an anecdote, offers to make an apology if two witnesses attest to having heard him tell it, and adds, "Note the difference in tone between my letter and yours" (*Corr.*, VI: 55). Kahn must have recognized his error, as later we find Mallarmé sending him a poem he had requested, and by February 1895 the tone is again one of friendship: "Thanks, Kahn: they come from past ages and from a heart, these poems that are so marvelously direct" (*Corr.*, VII: 147). Yet that kind of misinterpretation of Mallarmé's nature makes for an appreciable difference between the letters to Kahn and those to Régnier, and the lack of deep understanding between the two men may well have contributed to Kahn's relegation to a minor role in the list Mallarmé gave of those whose writing had developed *vers libre*.

The last six paragraphs of "Crise de vers" initially formed part of a preface written for yet another Mardiste, René Guilbert, who wrote under the pseudonym René Ghil. Founder of what he called the "école instrumentiste" (instrumentist school), Ghil is now remembered mainly for his extraordinary and largely unreadable *Traité du verbe* (Treatise on the word), which pushed to extremes Baudelairean correspondences and Mallarméan ideas on the relationship of music and literature.[29] Ghil and Mallarmé were soon to part, not in any bitterness, but as a result of temperamental differences that can be illustrated through the following anecdote. When Mallarmé affirmed that one could not live without the ideal that he sums up through the elliptical term "Eden," Ghil replied, "I believe one can, dear Master" (see *Corr.,* II: 285). Yet in 1885, when he read Ghil's poetry collection *La Légende d'âmes et de sangs* (The legend of souls and blood), Mallarmé saw in Ghil parallels with his younger self and praised in particular what he thought might be Ghil's goal of creating "a work whose architecture is already known to you, and not producing (even marvels) at random" (*Corr.,* II: 286). Given such a statement, given, too, that *La Légende* claimed to have found its principle inspiration in Mallarmé's "L'Après-midi d'un faune," it is hardly surprising that, in 1886, Ghil should have asked Mallarmé for a preface to the work in which he set forth his convictions about poetry. Nor is it surprising, in light of the extravagant nature of Ghil's treatise, with its attempt to establish exact parallels between colors and sounds, that Mallarmé should have suggested in his preface a far more subtle and flexible program. Mallarmé's opening sentence, while intimating that most poets prefer to keep to themselves the rules and patterns they establish for their creative writing, nevertheless credits Ghil for having established such a set of guidelines, the laws that, as he puts it, fix the mind's spoken instrumentation (*OC,* 857). In many letters and in other articles and prefaces, Mallarmé insists on the importance of creating such a framework, and establishing an architecture that would sustain a lifetime's work. I believe that by this Mallarmé is thinking more in terms of foundations than of an unchangeable and unadaptable structure. Although many critics believe that he continued to follow throughout his poetic career the ground rules he established while in the provinces, I think that what he is suggesting here, and what is in fact the case for his own writing, is a kind of underpinning that was strong enough, while remaining flexible enough, to respond to changing possibilities and conceptions. A theme that runs through his letters to younger poets and resurfaces here is that these laws should remain private and internalized. He suggests in his preface to Ghil's *Traité du verbe* that locking oneself into a published framework, however praiseworthy the desire to create such a framework might be, is in itself an error. In this he is close to Baudelaire's rueful confession about a system's simultaneous attraction and unworkability:

A SYSTEM IS A FORM OF DAMNATION that drives us into perpetual abjuration; you always have to invent yet another one and that is a wearisome and cruel punishment. And my system was always beautiful, vast, spacious, commodious, clean and above all polished, or at least so it seemed to me, and always some spontaneous and unexpected product, an aspect of the universal life force, would come along to show the weakness of my puerile and elderly knowledge, that deplorable daughter of utopia.[30]

The image of his manner of thinking provided by those who have described the Mardis, together with the traces remaining in his letters, points much more to a mind continuously evolving its methods on the basis of a preestablished set of triggers or departure points. This is reinforced, I would argue, by the fact that he sums up Ghil's treatise as representing "the particular point his thought has reached *at the moment when he intends to publish it*" (*OC,* 857; my italics), in a formula that makes clear his concept of an evolving thought moving through many points but captured here by a desire for publicity. Moreover, he presents Ghil's treatise as "made to vanish away amidst the obsolescence of cushions crushed under the habit of the Castle of Usher, or to don a rare binding marked with the seal of des Esseintes" (*OC,* 857). The allusion to Usher indirectly recalls Poe's treatise, *The Philosophy of Composition,* while the reference to Des Esseintes, the protagonist of Joris-Karl Huysmans's novel *A rebours,* strengthens the image of an effete readership.

Rather than use the preface to present, explore, or comment on Ghil's theories, Mallarmé launches into what is now familiar territory for him: the essential difference between the language of everyday communication and that of literature. In a sentence that has been frequently quoted but that is worth quoting again, since it sums up with great beauty and force an essential plank in Mallarmé's poetics, he asserts, "What, however, is the point of that marvel that transforms a fact of nature almost into its vibratory disappearance in accordance with the play of words, if it's not to liberate, free of the annoyance of a close or concrete echo, the pure notion?" (*OC,* 857). Placed within the context of Ghil's treatise, this miraculous formulation, which points to a desired end product rather than belaboring the means of achieving it, acts as a subtly ironic warning to the reader and to other poets.

Whatever hesitations Mallarmé may have had about the nature of Ghil's theories, there can be no doubt that he delighted in and welcomed the wide-ranging discussion about the nature and purpose of poetry. The final sentence in his preface makes this clear, as it insists on the fact that the time for such debates is propitious, which indeed it was. The flowering of periodicals devoted to aesthetics in general and to poetry in particular is a remarkable feature of these final decades of the nineteenth century. Many of the Mardistes were closely associated with one or more of these periodicals, and the discussions that took place on the rue de Rome no doubt find an extension in such volumes as La *Revue wagnérienne,* edited by Edouard Dujardin; La *Plume,* created by Léon Dechamps, whose enlightened and open-minded leadership made it the center of the young literary movement in the 1890s; *La Conque,* founded by Pierre Louÿs; and *La Revue indépendante,* which, under the editorship of Mallarmé's disciple Dujardin, was to become the richest and most interesting of the era's literary periodicals. Remy de Gourmont, closely involved in the founding of the prestigious and long-lived *Mercure de France,* and who himself had attempted to create a new art of rhetoric in his essay on the aesthetics of language and the problem of style, examined this rich vein of periodicals in his study *Les Petites Revues: Essai de bibliographie* (The little reviews: an attempt at a bibliography). Gourmont was an enthusiastic supporter of Mallarmé, eager to defend him, as he himself puts it, from the "relative stupidity of the philistines" (*Corr.,* IV: 69). While that stupidity is indeed reflected in some of the publications he mentions, what Gourmont's bibliography reveals is the astounding richness and variety of the contemporary aesthetic debates enabled by the creation of so many reviews.

La Conque was in many ways typical of these publications. Founded by Louÿs when the poet was barely twenty, it set out to provide an anthology of original work by the most recent poets, and its opening statement presented it as both exclusive and of the highest quality.[31] Only twelve issues were planned (in fact, only eleven appeared), each with a run of only one hundred copies, and as it proudly proclaimed, "It will never be continued or reprinted." Its title was inspired by Henri de Régnier's lines "La Conque / où je souffle un appel à quelque dieu qui passe" (The conch shell / through which I trumpet an appeal to some passing god), but its exclusivity and the luxury quality of its paper and presentation were clearly indicative of Mallarmé's influence. As the prolific ballad writer Paul Fort put it in his memoirs, Mallarmé was seen as "the image of pure art, sequestering himself from all foreign elements and enclosing himself jealously within himself, in immutable and solitary serenity, as in a temple forbidden to the profane."[32] As his remarks to those who accused him of obscurity reveal, Mallarmé believed that literature should demand of its readers an intellectual effort all the stronger in that language, the vehicle of literary expression, doubles as the current coin of daily exchanges, unlike the oils and notes of painting and music. And as Alphonse Daudet discovered when he asked, "as circumspectly as possible," if Mallarmé was not working at being more abstruse than ever, such questions and accusations were not accepted submissively: "With that lightly affectionate voice that at times seems, as someone [Georges Docquois] has said, to drop down half a tone in irony—after many muddled sentences like this one: 'One doesn't write in white'—Mallarmé concludes his nebulous amplification by confessing that at the present time, he considers a poem as a mystery to which the reader must seek the key."[33] While Louÿs clearly accepted the premise of the hermetic nature of all great art and was himself a great lover of hoaxes and mysteries, as is shown by his publication of *Les Chansons de Bilitis* (Songs of Bilitis), which purported to be translations of previously unknown Greek poets, his first Mardi was not a success. His diary entry for June 24, 1890, notes crossly that "Mallarmé pontificates in an unbearable way."[34] Like so many others, Louÿs soon succumbed to Mallarmé's charm, and we find him writing to request a poem for *La Conque* and receiving warm praise for the review: "The last number of *La Conque,* including 'La Femme qui danse' [Woman dancing], charmed me: you will have, all of you, created something rare" (*Corr.,* IV:

244). The richness and variety of *La Conque*'s stable of contemporary poets, running the gamut from the Parnassianism of Leconte de Lisle, Heredia, and Léon Dierx through the Symbolism of Mallarmé, Maurice Maeterlinck, and Régnier, and including Paul Verlaine, Algernon Swinburne and Judith Gautier, makes it exemplary of the poetic reviews of the time. Mallarmé clearly appreciated both the panache of its young editor and the warmth of his admiration and friendship. When Louÿs sent Mallarmé a sonnet in honor of his fiftieth birthday, the older poet replied:

> LOUÿS, I CANNOT REMEMBER ANYTHING that has touched me so much; and this sonnet, which is not only beautiful but mysterious and triumphal, possesses even this aspect of the work of art, in which everything must appear miraculous, its unexpectedness. How were you able to think in such a way of such a date. . . . It gives me heart because my golden wedding anniversary with the Muse seems to open with a breakdown of my health; say rather it gives me back my faith. I've staked my life on something, as a hermit; and you show me that it interests people; I can't lose! Touched, I thank you, dear friend. (*Corr.,* V: 56–57)

Igitur and the Captain, casting the dice; the figure of the hermit that he told Odilon Redon he saw as symbolizing his ideal self; poetry as mystery, triumph, and surprise: This is a letter that encapsulates much of Mallarmé's thinking and indicates the extent to which conversations with other poets were also conversations with himself. Louÿs, "precise, fleeting, gemlike, and musical" (*Corr.,* V: 64), as Mallarmé was to define him in a description identifying him with the ideal poet, strikes us now as primarily Parnassian, his verse, its subject, and its language far removed from Mallarméan Symbolism. Through *La Conque,* however, Louÿs did indeed, in Régnier's terms, "trumpet an appeal to a passing god" and exemplified a historical and artistic moment.

One of the by-products of the multiplicity of publications dedicated to aesthetic questions was the plethora of interviews conducted with poets and novelists. As Dieter Schwarz argues in the preface to his collection of Mallarmé's interviews, "Towards the end of the nineteenth century, the press began to discover literature and the fine arts as a part of current events."[35] Many of these interviews seem an extension of the Mardis, part of Mallarmé's broader image of the role of oral literature. As with his delight in writing occasional verse, formulating complex aesthetic convictions in the form of conversation was a type of exercise for him, a limbering up for the more serious business of writing; it was also intrinsically valuable, however. Thus his 1891 reply to Jules Huret's inquiry on the evolution of literature allows another means of exploring the question of *vers libre.* We have the same themes, the same attribution to Hugo's death of the freeing of poetry, the same musical analogies that show the poet playing his own flute in his own corner instead of "the great organs of official meter" (*OC,* 866). What we find in the interviews and in the records of the Mardis is a reflection of the continuing debate that Mallarmé maintained on a range of artistic subjects and that he also conducted in his letters.

This was a time when many young writers approached him for comments or advice and when his role as mentor assumed great importance for the future development of literature, both within and outside France. Many years later Paul Valéry would meditate on the particular nature of this kind of relationship, asserting that "we rarely give much thought to the nature and importance of the relationships that exist in a particular epoch between *young* and *old.* The admiration, the envy, the incomprehension, the meetings; the precepts and procedures handed down or disdained; the judgements each makes of the other; reciprocal denials, scorn, changes of mind. . . . All this, which *would be* one of the most lively aspects of the *Intellectual Comedy,* are well worth not passing over in silence. [. . .] What can be more interesting than these reciprocal opinions?" [36] Valéry himself was one of the generation of poets who were most influenced by Mallarmé's presentation of the poet's role and nature. Early in 1888, the seventeen-year-old Valéry, at that stage still resolutely Parnassian, according to his biographer, Denis Bertholet, began copying into his notebook various pieces by Mallarmé—the reverie on Wagner, the poem written for Geneviève's fan, "Les Fleurs" (The flowers). [37] Looking back at his discovery of what he was to term the "secret splendor" [38] of Mallarmé's poetry, Valéry reported, "At the still fairly tender age of 20 and at a critical moment in a strange and profound intellectual transformation, I experienced the shock of Mallarmé's work; I felt the surprise, the instant, intimate scandal; and was dazzled. It ruptured all my links with my current idols. I felt myself become fanatical. I experienced the stunning progression of a decisive spiritual conquest." [39] By an extraordinary stroke of luck, the young man, "lost in the provinces" [40] as he was to put it in his first letter to Mallarmé, met Pierre Louÿs on a date he was always to remember as decisive, May 26, 1890. This led to another important meeting, that with André Gide, and encouraged by his two new friends, Valéry found the courage to write to Mallarmé, sending him a copy of two of his poems and asking for his advice. The answer he received has often been quoted, and it deserves to be, both because it is so typical of the older Mallarmé and because it is so exemplary of the mentor's art: "The gift of subtle analogy, with adequate music, you certainly possess that, and that is everything. I said as much to our friend M. Louïs [*sic*]; and I repeat it, before your two brief and rich poems. As for giving advice, solitude alone gives that, and I envy you your solitude as I remember the hours of my youth spent in the provinces, down there near where you are; and which I'll never find again" (*Corr.,* IV: 152–54). In an elated letter to Pierre Louÿs, Valéry was to comment that Mallarmé's letter contained "a subtle marrow." [41] Mallarmé's recommendation of the value of solitude, Valéry tells his friend, had allowed him to perceive, "like a lightning bolt that tears aside the unquiet darkness, the entire secret of that strange and luxurious work." [42] In an amazingly perceptive and dense formulation, he asserts, "[Mallarmé's] style is the very essence of what he writes, the

invisible network of distant correspondences, and appropriate assonances, the unexpected awakening of ideas, exactly what is needed to summon to the soul of the
reader, the white, weightless flight of dreams."

In a letter written in April 1891, Valéry raises a question about the function of
poetry, one that accords closely with Mallarmé's own vision of the poet's role consisting in the orphic explanation of the earth. As Lloyd Austin comments, this letter
and Mallarmé's response constitute a "crystallization of symbolist theory" (*Corr.,* IV:
233). Poetry, asserts Valéry, "seems to me like a delicate, beautiful explanation of the
world. Whereas metaphysical art sees the universe as constructed of pure and absolute ideas, and painting sees it in terms of colors, poetic art will consist in considering it clad in syllables, organized into sentences."[43] Valéry's central premise is even
closer to Mallarmé, although it has its roots in Poe, whom the young poet acknowledges, and, even more so, though Valéry doesn't mention him, in Baudelaire:

> THIS MAKES INEVITABLE THE SUPREME conception of a high symphony, unit-
> ing the world around us and the world that haunts us, a symphony con-
> structed according to the rigorous rules of architecture, fixing simplified types
> of a background of gold and azure, and liberating the poet from the weighty
> assistance of banal philosophies, and false expressions of tenderness, and life-
> less descriptions. . . .
>
> In France, the afternoon of a faun is the only work that has realized this aes-
> thetic ideal, and the peerless perfection that it demands demonstrates the fu-
> ture disappearance of exasperated false poets, destroyed more or less mechan-
> ically by their own mediocrity.[44]

Mallarmé's reply, dated May 5, 1891, confirms Valéry's beliefs, and does so in terms
that echo so many of his statements, scattered through the letters and the published
work, as to indicate how close Valéry had come to the heart of Mallarméan Symbolism: "Yes, my dear poet, to comprehend literature and for it to have a reason, one
must attain that 'high symphony' that, perhaps, no one will create; but it has haunted
even the least conscious of us and its main features, vulgar or subtle, stamp every
written work. Music, in the strict sense, which we must pillage, demarcate, if our
own music, kept silent, is not enough, suggests such a poem" (*Corr.,* IV: 233). Just
as he did in the autobiographical notes for Verlaine, Mallarmé sketches in here his
image of a single work of literature, an ideal work on which all writers were engaged,
consciously or not. In the same way that Valéry, in his letter, brings together notions
of architecture and music, so Mallarmé had spoken of

> a book, quite simply, in many volumes, a book that would be a book, architec-
> tural and premeditated, and not a gathering of chance inspirations, however
> wonderful. . . . I would go further and say: The Book, persuaded that when

all's said and done, there is only one, attempted unawares by whomsoever has written, even geniuses. The Orphic explanation of the Earth, which is the poet's sole duty, and the literary game, *par excellence:* for the very rhythm of the book which would then be impersonal and alive, even in its pagination, juxtaposes with the equations of this dream, or Ode. (*OC,* 663)

The close friendship that developed between the two men, the pleasure they took in each other's company, is evident in their subsequent letters. But Valéry was entering a phase in which he turned away from writing literature and focused on what he considered more intellectually demanding tasks (a diary note lists as the famous men still alive whom he most admires Jules-Henri Poincaré, W.T. Kelvin, Mallarmé, Huysmans, Degas, "and perhaps Cecil Rhodes"),[45] and although there is little doubt that the two men continued to discuss their concept of writing and poetry when they met, the correspondence itself bears little trace of it. Valéry's numerous, sensitive, and highly intelligent evocations of Mallarmé after the latter's death played an essential role in keeping him firmly in the public eye, in accordance with the vow he made in his letter to Mme Mallarmé and Geneviève when Mallarmé died:

I BELIEVE THERE IS AN IMMENSE intellectual labor of ideas in his work, still in the shadow, and unknown by the majority of his best readers. I believe this, because I've so often spoken with him, and because a natural disposition of my mind always brought me back to questioning him passionately about that research of which his written work is only the visible result. On Sunday, over there [that is, at the cemetery], I resolved that this enormous work done by so admirable an intelligence would not be completely lost. It seems to me that if I succeeded in doing something in this vein, I would be more worthy of the affection he so often showed me. (*Corr.,* IX: 318)

It was a promise amply fulfilled.

Among the many others who attended the Mardis—the future novelist André Gide, who in those years was known to his friends as "The Symbolist," Stuart Merrill and Francis Viélé-Griffin, Paul Claudel and Francis Jammes—or who wrote to Mallarmé from Europe, as in the case of Stefan George and Edvard Munch, or from places as far a field as Australia, where Christopher Brennan was writing his intricate and complex poems in the Symbolist manner, one expected voice is absent: that of Marcel Proust. Proust could certainly have attended these gatherings. He was of the right age, he and Mallarmé had mutual friends, and of course they had many interests in common. But Proust's desire to stamp his own mark on the age and to establish his differences from the dominant older figures of the time, together with his personal attachment to Anatole France, kept him away and inspired him to write his article attacking the obscurity of the Symbolist movement, which he published in *La*

Revue blanche in 1896. Six weeks later Mallarmé's response, "Le Mystère dans les lettres" (Mystery in literature), appeared in the same periodical. It is in this article that Mallarmé's often quoted riposte to such attacks of incomprehensibility appeared: "I prefer, when faced with such aggression, to reply that our contemporaries do not know how to read—except for the newspaper; which certainly provides the advantage of not interrupting the chorus of preoccupations" (*OC,* 386). Reading profoundly, he argues, requires the individual to penetrate through the necessary stratum of intelligibility to find beneath it the boundless treasure that the true work of literature offers the intellect. Ironically, few readers of Mallarmé's time were better equipped than Proust himself to read in this way, as *A la recherche du temps perdu* makes abundantly clear. And as his biographer, Jean-Yves Tadié, reminds us, it was "Le Vierge, le vivace et le bel aujourd'hui" (The virgin, lively and beautiful today), Mallarmé's sonnet about the swan, that Proust's narrator inscribed on Albertine's yacht, as Proust himself inscribed it on the wing of his lover's plane.[46] Among all Mallarmé's relationships with younger writers, the absence of Proust appears as a kind of phantom, revealing all the more clearly the vital importance of Mallarmé's great gift of friendship for both the individuals and the period.

"A Passerby Seeking Refuge":
Poetry, Politics, and Bombs

La très vaine divinité universelle, sans extérieur ni pompes.
—Œuvres complètes, 398

There is reported to be an old Chinese curse: "May you live in interesting times." Mallarmé certainly lived in interesting times, not just for aesthetics and culture but also for politics and scientific discovery. When he was born, just over fifty years had passed since the French Revolution had brought an end to absolute monarchy, a dramatic change that continued to create traumatic aftershocks through much of the second half of the nineteenth century. The revolution of 1848, the short-lived republic that followed it, the coup d'état that brought to power Napoleon III, the waves of repression and relative tolerance that marked his twenty-year reign, the French defeat in the Franco-Prussian War in 1870, the violence of the Commune that followed that defeat, and the changes of power and the surges of anarchy that marked the first decades of the Third Republic are merely the most obvious elements of this complex development. The world was rapidly changing, not just politically and socially but materially and intellectually, with scientific and technical discoveries bringing previously unimaginable innovations to everyday existence. And if a Jules Verne or a Villiers de l'Isle-Adam was able to translate into fictional terms some of the extraordinary potential of these changes, there were many others who felt threatened to the very core of their social, sexual, and national identity. To what extent do Mallarmé's letters and friendships bear witness to his response to all this ferment? Who did he vote for, what periodicals did he read, what side did he take—morally and intellectually if not actively—in that most divisive of all cases, the Dreyfus Affair?

The image Paul Valéry has given us of an ascetic, living apart from society and the world in order better to grasp its complexities—"those who renounce the world place themselves in a position to understand it"[1]—and above all better to represent art in its pure form, is, of course, partly true. As Mallarmé himself argues in a letter to James McNeill Whistler, written during the height of the World Fair that was held in Paris in 1889, "I haven't yet gone to see the Fair, because I'm working a great deal and it would devour me" (*Corr.,* III: 313), a claim he repeated almost verbatim a few days later, when, in a letter to Henri Cazalis, he explained that he had at last visited the fair, because he had been asked to write an article on its most famous symbol, but asserted, enigmatically, that the only thing he could find to say about it was that "the Eiffel Tower surpasses my hopes" (*Corr.,* IV: 542). But Valéry is also right—is indeed drawing on one of Mallarmé's best-known maxims—when he claims that for the poet the universe has no other conceivable destiny than to find expression. Humanity's duty, as Mallarmé put it, was to translate the external world through images made possible by the richness of our internal world, our imagination. While he may have held back from these events for fear of being swept up by them, and while the masses as such had little appeal for him, it is also the case that he loved public holidays, saw them, indeed, as a kind of poetry, and believed that part of the poet's task was to extract from such fleeting moments the eternal elements that make sense of contemporary existence. Like the shimmering excitement and pleasure Claude Monet depicts in *Flags in the Rue Montorgueil,* Mallarmé's prose poem "La Déclaration foraine" (The declaration at the fair), in which the narrator, at the instigation of his female companion, is driven to present his own offering, a sonnet, to the assembled throng, develops the passion that Baudelaire and Théodore de Banville felt for public celebrations, presenting them as the ideal forum for literature, the venue in which the masses could become empowered by culture.

In 1862 a twenty-year-old Mallarmé wrote the article "Hérésies artistiques: L'Art pour tous" (Artistic heresies: art for all), which, as the critic Emilie Noulet asserts,[2] he never later acknowledged when referring to the works he had published. In this article he presents art as demanding an initiation and uses as his central example the encoding of music. Mallarmé insists that all art should transform itself into "a mystery accessible only to rare individuals" (*OC,* 259), not to the multitude that is incapable of recognizing its beauty. He goes on to argue that the individual can be a democrat, but when that individual writes, he or she must become double and allow the aristocrat within to dominate. He concludes with an intransigent call for the masses to be given moral tracts to read, but stipulates that they not be allowed to spoil poetry: "Poets," he adds, in a veritable call to arms, "you have always been full of pride: go further and become full of disdain" (*OC,* 260). While Emilie Noulet and many other critics have seen this statement as underpinning all of Mallarmé's future development, it is at least worth asking the question of whether the reason for his keeping it hidden in later years is less because it was too specific than that it showed a brash insensitivity that a later Mallarmé came to modify. After all, in the early 1860s Mallarmé must have been only too aware of the interest accorded the so-called worker poets, at a time when poetry was often equated with the mere ability to follow a rhythmical pattern and produce acceptable rhymes.[3] The verse of the worker poets presented a transparency that demanded little of the reader and clearly irked the young Mallarmé enough for him to indulge in a somewhat pretentious snobbery. While all his writing does indeed demand an energetic act of imaginative interpretation on the part of the reader, works such as "La Déclaration foraine," however ironic or utopian, suggest that the older Mallarmé, through conversing with artist and writer friends, came to realize the inspirational force provided by the crowd. And it of course remains the case that the terms he uses in his early article—*democrat, aristocrat*—are not to be understood in their habitual social sense but refer to the world of art, accessible to all, regardless of birth, who are willing to make the intellectual and imaginative effort to comprehend. Moreover, as the years passed, Mallarmé's growing prominence, and that of his friends, forced him, at least from time to time, to react to public events and participate in public ceremonies.

An August 1886 letter to his young cousin Victor Margueritte conveys much of his position in regard to public life and to his correspondents' or his interlocutors' right to their own opinions. Margueritte, a budding writer struggling with his failure to live up to his ideal, and thus offering to the older poet a mirror of his own earlier condition, had written to Mallarmé announcing that he was going to join the army in Algeria, but at the end of his letter he added the touching question, "What advice have you got for your little friend?" One might think that a man as moved by beauty as Mallarmé was, a man to whom, as his reaction to some of Edgar Degas's displays of temper reveals, even minor violence was not only so alien but also so demeaning, would urge his cousin not to adopt the military life. After all, it was barely three years since a major uprising in Algeria had been brutally put down following two years of bloodshed. It may be that Mallarmé felt that out of respect for Margueritte's father, a hero of the 1870 war, he should avoid any argument based on the barbarism of war. Instead he focuses entirely on what will be best for the young man's personal development and subsequent career hopes. While he makes it fairly plain that for him the only possible solution to a loss of faith in his abilities as a writer would be to set "elbows on the table, and gaze at the famous white paper of his soul, under a lamp" (*Corr.*, III: 50), he is careful to avoid laying any blame on Margueritte for not doing so of his own accord. Of the two possibilities he sees for the young man—devoting himself for life to the army or, as he puts it, suffering the despair of a literary dream—all Mallarmé can say is that his own choice fills him with suffering, while the military life has its noble side: Two suicides, he concludes. The question of the rights and wrongs of colonialism, war, and aggression does not appear to enter into Mallarmé's thinking, or at least into what he is willing to discuss in a letter. What matters above all, he asserts, is that a writer have a refuge. What he has learnt from bitter experience is that time does its utmost to destroy that refuge. The real solution, he suggests, would be to have a vigorous genius and impose yourself with such power that the crowd would grant you a livelihood; but, he adds wistfully, it would take a god to do that.

In letters like this, Mallarmé seems a long way from the awareness of social realities that we find in his contemporaries Jules Vallès and Louise Michel, or even Emile Verhaeren and Emile Zola. It is this kind of attitude that led the contemporary left-wing social historian Prosper-Oliver Lissagaray to accuse Mallarmé of decadence and to compare his work unfavorably with Louise Michel's socially conscious writings (see *Corr.*, IV: 119). While Mallarmé not surprisingly disliked being associated with the so-called Decadent school, complaining wearily, "J'ai mal au dent / D'être décadent" (What a fag / Is this Decadent tag) (*OC,* 167), he took little part in such polemics, seeing them as remote from the central interests of art.

While Mallarmé's principal meditations centered on language and beauty, his letters reveal that he was neither as ascetic nor as removed from everyday considerations as many have argued, taking the thinking of "L'Art pour tous" and Valéry's arguments to their extreme position. Although neither the assassination of the French president Sadi Carnot nor the devastation wreaked on the French wine industry by phylloxera (an outbreak that reached its heights in 1876, the year in which, by an irony of fate, Mallarmé published his "Après-midi d'un faune," with its paean to grapes), neither the expulsion and dissolution of the Jesuits in 1880 nor the sweeping electoral reforms in the United Kingdom in 1884 leave a ripple in his letters, or in the letters of those who wrote to him, we do get glimpses of his awareness of this rapidly changing world, both in his letters and in his responses to questions by journalists. The slightly nostalgic conservatism that marks his approach to material existence (though not to art and culture) can, perhaps, be perceived in the fact that he mentions neither Ernest Michaux's invention, in 1867, of the bicycle nor John Boyd Dunlop's invention of the inflatable tire in 1888; we do, however, find him discussing the shining splendor of the bicycle in a reply to a question about beauty and utility, and replying to the journalist who asked what his feelings were about the costume women cyclists should adopt: "Your question puts me in the same position as when I'm faced with those who ride the steel horse, making me a passerby seeking refuge, but if their motive is to show their legs, I prefer them to do so by means of a raised skirt, which is at least a vestige of femininity, rather than with the boyish trousers, so that the lightning dart strikes me, overthrows me and pierces me" (*OC,* 881). Aesthetics and eroticism rather than science and society are at the heart of his response to the modern world.

It is difficult to tell from his letters how much he was aware of the suffering of the poor, particularly of children, just as the paintings made by Manet, Monet, and Renoir at Argenteuil give no hint that human waste was being pumped into the river that they transformed into such visions of beauty. If Mallarmé mentions Jules Ferry, it is in reference to a possible improvement in his personal position rather than to the education minister's introduction of a law—based on his conviction that the book was the means of liberating the intellect—making school compulsory, free, and secular. Perhaps the jaundiced teacher Mallarmé had become viewed with a skeptical eye the influx of so many more of the nation's children into its classrooms.

Yet for all his determination not to let the external and the circumstantial devour him, Mallarmé could not remain unmoved by the suffering caused by the Franco-Prussian War. His letter to Frédéric Mistral of September 4, 1870, when he had just learned of the disastrous defeat of the French forces at Sedan but before he had heard that, in Paris, Léon Gambetta had declared France a republic, reveals the intensity of his feelings and indicates a political response founded in pragmatism:

I ADMIT THAT READING THIS MORNING'S DISPATCH, which you by this time know about, don't you? (40,000 French soldiers taken prisoner, among them the Emperor, and Prime Minister Mac-Mahon seriously wounded) was brutal! To-day's atmosphere has an unknown dose of misfortune and insanity. And all that, already, just because a handful of stupid fools, five weeks ago, proclaimed themselves insulted, and misread modern history, which consists of something quite different from those childish and worn-out ideas. Never have I so completely detested Stupidity. (*CC*, 487)

The ostensible trigger for this destructive war was the Hohenzollern candidacy for the Spanish throne, which the French foreign minister Louis de Gramont chose to use as a means of attempting to humiliate Prussia. Mallarmé was clearly convinced that modern Europe had little to do with ancient monarchies and entrenched nationalism. Indeed, his own support for republicanism can be detected when he followed up his letter to Mistral later that same day, after hearing of Gambetta's move, by suggesting, "It should have been you who went out on the balcony of the Avignon Town Hall to proclaim the Republic to Provence. But things never happen as they should" (*CC*, 488).

The Prussian army pushed on into France, setting siege to Paris on September 19. Gambetta escaped from the city by balloon, in a scene transformed by the artist Pierre Puvis de Chavannes into pure myth, but socialist and radical forces within Paris held out until the end of January, when starvation more than bombardments forced them to capitulate. From March to May, however, radical Paris, disturbed by the peace terms and alarmed by the composition of the National Assembly, seized cannons from the French army and attempted to establish a communist government within Paris. A week of ferocious fighting at the end of May, in which French troops were ordered into the capital, brought the commune to a violent end. If the regime that arose from this bloody beginning was republican rather than monarchist, it was mainly because of the disarray of the royalists and the Count de Chambord's insistence on returning to the white flag of the Bourbons, a decision that revealed how little he had learned from the radical changes that had taken place since the Bourbon flag last flew. But what seems to have propelled Mallarmé out of the deep sense of impotence from which he had been suffering was less the blow struck to the nation by the war and civil strife than the death of his close friend Henri Regnault. When he writes to Henri Cazalis on March 3, 1871, his letter opens with a cry of pain for the death of Regnault, then moves into what is in fact the only possible positive response to such a meaningless destruction of artistic promise—the determination to live entirely for art, to set aside the metaphysical questioning that had been plaguing and hampering him, and that he may well have come to see as self-indulgent in the face of death, and to become purely and simply a writer: "un littérateur pur et simple" (*CC,* 496).

During the 1870s and early 1880s Mallarmé increasingly came into contact with various groups of people whose political convictions, while he may not always have shared them, were nevertheless to some extent in accord with his own. Many of the artists, intellectuals, and writers who were part of his extended circle were as liberal in their thinking about politics, or at least about society, as they were in their conception of art and literature. Moreover, from the mid-1880s to the mid-1890s, Symbolism allied itself closely with anarchism, which was not yet, as Richard Sonn points out, the strictly working-class movement it was to become but rather "a collection of marginal and *déclassé* elements of the population that could easily incorporate bohemian artists as well as tradespeople, intellectuals as well as manual workers."[4] The profoundly bourgeois nature of the Third Republic, its philistinism and its materialism, quickly alienated the most imaginative and individualistic thinkers, since it was as suspicious of any new tendencies in art and literature as it was hostile to the demands of the working classes.

Through Manet, Mallarmé came into contact with artists whose work was seen as subversive by the bourgeois, or at least by the art critics who guided their thinking. Of course not all Impressionist paintings are as overtly political as Manet's powerful depiction of the execution of Emperor Maximilian, who had been proclaimed emperor of Mexico in 1863 by the French but was abandoned by his European allies under pressure from the United States in 1866 and shot by firing squad the following year. Yet even in their choice of subjects—workers, bars, entertainers and prostitutes, the outer suburbs—and in their changing perspectives—which direct attention away from the individual and onto the masses, or place on the same plane audience and stage, clients and barmaids—the Impressionists were reflecting a change in power structures and in concepts that the middle classes found all the more threatening for being indirect.

Nevertheless, when Mallarmé supports the Impressionists in 1876, his article stresses the solidarity of artists rather than that of thinkers. It is a plea for freedom for the artist and for openness from the viewer. There is no indication here of a political agenda or even of a social awareness. In other cases, too, in this first decade of the Third Republic, when Mallarmé seems to take a political stand, it appears primarily, at least in his eyes, as a personal stand, a defense of a friend or of some-one he admires. This is the case in 1879, for example, when he signed a petition in favor of the exiled Peruvian poet Della Rocca de Vergalo, who had sent him a copy of his recent volume *Le Livre des Incas* (The book of the Incas). The petition pleads with the Peruvian government to grant the penniless exile financial aid. Mallarmé's letter to Della Rocca de Vergalo concludes with a paragraph that shows how deeply he still felt the scars of what he considered his own exile: "Are you not, moreover, you who drive away from yourself all the suffering that causes your tears, a mother for that dear child, your son, invoked by your finest poems! From the bottom of my soul I wish you the chance to return home, bringing back from exile, instead of death and despair, the proud work that bears witness of a new future" (*Corr.*, II: 196). Throughout his life Mallarmé would go out of his way, whenever he could, to help writers and artists in financial or other difficulties, frequently drawing on his rela-tions with those in power.

While actions such as this are clearly not political in motive, Mallarmé was be-ginning to move in circles where he would meet people with strong political beliefs. By 1883, in particular, we find him writing to a woman whose many friends and acquaintances were in general strongly republican. Juliette Adam (1836–1936) was born Juliette Lamber, a name she was also to give to the private road that led to her house in Paris.[5] According to her highly romanticized autobiography, Juliette Adam, whom Gustave Flaubert was to describe, at the height of her influence over Gam-betta, as "more powerful than any minister,"[6] experienced a tumultuous and highly politicized childhood, married disastrously at the age of sixteen, and in 1868, after her first husband's death, married the left-wing freethinker Edmond Adam. In the 1860s her salons attracted such figures as the novelist, historian, and art critic Marie d'Agoult; the socialist theorist Louis Blanc; and the charismatic politician Léon Gam-betta. The first few years of the Third Republic brought such writers as Flaubert, Anatole France, Ernest and Alphonse Daudet, François Coppée, and Edmond de Goncourt to her home. Later on she attracted to her salon the writer Jean Aicard; the actor Mounet-Sulley; the composers Charles-François Gounod and Jules Massenet; the artists Carolus Duran, Bastien Lepage, Antonin Mercié, and Ernest Dubois; and the sculptor Auguste Rodin. Most important, Juliette Adam was the energetic and influential editor of the republican periodical *La Nouvelle Revue,* which published essays by Paul Bourget and Paul Valéry and, in serial form, novels by, among others, Anatole France, Jules Vallès, and Pierre Loti (Juliette Adam always claimed to have launched Loti's career ex nihilo). She appears to have been present at some of the Mardis in the 1880s, and, although relations between Adam and Mallarmé seemed to have cooled later on, she did contact the poet again at the end of September 1897, using as intermediary Camille Mauclair, requesting him to participate in her cele-bration of the Portuguese explorer Vasco da Gama. It was for this memorial volume that he wrote his magnificent sonnet "Au seul souci de voyager" (With the sole aim of traveling), the last poem he was to complete:

Au seul souci de voyager
Outre une Inde splendide et trouble
—Ce salut soit le messager
Du temps, cap que ta poupe double

Comme sur quelque vergue bas
Plongeante avec la caravelle
Ecumait toujours en ébats
Un oiseau d'annonce nouvelle

Qui criait montonement
Sans que la barre ne varie
Un inutile gisement
Nuit, désespoir et pierrerie

Par son chant reflété jusqu'au
Sourire du pâle Vasco.

(With the sole aim of traveling
Beyond a splendid and shadowy India
—Let this greeting be the messenger
Of time, cape that your prow rounds

As if on some low yardarm
That plunges with the caravel
Foaming ceaselessly in ecstasy
A bird bringing a new message

Monotonously cried
While the wheel never changed
Of a useless reef
Night, despair and gemstones

By its song reflected even to
The smile of the pale Vasco.) (*OC*, 72)

In this sonnet Mallarmé removes any hint of a political or mercantile agenda from Vasco da Gama's voyage, made to discover a passage to India for Portuguese traders, and transforms him into the ideal adventurer—explorer, artist, or intellectual—setting out into the unknown solely to go beyond the limits that others have accepted. There is an evident but perhaps unperceived irony in Mallarmé's sending this poem, at the height of the Dreyfus Affair, to Juliette Adam and her friends, whose ardent republicanism led them to develop a bigoted nationalism coupled with anti-Semitism. While Mallarmé certainly knew many of the actors, artists, and writers who gathered around Juliette Adam, they are not those who were closest to him, and even in the early 1880s her republicanism was beginning to border on the bellicose and the chauvinistic in ways that could have little deep appeal to the man who had sought to set up an international society of writers. Mallarmé's treatment of Vasco da Gama's journey can be read in this context as an icy rejection of the home-bound and unadventurous mentality of Juliette Adam and her circle.

By the mid-1880s, moreover, the political atmosphere of the artistic groups to which Mallarmé more centrally belonged was beginning to change. The growing economic crisis at home; the rise of political terrorism abroad, particularly in Russia, where Czar Alexander II had been assassinated in 1881; and the 1883 trial of sixty-six anarchists in Lyon all led to increased tensions and to a more strident nationalism among the bourgeoisie, while among artists it encouraged a more active questioning of the status quo. Prince Pyotr Kropotkin, the mentor of French anarchism, as Eugenia Herbert calls him,[7] openly invited the political participation of the avant-garde in his *Paroles d'un révolté* (Words of a rebel) of 1885: "You, poets, painters, sculptors, musicians, if you have understood our true mission and the interests of art itself, place your pen, your brush, your chisel at the service of the revolution."[8]

What moved many of the Symbolists to participate in rather than just theorize about politics was the amazing episode of General Georges Boulanger, a man who seems to have had the extraordinary gift of being all things to all people. As John Hutton affirms, "Boulanger drew support broadly from the disaffected: from disgruntled Blanquists, frustrated republicans, self-styled socialists, and die-hard monarchists."[9] Appointed minister of war in January 1886, this charismatic figure quickly gained sympathy for his eloquent attacks on German expansionism and became the symbol of French desires for revenge after the country's humiliating defeat in the Franco-Prussian War. On May 18, 1887, the French cabinet fell. When a new cabinet was formed under Maurice Rouvier, Boulanger was excluded, no doubt because he was stirring up nationalist and specifically anti-German feelings that the government believed to be of dangerous intensity in the years leading up to the centennial of the French Revolution. On July 14, 1887, there was a popular demonstration in his favor, to which Mallarmé refers in a letter to Edouard Dujardin, mentioning the enthusiasm he felt during the festivities for this charismatic statesman. Lloyd Austin points out a curious aspect of this story when he quotes a card from the general, apparently responding to a letter sent by Geneviève (*Corr.,* III: 126–27). In March of 1888 the government, alarmed by Boulanger's growing power, put him on the retired list, which enabled him to be elected to the chamber. In this position he campaigned for a revision of the constitution, remaining vague about the details of such a revision, and demanded dissolution of the chamber. He resigned from the chamber and was returned in three constituencies simultaneously. In the January 1889 elections he won a striking victory, but his popularity rapidly declined, and he fled into exile barely two months later. In February we find Mallarmé informing Eugène Manet that he had "voted for the General, bowing to the wishes of my daughter" (*Corr.,* III: 291). Of course, as a woman, Geneviève could not vote.

The collapse of Boulangism left a vacuum that socialist and anarchist thinkers were quick to seize on and fill. Although on March 5, 1892, the radically right-wing Gyp (Sybille de Mirabeau)[10] invited him to her exhibition of cartoons, Mallarmé's sensitivities were closer to the left, and the Mardis now included a critical mass of writers and thinkers who were either sympathetic to anarchist beliefs or overtly in support of them. The journalists Paul Adam and Adolphe Retté; the poets Stuart Merrill, Pierre Quillard, Henri de Régnier, and Francis Viélé-Griffin; the satirist Laurent Tailhade; and above all the superbly gifted art critic, the enigmatic Félix Fénéon, for example, were all Mardistes more or less closely associated with the movement. For Merrill, indeed, the Symbolist was the anarchist of literature.[11]

Many of the periodicals with which Symbolism was associated and to which Mallarmé contributed were anarchist in sympathy, especially *Entretiens politiques et littéraires, L'Ermitage, La Plume,* and *La Revue indépendante.* In 1891 Mallarmé authorized the militant anarchist Jean Grave to publish Villiers de l'Isle-Adam's tale *Les Brigands* in his tellingly titled periodical *La Révolte* (*Corr.,* IV: 186), and a letter from Grave to Mallarmé indicates that the poet had written to him congratulating him on his book, *La Société mourante et l'anarchie* (Dying society and anarchy) (see *Corr.,* VI: 115n2). Moreover, on May 1, 1893, *La Plume,* over whose banquet Mallarmé had presided in February of that year, devoted an entire issue to anarchism and included forceful, anticapitalist drawings by Camille Pissarro and Maximilien Luce and articles by Kropotkin, Jean Grave, and the brilliant geographer and freethinker Elisée Reclus. The issue also contained a posthumous poem by Léon Cladel, who had died in July 1892, and whom Mallarmé had termed in a letter of January 1891 his "old and dear Cladel" (*Corr.,* IV: 187).

Of course the relationship between Symbolism and the ideas expressed in such a journal is complex. As Richard Sonn maintains, "The Symbolists' relation to anarchism was doubly determined by their perception of formal homologies between their art and elements of anarchist ideology, and by the sense of opposition they felt between their transcendental pretensions and the anarchists' social concerns."[12] Nevertheless, when the periodical *L'Ermitage* conducted a poll of artists, writers, critics, and composers in 1893, more than half were sympathetic to anarchist ideals. Although the political tendency of the periodical itself makes these findings not entirely neutral, it remains the case that they do concur with the general atmosphere of the Mardis of that date.

In addition to these anarchist circles in Paris, Mallarmé was in touch with various Belgian freethinkers, anarchists, and socialists. Among these was Emile Picard, who, like the art critic Gustave Geffroy and the later Emile Zola, espoused evolutionary socialism, building on Karl Marx and on French theorists to envisage the gradual development of an equitable society. Picard's position as the moving force behind the influential Belgian periodical *L'Art moderne;* his work for the *Université nouvelle,* which sought to make the appreciation of literature and the arts available to all classes; and his dominant role in the Belgian renaissance made him an attractive and appealing figure to French Symbolists. He had been on friendly terms with Mallarmé since at least 1887, when he received an inscribed copy of "L'Après-midi d'un faune." When Picard was imprisoned in April of 1893, accused of having encouraged violence both in his article "La Poussée nécessaire" (The necessary push), published the previous year, and in subsequent public addresses,[13] Mallarmé sent him the following sympathetic letter: "Oh, my dear Picard! How you find yourself wherever you have to be, even in prison: my one thought is that there's nothing of beauty or justice to which you do not belong, mind and matter. All our hands here take yours firmly and wish you the least possible vexation" (*Corr.*, VI: 82–83). That firm handshake sent to a man in prison was in itself a courageous act, attracting to the poet the attention of the police.

While Picard was soon released, other friends of Mallarmé ran greater risks. The talented young writer Félix Fénéon, for instance, had since the mid-1880s attracted attention to himself through his inspired and incisive editorship of La *Revue indépendante* and above all for the extraordinary quality of his art criticism in such articles as "Les Impressionnistes en 1886" (The Impressionists in 1886), which he published in *La Vogue.* Fénéon's punchy style, technical knowledge, and perceptive insights into contemporary art made him a striking contrast with the mass of art critics. His eloquent support of the Impressionists and above all those for whom he coined the term "post-Impressionists"—the more politically motivated younger generation, including Paul Signac, Camille Pissaro, and Georges Seurat—also made him a man after Mallarmé's own heart. In September 1888 he published the pithy essay "Poe et M. Mallarmé," in which he made the following assertion about Mallarmé's translation of the American writer:

WHETHER YOU READ M. MALLARMÉ OR POE, *Ulalame, To Helen, The Sleeper* (compared with these wonders "The Raven" would seem feeble, for it condemns them: fancy allowing yourself to give so servile an analysis, and one moreover that's an attempt to dupe us!), the sensation will be identical. The surge of thought, the variations in transparency, the formal echoes, the hesitations at the end of such strophes,—you can find them all in M. Mallarmé. [. . .] M. Mallarmé has caught the prismatic magic of the original verse. The only traces of his collaboration: a certain hieratical quality and a deeper music in his prose writing.[14]

To this warm and intelligent assessment, Mallarmé responded with a delighted letter, which no doubt also delighted its recipient: "If I had requested a preface for my Poe, it would have been in such clear, definitive words as yours that I would have wanted it to be written. What a lapidary critic you are, and a friend" (*Corr.*, III: 267). The two men maintained cordial relations until the poet's death, although their friendship can be said to have reached a high point in the summer of 1894, which, as John Hutton puts it, "marked the apogee of the war against the French anarchists."[15]

On April 4 of that year an anarchist attack on the Foyot Restaurant blinded in one eye Laurent Tailhade—famous for his earlier apothegm "What does the victim matter, provided the attempt is beautiful?"—and led to the arrest of thirty anarchists suspected of involvement in the wave of terrorism that had seized Paris for the past few years. Among those arrested was Félix Fénéon. Mallarmé wrote to Octave Mirbeau, who himself was obliged to flee the country to escape arrest, "What infamy has burst over that poor Fénéon; and what grim consequences" (*Corr.,* VI: 263). Although Fénéon never admitted it, his biographer Joan Halperin provides convincing evidence that he did indeed throw the Foyot bomb. The court, however, did not find such evidence, and all thirty anarchists were eventually acquitted. The risks they ran were high. After all, François-Claudius Koenigstein, who used the pseudonym Ravachol, accused of setting off three bombs in March 1892, had been executed. Mallarmé's name was already on the police records because of his association with left-wing periodicals, yet he visited his imprisoned friend,[16] spoke up for Fénéon in an interview published in *Le Soir,* and testified at the trial. Mallarmé's interview, in which he is described as the recognized head of *la jeune littérature,* suggests that he did not believe that Fénéon would have resorted to physical violence, but what he says nevertheless has interesting political and certainly moral connotations. "There is talk," Mallarmé is reported as saying, "of detonators. Of course Fénéon had no better detonators than his articles. And I do not believe one can use any arms that are more efficient than literature" (*Corr.,* VI: 287). There is nothing anodyne in Mallarmé's reaction—no denial of hostility to the status quo, no underplaying of the power of Fénéon and other writers—making it exactly the kind of representation of the writer's potency that caused such an uproar when it was given a physical manifestation in Rodin's statue of Balzac, a statue that unambiguously reveals the immense might of that writer and by extension of all writers. Mallarmé apparently made this even more explicit during one of his Mardis, announcing to his friends that "there is only man who has the right to be an anarchist, Me, the Poet, because I alone create a product that society does not want, in exchange for which society does not give me enough to live on" (*Annales,* April 1894).

The acquittal of the thirty saw the virtual end of the anarchist movement, overtaken in public interest by another affair that was to cause even greater divisions among French city-dwellers, although it left those in the country more or less untouched. In September 1894 a memorandum providing French military information was discovered in the German embassy in Paris. Examination of the handwriting led suspicion to fall on a Jewish officer, Captain Alfred Dreyfus, who despite his assertions of innocence was found guilty, publicly degraded, and sent to the French penal settlement on Devil's Island. The trial fed into the anti-Semitic notions bandied about by the popular press and shared by a large segment of the French people, providing another in the series of bugbears that the nation had found to terrorize itself with throughout the century, beginning with the criminal class, moving on to the anarchists, and now finding its target in the Jews. In 1896, however, the new chief of army intelligence, Georges Picqart, reexamined the handwriting and recognized it as that of a French officer, Ferdinand Esterhazy. The next three years were marked by rabid anti-Semitism, intrigue, and forgeries, as the French establishment fought to keep the truth from coming out. When Esterhazy was acquitted in January of 1898, Zola published his famous article "J'Accuse" (I accuse), a courageous and scathing attack on those who had kept Dreyfus on Devil's Island while acquitting Esterhazy. In 1899 Dreyfus was brought back to France and tried again in secret session. He was again found guilty but was granted amnesty in November.

Among Mallarmé's friends, as in the population at large, opinions were divided and intense. The impetuous Degas gave vent to violent anti-Semitism, Renoir attempted to remain neutral, whereas others came to the defense of the captain and of Zola. Monet, writing to Zola from Giverney on the day after the trial, made clear his allegiance: "Ill and surrounded by invalids, I was unable to attend your trial and could not shake your hand, as I would have liked to do. I followed all the phases of the trial no less passionately for that and want to tell you how much I admire your courageous and heroic behavior. You're admirable, and once people calm down again all sensible and honest minds will render homage to you."[17] The novelist, indeed, was tried and condemned to a year's imprisonment for his article.

Mallarmé himself, immersed in work as he was, had not signed any of the public petitions in favor of his friend, but he did send an eloquent telegram to Zola on the evening after the trial:

> PENETRATED WITH THE SUBLIMITY that gleams forth in your Act, I didn't believe I could come with applause to distract or break a silence that grows more poignant by the hour. The spectacle has been given, definitively, of the limpid intuition a genius opposes to massed power. I venerate your courage and admire the way in which, with the glorious struggle of a task that would have worn out or satisfied anyone but you, a man has been able to come out of this, new, entire and so heroic! It's of him, the condemned man, that I ask as if I didn't already know you, because of the honor it arouses, the permission to shake your hand, passionately. (*Corr.,* X: 108)

"The limpid intuition a genius opposes to massed power": this pregnant expression speaks volumes for Mallarmé's concept of the artist's role, and it goes a long way in explaining what was at stake for him in his apparent abnegation of any political stance. It seems that his image of the artist and of the artist's power to change social structures is far more concerned with the timeless to be bothered with party politics or current events.

Julie Manet's diary, while it indicates numerous discussions between Renoir and Mallarmé about the Dreyfus Affair, gives us no idea of what the poet actually said. She herself was strongly anti-Dreyfussard, and her silence may well cover comments with which she was not in sympathy. But Mallarmé's telegram is above all an expression of enthusiasm and respect for Zola's transformation of conviction into action, rather than any clear statement of agreement with the conviction itself.[18]

What Mallarmé's correspondence reveals, therefore, is that for a man who is often seen as remote from quotidian existence, removed from politics, and isolated in his ivory tower, he was nonetheless driven, above all by friendship and sympathy, to participate, actively or from the sidelines, in many more public issues than one might have predicted. While not as politically active as many of his friends, Mallarmé is still a man whose life needs to be set in the context of the social and political fervor of the age, in the same way that it cannot be understood without the cultural background that colored and shaped it. Indeed, Mallarmé's response to such events as Regnault's death, Fénéon's gesture, and Zola's accusation is to attempt to make meaning of them not in any social or political way but in aesthetic terms. This tendency is most clearly illustrated in his response to the Panama Canal scandal, when the collapse of diplomat Ferdinand de Lesseps's company in 1888 led both to severe financial losses for many small investors and to the discovery that powerful political figures, notably Georges Clemenceau, had been involved in taking bribes in exchange for supporting Lesseps's company. In a February 25, 1893, article for London's *National Observer,* Mallarmé makes clear what he considers to be the poet's duty in regard to such sordid current events:

A PART FROM THE TRUTHS the poet can extract and keep secret within himself, except for conversation, planning to produce them, transfigured, at an opportune moment, nothing, in this collapse of Panama interests me, through its scandal. In comparison with the phantasmagoric sunsets, when it is only the clouds that collapse, (together, probably, with what, unbeknownst, we entrust to them in the form of dreams), when a liquefaction of treasures flows, spreads out, glows ruddily on the horizon, I have the feeling that the sums, hundreds of millions, or more, enumerated in the closing speech for the prosecution and in the superb defense proposed by the lawyers, during the trial, leave me, where their existence is concerned, incredulous. Yet, that gold exists, and you can even find it everywhere, in small doses! but the failure of figures, however grandiloquent, to translate it, truly comes from a situation in which no one was pleased to be placed. (*OC,* 1577–78)

A passerby taking refuge, Mallarmé seems to have cast a somewhat sardonic gaze on the world of finance and politics, preferring to all that, like Baudelaire before him, "the clouds . . . the clouds floating by . . . over yonder . . . the marvelous clouds."[19]

Remembering the Dead

> Grief fills the room up of my absent child,
> Lies in his bed, walks up and down with me,
> Puts on his pretty looks, and repeats his words,
> Remembers me of all his gracious parts,
> Stuffs out his vacant garments with his form.
> —*Shakespeare,* King John, 3.4.93–97

Loss, suggests Richard Stamelman in his study *Lost beyond Telling,* "may be beyond telling in that the object of loss cannot be fully represented; but grief for that loss is its sign. Emptiness becomes *significant.*"[1] The absence of Mallarmé from Stamelman's study is somewhat surprising, since so much of the poet's work, published and private, bears eloquent witness to the desire to make loss and emptiness significant. From the time of his adolescence, Mallarmé can be seen attempting to make his creative writing respond to the anguish of loss and to the knowledge of mortality. There is, for example, every indication that in a short story, untitled but generally referred to as "Ce que disaient les trois Cigognes" (What the three storks said), he was responding, at least in part, to the death of his thirteen-year-old sister Maria, although as both Lloyd Austin and Austin Gill point out, the version we possess contains reminiscences of poems by Baudelaire and Hugo that he could not have read at that date.[2] Whatever the event that triggered it, the piece poignantly raises the question of the "nevermore": "Oh my dear dead one, will you never let me hear again that far-off caroling? Those lilacs, those lilies, those verbenas that you stripped of their leaves and threw into the air intoxicated with your voice, you lived no longer than they did! And yet, it was a song of hope: everyone smiled at you and you laughed at everyone."[3] And the narrative voice adds, in terms that suggest a powerful and very physical imagination, "I pity the poor dead, who, sewn into their pale shrouds, which they cannot lift even with a finger, feel oozing through the cracks in their coffins the slow, mysterious drops of melted snow. I am sure they feel so cold that they would be happy to hear Joshua's trumpet blow to awaken the lightning bolts, and the thunderous voice of God fling them into the flames of Satan."[4] The tale ends with this affirmation of emptiness: "Then he heard no more . . . . Except for shivering dawn's light step on the snow and the cracking of branches that had died under their white burden."[5] Henri Mondor, the first to publish this tale, presents it rather apologetically, and it's true that there is little in it that clearly indicates Mallarmé's subsequent poetic development. There is nevertheless some foretaste of his eventual preoccupation with loss and the poet's task in response to what he would later call "l'avare silence et la massive nuit" (miserly silence and massive night) (*OC*, 55).[6] Tracing that preoccupation through his letters reveals the growing urgency with which he pursued it.

The death of Henri Regnault, who threw his life away in an act of heroic futility in the last moments of the Franco-Prussian War, prompted in Mallarmé the same need as in "Les Trois Cigognes" to somehow force language, if not to make sense of loss, at least to compensate in some measure for it. The letter he wrote to Henri Cazalis on receiving news of Regnault's death is a raw outburst of despair and revolt:

> YOU KNOW, AT THIS MOMENT, from what you yourself are feeling what a lasting wound this has made in our affection. And what feelings of revolt! There go 50 years of a life of love and glory, and with it all the deep thought of a youth spent in preparing it. And even if it hadn't been him (that exquisite being), what unforeseen suffering this first gap in our ranks creates, and how much we now know what it is to lose a friend! You know from the few lines read over and over, that even his corpse has been lost, buried under the remains of soldiers.[7] Would you, my dear friend, like at least to bury him in the folds of our finest thoughts? To dedicate to him, from both of us, certain pages telling of what he has not been able to do? (*CC*, 490–91)

While that particular joint project came to nothing, the desire to transform thoughts into shrouds, and the written word into the only suitable tomb, motivates many of Mallarmé's later poems as well as the "medallions" he wrote for lost friends. His long and profound meditation on death finds revealing echoes and reflections in his correspondence, setting up particularly close parallels between his letters and his literature.

The first of his memorial poems dates from 1873 and was written in response to a suggestion, initially proposed by the young poet Albert Glatigny, to publish a volume to commemorate Théophile Gautier, who had died on October 23, 1872. As Gardner Davies has shown,[8] Gautier's son-in-law, Catulle Mendès, seized control of the *Tombeau de Gautier* and established certain guidelines, most of which were ignored by the majority of contributors. In a letter to Coppée, Mendès explains, somewhat fussily, that

> for the book Lemerre is to publish, Leconte de Lisle and I have composed a collective poem (other poets: Heredia, Dierx, France, Silvestre), to which we're hoping you'll kindly contribute.

Subject:

After a prologue (which I have already written) in which I say that a certain number of poets, gathered around a memorial meal in honor of Théophile Gautier, all, one after the other, rose, and each celebrated a particular aspect of the talent of their dead master.—They addressed an image of Gautier. Therefore the informal "thou" is recommended at least in the first verse.

The eulogy we would like from you is of his *tenderness* . [. . .]

The poem should be about sixty lines long, and divided into verses. Each verse should begin with a feminine rhyme, and end with a masculine rhyme (so that all the poems will fit together).[9]

In a letter to Mendès, Mallarmé explains in lapidary terms how he conceives of his own contribution to the volume, which Lloyd Austin speculates he had been invited to write in celebration of Gautier's depiction of himself as "a man for whom the external world exists":[10]

BEGINNING WITH: O thou who . . . and ending with a masculine line, I want to sing, probably in couplets, of one of Gautier's glorious qualities:
the mysterious gift of seeing with the eyes.
(Remove: mysterious.) I will sing of the *seer* who, placed in this world, looked at it, something that is not done. I think that I've succeeded in aligning myself with the general point of view. (*Corr.,* XI: 25)

The result, "Toast funèbre" (Funereal toast), presents Gautier as archetypal poet, living on through the only true monument that can be erected to him—his own works. Moreover, this piece allows Mallarmé to explore what it means to be a poet, and in so doing to begin to chart in poetry what he had begun expressing in letters—the conviction that the writer's task consists in responding to the great question "Qu'est-ce, ô toi, que la Terre?" (What, oh soul, do you know of the Earth?) (*OC,* 55); in other words, supplying the Orphic explanation of the earth (compare *OC,* 663). This alone confers meaning on our existence and offers some kind of valid response to mortality, decay, and loss. While it may not bring back what Wordsworth had poignantly termed "the hour of splendor in the grass," it does confer on the transient and fragile, Mallarmé argues, the "mystery of a name," and by reconstituting it in language lends it a permanence that will last until the "heure commune et vile de la cendre" (that vile hour when all will come to ashes) (*OC,* 54).[11]

In addition to allowing him to pay tribute to a poet who, as he had put it some eight years earlier in a letter to Cazalis, was "a soul living in Beauty" (*CC,* 179) and who had inspired part of his "Symphonie littéraire," the volume to Gautier appealed to Mallarmé because it brought together a group of poets with a common purpose. As we have seen, Mallarmé's letter to Frédéric Mistral, proposing an international federation of poets, insists on the value of this role and presents the *Tombeau de Gautier* as containing the seed of the much larger project (*CC*, 544).

The same sense of community, of working together with other creative minds to respond to absence and death, and to attempt to build a monument to a much-admired poet, underlines Mallarmé's initially warm response to Sara Sigourney Rice's invitation to contribute to the memorial for Edgar Allan Poe. His sonnet for Poe was the direct result of this invitation:

> Tel qu'en Lui-même enfin l'éternité le change,
> Le Poëte suscite avec un glaive nu
> Son siècle épouvanté de n'avoir pas connu
> Que la mort triomphait dans cette voix étrange!
>
> Eux, comme un vil sursaut d'hydre oyant jadis l'ange
> Donner un sens plus pur aux mots de la tribu
> Proclamèrent très haut le sortilège bu
> Dans le flot sans honneur de quelque noir mélange.
>
> Du sol et de la nue hostiles, ô grief!
> Si notre idée avec ne sculpte un bas-relief
> Dont la tombe de Poe éblouissante s'orne
>
> Calme bloc ici-bas chu d'un désastre obscur
> Que ce granit du moins montre à jamais sa borne
> Aux noirs vols du Blasphème épars dans le futur. (*OC*, 70)

> (Such as into himself at last Eternity changes him,
> The Poet arouses with a naked hymn
> His century overawed not to have known
> That death extolled itself in this strange voice!
>
> But, in a vile writhing of the hydra, (they) once hearing the Angel
> To give too pure a meaning to the words of the tribe
> They (between themselves) thought (by him) the spell drunk
> In the honorless flood of some dark mixture.
>
> Of the soil and the ether (which are) enemies, O Struggle!
> If with it my idea does not carve a bas-relief
> Of which Poe's dazzling tomb be adorned
>
> Stern block here fallen from a mysterious disaster
> Let this granite at least show forever their bound
> To the old flights of Blasphemy (still) spread in the future.)
>   (Mallarmé's translation: *Corr.*, II: 155)

The loss of Baudelaire, which Mallarmé felt so sharply and of which he wrote movingly from the provinces to his friends, clearly plays a role in his decision to translate Poe's poetry and thus to complete a task Baudelaire himself had undertaken —that of bringing the American writer to the attention of a French audience. Mallarmé's subsequent disappointment when he discovered that the volume was not after all an anthology of poems reinforces the importance he placed on this joint activity, which can be seen as yet another aspect of the desire for impersonality, another version of his conviction that all writers undertook one joint task, the creation of what he terms "The Book."

Mallarmé comments on his poem for Poe in letters to Sarah Helen Whitman, who had translated it into English, producing what the poet himself described as "a very fine imitation" (*Corr.,* II: 148). His explanation of a line she had misread emphasizes the extent to which he followed Baudelaire's lead in presenting Poe's life as exemplary and his apparent alcoholism as a form of inspirational mnemonics, a way of recalling lost images and inspirations. While Baudelaire insists that "the poet had learned to drink, as careful writers train themselves to take books of notes," so that "part of what today creates our joy is what killed him,"[12] Mallarmé goes further: "I mean that the age he lived in accused Poe of having found in alcohol and delirium the cause of an inspiration that is too subtle and too pure for our understanding" (*Corr.,* II: 149). In a sense, both Baudelaire and Mallarmé transform Poe into idealized images not merely of the poet in general but more precisely of themselves as individuals. A further letter to Whitman gives Mallarmé's English translation of his poem, with brief explanatory notes. Of these the most interesting is the comment that the poet's "naked hymn" is so designated because in death the words take "their absolute value" (*Corr.,* II: 155). Like the poet himself, transformed into his absolute image—"Tel qu'en lui-même enfin l'Eternité le change" (Such as into himself at last Eternity changes him) (*OC,* 70)—his poetry has assumed its absolute form, conferring on the words of everyday speech a purer sense. There are close parallels here with the image of Gautier, conferring names on the world's beauty and thus achieving the status of archetypal poet.

In writing his meditations on the deaths of Gautier and Poe, Mallarmé was able, whatever the nature and intensity of his own feelings about them, to remain on the level of impersonality that such public responses require. Other deaths were much closer to him, and demanded not so much a public and jointly created monument as an intensely private reaction. The painful illness and death of his son, Anatole, in 1879 left Mallarmé distraught, in a sorrow he sought to alleviate by urgently trying to create some kind of memorial to the child. Victor Hugo, responding to the loss of his daughter, who had drowned while on her honeymoon, had been able to create his complex and beautiful memorial to her, which is at the same time a long meditation on death and the possibility of an afterlife. But in writing *Les Contemplations* Hugo was supported by religious convictions that Mallarmé did not share, and even so, Hugo, that most prolix of poets, recorded his child's actual death only by a blank space. What words could ever convey a parent's terrible despair at the loss of a child? Mallarmé struggled to create a verbal "tomb" for Anatole, but abandoned the attempt, leaving only fragments.[13] Regnault, Gautier, and Poe had, after all, left behind them their own monument, the works they had created, and were thus able to respond to the question Mallarmé raises in his memorial toast to Gautier: "What do you know of the Earth?" The fragments of the poem for Anatole reveal how bitterly Mallarmé swung between, on the one hand, despair that the child had died without knowing either the answer to that question or even that he was dying, and, on the other, fear that he may have been aware of his impending death.

Ten years later, the death of a friend he had admired and cherished since his early twenties again demanded from him a response to mortality. He had met Villiers de l'Isle-Adam (Figure 3) through their mutual friend Catulle Mendès in 1863, and the two remained friends throughout Villier's life. Alan Raitt, Villier's biographer, goes so far as to argue that "it is no exaggeration to say that Villiers changed the course of Mallarmé's existence, both as a man and as a poet (no doubt the two cannot be separated in his case), and Mallarmé undoubtedly understood and loved Villiers more than any other contemporary did."[14] An extravagant, eccentric figure, with a truly remarkable gift for prose style, Villiers has nevertheless not really achieved the renown he and his friends predicted for him. Although his play *La Révolte* (Revolt) is regularly performed; although *Axël* so struck the critic Edmund Wilson as encapsulating fin-de-siècle thinking that it inspired the title of his study of the period, *Axël's Castle*; although his short-story collection *Contes cruels* (Cruel tales) is widely read; and although feminist readings in particular have drawn attention to his novel *L'Eve future* (The future Eve), Villiers never really found the subject matter that would have merited his great stylistic gifts. His eccentricity and his misogyny, the fact that his life's work, *Axël,* was left unfinished at his death, and perhaps, too, the way in which his work is stamped with the thinking of his time rather than achieving any kind of transcendent universality have denied him the destiny he had believed from childhood to be his. Remy de Gourmont, who also knew him well, commented, "He felt he had had a destiny and that he had missed it."[15] One can't help thinking, in reading this comment, of Mallarmé's last note to his wife and daughter: "There is no literary heritage here, my children. . . . Believe me when I say it was meant to be very beautiful" (*CC,* 642).

When Mallarmé first met him, however, Villiers had all the prestige of a friend of Baudelaire and Gautier (he had at one stage wanted to marry Gautier's younger daughter), and above all of a writer with enormous ambitions and a radiant vision of his future glory. He embodied, far more than anyone else Mallarmé was ever to meet, a mind utterly devoted to literature, refusing to compromise in any way, determined to live by his pen alone, and unwavering in his vision of what it meant to be a poet. By 1865 Mallarmé was including him, together with Mendès and Lefébure, in the triumvirate of young poets who were part of his spiritual family (*CC,* 228). For nearly thirty years they would be close friends, and when it became clear that Villiers was dying, in abject poverty, with what he saw as his masterpiece *Axël* unfinished, Mallarmé did all he could to ensure not only the future of Villiers's works and reputation but also the financial situation of Villiers's son, Victor, insisting that Villiers make the boy legitimate through a deathbed wedding to Victor's mother. With Joris-Karl Huysmans, another of Villiers's close friends, Mallarmé worked to ensure the publication of *Axël,* and in February 1890 he made a lecture tour of Belgium, speaking to largely uncomprehending and at times downright rude audiences of his friend, "a man accustomed to dream" (*OC,* 495).

The role Villiers played in Mallarmé's concept of the artist can be detected from many of his letters. Thus in 1865 we find Mallarmé urging Eugène Lefébure to read the prose drama *Elën,* a work A. W. Raitt describes as juvenile in its conception but containing nevertheless "an unrestrained cry of individual anguish."[16] Mallarmé presents it as grandiose, the "eternal story of Man and Woman," and claims that its style is such that the reader will "feel a sensation at each of the words, as when you read Baudelaire. There is not a single syllable in it that has not been thought out in a night of reverie." He continues, "In a word, the thought, the feeling for Art, the voluptuous desires of the spirit (even the most blasé) will find in this a magnificent feast. Taste drop by drop this precious flask" (*CC,* 225). The letter he sent to wish Villiers well in the approaching new year of 1866 is an extraordinary record of friendship and a lucid and optimistic statement of Mallarmé's image of poetry:

> A LETTER BETWEEN THE TWO OF US is a banal melody which we allow to wander at will, while our two souls, which understand each other wonderfully well, create a natural and divine continuo for its vulgarity. [. . .] I'm getting back to work again, and with joy! I have the plan of my work, and its poetical theory which will be the following: "to create the strangest impressions, certainly, but without letting the reader forget for a single moment the enjoyment provided by the beauty of the poem." In a word, the subject of my work is Beauty and its ostensible subject is merely a pretext for approaching Beauty. That, I believe, is the clue to Poetry. (*CC,* 278–79)

In a letter of September 1867, when Mallarmé had not yet fully recovered from the deep depression that inspired his "my Thought has thought itself" letter to Cazalis in May of that year, he takes his concept of pure poetry considerably further, but in terms of a goal that is beyond his power to achieve: "Thanks to an extreme sensibility, I was able to understand the intimate correlation of Poetry and the Universe, and, to make poetry pure, I had conceived the plan of removing it from the realms of Dream and Chance and of juxtaposing it with the conception of the Universe. Unfortunately, as a soul organized uniquely for poetic pleasure, I could not, in the task needed to prepare that conception, emulate you and dispose of an Intelligence" (*CC,* 366). In Mallarmé's eyes, then, Villiers clearly stood for a high concept of poetry and of art, for a rejection of the haphazard and of empty reverie. The word *dream* is complex and multilayered in Mallarmé's writing, both in his correspondence and in his published writings, but here it seems to stand for the idle reverie in contradistinction to the determined expansion of the dreams of the poet's imagination. His presentation of Villiers as a man accustomed to dream suggests this difference quite forcefully. When he claims in his letter that Villiers has been able to dispose of an intelligence, he seems to mean that his friend has succeeded in setting aside his own personality to allow the universe to speak through him, as Mallarmé claimed in his letter to Cazalis that he himself wanted to do. The extent to which Villiers had shaped his conviction of the poet's task at this stage of his development is clear in a letter to Lefébure of May 1868, in which he quotes a line from *Isis* to reinforce his assertion that he has returned from the Absolute and will not use it to create poetry or to unfold "the living panorama of the forms of what will be" (*CC,* 384–85). The desire to find in Villiers a model or archetype of the poet may surprise us today, but what seems to me to be really at issue here is that Mallarmé is seeking among all the poets he knew images, formulas, and possibilities that would give form to his as yet rather inchoate ambitions. In a similar way, his threnody for Villiers was simultaneously a lament for the passing of a friend and an attempt to explore a universal image of the artistic mind, "the character of the authentic writer" (*OC,* 481).

The generalizing nature of his meditation is evident from the opening passages: "Is it known what it means to write? An ancient and very vague, but jealous practice, whose meaning lies in the heart's mysteries" (*OC,* 481). Writing is a mad gamble, an attempt to prove that one exists, and that the universe exists, by a series of reminiscences captured in an ink whose blackness is symbolically associated with that of night itself. What we have here is a statement that recalls the faun, attempting, in the face of his own doubts, or what he terms the "night's ancient hoard,"[17] to prove through his memories and anecdotes that something external to himself exists.

Mallarmé's lecture seizes briefly on aspects of Villiers as individual. We see him hastening off, scarf around his neck, to mysterious meetings and rendezvous, kept secret even from his closest friends, or stopping in the street to share with an acquaintance a comment described as "glittering, new, abrupt, leaping forth to surprise you by its disparity with everything around it" (*OC,* 482). We hear something of his famous witticisms: "Truly I have a name that makes everything difficult," he's reported as commenting, "and accursed, what's more! One of my ancestors having dared to flirt a little with Joan of Arc" (*OC,* 484). But Villiers's defiance of mediocrity was above all intellectual, and Mallarmé focuses on that defiance in attempting to pay him tribute. So intense was his desire to reign, if not as a king of some country or other then as "a great writer" (*OC,* 489), that from the moment he first arrived in Paris his bewitched friends could perceive him waving flags of victory, won either long ago or still in the future: "I swear," Mallarmé adds admiringly, "that we saw them" (*OC,* 489), and so clearly that all those who met him in those days understood him to be a genius.

For Mallarmé, that genius clearly lay in Villiers's manipulation of language, in his shared perception that the line of poetry was nothing more or less than a "perfect word," in the lapidary nature of his poems, and above all in that intense awareness of the task he believed it was his destiny to accomplish. Indeed, Mallarmé suggests, Villiers's tragedy lies precisely in the fact that he was so dazzled by the intensity and glory of the task that he remained "consumed by that youth, the time when he fell violently in love with himself" (*OC,* 496). Dying, he realized that he had let time slip through his fingers, without creating the great work that would have transformed promise into reality. Yet, Mallarmé affirms, since every work of art creates its artist's sepulcher, Villiers has traced out an extraordinary tale, even if at the end there is merely a tomb: "but what a tomb! Massive porphyry and clear jade, the jaspered marble beneath the passing clouds, and new metals" (*OC,* 502).

If the image of the work as tomb recalls the funereal toast to Gautier, another paragraph in the lecture evokes the sonnet in memory of Poe, reinforcing the impression that Mallarmé's meditations on the dead are also meditations on death, and that the impersonality of death serves to enhance the individuality not of the artist but of the work. It's a paragraph that also continues Mallarmé's questioning of the relationship between word and music, as if all of his production, whatever the genre, whether written or spoken, public or private, were one seamlessly continuing conversation. "Thus," he states in a passage whose syntactical difficulty and figurative complexity are intensified by his assumption that his audience is familiar with these central tenets of his aesthetics,

restored at last in all its integrity, durable, all of it an effigy of an enigmatic man whose presence in this age is a fact, the Work which will evoke the name of Villiers de l'Isle-Adam. A Work that, because it leaves an impression, when all is said and done, that resembles nothing else, a clash of triumphs, of abstract sadness, wild laughter, or worse, when he fell silent, and the bitter infiltration of shadows and evenings, with a gravity previously unknown, and peace, recalls the enigma of the orchestra. Here, then, is my final opinion: it seems that through an order proclaimed by the spirit of literature, and by foresight, at the exact moment when music appears better suited than any rite to what is present in the masses, though latent and incomprehensible, it has been shown that there is nothing, in the inarticulation or anonymity of those cries, that jubilation, that pride, those transports, that can not with equal magnificence, and what's more with that clarity that is our conscious knowledge, be rendered by that old and holy elocution; or Words, when it's someone special who pronounces them. (*OC,* 507)

Here, in his complex structures and densely packed syntax, Mallarmé reasserts the immortality of art, presents it as the only immortality we have, and triumphantly proclaims that Villiers's writing reveals what he himself has long argued—that language has all the magnificence of music, but that unlike music, which he sees as primarily sensual, language draws on that blaze of light that is human consciousness.

While Mallarmé was to write other evocations of the dead, among them Baudelaire and Wagner, Manet, Berthe Morisot, Banville, and Verlaine, his memorial lecture for Villiers epitomizes his image of the relationship between art and immortality, the individual and the work, and the primacy of the intellect over the senses, poetry over music. While his letters show that he also took the time and trouble to try to alleviate personal and financial suffering, they continue to debate these great themes, and his last letter, the unfinished note to Geneviève and his wife written when he feared death was near, shows how deeply held those convictions were. Because what remains is the artist's work, Mallarmé wanted nothing of his fifty-year accumulation of notes and drafts to survive him, preferring instead the record left by his publications. "Burn my letters," he had told Cazalis, as he was to instruct his wife and daughter to burn his notes. "You alone will see into the depths of my heart" (*CC*, 141).

In a letter written only weeks before his death, Mallarmé was to provide a more optimistic summary of his life. The journalist Jean-Bernard Passerieu, author of a series of documentary studies, *La Vie Parisienne* (Parisian life), and of a regular chronicle in the periodical *Figaro*, had launched a detailed investigation into what he named "L'Idéal à vingt ans" (The ideal at age twenty). Various leading figures in the arts and sciences were asked two questions: "At 20, what was your life ideal, your dream? In maturity, have you fulfilled that ideal?" (*Corr.*, X: 251–52n3). Mallarmé's reply can serve as a summary both of his life and of the man himself:

W*HAT WAS MY IDEAL AT 20*, it wouldn't be surprising if I'd even given expression to it, feebly, since the act I chose for myself was that of writing. Now, *has maturity fulfilled it,* this judgment can be made only by those who have maintained their interest in me. As for an intimate autobiographical appreciation, of the sort in which one indulges, notably, alone or in the presence of a rare friend, I'll add, in the newspaper, according to your wishes, and in the hope of offering something, that I was sufficiently true to myself for my humble life to have retained a meaning. The means, I'll let the world know that the way to do this consists in using my inborn illumination to dust off every day the chance accumulation provided by the external world, that one gathers, rather, under the name of experience. Fortunate or vain, the wish I formulated at 20 has survived intact. (*CC*, 640–41)

It is a joyous and optimistic affirmation, one that reflects above all the determination Mallarmé always felt to control his life, and with it his posthumous image. The aleatory, the haphazard, the coincidental is the great shadow against which he battles, however much he knows that the throw of the dice can never abolish chance.

"Crise de vers"

Mallarmé's "Crise de vers" is so central to much of his later thinking on the future direction of poetry that it seemed useful to include a translation of this seminal article. Based in part on a lecture given in Oxford and Cambridge, "Crise de vers" shows the extent to which Mallarmé, fascinated by the experiments with free verse but personally convinced of the value of the constraints imposed by fixed forms such as the sonnet, is willing to enter into the thinking of his contemporaries and to respond with warmth and support to what they were doing. Nevertheless, the article makes it clear that he believes *vers libre* is not free of all constraints, but that, like fixed form verse itself, it is limited in its possibilities and requires, particularly, tact and control if it is to gain ifs full value. It is typical of Mallarmé that, while he never abandoned the fixed forms, he does offer "Un coup de dés" as a contribution to the experiments that are part of the exploration of "*vers libre.*"

Just now, abandoning any possibility of action, with the lassitude brought about by one afternoon after another of distressing bad weather, I let fall, without any curiosity but with the feeling of having read it all twenty years ago, the thread of multicolored pearls that stud the rain, once more, in the glimmer of booklets in the bookshelves. Many a work under the bead-curtain will send out its own scintillation: as, in a mature sky against the window pane, I love to follow the lights of a storm.

Our phase, which is recent, is, if not closing, taking breath or perhaps stock: considering it attentively reveals the creative and fairly sure will power driving it.

Even the press, which usually needs twenty years to discover the news, is suddenly preoccupied with the subject, and on time.

Literature here is undergoing an exquisite crisis, a fundamental crisis.

Whoever grants that function a place, whether or not it be the first place, recognizes in this the substance of current affairs. We are observing, as a finale to the century not what last century observed, not disruptions; but, outside the public arena, a trembling of the veil in the temple revealing significant folds, and to some extent, its tearing down.

French readers, their habits disrupted by the death of Victor Hugo, cannot fail to be disconcerted. Hugo, in his mysterious task, turned all prose, philosophy, eloquence, history, to verse, and as he was verse personified, he confiscated from any thinking person, anyone who talked or told stories, all but the right to speak. A monument in this desert, with silence far away; in a crypt, thus lies the godhead of a majestic and unconscious idea, to whit that the form we call verse is simply in itself literature; that there is verse as soon as diction is stressed, that there is rhythm as soon as style is emphasized. Poetry, I believe, waited respectfully until the giant who identified it with his tenacious hand, a hand stronger than that of a blacksmith, ceased to exist; waited until then before breaking up. The entire language, tailored to metrics, now recovered its vital rhythms and escaped, in a free disjunction of thousands of simple elements; and, as I'll show, it was not unlike the multiplicity of cries in an orchestra, but an orchestra remaining verbal.

The change dates from then: although it was surreptitiously and unexpectedly prepared beforehand by Verlaine, who, fluid as he was, was called back to primitive forms.

A witness to this adventure, in which people have asked me to play a more efficacious role although such a role suits no one, I did at least take a fervent interest in it and the time has come to talk about it, preferably from a distance, since what took place did so almost anonymously.

Let's grant that French poetry, because of the primary role played by rhyme in creating its enchantment, has, in its evolution up to our time, proved to be intermittent: for a time it gleams, then fades and waits. Extinct, or rather worn threadbare by repetition. Does the need to write poetry, in response to a variety of circumstances, now mean, after one of those periodical orgiastic excesses of almost a century comparable only to the Renaissance, that the time has come for shadows and cooler temperatures? Not at all! It means that the gleam continues, though changed. The recasting, a process normally kept hidden, is taking place in public, by means of delicious approximations.

I think one can separate under a triple aspect the treatment given to the solemn canon of poetry, taking each in order.

That prosody, with its very brief rules, is nevertheless untouchable: it is what points to acts of prudence, such as the hemistich, and what regulates the slightest effort at simulating versification, like codes according to which abstention from flying is for instance a necessary condition for standing upright. Exactly what one does not need to learn; because if you haven't guessed it yourself beforehand, then you've proved the uselessness of constraining yourself to it.

The faithful supporters of the alexandrine, our hexameter, are loosening from within the rigid and puerile mechanism of its beat; the ear, set free from an artificial counter, discovers delight in discerning on its own all the possible combinations that twelve timbres can make amongst themselves.

It's a taste we should consider very modern.

Let's take an intermediate case, in no way the least curious:

The poet who possesses acute tact and who always considers this alexandrine as the definitive jewel, but one you bring out as you would a sword or a flower only rarely and only when there is some premeditated motive for doing so, touches it modestly and plays around it, lending it neighboring chords, before bringing it out superb and unadorned. On many occasions he lets his fingering falter on the eleventh syllable or continues it to the thirteenth. M. Henri de Régnier excels in these accompaniments, of his own invention, I know, an invention as discrete and proud as the genius he instills into it, and revelatory of the fleeting disquiet felt by the performers faced with the instrument they have inherited. Something else, which could simply be the opposite, reveals itself as a deliberate rebellion in the absence of the old mold, grown weary, when Jules Laforgue, from the outset, initiated us into the unquestionable charm of the incorrect line.

So far, in each of the models I've just mentioned, nothing apart from reserve and abandon, because of the lassitude caused by excessive recourse to our national rhythm; whose use, like that of the flag, ought to remain an exception. With this nevertheless amusing particularity that willful infractions or deliberate dissonances appeal to our delicacy, whereas, barely fifteen years ago, the pedant that we have remained would have felt as exasperated as if confronted with some ignorant sacrilege! I'll say that the memory of the strict line of poetry haunts these games on the side and confers on them a certain benefit.

The entire novelty, where free verse is concerned, resides not as the seventeenth century attributed verse to the fable or the opera (that was merely a non-strophic arrangement of diverse famous meters) but in what it might be suitable to call its "polymorphous" nature: and we should now envisage the dissolution of the official number into whatever one wishes, as far as infinity, provided that it contains a renewed source of pleasure. Sometimes it's a euphony fragmented with the consent of an intuitive reader, someone with inborn and precious good taste—just now, M. Moréas; or a languishing gesture of dream, leaping up in passion and finding the right beat—that's M. Viélé-Griffin; beforehand it was M. Kahn with a very erudite notation of the tonal value of words. I'm giving names, for there are others who are typical, MM Charles Morice, Verhaeren, Dujardin, Mockel and all, only as a proof of what I'm saying, so that you can consult their publications.

What's remarkable is that, for the first time in the course of any nation's literary history, concurrently with the great general and secular organs, in which, following an inborn keyboard, orthodoxy expresses its exaltation, whoever wishes to use his or her own techniques and individual hearing can create a personal instrument on which to breathe, to touch or stroke with skill; and it can be used on its own, and also be dedicated to the Language in general.

A high freedom has been acquired, the newest: I don't see, and this remains my own intensely felt opinion, that anything that has been beautiful in the past has been eliminated, and I remain convinced that on important occasions we will always conform to the solemn tradition, that owes its prevalence to the fact that it stems from the classical genius; only, when what's needed is a breath of sentiment or a story, there's no call to disturb the venerable echoes, so we'll look to do something else. Every soul is a melody, which needs only to be set in motion; and for that we each have our own flute or viola.

In my view this is the belated eruption of a real condition or of a possibility, that of not only expressing ourselves, but of bursting into song, as we see fit.

Languages, which are imperfect in so far as they are many, lack the supreme language: because thinking is like writing without instruments, not a whispering but still keeping silent, the immortal word, the diversity of idioms on earth, prevents anyone from proffering the words which otherwise would be at their disposal, each uniquely minted and in themselves revealing the material truth. This prohibition flourishes expressly in nature (you stumble upon it with a smile) so that there is no reason to consider yourself God; but, as soon as my mind turns to aesthetics, I regret that speech fails to express objects by marks that correspond to them in color and movement, marks that exist in the instrument of the voice, among languages and sometimes in a single language. Compared to the word *ombre* (shadow) which is opaque, *ténèbres* (darkness) is not much blacker; how disappointing to discover the perversity that in contradictory fashion bestows on the word *jour* (day, light) sounds that are dark, while those of *nuit* (night) are bright. We desire a word of brilliant splendor or conversely one that fades away; and as for simple, luminous alternatives. . . . *But,* we should note, *otherwise poetry would not exist:* philosophically, it is poetry that makes up for the failure of language, providing an extra extension.

Strange mystery; and from intentions no less strangely mysterious metrics burst forth in the days when everything was coming into being.

Let an average group of words, under the comprehension of the gaze, line up in definitive traits, surrounded by silence.

If, in the French case, no private invention were to surpass the prosody that we've inherited, there would be an outpouring of displeasure, as if a singer were unable, away from others or walking where he pleased among the infinite number of little flowers, wherever his voice met a notation, to pluck it. . . . This attempt took place just recently, and, leaving aside the erudite research in the same direction, accentuation and so forth, that has been announced, I know that a seductive game leads, together with shreds of the old still recognizable line, to the possibility of eluding it or revealing it, rather than to a sudden discovery of something entirely alien. It just takes the time needed to loosen the constraints and whip up some zeal, where the school went astray. And it's very precious: but to go from that freedom to imagine more, or simply to think that each individual brings a new prosody arising from their own way of breathing—which is certainly how some people spell—well it's a joke to cause much laughter and to inspire the preface-writers to build their platforms. Similarity between lines of poetry and old proportions, this will provide the regularity that will last because the poetic act consists in suddenly seeing that an idea splits into a number of motives of equal value and in grouping them; they rhyme: and to place an external seal upon them we have their common metrics which the final beat binds together.

It is in the very interesting treatment meted out to versification in this age of recess and interregnum, no less than in our virginal mental circumstances, that lies the crisis.

To hear the unquestionable ray of light—as features gild or tear a meander of melodies: or Music rejoins Verse, to form, since Wagner, Poetry.

It's not that one element or another moves away, advantageously, towards an integrity triumphing somewhere else, in the form of a concert that remains mute if it is not given voice, and the poem, enunciator: of their community or their new form, illuminating the instrumentation until it's obvious under the veil, as elocution descends from the sky of sounds. That modern meteor, the symphony, at the pleasure of the musicians or unbeknownst to them, draws closer to thought, but a thought which no longer draws on current expressions.

Some explosion of Mystery into all the skies of its impersonal magnificence, where the orchestra should not have failed to influence the ancient effort which has long sought to extract it from the mouth of the race.

A double indication arises from this—

Decadent or mystic, the schools describe themselves or are given labels hastily by our news media, and adopt, as meeting point, an Idealism which (like fugues or sonatas) refuses the natural materials and brutally demands an exact thought to put them in order, so as to keep nothing but the mere suggestion. To create an exact relationship between the images, in such a way that a third aspect, fusible and light, and whose presence can be divined, will break free . . . We've abolished the pretension—an aesthetic error, although one that has commanded masterpieces—of including on the subtle paper of the volume anything other than for instance the horror of the forest or the silent thunder scattered through the foliage, not the intrinsic and dense wood of the trees. A few bursts of the intimate pride truthfully trumpeted awaken the architecture of the palace, the only place where one can dwell; no stone, on which the pages would have difficulty closing.

"Monuments, the sea, the human face, in their plenitude, and as they are, preserving a virtue which is more attractive than if they were veiled by a description, call it *evocation*, or *allusion, suggestion*: that somewhat random terminology bears witness to the tendency, a very decisive tendency perhaps, that literary art has experienced, a tendency that limits it and dispenses it. Literature's witchery, if it is not to liberate from a fistful of dust or reality without enclosing it in the book, even as a text, that volatile dispersion which is the mind, which has nothing to do with anything but the musicality of everything."

Speech has no connection with the reality of things except in matters commercial; where literature is concerned, speech is content merely to make allusions or to distill the quality contained in some idea.

On this condition the song burst forth, as a lighthearted joy.

This ambition, I call Transposition—Structure is something else.

The pure work of art implies the elocutionary disappearance of the poet who yields the initiative to words, set in motion by the clash of their inequalities; they illuminate each other with reciprocal lights like a virtual trail of fire on precious stones, replacing the perceptible breath of the old lyric or the individual enthusiastic direction of the sentence.

An order of the book of verse springs from it, innate or pervasive, and eliminates chance; such an order is essential, to omit the author: well, a subject, destined, implies amongst the elements of the whole, a certain accord as to the appropriate place for it within the volume. This is a possibility brought about by the fact that each cry has its echo—in the same way motifs balance each other, from a distance, producing neither the incoherent sublimity of the romantic pagination, nor that artificial unity of more recent times, measured out to the book en bloc. Everything becomes suspense, a fragmentary disposition with alternations and oppositions, all working towards the total rhythm of the white spaces, which would be the poem silenced; but it is translated to some extent by each pendant. I want to consider it as instinct, perceived in these publications and, if the supposed type does not remain separate from complementary types, youth, for once, in poetry where a dazzling and harmonious plenitude imposes itself, has stuttered the magic concept of the Work. Some symmetry, in parallel fashion, which, from the situation of the lines in the poem that are linked to the authenticity of the poem within the volume, fly beyond it, several of them inscribing on the spiritual plane the amplified signature of the genius, anonymous and perfect as an artistic existence.

A chimera, having thought of it proves, from the reflection of its scales, how much the current cycle or this last quarter century, is undergoing some absolute illumination—whose wild shower on my window panes wipes away the dripping murkiness sufficiently to illuminate those panes—that, more or less, all books contain the fusion of some counted repetitions: even if there were only one—the world's law—a bible of the kinds nations simulate. The difference from one work to another offers as many lessons set forth in an immense competition for the true text, between the ages termed civilized or—lettered.

Certainly I never sit down on the terraces to hear a concert without glimpsing amidst the obscure sublimity some sketch of one or other of humanity's immanent poems or their original state, all the more comprehensible for not being spoken, and I see that to determine its vast line the composer experienced that easy suspension of even the temptation to express it. I imagine, through a no doubt ineradicable prejudice of writers, that nothing will remain if it is not given form; a form we have reached the stage, precisely, of seeking out, faced with a break in the great literary rhythms (I discussed this above) and their dispersal into shivers articulated in ways close to instrumentation. An art of achieving the transposition in the Book of the symphony or simply to take back our own: for there is no question that it is not the elementary sounds produced by the brass, strings, woods, but the intellectual word at its purest point that must lead, with plenitude and undeniably as the ensemble of links existing within everything, to Music.

An undeniable longing of my time has been to separate as if for different purposes the double state of the word, raw and immediate on the one hand, on the other, essential.

Telling, teaching, even describing, that's all very well and yet all that would be needed perhaps for each of us to exchange our thoughts as humans would be to take from or leave in the hand of another a coin, in silence, but the elementary use of speech serves the universal reporting in which all the contemporary written genres participate, with the exception of literature.

What is the point of the marvel of transposing a fact of nature into its almost vibratory disappearance according to the action of the word, however, if it is not so that there emanates from it, without the predicament posed by a near or concrete reminder, the pure notion.

I say: a flower! And from the oblivion to which my voice relegates all contours, as something other than the unmentioned calyces, musically arises, the idea itself, and sweet, the flower absent from all bouquets.

Contrary to the facile numerical and representative functions, as the crowd first treats it, speech which is above all dream and song, finds again in the Poet, by a necessity that is part of an art consecrated to fictions, its virtuality.

The line of several words which recreates a total word, new, unknown to the language and as if incantatory, achieves that isolation of speech: denying, in a sovereign gesture, the abitrariness that clings to words despite the artifice of their being alternately plunged in meaning and sound, and causes you that surprise at not having heard before a certain ordinary fragment of speech, at the same time as the memory of the named object bathes in a new atmosphere.

Notes

Introduction: Corresponding

1. On Mockel, see Charles Conrardy, *Albert Mockel* (Brussels: Le Thyrse, 1953).
2. See Henri Mondor, *Autres Précisions sur Mallarmé et inédits* (Paris: Gallimard, 1961), 88.
3. Judith Gautier, *Le Collier des jours* (Paris: Juven, 1909), 1: 84.
4. Charles Baudelaire, *Œuvres complètes*, ed. Claude Pichois (Paris: Gallimard, 1975–76), 1: 497.
5. Henri Mondor, La *Vie de Mallarmé* (Paris: Gallimard, 1941–42); Kurt Wais, *Mallarmé: Dichtung, Weisheit, Haltung* (Munich: C. H. Beck, 1952); Austin Gill, *The Early Mallarmé*, 2 vols. (Oxford: Clarendon Press, 1979–86); Gordon Millan, *A Throw of the Dice: The Life of Stéphane Mallarmé* (London: Secker & Warburg, 1994); Jean-Luc Steinmetz, *Mallarmé: L'Absolu au jour le jour* (Paris: Fayard, 1998).
6. On this fan, see my article "Fan Autographs: Unfolding Relationships," *Australian Journal of French Studies* 32, I no. 3 (1995): 380–89.
7. Alison Fairlie, "'Entre les lignes': Mallarmé's Art of Allusion in His Thank-You Letters," in *Baudelaire, Mallarmé, Valéry: New Essays in Honour of Lloyd Austin,* ed. M. Bowie, A. Fairlie, and A. Finch (Cambridge: Cambridge University Press, 1982), 181–201.
8. See Michael Pakenham, "Mallarmé nous parle de Verlaine," *Europe* (April–May 1976): 119–25.
9. Paul Verlaine, *Œuvres poétiques*, ed. Jacques Robichez (Paris: Garnier, 1969), 25.
10. Baudelaire, *Œuvres complètes,* 1: 650.
11. See, for instance, Frances Yates, *The Art of Memory* (Chicago: University of Chicago Press, 1966).
12. *Vers libéré* refers to poetry that ignores such standard rules as the alternation of rhymes ending in a mute "e" and those ending in another letter, or the use of an even number of syllables in the line. *Vers libre* goes further still, rejecting the necessity of rhyme, using unstable rhythms, and throwing into doubt the primacy of syllabism. On these questions see Clive Scott, *Vers Libre: The Emergence of Free Verse in France, 1886–1914* (Oxford: Clarendon Press, 1990), and *The Poetics of French Verse* (Oxford: Clarendon Press, 1998).

Interlude 1. Reading in Mallarmé's Letters

1. A considerable body of theoretical literature is devoted to studies of reading practice, but here I am concerned with the specific reading practice of one individual, Mallarmé.
2. A. S. Byatt, *Possession: A Romance* (New York: Vintage, 1991), 470.
3. Marcel Proust, *A la recherche du temps perdu* (Paris: Pléaide, 1945), 1: 3.
4. Wallace Stevens, *The Palm at the End of the Mind,* ed. Holly Stevens (New York: Vintage Books, 1990), 358.

5. Stevens, The *Palm at the End of the Mind,* 146–47.

6. I explore this question of childhood reading in my *Land of Lost Content* (Oxford: Clarendon Press, 1991).

Chapter 1. Writing in Exile

1. For Mallarmé's youthful reading, see Austin Gill, *The Early Mallarmé,* 2 vols. (Oxford: Clarendon Press, 1979–86).

2. See on this Marshall Olds, "Mallarmé and Internationalism," in *Kaleidoscope: Reading in Barbey's "Les Diaboliques,"* ed. Graham Falconer and Mary Donaldson-Evans (Toronto: Centre d'Etudes Romantiques/Joseph Sable, 1996), 156–67.

3. The clock is now preserved in the Musée Mallarmé at Valvins. It appears in Mallarmé's prose poem "Frisson d'hiver" (Winter shiver).

4. On this see Bertrand Marchal's splendid study, *La Religion de Mallarmé* (Paris: Corti, 1988).

5. The expression is that of Peter Laslett, "The Wrong Way through the Telescope," *British Journal of Sociology* 27 (September 1976): 319–42.

6. For this, see *HC* and the two letters from Proust to Cazalis published there on pp. 271–72. It should perhaps be added that Jean-Yves Tadié's monumental biography of Proust makes no mention of Cazalis.

7. Compare Henry James's interest in Cazalis for similar reasons in *The Notebooks of Henry James,* ed. F. O. Matthiessen and Kenneth B. Murdoch (New York: Oxford University Press, 1961), 231.

8. See, for instance, Marcel Proust, *A la recherche du temps perdu* (Paris: Gallimard, 1954), 3: 701.

9. Proust, *A la recherche du temps perdu,* 1: 67.

10. For this attribution, see *HC,* 27, note.

11. Quoted *HC,* 87.

12. Compare, for example, his first letter to Sara Sigourney Rice (*Corr.,* II: 110).

13. To understand this comment in the context of a time in which everyone wrote verse, see Graham Robb, *La Poésie de Baudelaire* (Paris: Aubier, 1993).

14. Baudelaire, *Œuvres complètes* (Paris: Gallimard, 1976), 1: 83.

15. Quoted in Mallarmé, *Œuvres complètes,* vol. 1, *Poésie,* ed. Carl P. Barbier and G. Millan (Paris: Flammarion, 1983), 222.

16. W. B. Yeats, *Collected Works* (New York: Macmillan, 1989), 1: 92.

17. Quoted in Henri Mondor, *Histoire d'un faune* (Paris: Gallimard, 1948), 75.

18. See Chapter 2, p. 81.

19. Lawrence A. Joseph has published the correspondence in *Documents Stéphane Mallarmé,* 7: 417–33, together with a detailed introduction and other materials.

20. Joseph includes one letter written from the Villa Medicis and dated April 25, 1867.

21. See Gordon Millan, *A Throw of the Dice: The Life of Stéphane Mallarmé* (London: Secker & Warburg, 1994), 189, and Geneviève Bréton, *Journal, 1867–1871* (Paris: Ramsay, 1985).

22. Quoted in Luc Decaunes, *La Poésie parnassienne* (Paris: Seghers, 1977), 204.

23. Millan, *A Throw of the Dice,* 127.

24. Marchal, *La Religion de Mallarmé,* 80.

25. See Introduction, p. 9.

26. On this, see my *Baudelaire's Literary Criticism* (Cambridge: Cambridge University Press, 1981).

27. See Lloyd Austin, "Mallarmé and Gautier: New Light on *Toast funèbre,*" in *Balzac and the Nineteenth Century,* ed. D. G. Charlton, J. Gaudon, and Anthony R. Pugh (Leicester: Leicester University Press, 1972).

28. See in particular his letters to Cazalis dated March 23, 1864 (*CC,* 173), and April 25, 1864 (*CC,* 177); to Albert Collignon dated April 11, 1864 (*CC,* 175); as well as many later letters.

29. Verlaine, *Lettres inédites à Charles Morice,* ed. Georges Zayed (Geneva: Droz, 1976), 17. The word Verlaine uses, *épatarouflances,* is a portmanteau term that includes *époustoufler* (amaze) and *épater* (astonish: frequently used in the phrase *épater les bourgeois*).

30. Verlaine, *Lettres inédites à Charles Morice,* 25. The poems alluded to are "L'Après-midi d'un faune"; "Toast funèbre," the poem Mallarmé wrote in memory of Gautier; and his prose poem "Le Démon de l'analogie," which hinges on a sentence haunting the narrator: "La pénultième est morte" (The penultimate one is dead).

31. Verlaine, *Lettres inédites à Charles Morice,* 107.

32. Verlaine, *Lettres inédites à Charles Morice,* 110–11.

Interlude 2. Depression

1. See Bertrand Marchal, *La Religion de Mallarmé* (Paris: Corti, 1988).

2. Enid Starkie, *Baudelaire* (Norfolk, Conn.: New Directions, 1958), 57.

3. Jean-Yves Tadié, *Marcel Proust* (Paris: Gallimard, 1996), 138 ff.

4. See Mallarmé, *Œuvres complètes,* vol. 1, *Poésie,* ed. Carl P. Barbier and G. Millan (Paris: Flammarion, 1983), 145.

5. Roger Pearson, *Unfolding Mallarmé: The Development of a Poetic Art* (Oxford: Clarendon, 1996), 11.

Chapter 2. Finding a Voice

1. Quoted in Henri Mondor, *L'Affaire du Parnasse: Stéphane Mallarmé et Anatole France* (Paris: Fragrance, 1951), 55.

2. Mondor, *L'Affaire du Parnasse,* 57.

3. Published by Slatkine under the general editorship of Peter Edwards.

4. Baudelaire, *Correspondance,* ed. Claude Pichois and Jean Ziegler (Paris: Gallimard, 1973), 1: 676. The letter is to Armand Fraisse.

5. Léon Deffoux, *Dix-neuf lettres de Stéphane Mallarmé à Emile Zola* (Paris: Jacques Bernard, 1929), 13.

6. Frederick Brown, *Zola: A Life* (New York: Farrar, Straus & Giroux, 1995), 307.

7. Emile Zola, *Œuvres complètes,* ed. H. Mitterand, 15 vols. (Paris: Cercle du livre précieux, 1966–70), 12: 379.

8. See Roland de Renéville, "Correspondance inédite de Huysmans et de S. Mallarmé," in *L'Univers de la parole* (Paris: Gallimard, 1944), 40–42.

9. Renéville, "Correspondance," 44.

10. For a detailed study of such presentations of women, see Bram Dijkstra, *Idols of Perversity* (Oxford: Oxford University Press, 1986), especially the chapter "Women with Broken Backs."

11. Gordon Millan, *A Throw of the Dice: The Life of Stéphane Mallarmé* (London: Secker & Warburg, 1994), 213.

12. On this friendship, see Marianne Ryan, "John Payne et Mallarmé: Une longue amitié," *Revue de littérature comparée* 32 (1958): 377–89.

13. Thomas Wright, *The Life of John Payne* (London: T. Fisher Unwin, 1919), 76.

14. John Payne, *Poetical Works,* 2 vols. (1902; New York: AMS Press, 1970).

15. Wright, *The Life of John Payne,* 22.

16. Stéphane Mallarmé, *Les "Gossips" de Mallarme,* ed. Henri Mondor and Lloyd Austin (Paris: Gallimard, 1962), 80.

17. Arthur O'Shaugnessy, *Poems,* sel. and ed. William Alexander Percy (New Haven, Conn.: Yale University Press, 1923), 39.

18. O'Shaugnessy, *Poems,* 43.

19. O'Shaugnessy, *Poems,* 29.

20. O'Shaugnessy, *Poems,* 28.

21. For a discussion of this seminal article, see Chapter 3, p. 124.

22. Payne, *Poetical Works,* 2: 27.

23. Charles Algernon Swinburne, *Letters,* ed. Cecil Y. Lang (New Haven, Conn.: Yale University Press, 1959–60), 3: 84.

24. Swinburne, *Letters,* 3: 128.

25. Sarah Helen Whitman, *Edgar Poe and His Critics* (Providence, R.I.: Tibbitts & Preston, 1885), 69.

26. On the question of Mallarmé's translations of Poe, see Haskell Block, "Poe, Baudelaire, Mallarmé, and the Problem of the Untranslatable," *Translation Perspectives* 1 (1984): 104–12.

27. Quoted in Caroline Ticknor, *Poe's Helen* (New York: Charles Scribner's Sons, 1916), 260.

28. Whitman, *Edgar Poe and His Critics,* 56.

29. Baudelaire, *Œuvres complètes,* 2: 347.

30. See Evlyn Gould, *Virtual Theater from Diderot to Mallarmé* (Baltimore: Johns Hopkins University Press, 1989), and Mary Lewis Shaw, *Performance in the Texts of Mallarmé: The Passage from Art to Ritual* (University Park: Pennsylvania State University Press, 1992).

31. One volume of these, *More Bed-Time Stories,* is now housed in the Musée Mallarmé in Valvins, side by side with O'Shaugnessy's *Toyland.*

32. For a study of his relationships with these artists, see Chapter 3.

33. Louise Chandler Moulton, *Lazy Tours in Spain and Elsewhere* (London: Ward, Lock & Co., 1896), 166.

34. Moulton, *Lazy Tours,* 166–67.

35. Marshall Olds, "Mallarmé and Internationalism," in *Kaleidoscope: Reading in Barbey's "Les Diaboliques,"* ed. Graham Falconer and Mary Donaldson-Evans (Toronto: Centre d'Etudes Romantiques/Joseph Sable, 1996), 163.

36. C. Lefèvre Roujon, *Correspondance inédite de Stéphane Mallarmé et Henry Roujon* (Geneva: Pierre Cailler, 1949), 87.

37. Ruth Z. Temple, *The Critic's Alchemy: A Study of the Introduction of French Symbolism into England* (New York: Twayne Publishers, 1953), 111.

38. Swinburne, *Letters,* 3: 41.

39. Swinburne, *Letters,* 3: 51.

40. Swinburne, *Letters,* 3: 42. For Baudelaire's expression, see his *Œuvres complètes,* 2: 298.

41. Swinburne, *Letters,* 3: 115.

42. Swinburne, *Letters,* 3: 134.

43. Swinburne, *Letters,* 3: 137.

44. Swinburne, *Letters,* 3: 193

Interlude 3. Father and Daughter

1. Gordon Millan, *A Throw of the Dice: The Life of Stéphane Mallarmé* (London: Secker & Warburg, 1994), 232.

2. Jean-Paul Sartre, *Mallarmé: La Lucidité et sa face d'ombre* (Paris: Gallimard, 1986), 78.

3. Kurt Wais, *Mallarmé: Dichtung, Weisheit, Haltung* (Munich: C. H. Beck, 1952), 284.

4. Geneviève Bonniot-Mallarmé, "Mallarmé par sa fille," *La Nouvelle Revue française* (November 1926): 517.

5. Bonniot-Mallarmé, "Mallarmé par sa fille," 517.

6. Edmond de Goncourt and Jules de Goncourt, *Journal* (Paris: Robert Laffont, 1989), 3: 827.

7. Bonniot-Mallarmé, "Mallarmé par sa fille," 519.

8. Bonniot-Mallarmé, "Mallarmé par sa fille," 519.

Chapter 3. Forging an Aesthetic

1. Berthe Morisot, *Correspondance,* ed. Denis Rouart (Paris: Quatre-Chemins-Editart, 1950), 154.

2. For a detailed study of the traces of these friendships on Mallarmé's poetry and criticism, see James Kearns, *Symbolist Landscapes: The Place of Painting in the Poetry and Criticism of Mallarmé and His Circle* (London: Modern Humanities Research Association, 1989).

3. On this, see my "Fan Autographs: Unfolding Relationships," *Australian Journal of French Studies* 32, no. 3 (1995): 380–89.

4. For a detailed and illuminating study of Mallarmé's article, see Penny Florence, *Mallarmé, Manet, and Redon: Visual and Aural Signs and the Generation of Meaning* (Cambridge: Cambridge University Press, 1986).

5. Monet's *La Japonaise* (The Japanese woman) dates from this year (1876), confirming an increasing interest in this new form of representation that had been growing in popularity with European artists since the 1860s. See, among many other studies, Jacques Dufwa, *Winds from the East: A Study in the art of Manet, Degas, Monet, and Whistler, 1856–86* (Stockholm: Almqvist & Wiksell International, 1981).

6. For a subtle reading of this poem, see Sergio Sacchi, "'Imiter le Chinois au cœur limpide et fin. . .': La Chine en France aux environs de 1860," *Patterns of Evolution in Nineteenth-Century French Poetry,* ed. Lawrence Watson and Rosemary Lloyd (Deddington: The Tallents Press, 1990), 161–70.

7. See Harry Rand's valuable study, *Manet's Contemplation at the Gare Saint-Lazare* (Berkeley: University of California Press, 1987), 6.

8. Françoise Cachin, Introduction to *Manet, 1832–1883* (New York: Metropolitan Museum of Modern Art/Abrams, 1983), 13.

9. Charles Baudelaire, *Correspondance* (Paris: Gallimard, 1973), 2: 496–97.

10. For the story of this publication, see Michael Pakenham, *Edgar Poe: Le Corbeau, Traduction de Stéphane Mallarmé, Illustré par Edouard Manet* (Paris: Séguier, 1994).

11. On this, see Thomas Monro, "*The Afternoon of a Faun* and the Interrelation of the Arts," *Journal of Aesthetics and Art Criticism* 10 (1951–52): 95–111, and Pamela Genova, "Word, Image, Chord: Stéphane Mallarmé and the Interrelationship of the Arts in Late Nineteenth-Century French Symbolist Reviews," *Dalhousie French Studies* 36 (Fall 1996): 79–102.

12. Rand, *Manet's Contemplation,* 147.

13. Quoted in Rand, *Manet's Contemplation,* 145.

14. Quoted in Anne Higgonet, *Berthe Morisot's Images of Women* (Cambridge, Mass: Harvard University Press, 1992), 19.

15. Morisot, *Correspondance,* 99.

16. Morisot, *Correspondance,* 178.

17. Julie Manet, *Journal,* Introduction by Rosalind de Boland Roberts and Jane Roberts (Paris: Scala, 1987), 112.

18. Mallarmé's quatrain for Paule suggests something of her character: "N'allez pas, en le fuyant, Paule, / Même par vagabonde humeur / Tourner une jolie épaule / Au vieil hommage du rimeur" (Paule, do not flee, / even in a vagabond mood, / turning your pretty shoulder / to the rhymer's old homage) (*OC,* 124).

19. Morisot, *Correspondance,* 133.

20. Virginia Spate, *Claude Monet: Life and Work* (New York: Rizzoli, 1992), 190.

21. Morisot, *Correspondance,* 134.

22. Morisot, *Correspondance,* 141.

23. Quoted in Morisot, *Correspondance,* 144.

24. Julie Manet, *Journal.* For the series of Moret church pictures, see MaryAnne Stevens et al., *Alfred Sisley* (New Haven, Conn.: Yale University Press, 1992), 236–49.

25. Morisot, *Correspondance,* 184.

26. Mallarmé had given this dog to Julie.

27. See also Reynaldo Hahn's memoirs, *L'Oreille au guet* (Paris: Gallimard, 1937).

28. Julie Manet, *Journal,* 141.

29. Jean Renoir, *Renoir, My Father,* trans. Randolph Weaver and Dorothy Weaver (Boston: Little, Brown, 1962), 300.

30. See, for instance, the photo in Julie Manet's *Journal,* 69.

31. Julie Manet, *Journal,* 122.

32. Julie Manet, *Journal,* 130.

33. See Interlude 5.

34. Quoted in Daniel Wildenstein et al., *Claude Monet: Biographie et catalogue raisonné,* 4 vols. (Lausanne: Bibliothèque des Arts, 1974–85), vol. 2, letter 388. See also Spate, *Monet,* 165.

35. Wildenstein, vol. 2, letter 383.

36. See Wildenstein, vol. 2, letter 383.

37. Reproduced in Wildenstein, catalog number 912.

38. Although possibly written a year later; see *Corr.,* IV: 119n. 1.

39. See Spate, *Monet,* 221.

40. Wildenstein, vol. 3, letter 1208.

41. *Correspondance Mallarmé-Whistler,* ed. Carl Paul Barbier (Paris: Nizet, 1964), 66.

42. *Correspondance Mallarmé-Whistler,* 77.

43. *Correspondance Mallarmé-Whistler,* 85.

44. Edmond Bonniot, "Notes sur les mardis," *Les Marges* 52 (1936): 12–13.

45. John Walker, *James McNeill Whistler* (New York: Abrams, 1987), 52.

46. *Correspondance Mallarmé-Whistler,* 171.

47. *Correspondance Mallarmé-Whistler,* 171.

48. In Joshua Taylor, ed., *Nineteenth-Century Theories of Art* (Berkeley: University of California Press, 1987), 506–507.

49. Rosaline Bacou, *Odilon Redon* (Paris: Editions des Musées Nationaux, 1956), 1: 9.

50. See Baudelaire, *Œuvres complètes* (Paris: Gallimard, 1975–76), 2: 85–86, for Baudelaire's intense and highly perceptive reading of Flaubert's text, especially the lines "I would like above all to draw the reader's attention to that ability to suffer, an ability that's kept hidden and in revolt, and that runs through the entire work, like a dark thread that illuminates it, —what the English call a *subcurrent,*—and that serves to guide us through this pandemonic bedlam of solitude."

51. A third series reached Mallarmé in 1896, but the only letter concerning it begs time to allow the poet to "become magnificently penetrated" by Redon's illustrations (*Corr.,* VIII: 119). If a further letter contained his meditations on them, it has gone astray.

52. See *Lettres de Degas,* ed. Marcel Guérin, pref. Daniel Halévy (Paris: Editions Bernard Grasset, 1945), 209.

53. Julie Manet, *Journal,* 86.

54. Paul Valéry, *Œuvres complètes,* ed. Jean Hytier (Paris: Gallimard, 1958–60), 2: 1181.

55. Michael Tilby, "Le Monde vu de (trop?) près: Le Degas de J.-K. Huysmans," in *Le Champ littéraire,* ed. K. Cameron and J. Kearns (Amsterdam: Rodopi, 1996), 100.

56. Quoted in Valéry, *Œuvres complètes,* 2: 1164.

57. Valéry, *Œuvres complètes,* 2: 1165.

58. Roy McMullen, *Degas: His Life, Times, and Work* (Boston: Houghton Mifflin, 1984), vii.

59. Degas, *Lettres,* 273. Bouguereau and Girod were academic painters of the kind now referred to as "Pompier."

60. Baudelaire, *Œuvres complètes,* 2: 578; cf. 302.

61. See Michel Deguy, *Choses de la poésie et affaire culturelle* (Paris: Hachette, 1986), 63–65.

62. Aimée Brown Price, *Pierre Puvis de Chavannes* (New York: Rizzoli, 1994), 45.

63. Kurt Wais, *Mallarmé: Dichtung, Weisheit, Haltung* (Munich: C. H. Beck, 1952), 539.

64. Mallarmé, *Collected Poems,* trans. Henry Weinfield (Berkeley: University of California Press, 1994), 75.

65. Edouard Dujardin, *Mallarmé par un des siens* (Paris: Messein, 1936), 39.

66. Quoted in Suzanne Bernard, *Mallarmé et la musique* (Paris: Nizet, 1959), 21. On this question see also David Hillery, *Music and Poetry in France from Baudelaire to Mallarmé* (Berne: Lang, 1980).

67. Bernard, *Mallarmé et la musique,* 21.

68. Valéry, *Œuvres complètes,* 2: 1276.

69. Valéry, *Œuvres complètes,* 2: 1276.

70. Valéry, *Œuvres complètes,* 2: 1272.

71. On this remarkable woman, see Gérard Gefen, *Augusta Holmès: L'Outrancière* (Paris: Belfond, 1987).

72. André Fontainas, *De Stéphane Mallarmé à Paul Valéry: Notes d'un témoin, 1894–1922* (Paris: Edmond Bernard, 1928), entry for January 18, 1895.

73. Gide and Mockel, *André Gide et Albert Mockel: Correspondance,* ed. Gustave Vanwelken-huyzen (Geneva: Droz, 1975), 85. Remy wrote a biography of César Franck.

74. Gide-Mockel, *Correspondance,* 112.

75. Quoted in Stefan Jarocinski, *Debussy: Impressionism and Symbolism,* trans. R. Myers (London: Eulenberg Books, 1976), 93.

76. Quoted in Jarocinski, *Impressionism and Symbolism,* 96.

77. See Jarocinski, *Impressionism and Symbolism,* 90; Debussy's presence at the Mardis is also mentioned in Edward Lockspeiser, *Debussy: His Life and Mind* (Cambridge: Cambridge University Press, 1978).

78. See A.-F. Hérold, "Quelques mots sur Stéphane Mallarmé," *L'Ere nouvelle,* 21 December 1925.

79. As part of the award to him of the coveted Prix de Rome.

Interlude 4. Love and Friendship

1. David Lodge, *Small World* (London: Secker & Warburg, 1984), 200.

2. See Roger Chartier, *La Correspondance: Les Usages de la lettre au XIXe siècle* (Paris: Fayard, 1991).

3. Questions concerning Mallarmé's use of occasional verse and his experiments across the genres of letters, light verse, and more formal verse are raised by both Ross Chambers, "An Address in the Country: Mallarmé and the Kinds of Literary Context," *French Forum* 11, no. 2 (May 1986): 199–215, and Marian Zwerling Sugano, *The Poetics of the Occasion: Mallarmé and the Poetry of Circumstance* (Stanford, Calif.: Stanford University Press, 1992).

4. On this, see Charles Chadwick, "Méry Laurent dans la poésie de Mallarmé," *Revue des sciences humaines* 27, no. 106 (April–June 1962): 251–61.

Chapter 4. Becoming a Symbol

1. On this endearing figure, see P. Delsemme, *Teodor de Wyzewa* (Brussels: Presses Universitaires de Bruxelles, 1969).

2. *La Vogue* 12 (13–20 July 1886).

3. On this see the Conclusion.

4. John Donne, *Selections,* ed. John Carey (Oxford: Oxford University Press, 1990), 101.

5. Emilie Noulet, "Remémoration d'amis belges," *Australian Journal of French Studies* 1 (1964): 100.

6. See François Ruchon, *L'Amitié de Stéphane Mallarmé et de Georges Rodenbach* (Geneva: Pierre Cailler, 1949).

7. See Georges Rodenbach, *Du Silence: Poésies* (Paris: Alphonse Lemerre, 1888).

8. While Mallarmé's letters and occasional verse are equally courteous toward Rodenbach's wife, she seems to have regarded him in less friendly fashion, if an anecdote in Edmond de Goncourt's diary for 1891 is to be believed. Goncourt relates that at a dinner at the Daudets', Mme Rodenbach murmured to him that Mme Mallarmé had confided in her that Mallarmé had suffered a stroke a few years previously, information that prompts the antagonistic Goncourt to ask, "So, could he be sincere in his logogryphic language?" (Goncourt, *Journal* [Paris: Laffont, 1989], 3: 556).

9. Charles Baudelaire, *Œuvres complètes* (Paris: Gallimard, 1975–76), 2: 786.

10. Baudelaire, *Œuvres complètes,* 1: 275–76.

11. Paul Verlaine, *Œuvres poétiques,* ed. Jacques Robichez (Paris: Garnier, 1969), 261.

12. Edouard Dujardin, *Mallarmé par un des siens* (Paris: Messein, 1936), 24.

13. Goncourt, *Journal,* 3: 1070.

14. Goncourt, *Journal,* 3: 1160.

15. See Gordon Millan, *A Throw of the Dice* (London: Secker & Warburg, 1994), 245–46.

16. See Chapter 3.

17. The series of meditations on a variety of themes that Mallarmé published under this title.

18. André Gide, *Si le grain ne meurt* (Paris: Gallimard, 1928), 263–64.

19. Henri Mazel, *Aux beaux temps du Symbolisme* (Paris: Mercure de France, 1943).

20. Goncourt, *Journal,* 3: 1093.

21. Quoted in H. P. Clive, *Pierre Louÿs* (Oxford: Clarendon Press, 1978), 47.

22. Gide, *Si le grain ne meurt,* 265.

23. For a fascinating study of this period, see Jean Lacouture, *Une adolescence du siècle: Jacques Rivière et la NRF* (Paris: Seuil, 1994).

24. On the history and development of *vers libre,* see Clive Scott, *Vers libre: The Emergence of Free Verse in France, 1886–1930* (Oxford: Clarendon Press, 1990).

25. Henri de Régnier, *Œuvres poétiques* (Geneva: Slatkine, 1978), 3: 46.

26. Régnier, *Œuvres poétiques,* 3: 60.

27. Régnier, *Œuvres poétiques,* 3: 84.

28. The publishing details of "Crise de vers" are complex. Mallarmé himself comments on the history of the various elements of this essay in the "Bibliography" of *Divagations,* reproduced in *OC,* 1574. The paragraph announcing the crisis that French poetry was traversing dates from 1892.

29. See René Ghil, *Traité du verbe,* ed. Tiziana Goruppi (Paris: Nizet, 1978), and Anna Balakian, "Mallarmé's Préface to René Ghil's *Traité du verbe,*" *L'Esprit créateur* 27, no. 3 (Fall 1987): 58–67.

30. Baudelaire, *Œuvres complètes,* 2: 578.

31. On Louÿs and his relationships with Mallarmé, see Gordon Millan, *Pierre Louÿs ou le culte de l'amitié* (Aix-en-Provence: Pandora, 1979).

32. Paul Fort, *Mes mémoires* (Paris: Flammarion, 1944), 58.

33. Related in Goncourt, *Journal,* 3: 800. For the reference to Mallarmé's voice, see Georges Docquois, *Bêtes et gens de lettres* (Paris: Flammarion, 1895), 84.

34. Louÿs, *Œuvres complètes* (Geneva: Slatkine, 1973), ix, 293.

35. *Les Interviews de Mallarmé*, ed. Dieter Schwartz (Neuchâtel: Ides et Calendes, 1995), 11.

36. Paul Valéry, *Œuvres*, ed. Jean Hytier (Paris: Gallimard, 1957–60), 1169.

37. Bertholet, *Paul Valéry* (Paris: Plon, 1995), 32.

38. Paul Valéry, *Lettres à quelques-uns* (Paris: Gallimard, 1952), 28.

39. Quoted in Henri Mondor, *L'Heureuse Rencontre de Valéry et Mallarmé* (Lausanne: La Guilde du Livre, 1948), 22.

40. Valéry, *Lettres à quelques-uns*, 28.

41. Valéry, *Lettres à quelques-uns*, 32. The expression alludes to Rabelais's famous formula in which he refers to his novel as offering a "substantific" marrow.

42. Valéry, *Lettres à quelques-uns*, 32.

43. Valéry, *Lettres à quelques-uns*, 46.

44. Valéry, *Lettres à quelques-uns*, 47.

45. Paul Valéry, *Cahiers, 1894–1914* (Paris: Gallimard, 1987), 204.

46. See Jean-Yves Tadié, *Marcel Proust: Biographie* (Paris: Gallimard, 1996), 307–10, for a study of the relationship between Mallarmé and Proust.

Interlude 5: *"A Passerby Seeking Refuge": Poetry, Politics, and Bombs*

1. Paul Valéry, *Ecrits divers sur Stéphane Mallarmé* (Paris: Gallimard, 1950), 11.

2. Emilie Noulet, *L'Œuvre poétique de Stéphane Mallarmé* (Paris: Droz, 1940), 36–37.

3. See Graham Robb, *La Poésie de Baudelaire* (Paris: Nizet, 1993).

4. Richard Sonn, *Anarchism and Cultural Politics* (Lincoln: University of Nebraska Press, 1989), 7. On the anarchist movement, see Jean Maitron, *Le Mouvement anarchiste en France*, 2 vols. (Paris: François Maspero, 1975).

5. On this dynamic woman, see Saad Morcos, *Juliette Adam* (Beirut: Dar Al-Maaref-Liban, 1962).

6. Gustave Flaubert, *Correspondance* (Paris: Conard, 1926–33), vol. 13, letter of June 6, 1878.

7. Eugenia Herbert, *The Artist and Social Reform: France and Belgium, 1885–1898* (Freeport, N.Y.: Books for Libraries Press, 1971), 13.

8. Quoted Herbert, *The Artist and Social Reform*, 1.

9. John Hutton, *Neo-Impressionism and the Search for Solid Ground: Art, Science, and Anarchism in Fin-de-Siècle France* (Baton Rouge: Louisiana State University Press, 1994), 70–71.

10. On this extraordinary figure, see Willa Silverman's *The Notorious Life of Gyp* (Oxford: Oxford University Press, 1995).

11. Herbert, *The Artist and Social Reform*, 59–60.

12. Sonn, *Anarchism and Social Politics*, 220.

13. On this, see Alex Pasquier, *Une grande figure belge contemporaine: Edmond Picard* (Brussels: Office de Publicité, 1945).

14. Félix Fénéon, *Œuvres plus que complètes*, ed. Joan Halperin (Geneva: Droz, 1970), 2: 846–47.

15. Hutton, *Neoimpressionism*, 49.

16. Joan Halperin, *Félix Fénéon: Art et Anarchie dans le Paris fin de siècle* (Paris: Gallimard, 1988), 315–16.

17. Daniel Wildenstein et al., *Claude Monet: Biographie et catalogue raisonné*, 4 vols. (Lausanne and Paris: Bibliothèque des Arts, 1974–85), 3: 296.

18. On this question, see Jean-Luc Steinmetz, "Interscriptions (Mallarmé-Zola)," *Revue des sciences humaines* 160 (October–December 1975): 597–617.

19. See Charles Baudelaire, *Œuvres complètes* (Paris: Gallimard, 1975–76), 1: 276. On the

Panama article and the difference between Mallarmé's newspaper column and the piece he published in *Divagations,* see also Barbara Johnson, "Erasing Panama," in her *A World of Difference* (Baltimore: Johns Hopkins University Press, 1987), 57–67.

Conclusion: Remembering the Dead

1. Richard Stamelman, *Lost beyond Telling: Representations of Death and Absence in Modern French Poetry* (Ithaca, N.Y.: Cornell University Press, 1990), 13. Stamelman's sensitive and valuable study concentrates on twentieth-century poets after an initial chapter on Baudelaire.

2. Lloyd Austin, "Les 'Années d'apprentissage' de Stéphane Mallarmé," in *Essais sur Mallarmé,* ed. Malcolm Bowie (Manchester: Manchester University Press, 1995), 15, and Austin Gill, *The Early Mallarmé* (Oxford: Clarendon Press, 1979), 1: 95–99.

3. Henri Mondor, *Mallarmé plus intime* (Paris: Gallimard, 1944), 30.

4. Mondor, *Mallarmé plus intime,* 32.

5. Mondor, *Mallarmé plus intime,* 42.

6. The poem has been subjected to some rather heavy and surely inappropriate psychoanalytical digging. Austin Gill argues convincingly against the more exaggerated of these readings in *The Early Mallarmé,* 1: 96–97.

7. The body was later found and buried.

8. Gardner Davies, *Les Tombeaux de Mallarmé* (Paris: Corti, 1950), 13–14.

9. Quoted in Davies, *Les Tombeaux,* 13–14. "Feminine" rhymes are those which end in a mute "e," while masculine rhymes do not. Traditional French prosody demands the alternation of masculine and feminine rhymes, hence Mendès's concern.

10. See Lloyd Austin, "Mallarmé and Gautier," in *Balzac and the Nineteenth Century* (Leicester: Leicester University Press, 1972), 335–51.

11. For a very different reading, which sees the poem (to my mind, unjustifiably) as constituting a rejection of Gautier's poetry and his apparent gift for seeing the world, see Leo Bersani, *The Death of Stéphane Mallarmé* (Cambridge: Cambridge University Press, 1982), 28–33.

12. Charles Baudelaire, *Œuvres complètes* (Paris: Gallimard, 1975–76), 2: 315.

13. See *Pour un tombeau d'Anatole,* introduction de Jean-Pierre Richard (Paris: Seuil, 1961), and André Vial, *Mallarmé: Tétralogie pour un enfant mort* (Paris: Corti, 1976). Michel Deguy's "thrène" of 1995, *A ce qui n'en finit pas* (Paris: Seuil, 1995), offers both a moving tribute to the poet's wife and a counterpoint to Mallarmé's failure to write adequately of Anatole.

14. Alan Raitt, *The Life of Villiers de l'Isle-Adam* (Oxford: Clarendon Press, 1981), 50.

15. Quoted in Raitt, *Villiers,* 375.

16. Raitt, *Villiers,* 54.

17. This is Henry Weinberg's inspired translation of "amas de nuit ancienne": see his edition of *Collected Poems* (Los Angeles: University of California Press, 1994), 38.

Selected Bibliography

Works by Mallarmé

Collected Poems. Translated with a commentary by Henry Weinfield. Berkeley: University of California Press, 1994.

Correspondance. Edited by L. J. Austin, H. Mondor, and J. P. Richard. 11 vols. Paris: Gallimard, 1959–85.

Correspondance: Compléments et suppléments. Edited by Lloyd James Austin, Bertrand Marchal, and Nicola Luckhurst. Oxford: Legenda, 1998.

Correspondance (1862–1871): Suivie de Lettres sur la poésie (1872–1898). Preface by Yves Bonnefoy, edited by Bertrand Marchal. Paris: Folio, 1995.

Correspondance Mallarmé-Whistler. Edited by Carl Paul Barbier. Paris: Nizet, 1964.

Les "Gossips" de Mallarmé. Edited by Henri Mondor and Lloyd James Austin. Paris: Gallimard, 1962.

Les Interviews de Mallarmé. Edited by Dieter Schwartz. Neuchâtel: Ides et Calendes, 1995.

Lettres à Méry Laurent. Edited by Bertrand Marchal. Paris: Gallimard, 1996.

The Meaning of Mallarmé. Bilingual edition of *Poésies* and *Un coup de dés,* translated and introduced by Charles Chadwick. Aberdeen: Scottish Cultural Press, 1996.

Œuvres. Edited by Yves-Alain Favre. Paris: Garnier, 1985.

Œuvres complètes. Edited by Henri Mondor and Jean-Aubry. Paris: Gallimard, 1945.

Œuvres complètes, vol. 1, *Poésies.* Edited by Carl P. Barbier and Gordon Millan. Paris: Flammarion, 1983.

Poésies. Edited by Lloyd James Austin. Paris: Garnier-Flammarion, 1989.

Poésies. Edited by Bertrand Marchal. Paris: Gallimard, 1992.

Pour un tombeau d'Anatole. Introduction by Jean-Pierre Richard. Paris: Seuil, 1961.

Selected Letters. Translated and edited by Rosemary Lloyd. Chicago: University of Chicago Press, 1988.

Other Works

Abastado, Claude. *Expérience et théorie de la création poétique chez Mallarmé.* Paris: Minard, 1970.

———. "Le Livre de Mallarmé: Un autoportrait mythique." *Romantisme: Revue du dix-neuvième siècle* 14, no. 44 (1984): 65–81.

Alcoloumbre, Thierry. *Mallarmé: La Poétique du théâtre et l'écriture.* Paris: Minard, 1995.

Anderson, D. L. *Symbolism: A Bibliography of Symbolism as an International and Multi-Disciplinary Movement.* New York: New York University Press, 1975

Arico, Santo L. "The Arrangement of St. Preux's First Letter to Julie in *La Nouvelle Héloïse.*" *Studies on Voltaire* 249 (1987): 295–301.

Austin, Lloyd J. *Essais sur Mallarmé,* edited by Malcolm Bowie. Manchester, England: Manchester University Press, 1995.

———. "Mallarmé and Gautier: New Light on *Toast funèbre.*" In *Balzac and the Nineteenth Century,* edited by D. G. Charlton, J. Gaudon, and A. R. Pugh. Leicester, England: Leicester University Press, 1972.

————. *Poetic Principles and Practice.* Cambridge: Cambridge University Press, 1987.

Bacou, Rosaline. *Odilon Redon.* 2 vols. Paris: Editions des Musées Nationaux, 1956.

Badesco, Luc. *La Génération poétique de 1860: La Jeunesse de deux rives.* 2 vols. Paris: Nizet, 1971.

Balakian, Anna. "Mallarmé's Preface to René Ghil's *Traité du verbe.*" *L'Esprit créateur* 27, no. 3 (Fall 1987): 58–67.

————. *The Symbolist Movement: A Critical Appraisal.* New York: New York University Press, 1977.

Baldick, Robert. *La Vie de J.-K. Huysmans.* Paris: Denoël, 1958.

Bancquart, Marie-Claire. *Anatole France.* Paris: Julliard, 1994.

Banville, Théodore de. *Œuvres poétiques complètes.* Edited by Peter Edwards et al. Paris: H. Champion, 1994–96.

Barrot, Olivier, and Pascal Ory. *La Revue blanche: Histoire, Anthologie, Portraits.* Paris: C. Borgois, 1989.

Barzun, Jacques. *Berlioz and the Romantic Century.* 2 vols. Boston: Little, Brown, 1950.

Baudelaire, Charles. *Correspondance.* Edited by Claude Pichois and Jean Ziegler. 2 vols. Paris: Gallimard, 1973.

————. *Œuvres complètes.* Edited by Claude Pichois. 2 vols. Paris: Gallimard, 1975–76.

Bellanger, Claude, ed. *Histoire générale de la presse française.* Vol. 2. Paris: Presses Universitaires de France, 1969.

Bellet, Roger. *Stéphane Mallarmé: L'Encre et le ciel.* Seyssel, France: Champ Vallon, 1987.

Bénichou, Paul. *Selon Mallarmé.* Paris: Gallimard, 1995.

Bernard, Suzanne. *Mallarmé et la musique.* Paris: Nizet, 1959.

Berne-Joffroy, André. *Valéry.* Paris: Gallimard, 1960.

Bersani, Leo. *The Death of Stéphane Mallarmé.* Cambridge: Cambridge University Press, 1982.

Bertholet, Denis. *Paul Valéry.* Paris: Plon, 1995.

Bertrand, Antoine. *Les Curiosités esthétiques de Robert de Montesquiou.* 2 vols. Geneva: Droz, 1996.

Biester, James. "Samuel Johnson on Letters." *Rhetorica* 6, no. 2 (Spring 1988): 145–66.

Blanchot, Maurice. "L'Absence du livre." In *L'Entretien infini,* 620–36. Paris: Gallimard, 1969.

————. *L'Espace littéraire, 33–48, 133–49.* Paris: Gallimard, 1955.

————. *Faux pas, 117–31, 189–96.* Paris: Gallimard, 1943.

————. *Le Livre à venir, 326–58.* Paris: Gallimard, 1959.

————. *La Part du feu, 35–48.* Paris: Gallimard, 1949.

Block, Haskell M. *Mallarmé and the Symbolist Drama.* Detroit: Wayne State University Press, 1963.

————. "Poe, Baudelaire, Mallarmé, and the Problem of the Untranslatable." In *Translation Perspectives: Selected Papers,* edited by Rose Marilyn Gaddis. Binghamton, N.Y.: Translation Research and Instruction Program/State University of New York at Binghamton, 1982–83.

Bodenheimer, Rosemarie. *The Real Life of Mary Ann Evans: George Eliot, Her Letters, and Fiction.* Ithaca, N.Y.: Cornell University Press, 1994.

Bonniot, Edmond. "Notes sur les mardis." *Les Marges* 52 (1936): 12–13.

Bonniot-Mallarmé, Geneviève. "Mallarmé par sa fille." *La Nouvelle Revue française,* 27 November 1926, 517–23.

Bowie, Malcolm. *Mallarmé and the Art of Being Difficult.* Cambridge: Cambridge University Press, 1978.

Bowness, Alan. *Poetry and Painting: Baudelaire, Mallarmé, Apollinaire, and Their Painter Friends.* Oxford: Oxford University Press, 1994.

Bréton, Geneviève. *Journal, 1867–1871.* Paris: Ramsay, 1985.

Brown, Frederick. *Zola: A Life.* New York: Farrar, Straus & Giroux, 1995.

Buenzod, Emmanuel. *Une époque littéraire: 1890–1910.* Neuchâtel, France: Baconnière, 1941.

Byatt, A. S. *Possession: A Romance.* New York: Vintage Books, 1991.

Cachin, Françoise. Introduction to *Manet, 1832–1883.* New York: Metropolitan Museum of Modern Art/Abrams, 1983.

Camacho, Mathilde. *Judith Gautier: Sa Vie et son œuvre.* Paris: Droz, 1939.

Cameron, Keith, and James Kearns, eds. *Le Champ littéraire, 1860–1900.* Amsterdam: Rodopi, 1996.

Campion, Pierre. *Mallarmé: Poésie et philosophie.* Paris: Presses Universitaires de France, 1994.

Caws, Mary Ann. *The Eye in the Text: Essays on Perception, Mannerist, and Modern.* Princeton, N.J.: Princeton University Press, 1981.

Cellier, Léon. *Mallarmé et la morte qui parle.* Paris: Presses Universitaires de France, 1959.

Chadwick, Charles. *Mallarmé: Sa Pensée dans sa poésie.* Paris: Corti, 1962.

———. "Méry Laurent dans la poésie de Mallarmé." *Revue des sciences humaines* 27, no. 106 (April–June 1962): 251–61.

Chambers, Ross. "An Address in the Country: Mallarmé and the Kinds of Literary Context." *French Forum* 11 (2 May 1986): 199–216.

Chartier, R. *La Correspondance: Les Usages de la lettre au XIXe siècle.* Paris: Fayard, 1991.

Chastel, Guy. *J.-K. Huysmans et ses amis: Documents inédits.* Paris: Bernard Grasset, 1957.

Chisholm, A. R. *Mallarmé's Grand Œuvre.* Manchester: Manchester University Press, 1962.

Clark, T. J. *The Painting of Modern Life: Paris in the Art of Manet and His Followers.* London: Thames & Hudson, 1984.

Claudel, Paul. *Mémoires improvisés.* Paris: Gallimard, 1954.

Clive, H. P. *Pierre Louÿs (1870–1925): A Biography.* Oxford: Clarendon Press, 1978.

Cohn, R. G. *Toward the Poems of Mallarmé.* Berkeley: University of California Press, 1965.

Conrardy, Charles. *Albert Mockel.* Brussels: Le Thyrse, 1953.

Cornell, Kenneth. *The Symbolist Movement.* New Haven, Conn.: Yale University Press, 1951.

Dantzig, C. *Rémy de Gourmont: Cher vieux daim!* Monaco, France: Editions du Rocher, 1990.

Davies, Gardner. "Divagations on Mallarmé research." *French Studies* 40 (1 January 1986): 1–12.

———. *Mallarmé et la "couche suffisante d'intelligibilité."* Paris: Corti, 1988.

———. *Mallarmé et le drame solaire.* Paris: Corti, 1959.

———. "Stéphane Mallarmé: Fifty Years of Research." *French Studies* 1 (1947): 1–26.

———. *Les Tombeaux de Mallarmé.* Paris: Corti, 1950.

Dayan, Peter. *Mallarmé's Divine Transposition: Real and Apparent Sources of Literary Value.* Oxford: Oxford University Press, 1986.

Decaunes, Luc, ed. *La Poésie parnassienne.* Paris: Seghers, 1977.

Deffoux, Léon. *Dix-neuf lettres de Stéphane Mallarmé à Emile Zola.* Paris: Jacques Bernard, 1929.

Degas, Edgar. *Lettres de Degas.* Edited by Marcel Guérin, Preface by Daniel Halévy. Paris: Editions Bernard Grasset, 1945.

Deguy, Michel. *A ce qui n'en finit pas: Thrène.* Paris: Seuil, 1995.

———. *Choses de la poésie et affaire culturelle.* Paris: Hachette, 1986.

Delsemme, P. *Teodor de Wyzewa et la cosmopolitisme littéraire en France à l'époque du symbolisme.* Brussels: Presses Universitaires de Bruxelles, 1969.

Delvaille, Bernard. *La Poésie symboliste: Anthologie.* Paris: Seghers, 1971.

Derrida, Jacques. *La Dissémination.* Paris: Seuil, 1972.

Dierx, Léon. *Les Lèvres closes.* Paris: Lemerre, 1867.

Dijkstra, Bram. *Idols of Perversity: Fantasies of Feminine Evil in Fin-de-Siècle Culture.* Oxford: Oxford University Press, 1986.

Docquois, Georges. *Bêtes et gens de lettres.* Paris: Flammarion, 1895.

Documents Stéphane Mallarmé. Edited by Carl Paul Barbier et al. Vols. 1–7. Paris: Nizet, 1968–80.

Donne, John. *Selections.* Edited by John Carey. Oxford: Oxford University Press, 1990.

Druick, Douglas, et al. *Odilon Redon: Prince of Dreams.* New York: Harry Abrams, 1994.

Dufwa, Jacques. *Winds from the East: A Study in the Art of Manet, Degas, Monet, and Whistler, 1856–86.* Stockholm: Almqvist & Wiksell International, 1981.

Dujardin, Edouard. *Mallarmé par un des siens.* Paris: Messein, 1936.

Duret, Théodore. *Manet and the French Impressionists.* London: J. B. Lippincott, 1912.

Fairlie, Alison. "'Entre les lignes': Mallarmé's Art of Allusion in His Thank-You Letters." In *Baudelaire, Mallarmé, Valéry: New Essays in Honour of Lloyd Austin.* edited by M. Bowie, A. Fairlie, and A. Finch, 181–201. Cambridge: Cambridge University Press, 1982.

Fénéon, Félix. *Œuvres plus que complètes.* Edited by Joan Halperin. 2 vols. Geneva: Droz, 1970.

Ferré, André. *Les Années de collège de Marcel Proust.* Paris: Gallimard, 1959.

Flaubert, Gustave. *Correspondance.* Paris: Connard, 1926–33.

Fleming, Marie. *The Geography of Freedom: The Odyssey of Elisée Reclus.* Montreal: Black Rose Books, 1988.

Florence, Penny. *Mallarmé, Manet, and Redon: Visual and Aural Signs and the Generation of Meaning.* Cambridge: Cambridge University Press, 1986.

Fontainas, André. *De Stéphane Mallarmé à Paul Valéry: Notes d'un témoin, 1894–1922*. Paris: Edmond Bernard, 1928.

Fort, Paul. *Mes mémoires, toute la vie d'un poète, 1982–1943*. Paris: Flammarion, 1944.

Frappier-Mazur, Lucienne. "Narcisse travesti: Poétique et idéologie dans *La Dernière Mode* de Mallarmé." *French Forum* 11 (1 January 1986): 41–57.

Fulcher, Jane. *Le Grand Opéra en France: Un art politique, 1820–1870*. Translated by Jean-Pierre Bardos. Paris: Belin, 1988.

Furet, François, and Jacques Ozouf. *Lire et Ecrire: L'Alphabétisation des Français de Calvin à Jules Ferry*. Paris: Minuit, 1977.

Gautier, Judith. *Le Collier des jours: Souvenirs de ma vie*. 3 vols. Paris: Juven, 1909–11.

Gavoty, Bernard. *Reynaldo Hahn: Le Musicien de la Belle Epoque*. Paris: Buchet/Chastel, 1976.

Gefen, Gérard. *Augusta Holmès: L'Outrancière* Paris: Belfond, 1987.

Genette, Gérard. *Palimpsestes: La Littérature au second degré*. Paris: Seuil, 1982.

Genova, Pamela. "Word, Image, Chord: Stéphane Mallarmé and the Interrelationship of the Arts in Late Nineteenth-Century French Symbolist Reviews." *Dalhousie French Studies* 36 (Fall 1996): 79–102.

Ghil, René. *Ecrits pour l'art,* no. 6, 7 June 1887.

———. *Traité du verbe: Etats successifs*. Edited by Tiziana Goruppi. Paris: Nizet, 1978.

Gide, André. *Cahiers d'André Walter: Œuvre posthume*. Paris: Librairie de l'Art Indépendant, 1891.

———. *Correspondance avec sa mère, 1880–1895*. Edited by Claude Martin. Preface by Henri Thomas. Paris: Gallimard, 1988.

———. *Si le grain ne meurt*. Paris: Gallimard, 1928.

Gide, André, and Albert Mockel. *André Gide et Albert Mockel: Correspondance*. Edited by Gustave Vanwelkenhuyze. Geneva: Droz, 1975.

Gill, Austin. *The Early Mallarmé*. 2 vols. Oxford: Oxford University Press, 1979–86.

Glatigny, Albert. *Les Flêches d'or: Poésies*. Paris: Frédéric Henry, 1864.

Goffin, Robert. *Mallarmé vivant*. Paris: Nizet, 1956.

Goncourt, Edmond, and Jules de Goncourt. *Journal: Mémoires de la vie littéraire*. Vol. 3. Paris: Robert Laffont, 1989.

Goodkin, Richard E. *The Symbolist Home and the Tragic Home: Mallarmé and Oedipus*. Amsterdam: J. Benjamins, 1984.

Gosse, Edmund. "Symbolism and M. S. Mallarmé." In *Questions at Issue,* 217–34. London: Heinemann, 1893.

Gould, Evlyn. *Virtual Theater from Diderot to Mallarmé*. Baltimore: Johns Hopkins University Press, 1989.

Gourmont, Remy de. *Les Petites Revues: Essai de bibliographie*. Paris: Mercure de France, 1900.

———. *Promenades littéraires*. 4th series. Paris: Mercure de France, 1912.

Gregh, Fernand. *L'Age d'or*. Paris: Grasset, 1947.

Hahn, Reynaldo. *L'Oreille au guet*. Paris: Gallimard, 1937.

Halperin, Joan. *Félix Fénéon: Art et anarchie dans le Paris fin de siècle*. Paris: Gallimard, 1991.

Hamilton, George Heard. *Manet and His Critics*. New Haven, Conn.: Yale University Press, 1954.

Hemmings, F. W. J. *Culture and Society in France, 1848–1898*. New York: Scribner, 1971.

Herbert, Eugenia. *The Artist and Social Reform: France and Belgium, 1885–1898*. Freeport, N.Y.: Books for Libraries Press, 1971.

Herbert, Robert. *Impressionism: Art, Leisure, and Parisian Society*. New Haven, Conn.: Yale University Press, 1988.

Hérold, A.-F. "Quelques mots sur Stéphane Mallarmé." *L'Ere nouvelle,* 21 December 1925.

Higgonet, Anne. *Berthe Morisot's Images of Women*. Cambridge, Mass.: Harvard University Press, 1992.

Hillery, David. *Music and Poetry in France from Baudelaire to Mallarmé: An Essay on Poetic Theory and Practice*. Berne: Lang, 1980

Houston, John Porter. *French Symbolism and the Modernist Movement: A Study of Poetic Structures*. Baton Rouge: Louisana State University Press, 1980.

Hutton, John G. *Neo-Impressionism and the Search for Solid Ground: Art, Science, and Anarchism in Fin-de-siècle France*. Baton Rouge: Louisiana State University Press, 1994.

Hutton, Patrick, et al. *Historical Dictionary of the Third Republic.* 2 vols. New York: Greenwood Press, 1986.

Jackson, A. B. *La Revue blanche (1889–1903): Origine, influence, bibliographie.* Paris: Minard, 1960

Jackson, Susan Klem. "Disengaging Isabelle: Professional Rhetoric and Female Friendship in the Correspondence of Mme de Charrière et Mlle de Gélieu." *Eighteenth-Century Life* 13, no. 1 (February 1989): 26–41.

James, Henry. *The Notebooks of Henry James.* Edited by F. O. Matthiessen and Kenneth B. Murdoch. New York: Oxford University Press, 1961.

Jarocinski, Stefan. *Debussy: Impressionism and Symbolism.* Translated by Rollo Myers. London: Eulenberg Books, 1976.

Johnson, Barbara. *A World of Difference.* Baltimore: Johns Hopkins University Press, 1987.

Joseph, Lawrence A. *Henri Cazalis: Sa vie, son œuvre, son amitié avec Mallarmé.* Paris: Nizet, 1972.

Jutrin, M. *Marcel Schwob: "Cœur double."* Lausanne: Editions de l'Aire, 1982.

Kahn, Gustave. *Symbolistes et décadents.* Paris, Vanier, 1902.

Kearns, James. *Symbolist Landscapes: The Place of Painting in the Poetry and Criticism of Mallarmé and His Circle.* London: Modern Humanities Research Association, 1989.

Kendall, Richard, and Griselda Pollock, eds. *Dealing with Degas: Representations of Women and the Politics of Vision.* New York: Universe, 1992.

Klein, R. "'Je suis véritablement décomposé': Sur une lettre de Mallarmé." *Romantisme* 18, no. 61 (1988): 47–57.

Kristeva, Julia. *La Révolution du langage poétique.* Paris: Nizet, 1974.

Kuhn, Reinhard. *Return to Reality: A Study of Francis Viélé-Griffin.* Geneva: Droz, 1962.

Kyria, Pierre. *Jean Lorrain.* Paris: Seghers, 1973.

Lacomblé, E. E. B. *Perles de la poésie contemporaine.* Brussels: J. Lebègue, s.d.

Lacouture, Jean. *Une adolescence du siècle: Jacques Rivière et la NRF.* Paris: Seuil, 1994.

Laforgue, Jules. *Lettres à un ami.* Paris: Mercure de France, 1941.

Laslett, Peter. "The Wrong Way through the Telescope." *Journal of Sociology* 27, no. 3 (September 1976): 319–42.

Laude, Patrick. "Rodenbach and Mallarmé: Le Miroir, la profondeur, et les sens." *Romance Notes* 27, no. 3 (1987): 223–30.

Lawler, James. *The Language of French Symbolism.* Princeton, N.J.: Princeton University Press, 1969.

Lecercle, Jean-Pierre. *Mallarmé et la mode.* Paris: Seguier, 1989.

Lefèvre-Roujon, C., ed. *Correspondance inédite de Stéphane Mallarmé et Henry Roujon.* Geneva: Pierre Cailler, 1949.

Lind, Melva. *Un parnassien universitaire: Emmanuel Des Essarts.* Paris: Presses Universitaires de France, 1928.

Lloyd, Rosemary. "The Art of Distilling Life: Mallarmé, Misogyny, and the Seduction of the Feminine." *Australian Journal of French Studies* 31, no. 1 (1994): 97–112.

———. "Christopher Brennan." *Yearbook of Comparative and General Literature* 42 (1995): 9–13.

———. "Fan Autographs: Unfolding Relationships." *Australian Journal of French Studies* 32, no. 3 (September–December 1995): 380–89.

———. *Mallarmé: Poésies.* London: Grant & Cutler, 1984.

Lloyd, Rosemary, et al. *Mallarmé and His Circle: Music and Letters in France and Belgium, 1870–1900.* Exhibition catalog. Bloomington, Ind.: Lilly Library, 1994.

Lockspeiser, Edward. *Debussy: His Life and Mind.* 2 vols. Cambridge: Cambridge University Press, 1978.

Lodge, David. *Small World.* London: Secker & Warburg, 1984.

Loncke, Joycelynne. *Baudelaire et la musique.* Paris: Nizet, 1975.

Lorrain, Jean. *Correspondance.* Paris: Editions Baudinière, 1929.

———. *Lettres inédites à Gabriel Mourey et à quelques autres.* Edited by Jean-Marc Ramos. Lille, France: Presses Universitaires de Lille, 1987.

Louÿs, Pierre. *Œuvres complètes.* 13 vols. Geneva: Slatkine, 1973.

Lund, Hans Peter. *L'Itinéraire de Mallarmé.* Copenhagen: Akademisk Forlag, 1969.

Maitron, Jean. *Le Mouvement anarchiste en France.* 2 vols. Paris: François Maspero, 1975.

Manet, Julie. *Journal*. Introduction by Rosalind de Boland Roberts and Jane Roberts. Paris: Scala, 1987.

Marchal, Bertrand. *Lecture de Mallarmé: Poésies, "Igitur," "Un coup de dés."* Paris: Corti, 1985.

———. *La Religion de Mallarmé: Poésie, mythologie, et religion*. Paris: Corti, 1988.

Margueritte, Paul. *Nos Tréteaux*. Paris: Dorbon Aîné, 1910.

Mathews, Andrew Jackson. *La Wallonie, 1886–1892: The Symbolist Movement in Belgium*. New York: King's Crown Press, 1947.

Mauclair, Camille. *Mallarmé chez lui*. Paris: Grasset, 1935.

———. *Le Soleil des morts: Roman contemporain*. Paris: P. Ollendorff, 1898.

Mauron, Charles. *Mallarmé par lui-même*. Paris: Seuil, 1964.

Mazel, Henri. *Aux beaux temps du Symbolisme*. Paris: Mercure de France, 1943.

McMullen, Roy. *Degas: His Life, Times, and Work*. Boston: Houghton Mifflin, 1984.

Meitinger, Serge. *Stéphane Mallarmé*. Paris: Hachette, 1995.

Mendès, Catulle. *Soirs moroses*. Paris: Dentu, 1887.

———, ed. *Le Tombeau de Théophile Gautier*. Paris: Lemerre, 1872.

Merrill, Stuart. Manuscript letters to his family. Bloomington, Ind.: Lilly Library.

———. *Poèmes*. Paris: Mercure de France, 1897.

Michaud, Guy. *Mallarmé: Nouvelle édition refondue et mise à jour*. Paris: Hatier, 1971.

———. *Le Message poétique du symbolisme*. Paris: Nizet, 1947.

Millan, Gordon. *Pierre Louÿs ou le culte de l'amitié*. Aix-en-Provence, France: Pandora, 1979.

———. *A Throw of the Dice: The Life of Stéphane Mallarmé*. London: Secker & Warburg, 1994.

Minahen, Charles D. "Whirling toward the Void at Dead Center: Symbolic Turbulence in Mallarmé's *Un coup de dés*." *Romanic Review* 78, no. 1 (1987): 102–13.

Miner, Margaret. *Resonant Gaps between Baudelaire and Wagner*. Athens: University of Georgia Press, 1995.

Mockel, Albert. *Stéphane Mallarmé, un héro*. Paris: Mercure de France, 1899.

Mondor, Henri. *L'Affaire du Parnasse: Stéphane Mallarmé et Anatole France*. Paris: Fragrance, 1951.

———. *Autres précisions sur Mallarmé et inédits*. Paris: Gallimard, 1961.

———. *Eugène Lefébure: Sa vie, ses lettres à Mallarmé*. Paris: Gallimard, 1951.

———. *L'Heureuse Rencontre de Valéry et Mallarmé*. Lausanne: La Guilde du Livre, 1948.

———. *Histoire d'un faune*. Paris: Gallimard, 1948.

———. *Mallarmé plus intime*. Paris: Gallimard, 1944.

———. *Vie de Mallarmé*. Paris: Gallimard, 1941.

Monneret, Sophie. *L'Impressionnisme et son époque: Dictionnaire international*. 2 vols. Paris: Denoël, 1981.

Monro, Thomas. "*The Afternoon of a Faun* and the Interrelation of the Arts." *Journal of Aesthetics and Art Criticism* 10, no. 2 (December 1951): 95–111.

Montesquiou-Fézensac, Robert de. *Les Perles rouges: 93 sonnets*. Paris: Eugène Fasquelle, 1899.

Montesquiou-Fézensac, Robert de, and James McNeill Whistler. *La Chauve-Souris et le Papillon: Correspondance Montesquiou-Whistler*. Edited by Joy Newton. Glasgow: University of Glasgow French and German Publications, 1990.

Morcos, Saad. *Juliette Adam*. Beirut: Dar Al-Maaref-Liban, 1962.

Morisot, Berthe. *Correspondance*. Edited by Denis Rouart. Paris: Quatre-Chemins-Editart, 1950.

Morris, Bruce. "Mallarmé's Letters to Arthur Symons: Origins of the Symbolist Movement." *English Literature in Transition* 28, no. 4 (1985): 346–53.

Morris, D. Hampton. *Stéphane Mallarmé: Twentieth-Century Criticism (1901–1971)*. Columbia: University of Missouri Romance Monographs, 1977.

———. *Stéphane Mallarmé: Twentieth-Century Criticism (1972–1979)*. Columbia: University of Missouri Romance Monographs, 1989.

Mossop, D. *Pure Poetry: Studies in French Poetic Theory and Practice, 1746–1945*. Oxford: Clarendon Press, 1971.

Moulton, Louise Chandler. *Lazy Tours in Spain and Elsewhere*. London: Ward, Lock & Co., 1896.

Nectoux, Jean-Michel. *Mallarmé. "Un clair regard dans les ténèbres," poésie, peinture, musique*. Paris: Adam Biro, 1998.

Newmark, Kevin. "Beneath the Lace: Mallarmé, the State, and the Foundation of Letters." *Yale French Studies* 77 (1990): 243–75.

Noulet, Emilie. *L'Œuvre poétique de Stéphane Mallarmé*. Paris: Droz, 1940.

———. "Remémoration d'amis belges." *Australian Journal of French Studies* 1 (1964): 96–103.

Olds, Marshall. "Mallarmé and Internationalism." In *Kaleidoscope: Reading in Barbey's "Les Diaboliques,"* edited by Graham Falconer and Mary Donaldson-Evans, 156–67. Toronto: Centre d'Etudes Romantiques/Joseph Sable, 1996.

O'Shaugnessy, Arthur. *Poems*. Selected and edited by William Alexander Percy. New Haven, Conn.: Yale University Press, 1923.

Pakenham, Michael. *Edgar Poe: Le Corbeau, Traduction de Stéphane Mallarmé, Illustré par Edouard Manet*. Paris: Séguier, 1994.

———. "Mallarmé nous parle de Verlaine." *Europe* (April–May 1976): 119–25.

Parnasse contemporain. Vol. 1. Paris: Alphonse Lemerre, 1866.

Parnasse contemporain. Vol. 2. Paris: Alphonse Lemerre, 1871.

Pasquier, Alex. *Une grande figure belge contemporaine: Edmond Picard*. Brussels: Office de Publicité, 1945.

Payne, John. *Poetical Works*. 1902. 2 vols. New York: AMS Press, 1970.

Pearson, Roger. *Unfolding Mallarmé: The Development of a Poetic Art*. Oxford: Clarendon Press, 1996.

Poe, Edgar Allan. *Le Corbeau*. Translated by Stéphane Mallarmé with illustrations by Edouard Manet. Paris: Lesclide, 1875.

Poulet, Georges. *La Distance intérieure*. Paris: Plon, 1952.

Price, Aimée Brown. *Pierre Puvis de Chavannes*. New York: Rizzoli, 1994.

Prick, Harry G. M. "La Rencontre de Stéphane Mallarmé et François Erens." *Maatstaf* 39, no. 4 (April 1991): 1–13.

Prince, Gerald. "Fragments of a Loving Discourse." *L'Esprit créateur* 29, no. 4 (Winter 1989): 33–41.

Proust, Marcel. *A la recherche du temps perdu*. 3 vols. Paris: Gallimard, 1954.

———. "Contre l'obscurité." In *Contre Sainte-Beuve, edited by Pierre Clarac with Yves Saudre,* 390–95. Paris: Gallimard, 1971.

———. *Correspondance*. Vol. 2 (1896–1901). Edited by Philip Kolb. Paris: Plon, 1976.

Raitt, A. W. *The Life of Villiers de l'Isle-Adam*. Oxford: Clarendon Press, 1981.

Rancière, Jacques. *Mallarmé: La Politique de la sirène*. Paris: Hachette, 1996.

Rand, Harry. *Manet's Contemplation at the Gare Saint-Lazare*. Berkeley: University of California Press, 1987.

Raynaud, Ernest. *La Mêlée Symboliste 1918–1922*. Paris: Nizet, 1971.

Regnault, Henri. *Correspondance*. Edited by Arthur Duparc. Paris: Charpentier, 1872.

Régnier, Henri de. *Annales psychiques et occulaires*. Unpublished diaries. Paris: Bibliothèque Nationale, MSS Nouvelles Acquisitions Françaises 14974–80.

———. *Lettres à André Gide*. Preface and notes by David J. Niederauer. Geneva: Droz, 1972.

———. *Nos Rencontres*. Paris: Mercure de France, 1931.

———. *Œuvres poétiques*. 4 vols. Geneva: Slatkine, 1978.

Renéville, Roland de. "Correspondance inédite de Huysmans et de S. Mallarmé." In *L'Univers de la parole,* 40–49. Paris: Gallimard, 1944.

Renoir, Jean. *Renoir, My Father*. Translated by Randolph Weaver and Dorothy Weaver. Boston: Little, Brown, 1962.

Rice, Sara Sigourney, ed. *Edgar Allan Poe: A Memorial Volume*. Baltimore: Turnbull Brothers, 1877.

Richard, Jean-Pierre. *L'Univers imaginaire de Stéphane Mallarmé*. Paris: Seuil, 1961.

Richard, Noël. *A l'aube du symbolisme: Hydropathes, fumistes, et décadents*. Paris: Nizet, 1961.

———. *Le Mouvement décadent: Dandys, esthetes, et quintessents*. Paris: Nizet, 1968.

———. *Profils symbolistes*. Paris: Nizet, 1978.

Richardson, Joanna. *Judith Gautier: A Biography*. New York: F. Watts, 1987.

Robb, Graham. *La Poésie de Baudelaire et la poésie français, 1838–1852*. Paris: Aubier, 1993.

———. *Unlocking Mallarmé*. New Haven, Conn.: Yale University Press, 1996.

Robichez, Jacques. *Le Symbolisme au théâtre: Lugné-Poe et les débuts de l'Œuvre*. Paris: L'Arche, 1957.

Rodenbach, Georges. *Bruges-la-morte*. Paris: Librairie Marpon et Flammarion, [1911?].

———. *Du Silence: Poésies*. Paris: Alphonse Lemerre, 1888.

———. *Œuvres*. 2 vols. Paris: Mercure de France, 1923–25.

———. *Le Règne du silence: Poème*. Paris: Bibliothèque Charpentier, 1891.

———. *Vies encloses: Poème*. Paris: Bibliothèque Charpentier, 1896.

Ruchon, François. *L'Amitié de Stéphane Mallarmé et de Georges Rodenbach.* Geneva: Pierre Cailler, 1949.

Ryan, Marianne. "John Payne and Mallarmé: Une longue amitié." *Revue de littérature comparée* 32 (1958): 377–89.

Sacchi, Sergio. "'Imiter le Chinois au cœur limpide et fin . . .': La Chine en France aux environs de 1860." In *Patterns of Evolution in Nineteenth-Century French Poetry,* edited by Lawrence Watson and Rosemary Lloyd, 161–70. Deddington, England: Tallents Press, 1990.

Sarda, Marie-Anne. *Stéphane Mallarmé à Valvins.* Vulaines sur Seine, France: Musée Mallarmé, 1995.

Sartre, Jean-Paul. *Mallarmé: La Lucidité et sa face d'ombre.* Paris: Gallimard, 1986.

Scott, Clive. *Vers libre: The Emergence of Free Verse in France, 1886–1914.* Oxford: Clarendon Press, 1990.

———. *The Poetics of French Verse.* Oxford: Clarendon Press, 1998.

Scott, David. *Pictorialist Poetics: Poetry and the Visual Arts in Nineteenth-Century France.* Cambridge: Cambridge University Press, 1988.

Sert, Misia. *Misia.* Paris: Gallimard, 1952.

Shaw, Mary Lewis. *Performance in the Texts of Mallarmé: The Passage from Art to Ritual.* University Park: Pennsylvania State University Press, 1992.

Silverman, Willa. *The Notorious Life of Gyp: Right-Wing Anarchist in Fin-de-Siècle France.* Oxford: Oxford University Press, 1995.

Sonn, Richard. *Anarchism and Cultural Politics in Fin-de-Siècle France.* Lincoln: University of Nebraska Press, 1989.

Spate, Virginia. *Claude Monet: Life and Work.* New York: Rizzoli, 1992.

Stamelman, Richard. *Lost beyond Telling: Representations of Death and Absence in Modern French Poetry.* Ithaca, N.Y.: Cornell University Press, 1990.

Starkie, Enid. *Baudelaire.* Norfolk, Conn.: New Directions, 1958.

Steiner, George. *After Babel: Aspects of Language and Translation.* Oxford: Oxford University Press, 1992.

Steiner, Wendy. *The Colors of Rhetoric: Problems in the Relation between Modern Literature and Painting.* Chicago: University of Chicago Press, 1982.

Steinmetz, Jean-Luc. "Interscriptions (Mallarmé-Zola)." *Revue des sciences humaines* 160 (October–Deccember 1975): 597–617.

———. *Mallarmé: L'Absolu au jour le jour.* Paris: Fayard, 1998.

Stevens, MaryAnne, et al. *Alfred Sisley.* New Haven, Conn.: Yale University Press, 1992.

Stevens, Wallace. *The Palm at the End of the Mind.* Edited by Holly Stevens. New York: Vintage Books, 1990.

Sugano, Marian Zwerling. *The Poetics of the Occasion: Mallarmé and the Poetry of Circumstance.* Stanford, Calif.: Stanford University Press, 1992.

Swinburne, A. C. *Letters.* Edited by Cecil Y. Lang. 6 vols. New Haven, Conn.: Yale University Press, 1959–60.

———. *Selected Poems.* Edited by L. M. Findlay. Manchester, England: Carcanet, 1982.

———. *Swinburne as Critic.* Edited by Clyde K. Hyder. London: Routledge & Kegan Paul, 1972.

Tadié, Jean-Yves. *Marcel Proust: Biographie.* Paris: Gallimard, 1996.

Taylor, Joshua T. *Nineteenth-Century Theories of Art.* Berkeley: University of California Press, 1987.

Temple, Ruth Z. *The Critic's Alchemy: A Study of the Introduction of French Symbolism into England.* New York: Twayne Publishers, 1953.

Thibaudet, Albert. *La Poésie de Stéphane Mallarmé.* Paris: Gallimard, 1926.

Ticknor, Caroline. *Poe's Helen.* New York: Charles Scribner's Sons, 1916.

Tilby, Michael. "Le Monde vu de (trop?) près: Le Degas de J.-K. Huysmans." In *Le Champ littéraire,* edited by K. Cameron and J. Kearns, 91–103. Amsterdam: Rodopi, 1996.

Valéry, Paul. *Cahiers, 1894–1914.* Edited by Nicole Celeyrette-Pietri and Judith Robinson-Valéry. Paris: Gallimard, 1987.

———. *Ecrits divers sur Stéphane Mallarmé.* Paris: Gallimard, 1950.

———. *Lettres à quelques-uns.* Paris: Gallimard, 1952.

———. *Œuvres.* Edited by Jean Hytier. 2 vols. Paris: Gallimard, 1957–60.

Verhaeren, Emile. *Œuvres.* 9 vols. Geneva: Slatkine, 1977.

Verlaine, Paul. *Lettres inédites à Charles Morice*. Edited by Georges Zayed. Geneva: Droz, 1964.

———. *Lettres inédites à divers correspondants*. Edited by Georges Zayed. Geneva: Droz, 1976.

———. *Œuvres poétiques*. Edited by Jacques Robichez. Paris: Garnier, 1969.

———. *Œuvres poétiques complètes*. Edited by Y. G. Le Dantec and Jacques Borel. Paris: Gallimard, 1962.

Vial, André. *Mallarmé: Tétralogie pour un enfant mort*. Paris: Corti, 1976.

Villiers de l'Isle-Adam, Mathias de. *Axël*. Paris: Maison Quantin, 1890.

———. *Contes cruels*. Paris: Calmann-Lévy, 1883.

———. *L'Eve future*. Paris: Brunhoff, 1886.

Wais, Kurt. *Mallarmé: Dichtung, Weisheit, Haltung*. Munich: C. H. Beck, 1952.

Walker, John. *James McNeill Whistler*. New York: H. N. Abrams, 1987.

Weinberg, Bernard. *The Limits of Symbolism: Studies of Five Modern French Poets*. Chicago: University of Chicago Press, 1966.

Whitman, Sarah Helen. *Edgar Poe and His Critics*. Providence, R.I.: Tibbitts & Preston, 1885.

Wildenstein, Daniel, et al. *Claude Monet: Biographie et catalogue raisonné*. 4 vols. Lausanne: Bibliothèque des Arts, 1974–85.

Wright, Susan. "Private Language Made Public: The Language of Letters as Literature." *Poetics* 18, no. 6 (December 1989): 549–78.

Wright, Thomas. *The Life of John Payne*. London: T. Fisher Unwin, 1919.

Wyzewa, Teodor de. *Nos Maîtres: Etudes et portraits littéraires*. Paris: Perrin, 1895.

Yates, Frances. *The Art of Memory*. Chicago: University of Chicago Press, 1966.

Yeats, William Butler. *Collected Works*. Edited by Richard J. Finneran and George M. Harper. Vol. 1. New York: Macmillan, 1989.

Zeldin, Theodore. *France, 1848–1945*. 2 vols. Oxford: Clarendon Press, 1973–77.

Zola, Emile. *Correspondance*. Edited by B. H. Bakker. Vols. 5 (1884–86) and 6 (1887–90). Montreal: Presses Universitaires de Montréal; Paris: Editions du CNRS, 1985, 1987.

———. *Œuvres complètes*. Edited by H. Mitterand. 15 vols. Paris: Cercle du Livre Précieux, 1966–70.

Index

Adam, Juliette, 179, 208–10
Adam, Paul, 211
Arsel, Allys, 133
Aubanel, Théodore, 17, 49, 50
Austin, Lloyd, 6, 14, 87, 95, 99, 111, 137, 150, 153, 199, 210, 217, 219

Bacou, Rosaline, 143
Bajut, Anatole, 63
Balzac, Honoré de, 24, 40, 86, 87, 155, 213
Banville, Théodore de
    friendship of, 82–84, 93, 165, 169, 226
    influence of, 24, 93, 184
    Lefébure's judgements on, 35
    writings of, 8, 12, 25, 34, 50, 80–81, 95, 106, 114, 146, 203
Barbier, Carl, 47
Baudelaire, Charles
    childhood of, 20, 67
    death of, 8, 24, 31, 153, 217, 221, 226
    influence of, 72, 87, 103, 105, 175, 183
    and Manet, 126, 148
    and Mallarmé, 82
    and other authors, 89, 106, 143, 184, 185, 199, 222
    and Poe, 30, 43, 48, 79, 99, 101–2
    writings of, 4, 9, 12, 14, 21, 23, 24, 25, 45, 55, 56, 83, 129, 134, 135, 147, 149, 151, 173, 176, 191, 194–95, 203
Beauvoir, Simone de, 20
Beckford, William, 79, 97, 115
Beethoven, Ludwig van, 149, 150
Béranger, Pierre-Jean de, 3
Bernard, Suzanne, 149
Bertholet, Denis, 198
Blake, William, 107
Bonnefoy, Yves, 7
Bonniot, Edmond, 24, 120, 135, 141, 178
Bouguereau, William, 92, 147
Boulanger, Georges, 113, 210
Brennan, Christopher, 116, 200
Bréton, Geneviève, 52, 151

Brown, Frederick, 84
Byatt, A. S., 19–20

Cachin, Françoise, 125
Carjat, Etienne, 105
Carnot, Sadi, 205
Cazalis, Henri
    and death of Regnault, 207, 218
    and Augusta Holmès, 150–51
    Mallarmé's early letters to, 14, 28–30, 34–53, 71–75, 95, 98, 183, 223–24, 226
    pseudonym of Jean Lahor, 27
    recommends books to Mallarmé, 67
Chabrier, Emmanuel, 153
Champsaur, Félicien, 158
Chateaubriand, François René, 73, 126
Chausson, Ernest, 153–54
Cladel, Léon, 89–90, 114, 211
Claudel, Paul, 200
Clemenceau, Georges, 215
Coppée, François, 7, 8, 28, 53–60, 62, 80–81, 186, 218
Coquelin, Constant, 50
Corbière, Tristan, 62–63
Courbet, Gustave, 19, 86
Cressonnois, J., 149

Daudet, Alphonse, 196
Davies, Gardner, 218
Debussy, Claude, 118, 154–55
Deffoux, Léon, 84
Degas, Edgar, 80, 109, 123, 131, 136, 146–48, 155, 204, 215
Delacroix, Eugène, 35
Derenne, Alphonse, 50, 105
Desbordes-Valmore, Marceline, 21, 23, 29, 36, 129
Deschamps, Léon, 195
Des Essarts, Emmanuel, 21–22, 27, 30, 37, 38, 44, 51, 71
Dierx, Léon, 81, 84, 183, 197, 218
Docquois, Georges, 196

Donne, John, 168
Dorian, Tola, 179
Dreyfus, Alfred, 136–37, 213–15
Droz, Gustave, 110
Dujardin, Edouard, 24, 148–49, 178, 192, 195,
    210, 220
Dukas, Paul, 154
Dunlop, John Boyd, 205
Duparc, Arthur, 51, 52
Durand-Ruel, Paul, 138, 139, 143, 144
Duret, Théodore, 115

Eliot, Thomas Stearns, 192
Elphinestone Hope, Mrs. C. W., 79
Esterhazy, Ferdinand, 214
Evans, Thomas, 157

Fairlie, Alison, 7
Fantin-Latour, Henri, 106
Fénéon, Félix, 211, 212, 213
Ferry, Jules, 15, 205–6
Flaubert, Gustave, 14, 15, 56, 90–91, 143, 208
Fontainas, André, 152
Fort, Paul, 196
France, Anatole, 80–82, 87, 200, 218
France, Marie de, 94
Franck, César, 151

Gaillard, Nina de, 80
Gallimard, Paul, 115
Gambetta, Léon, 206, 208
Gauguin, Paul, 21, 123
Gautier, Judith, 3, 150, 151, 197
Gautier, Théophile
  criticism by, 25, 148
  Lefébure's views of, 35–36
  Mallarmé's appreciation of, 24, 40, 82, 221
  Mallarmé's *Tombeau* for, 11, 55, 80, 105,
      217–219, 222, 225
  opposition to marriage of Judith Gautier and
      Mendès, 150
  and Swinburne, 106
  verse forms of, 12
Geffroy, Gustave, 122, 139, 211
Genette, Gérard, 21
George, Stefan, 200
Gerhard, Maria. *See* Mallarmé, Marie
Ghil, René, 63, 194–95
Gide, André, 152–53, 155, 179–80, 181, 198,
    200
Gill, Austin, 2, 4, 217
Girard, Edmond, 128
Girod, Victor, 147
Glatigny, Albert, 218
Gobillard, Paule, 129
Goncourt, Edmond de, 116, 178, 180, 181
Gosse, Edmond, 106
Gould, Evlyn, 103–4
Gourmont, Remy de, 195–96, 222

Goya y Lucientes, Francisco de, 143
Gramont, Louis de, 206
Grave, Jean, 211
Graves, Robert, 20
Griswold, Rufus, 106
Guérin, Charles, 7
Guilbert, René. *See* Ghil, René
Gyp, 211

Hahn, Reynaldo, 133–34
Halévy, Ludovic, 147
Halperin, Joan, 213
Hegel, Friedrich, 72
Hennique, Léon, 89
Herbert, Eugenia, 210
Heredia, José-Maria, 80, 84, 181, 186, 197,
    218
Herold, André-Ferdinand, 154
Holmès, Augusta, 47, 106, 150–52, 158
Horne, Richard Hengist, 121
Hoschédé, Germaine, 139
Hugo, Victor
  and choice of subject, 187
  and loss of child, 221–22
  Mallarmé's adolescent reading of, 24, 217
  and other writers, 21, 36, 175, 177, 182, 184
  and street jargon, 86
  and universal fraternity, 9
  and verse forms, 12, 106, 197, 227–28
Huret, Jules, 179, 197
Hutton, John, 210, 212
Huysmans, Joris Karl, 12, 24, 50–51, 88, 90–
    92, 143, 147, 195, 223

Ingram, John, 101, 102, 106

Jammes, Francis, 200
Joseph, Lawrence, 28, 29, 37, 47

Kahn, Gustave, 7, 188, 189–91, 193, 229
Koenigstein, François-Claudius (pseud. Rava-
    chol), 213
Kropotkin, Pyotr Alekseyevich, 210, 211
Krysinska, Marie, 188, 190

Laforgue, Jules, 191, 192, 229
Lahor, Jean. *See* Cazalis, Henri
Lamber, Juliette. *See* Adam, Juliette
Lamoureux, Charles, 149–50
Laurent, Méry, 29, 98, 112, 113, 116, 127–28,
    144, 156–65
Leconte de Lisle, Charles René, 8, 35, 53, 80–
    82, 93, 106, 116, 183, 197, 218
Lefébure, Eugène
  and Egyptology, 27, 73
  Mallarmé discusses his poetry with, 40–41,
      44–45, 48, 83
  Mallarmé visits at Cannes, 52, 61
  Mallarmé's early letters to, 27–36, 75

and music, 149
as part of Mallarmé's spiritual family, 222
Lemerre, Alphonse, 81, 218
Lesseps, Ferdinand de, 215
Lissagary, Prosper Olivier, 205
Lodge, David, 156
Loti, Pierre, 208
Louviot, Anne Rose Suzanne. *See* Laurent, Méry
Louÿs, Pierre, 155, 195–97, 198
Luce, Maximilien, 211

Mac-Mahon, Edme Patrice, 206
Maeterlinck, Maurice, 197
Mallarmé, Anatole, 2, 109–10, 221–25
Mallarmé, Geneviève, 2, 17, 25, 29, 46, 109–20, 144, 149, 151, 178, 210, 226
Mallarmé, Maria, 2, 217–18
Mallarmé, Marie (née Gerhard), 2, 17, 27, 29, 36, 46, 68–69, 72, 109–12, 145, 158, 226
Manet, Edouard
and Méry Laurent, 157–58
and Mallarmé, 27, 50, 92, 123–28, 135–36, 183, 226
and other writers, 100–101, 106, 126, 133, 148, 151
Manet, Eugène, 122, 132, 210
Manet, Julie, 123, 129, 132–34, 136–37, 139, 146, 214–15
Manet, Suzanne, 128
Marchal, Bertrand, 7, 14, 48, 50, 52, 53, 59, 66, 74, 156, 157
Margueritte, Blanche, 116
Margueritte, Paul, 114, 116, 144, 169–70
Margueritte, Victor, 116, 204–5
Marras, Jean, 111
Mauclair, Camille, 112–13, 116, 154, 178, 208
Mazel, Henri, 180–81
McMullen, Roy, 147
Mendès, Catulle, 8, 27, 36, 49, 76, 81, 82, 93, 105–6, 110, 121, 150–51, 218–19, 222
Merrill, Stuart, 153, 200, 211
Michaux, Ernest, 205
Michel, Louise, 205
Michelet, Jules, 36, 49, 110
Millan, Gordon, 4, 111, 179
Mirabeau, Sybille de. *See* Gyp
Mirbeau, Octave, 137, 139, 213
Mistral, Frédéric, 105, 206, 219–20
Mockel, Albert, 1, 152–53, 166, 229
Mondor, Henri, 4, 28, 29, 30, 111, 126, 127, 218
Monet, Claude, 122, 130–33, 137–39, 146, 165, 205, 214
Monet, Jean, 139
Montaigne, Michel, 19
Montesquiou, Robert Ferenzac de, 61, 90, 179
Moore, George, 142
Moréas, Jean, 229

Morice, Charles, 62, 63, 148, 229
Morisot, Berthe, 122, 128–34, 135, 137, 146, 148, 165, 179, 226
Moulton, Louise Chandler, 98, 101, 104–5
Munch, Edvard, 116, 122, 200
Musset, Alfred de, 69, 72

Nadar, Félix, 123
Nadar, Paul, 14
Nettleship, John Trivett, 94
Noulet, Emilie, 168, 203

Offenbach, Jacques, 8
Olds, Marshall, 105
O'Shaugnessy, Arthur, 94–99, 104

Passerieu, Jean-Bernard, 226
Payne, John, 83–84, 93–94, 99, 104
Pearson, Roger, 74–75
Picard, Emile, 211–12
Pichois, Claude, 29
Picquart, Georges, 214
Pissarro, Camille, 211, 212
Poe, Edgar Allan
Baudelaire's translations of, 21, 48, 79
and Fénéon, 212
Mallarmé's "tombeau" for, 220–22, 225
and Louise Chandler Moulton, 98, 104–6
and Sara Sigourney Rice, 99–100
and Sarah Helen Whitman, 100–104
and "Philosophy of Composition," 43, 195
and "The Raven," 32, 126–27
Ponson du Terrail, Pierre Alexis, 86, 127
Ponsot, Willy, 114
Popelin, Claudius, 80
Proust, Marcel, 20, 37, 67, 90, 157, 179, 200–201
Puvis de Chavannes, Pierre, 123, 148, 184, 206

Quillard, Pierre, 211

Rabelais, François, 99
Raffaelli, Jean-François, 123
Raitt, Alan, 222, 223
Rand, Harry, 125
Ravachol (pseud. of François-Claudius Koenigstein), 213
Reboux, Paul, 181
Reclus, Elisée, 211
Redon, Ari, 143–44
Redon, Camille, 144
Redon, Odilon, 115, 116, 123, 143–45, 154, 197
Regnault, Henri, 17, 38, 51–53, 123, 207, 218, 222
Régnier, Henri de
diary entries of, 30, 72, 82, 123, 127, 133, 136–37, 139, 151–52, 178

(Régnier, Henri de *continued*)
  poetry of, 7, 24, 129, 191–93, 196, 197, 211, 229
  reflections on Méry Laurent, 158–61
Remy, Marcel, 153
Renaud, Armand, 15, 39
Renoir, Jean, 135, 136
Renoir, Pierre-Auguste, 19, 109, 123, 129, 130, 131, 133, 134–37, 138, 146, 165, 205, 214
Retté, Adolphe, 211
Ricard, Louis-Xavier, 27
Rice, Sara Sigourney, 99–101, 220
Richepin, Jules, 114
Rimbaud, Arthur, 2, 20, 62–63, 67, 82–83
Rocca de Vergalo, Nicanor A. della, 208
Rodenbach, Anna-Maria, 123, 148
Rodenbach, Georges, 7, 24, 169–71
Rodin, Auguste, 114, 123, 155, 213
Roeg, Nicolas, 19
Roujon, Henri, 105, 147
Rousseau, Jean-Jacques, 127
Rouvier, Maurice, 210

Sainte-Beuve, Charles, 1, 64, 127
Sand, George, 15, 20
Sarcey, Francisque, 84
Sartre, Jean-Paul, 111
Schwarz, Dieter, 197
Seurat, Georges, 212
Shaw, Mary, 103–4
Signac, Paul, 212
Silvestre, Armand, 218
Sisley, Alfred, 132–33
Simon, Jules, 52
Sivry, Charles de, 154
Sonn, Richard, 207, 211
Spate, Virginia, 130
Stamelman, Richard, 217
Steinmetz, Jean-Luc, 4–5
Stevens, Wallace, 20
Strauss, Richard, 155
Swinburne, Algernon, 79, 94, 99, 100, 105–8, 197

Tadié, Jean-Yves, 201
Tailhade, Laurent, 53, 211, 213

Taine, Hipployte, 35
Temple, Ruth, 106
Tennyson, Alfred, Lord, 34–35, 99
Tilby, Michael, 147
Tolstoy, Leo, 8

Vacquerie, Auguste, 39, 106
Valéry, Paul, 7, 9, 76, 107, 144, 147, 149, 155, 198–200, 202–3, 205
Vallès, Jules, 8, 20, 205
Valotton, Félix, 123
Vanier, Léon, 63
Verhaeren, Emile, 7, 23, 24, 169, 171–78, 205, 229
Verlaine, Paul, 2, 4, 7–14, 17, 30, 53, 60–65, 81, 126, 154, 166, 175, 197, 226
Viélé-Griffin, Francis, 7, 142, 200, 211, 229
Vigny, Alfred de, 182
Villiers de l'Isle-Adam, 4, 17, 27, 72, 75, 76, 114–15, 136, 144, 146, 151, 165, 178–79, 222–26
Vitu, Auguste, 84
Voilquin, Suzanne, 8
Vollard, Ambroise, 115, 144
Vuillard, Edoard, 115

Wagner, Richard, 15, 93, 114, 126, 149, 151–52, 180, 183, 184, 191, 226, 231
Wais, Kurt, 4, 112, 148
Watts, Theodore, 107
Weinfield, Henry, 226
Whistler, James McNeill, 64, 106, 112, 114, 122, 123, 139–43, 146, 150, 152, 153, 203
Whistler, Trixie, 142
Whitman, Sarah Helen, 100, 101–4, 221
Whitman, Walt, 94, 99
Wilde, Oscar, 155
Wilson, Edmond, 222
Wordsworth, William, 219
Wright, Thomas, 94
Wyzewa, Theodor, 63, 166–67

Yapp, Ettie, 36, 37
Yeats, W. B., 49

Zola, Emile, 8, 84–88, 91, 92, 114, 127, 155, 205, 211, 214